Beyond Red Power

School for Advanced Research
Global Indigenous Politics series

James F. Brooks
General Editor

Beyond Red Power

American Indian Politics
and Activism since 1900

Edited by Daniel M. Cobb
and Loretta Fowler

School for Advanced Research
Global Indigenous Politics Book

School for Advanced Research Press
Post Office Box 2188
Santa Fe, New Mexico 87504-2188
www.sarpress.sarweb.org

Co-Director and Executive Editor: Catherine Cocks
Manuscript Editor: Kate Whelan
Design and Production: Cynthia Dyer
Proofreader: Sarah Soliz
Indexer: Catherine Fox
Printer: Edwards Brothers Printing

Library of Congress Cataloging-in-Publication Data:
Beyond red power : American Indian politics and activism since 1900 / edited by Daniel M. Cobb
and Loretta Fowler.
    p. cm. — (School for Advanced Research global indigenous politics series)
  Includes bibliographical references and index.
  ISBN 978-1-930618-86-2 (paper : alk. paper)
  1. Indians of North America—Politics and government. 2. Indians of North America—Civil rights.
3. Indian activists—United States. 4. Political participation—United States. 5. Social movements—
United States. 6. Self-determination, National—United States. 7. United States—Social policy.
8. United States—Race relations. 9. United States—Politics and government. I. Cobb, Daniel M.
II. Fowler, Loretta, 1944-

E98.T77B49 2007
323.1197'073—dc22

                    2007020709

Cover illustration: American Indians protest the Supreme Court's Puyallup decision. Poor People's
Campaign, Washington DC, 1968. Photo 2000-008-0086. Courtesy of the Karl Kernberger Collection,
Center for Southwest Research, University of New Mexico, Albuquerque, New Mexico.

Contents

Figures

Tables

Acknowledgments

The completion of this volume would not have been possible without a great deal of help from an even greater number of people. Foremost, we thank all of the contributors for a richly rewarding endeavor. A special debt of gratitude is owed to Miami University for making it possible to host a three-day symposium in which nearly all the authors gathered in Oxford, Ohio, to critique and elaborate on the connections between one another's work. The Department of History's McClellan Symposium Fund and the College of Arts and Science's John W. Altman Humanities Scholars-in-Residence Program provided generous resources. History department chair Charlotte Newman Goldy embraced the idea for "Beyond Red Power" from the first, and her successor, Mary Kupiec Cayton, proved no less an advocate. Allan Winkler and Andrew R. L. Cayton, also of the Department of History, shared information from their past experiences that made planning for the event much easier. A word of thanks must also be extended to former associate dean Dianne Sadoff, who received the initial proposal for the symposium and responded with encouragement to "think bigger."

In the end, the scholarly symposium, which culminated in a keynote address and roundtable discussion on "The Past and Future of Indian Sovereignty," was one of five components in a semester-long series of events at Miami University during the spring of 2006 that explored contemporary issues in Native America. It would be remiss not to acknowledge the help of Mary Jane Berman and the Center for American and World Cultures, Jane Goettsch and the Women's Center, Daryl Baldwin and the Myaamia Project, Bob Wicks, Edna Southard, and the Miami University Art Museum, Jenny Presnell, Bill Wortman, Janet Stuckey, and Lisa Santucci at King Library, Bobbe Burke, Lynn Eisele, and finally Dolph Greenberg and the Department of Anthropology for making the Hansen Fund available to host a talk by Spokane activist Charlene Teters. Miami University was fortunate to have her presence, along with that of Iola Hayden (Comanche), Julie Olds

(Miami), and Della Warrior (Otoe-Missouria) as part of the "Founding Mothers" speaker series celebrating women's activism.

This volume has benefited from careful readings and comments by the contributors and others. Drew Cayton and Judith Zinsser of Miami's Department of History offered helpful suggestions, as did the fourteen Miami students enrolled in HST 400Z, a senior capstone on twentieth-century American Indian political activism. They not only read and critiqued the essays but also gave us a much needed early indication of how our efforts would be received in the classroom and how we might improve these in anticipation of that. So Amber Beal, John Cahill, Brooke Conner, Heather Hall, John Irmen, Drew Johnson, Brittney Peters, Mike Poe, Aaron Pride, Chris Renner, Maggie Shell, Dan Watts, Andrew Wilson, and Kellen Wise, we thank you. George Ironstrack (Miami) served as a graduate assistant for the entire series of events, going far above and beyond the call of duty on multiple occasions. His many contributions included a thoughtful and much appreciated evaluation of the collection. And finally, we appreciate the careful cartographic work of geography department graduate student Joshua Sutterfield (Miami), who made two of the maps that appear in the volume.

SAR Press embraced *Beyond Red Power* from day one, and we are grateful to School for Advanced Research president James F. Brooks and SAR Press co-director and editor Catherine Cocks. Our copy editor, Kate Whelan, proved to be as patient as she was meticulous. Collaborating with her was a joy. Any mistakes that remain are, of course, ours alone.

DMC and LKF

For Nhon, Anna, and Molly
DMC

Introduction

Daniel M. Cobb and Loretta Fowler

The American Indian Movement (AIM) catapulted into public consciousness during the 1970s. With militant rhetoric, audacious confrontational strategies, and larger-than-life personalities, it immediately captivated popular and scholarly attention. Over the years, a surfeit of books, articles, documentary films, and major motion pictures has solidified its significance as a turning point in American Indian history. Today the dramatic events surrounding AIM constitute what is commonly called the era of Red Power. The story, as it is typically told, opens in November 1969 with a nineteen-month occupation of Alcatraz Island orchestrated by the Indians of All Tribes and reaches a critical turning point three years later, when a march on Washington (the Trail of Broken Treaties) led to a takeover of the Bureau of Indian Affairs. From there, the narrative climaxes with a seventy-two-day standoff at Wounded Knee, South Dakota, beginning in February 1973. It then closes with a period of violence on the Pine Ridge Reservation, a devastating "counter-insurgency" campaign coordinated by the federal government, and in 1978 a final mass demonstration known as the Longest Walk.[1]

The Red Power era has so complete a grasp on our historical imagination that it has come to symbolize the quintessence of Indian activism. This volume argues that such a limited view obscures as much as it reveals about the ways in which American Indians have engaged in politics since the late nineteenth century. These sixteen chapters situate a decade of concentrated militancy in the context of a century's worth of Native political action. The contributors address a question that may, at first, sound simple: how did Indians ensure the survival of their communities through the twentieth and into the twenty-first centuries? If this query appears simple, it is deceptively so—there are, in fact, many answers. The following pages illustrate that the politics of survival has played out across every conceivable scale of analysis, and continues to do so, and that activism often manifests itself in unexpected ways. From these chapters, we gain new perspectives on major historical eras (assimilation, Indian reorganization, termination, and self-determination), as well as on pressing contemporary issues such as gaming, acknowledgment, language revitalization, tribal jurisprudence, and sovereignty.

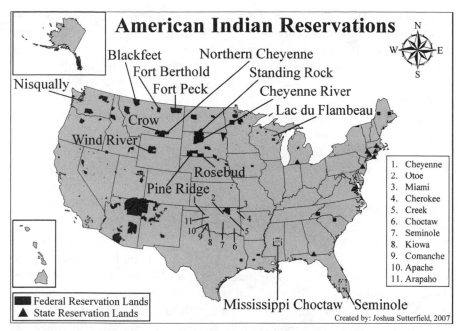

Figure 1. In 2006 there were more than 560 federally recognized tribes and Alaska Native villages occupying more than 100 million acres of land, and hundreds more state-recognized, unacknowledged, and Hawaiian Native communities. In addition, about two-thirds of the 4.3 million who identified themselves as American Indian or Alaska Native during the 2000 census lived in cities and small towns. The tribal communities that receive particular emphasis in this volume are highlighted. Map courtesy of Joshua Sutterfield.

Part I presents three perspectives on the evolution of American Indian political history. Don Fixico, Fred Hoxie, and Taiawagi Helton and Lindsay Robertson offer quite different but complementary chapters rooted in personal experience, historiography, and law, respectively. The chapters that constitute Parts II and III carry readers across a considerable expanse of space and time through focused, politically oriented case studies (figure 1). We have added introductions to Parts II and III in order to extend the geographical and interpretational reach of the volume. Concise chapter introductions locate the chapters in relation to existing scholarship and direct readers to tables containing additional information on legislation, Supreme Court decisions, and other pivotal events in the realms of both policy and political activism.

Through our collective efforts, we have attempted to outline the contours of a broadly conceived, multidisciplinary history of American Indian politics and activism. It is, of course, a history that has always been there and is still being written. This volume represents an effort to acknowledge and comprehend its tremendous diversity and import. In so doing, the authors carry readers beyond Red Power by situating that movement in the context of an American Indian political tradition that preceded, spanned the full breadth of, and extends past the close of the twentieth century. The politics of survival has deep roots. Thinking globally about one's self and others, forging pantribal networks, adopting the language of sovereignty, fostering local and regional interdependencies and reckoning with the consequences, and dealing internally with issues of representation and nation-building—none of these are new to Native North America. They are manifestations of a process that is as old as the colonial encounter itself.

Beyond Red Power grew out of a double session organized for the 2004 American Society for Ethnohistory meeting in Chicago. With enthusiastic support from James Brooks and Catherine Cocks of SAR Press, we sought out others who shared our interest in developing innovative ideas. We wanted to represent the perspectives of Native and non-Native men and women, emerging scholars and established full professors, formal academics and people who work in tribal communities. Ultimately, we pulled together a diverse group of historians, anthropologists, legal scholars, specialists in American Indian Studies, and individuals operating outside the academy. In March 2006 we gathered at Miami University in Oxford, Ohio, to discuss, critique, and reflect on the larger implications of one another's work. And, over the next several months, we set about revising our chapters, based on the time we spent together. What you are now reading, then, is not merely a collection of individual essays that have been cobbled together and proclaimed a book. Instead, it is the product of an extended and ongoing conversation—and we hope that that you will become a participant in it.

Note

1. For overviews, see Paul Chaat Smith and Robert Allen Warrior, *Like a Hurricane: The Indian Movement from Alcatraz to Wounded Knee* (New York: The New Press, 1996); Troy Johnson, Joane Nagel, and Duane Champagne, eds., *American Indian Activism: Alcatraz to the Longest Walk* (Urbana: University of Illinois Press, 1997); and Troy Johnson, *The Occupation of Alcatraz Island: Indian Self-Determination and the Rise of Indian Activism* (Urbana: University of Illinois Press, 1997). First-person accounts include Russell Means, *Where White Men Fear to Tread: The Autobiography of Russell Means* (New York: St. Martin's, 1995); Adam Fortunate Eagle, *Heart of the Rock: The Indian Invasion of Alcatraz* (Norman: University of Oklahoma Press, 2002); and Dennis Banks with Richard Erdoes, *Ojibwe Warrior: Dennis Banks and the Rise of the American Indian Movement* (Norman: University of Oklahoma Press, 2004). For a general review of the literature, see Sandra Baringer's "Indian Activism and the American Indian Movement: A Bibliographical Essay," *American Indian Culture and Research Journal* 21, no. 4 (1997): 217–250. A more wide-ranging interpretation of the post-1953 period is Charles Wilkinson's *Blood Struggle: The Rise of Modern Indian Nations* (New York: Norton, 2005).

Table 1. Assimilation and Allotment Era, 1871–1934

Year	Federal Policy	Political Activism
1871	Congress ends treaty making, acknowledges obligation to uphold existing treaties with tribes.	
1879	The Carlisle Indian Industrial School founded. By 1900 more than 20,000 students attend off- and on-reservation schools devoted to cultural assimilation.	Revitalization movements gain adherents throughout Indian Country.
1883	Courts of Indian Offenses established on reservations to enforce federal regulations banning dancing, traditional religion, polygamy, gift giving, and other customs.	Tribes sue United States in Court of Claims.
1885	Major Crimes Act extends federal jurisdiction over 7 (and later 16) crimes on reservations. Upheld in *United States v. Kagama* (1886).	Tribes begin plans to make Indian Territory an Indian state (1888).
1887	General Allotment (Dawes) Act authorizes division of communally held reservations into individually owned parcels of land. Unallotted "surplus land" opened to non-Native settlement.	Wounded Knee Massacre (1890); Sioux file Black Hills claim (1890s).
1898	Curtis Act extends Dawes Act to Cherokee, Choctaw, Chickasaw, Creek, and Seminole in Indian Territory, dissolves tribal governments.	Indian leaders protest allotment and land cessions through lobbying, public tours, litigation.
1903	*Lone Wolf v. Hitchcock* affirms and expands doctrine of "plenary power."	Tribes demand protection of religious freedom, reservation resources, and treaty provisions.
1906	Burke Act permits Indians to be declared "competent" for removal of trust status over allotments.	Society of American Indians founded (1911); Four Mothers Society founded (1912).
1908	*Winters v. United States* rules that Indians on reservation lands retain water rights.	Alaska Native Brotherhood founded (1912); Alaska Native Sisterhood founded (1915).
1916	*United States v. Nice* finds that federal government retains the role of guardian whether or not an Indian becomes a US citizen.	Native American Church incorporates in Oklahoma (1918).
1924	American Indian Citizenship Act grants US citizenship, recognizes rights to tribal citizenship and property.	Pueblos unite to stop massive land loss (1920s).

Table 2. Reorganization Era, 1934–1946

Year	Federal Policy	Political Activism
1934	Indian Reorganization Act ends allotment, extends trust status of Indian land indefinitely, recognizes tribal governments, and initiates economic development programs. Similar legislation written for tribes in Oklahoma and Native communities in Alaska passes in 1936. Although the rights to self-government, tribal courts, and freedom of religion are acknowledged, the federal government retains supervisory authority over tribes, the revolving loan fund is underfunded, and very little land is brought into trust.	Tribal representatives respond to IRA legislation during regional congresses.
1934	Interior Department solicitor Nathan Margold issues Powers of Indian Tribes opinion that distinguishes inherent and delegated powers.	Tribes hold referendums to vote on IRA, constitutions, and charters of incorporation.
1934	Johnson-O'Malley Act authorizes the secretary of the interior to contract with state and local governments to provide educational, medical, agricultural, and social welfare services to Indians.	Tribal communities that reject IRA form independent business councils and governments.
1935	Indian Arts and Crafts Board promotes economic self-determination through development of Indian arts and crafts, expansion of markets for the products of Indian art and craftsmanship, and support for Indian-controlled cultural institutions.	Unacknowledged tribes use IRA to seek federal recognition.
1938	Indian Mineral Leasing Act is amended, allows tribes to lease unallotted reservation lands or land otherwise under federal jurisdiction, seeks to increase tribal revenue and control over resources.	Cultural revitalization accompanies American Indian participation in World War II (1941–1945).
1941	Felix Cohen publishes his *Handbook of Federal Indian Law,* the first attempt to arrive at a comprehensive understanding of the subject.	Iroquois protest draft, declare war on Axis powers as a sovereign nation.
1941	*Hualapi Tribe v. Santa Fe Railroad* recognizes aboriginal title as equal to fee simple title.	National Congress of American Indians is founded (1944), defends treaty rights, promotes voting rights, advocates for claims process.

Table 3. Termination and Relocation Era, 1946–1961

Year	Federal Policy	Political Activism
1946	Indian Claims Commission Act creates legal mechanism for tribes to seek restitution for the illegal taking or undervaluing of land and the mismanagement of tribal funds. Between 1947 and 1978 the ICC settles nearly 300 claims against the government, valued at more than $800 million.	Tribes fight to limit federal government's use of ICC settlements to pay for past expenses, demand control over allocation of balance.
1952	Bureau of Indian Affairs establishes Voluntary Relocation Program to encourage individuals and families to leave reservation communities for cities.	Alaska Natives, Mississippi Choctaws, and Lumbees challenge segregation, racial discrimination.
1953	House Concurrent Resolution 108 articulates federal policy of termination, which seeks to eliminate the trust relationship and destroy tribal sovereignty. One hundred tribes, bands, and rancherias and 13,263 individual Indians are terminated; 1.3 million acres of tribal lands lost.	Tribal leaders insist on their right to hire lawyers without federal approval.
1953	Public Law 280 empowers California, Minnesota, Nebraska, Oregon, and Wisconsin to extend state legal and civil jurisdiction over Indian reservations without tribal consent.	Urban Indian centers grow.
1955	*Tee-Hit-Ton Indians v. United States* delivers blow to aboriginal property rights, ruling that Alaska Natives have occupancy or possessory instead of ownership rights to land.	Indian youth movement begins with the Southwest Regional Indian Youth Council and the Workshop on American Indian Affairs.
1958	Bureau of Indian Affairs initiates Indian Adoption Project to place children in non-Indian foster homes.	NCAI and other organizations halt coercive termination and compel federal government to seek tribal consent before severing trust relationship.
1960	United States Army Corps of Engineers continues massive dam-building projects begun during 1950s along major river systems in both the East and West, including the Pick-Sloan Plan for the Missouri River and the Kinzua Dam near the New York–Pennsylvania border. These projects lead to the flooding of ancestral villages and burial grounds and to the violation of treaty rights.	Tribes protest flooding of ancestral lands and environmental degradation due to construction of dams.

Table 4. Self-Determination Era I, 1961–1973

Year	Federal Policy	Political Activism
1961	John F. Kennedy is elected president. Congress begins making tribal governments eligible for programs such as the Area Redevelopment Administration.	American Indian Chicago Conference. National Indian Youth Council founded.
1962	Bureau of Indian Affairs funds Institute of American Indian Arts in Santa Fe, New Mexico.	Indians secure right to vote in New Mexico state elections.
1964	Economic Opportunity Act launches War on Poverty and provides federal money directly to tribal governments for programs such as Head Start, Neighborhood Youth Corps, and Community Action. Other federal agencies establish "Indian Desks."	Tribal governments grow, taking on increased responsibilities. Fish-in movement expands in Pacific Northwest. Survival of American Indians Association founded.
1966	Congress establishes right of tribes to bring suit in federal courts.	Alaska Native Federation founded.
1968	Lyndon Johnson presents "Forgotten American" address. American Indian Civil Rights Act provides model code for Indian courts, requires states to obtain tribal consent before assuming jurisdiction over Indian land, and imposes restrictions on acts of tribal governments toward their citizens.	Poor People's Campaign. American Indian Movement founded.
1968	Bilingual Education Act funds nearly 70 Native language projects during the 1970s.	Indians of All Tribes occupies Alcatraz Island (November 1969).
1969	Federal funding of Navajo Community College signals support for tribal control over education.	Taos Pueblos succeed in securing return of Blue Lake (1970).
1970	President Richard Nixon supports self-determination in Special Message to Congress.	Ada Deer and Menominee DRUMS press for federal restoration in wake of termination.
1971	Alaska Native Claims Settlement Act recognizes Native ownership of 44 million acres, awards monetary settlement and mineral royalties, and creates 13 Native regional corporations to administer monies and lands.	Native American Rights Fund founded (1970).
1973	Menominee Restoration Act repeals termination of federal trust responsibility for Menominees. Other restorations follow.	Trail of Broken Treaties (November 1972); Wounded Knee takeover (February 1973).

Table 5. Self-Determination Era II, 1974–1982

Year	Federal Policy	Political Activism
1974	*United States v. Washington* affirms treaty rights of Washington Indians to half the harvestable fish and mandates co-management by state and tribes. Supreme Court upholds Boldt decision (1979).	International Indian Treaty Council organized.
1974	*Morton v. Mancari* rules that Indian status is a political, not racial, classification and preserves Indian hiring preference within the BIA.	
1975	Indian Self-Determination and Education Assistance Act allows tribes to contract with federal government to administer federal programs.	Council of Energy Resources Tribes formed.
1978	Tribally Controlled Community College Act provides federal money to support creation of Indian-controlled institutions of higher education.	Tribes create colleges and culturally relevant curricula.
1978	Indian Child Welfare Act gives tribal courts jurisdiction over children of tribal members.	
1978	American Indian Religious Freedom Act establishes rights of Indians to practice Native religion; amended in 1994 to protect peyote religion.	Repatriation movement accelerates.
1978	Office of Federal Acknowledgment created within BIA, establishes criteria for tribes to obtain federal recognition (revised in 1994); now named the Branch of Acknowledgment Research.	AIM organizes Longest Walk.
1978	*Santa Clara Pueblo v. Martinez* rules that tribes can decide criteria for membership and tribal courts are appropriate forums for individuals to litigate civil rights claims against tribes.	
1978	*Oliphant v. Suquamish* decision leads to doctrine of "implicit divestiture," signals period of tension and ambivalence over federal support for tribal sovereignty.	
1980	*Sioux Nation v. United States* rules that the United States violated the Treaty of 1868 in taking possession of the Black Hills.	Sioux refuse monetary settlement, argue for return of land.
1981	*Montana v. United States* denies tribes civil jurisdiction over non-Indians on fee (non-trust) lands within Indian Country.	Tribes accelerate efforts to prevent destruction of land due to drilling, mining, nuclear waste, urban sprawl.
1982	Indian Mineral Development Act allows tribes to participate in mineral development as regulators, in joint ventures, and in negotiating mineral leases.	
1982	*Merrion v. Jicarilla* rules that tribes can tax oil and gas production on trust lands, bolsters tribal revenue.	Wisconsin Ojibwes arrested for spearfishing in off-reservation sites.

Table 6. Self-Determination Era III, 1983–1993

Year	Federal Policy	Political Activism
1983	*Voigt* decision affirms Wisconsin Ojibwe treaty rights to hunt and fish on ceded lands, denies state jurisdiction over tribal members.	Mashantucket Pequots secure federal acknowledgment.
1985	*Montana v. Blackfeet* disallows state taxation of tribes' income from mineral leases.	Klamaths secure restoration (1986).
1987	*California v. Cabazon Band of Mission Indians* holds that after a state legalizes gambling, Indian tribes can offer similar games on trust land, free from state regulation.	
1988	*Lyng v. Northwest Indian Cemetery Association* permits federal government to build logging road, though this will destroy sacred sites of California tribes. The road is not built, but a legal precedent is set.	Protests against derogatory sports mascots escalate.
1988	National Indian Gaming Regulatory Act establishes three classes of gaming, prohibits Class III unless tribes and states negotiate compacts, and creates national regulatory agency.	Increase in unacknowledged tribes seeking federal recognition.
1989	*Cotton Petroleum v. New Mexico* rules that states can tax oil and gas producers on reservations.	Native delegates contribute to UN's Draft Declaration on the Rights of Indigenous Peoples.
1990	Native American Language Act repudiates past policies aimed at eradicating Indian languages, declares Indians entitled to own languages, and promises assistance in language revitalization.	Tribes begin sending nonvoting delegations to UN.
1990	Native American Graves Protection and Repatriation Act requires federally supported institutions with human remains, funerary objects, or cultural patrimony to identify the descendants and provide opportunity for them to reclaim these.	Tribes pursue repatriation, invest in tribally controlled museums.
1990	*Oregon v. Smith* delivers blow to sacramental use of peyote.	NARF lobbies for amendment to counteract *Oregon v. Smith*.
1990	*Duro v. Reina* finds that tribes do not have jurisdiction over crimes committed on their reservations by Indians from other tribes. Congress passes the "*Duro* Fix" to override the Supreme Court.	Indian Studies programs at public and private colleges and universities increase.
1993	Congress passes the Religious Freedom Restoration Act, countering the *Smith* decision.	

Table 7. Self-Determination Era IV, 1993–2006

Year	Federal Policy	Political Activism
1993	Indian Tribal Justice Act strengthens tribal court system.	Mashantucket Pequots open Foxwoods casino (1992).
1994	Indian Self-Governance Act offers tribes greater leeway in managing federal monies via compacting; tribes negotiate directly with Congress, nation to nation.	Trust mismanagement suit against BIA launched.
1994	Indian Trust Management Reform Act addresses federal negligence regarding Individual Indian Money Accounts.	Grassroots campaigns to preserve sacred sites and protect the environment grow.
1996	*Seminole Tribe v. Florida* finds that states have sovereign immunity from suit in dealings with tribes.	Tribes invest gaming revenue in cultural and language revitalization programs, diversify economies.
2004	Circuit court upholds Bonnichsen decision (2002), allowing scientific research on the Ancient One (Kennewick Man), the 9,600-year-old human remains found in Washington State; tribes argue that the "inability to prove cultural affiliation" argument discounts the validity of oral traditions.	Native American Rights Fund represents organizations seeking amendments to NAGPRA.
2004	*United States v. Lara* supports "inherent legal authority" and upholds "*Duro* Fix" and right of tribes to prosecute nonmembers for crimes committed within their jurisdictional area.	Alaska Natives struggle to prevent drilling in wildlife refuge, call for revision of ANCSA.
2005	National Museum of the American Indian opens in Washington DC.	Hopi and Navajo secure closure of destructive mines, move toward settlement of land disputes.
2006	National Collegiate Athletic Association bans use of Indian mascots without the consent of tribes.	Tribes engage in litigation and negotiations with states over issues of taxation and jurisdiction.
2006	United Nations Human Rights Commission adopts Draft Declaration on the Rights of Indigenous Peoples (June). In December, the UN General Assembly votes to "defer consideration and action."	Native Hawaiians demand recognition of sovereignty.
2006		Florida Seminoles become the first tribe to own an international corporation with the purchase of Hard Rock.

Table 8. Number of State-Recognized Tribes, by State

State	Number of Tribes
Alabama	9
Arkansas	1
Connecticut	3
Delaware	1
Georgia	3
Kansas	2
Louisiana	6
Maine	2
Massachusetts	3
Michigan	4
Missouri	3
Montana	1
New Jersey	3
New York	2
North Carolina	6
Ohio	3
South Carolina	6
Tennessee	1
Virginia	9
TOTAL	63

Part I
Contexts

Witness to Change
Fifty Years of Indian Activism and Tribal Politics

Donald L. Fixico

The field of American Indian studies has gone through a series of upheavals since the late 1960s, with much of the debate revolving around research methodologies and the need to recognize Native agency and voice.[1] Donald L. Fixico, since 1969, when he began his college career, has been a central participant in this debate, and his work has been instrumental to the rewriting of twentieth-century American Indian history. Here he offers a personal reflection on the everyday experiences and formal literature that have shaped his thinking about the relationships between politics, activism, and scholarship. His argument for useable histories focused on the internal dynamics of Indian persistence charts a course for new studies of politics and activism.[2] Fred Hoxie, in chapter 2, builds upon this analysis with a critique of the Western historical canon.

Looking back at the years of growing up in Oklahoma, I am amazed that so much has happened in my part of Indian Country. The same can be said for the rest of Indian Country. What I remember most about my rural childhood during the 1950s and early 1960s involves going to stomp dances in eastern Oklahoma, yet so much occurred during this decade that threatened my four tribes (Shawnee, Sac and Fox, Muscogee Creek, and Seminole) and others. I did not fully realize this until I began my graduate studies at the University of Oklahoma in federal–Indian relations during the twentieth century. In my world of the Seminole and Muscogee Creeks, "Red Power" related naturally to the Red Stick warriors of the Creeks, and activism did not equate to much of anything relevant in my growing up years around the towns of Shawnee and Seminole.

When I focused my research on the policy of termination during the 1950s and 1960s, I came to the realization that most Indians knew very little about it—unless, that is, they were citizens of the tribes that had been terminated, like the Menominee of Wisconsin or the Klamath of Oregon. In fact, most Americans knew very little about termination when it was happening. And they still do not know. It is almost as if this dreadful Indian policy was and is a big secret.

I was born during the years of the Korean War and at about the same time as the federal government began its push for termination. In addition to ending tribes' trust relationships, it was offering relocation to all American Indians. The government hoped that if Indians left tribal communities and moved to big cities, they would lose their culture and their attachment to the land. As I mentioned, during my own childhood much of what mattered to me had little to do with termination, relocation, or how tribes responded to these. It took graduate study to sort out all of this much later. But during that time, I came to realize that these federal decisions were, in large measure, a response to the Second World War and to the onset of the Cold War.

My heroes were Uncle Telmond and Uncle Otis. I remember seeing their pictures on the walls in their houses as a youngster and admiring them in their uniforms. I never asked questions about their war experiences, but I thought that if they wanted to talk to me about them, I would be ready to listen. They were two of an estimated twenty-five thousand Native men and several hundred Native women who served in the armed forces during World War II. The United States was our country too, and there was no doubt about this as another ten-thousand-plus Indian men fought in Korea. Heroes emerged during both conflicts, such as the Navajo Code Talkers and Oklahoma Indians Ernest Childers, a Creek, and Jack Montgomery, a Cherokee, both of whom earned the Medal of Honor. Ironically, the Native patriotism of people like Childers, Montgomery, and my uncles is what convinced the United States government that a new policy of assimilating Indians into the American mainstream seemed right.

World War II changed attitudes about everything, including Indians. I remember saluting and saying the Pledge of Allegiance to the American flag in school every morning. I went to a rural public school, Bethel School, outside Shawnee, Oklahoma. My younger brother and I were about the only Indians at Bethel. I still recall writing with the big, thick pencils on heavy, dark red Big Chief tablets in the first and second grades. I was Indian, and everyone knew it because I looked Indian. Somehow I felt connected to the picture on the front of the Big Chief tablet, and this was not a good feeling.

In those days at a country school, it seemed that everyone used those tablets in the first and second grades. I was always the only Indian in class, and only years later did it dawn on me why I was seated toward the front of the class only once, in the second grade. My assigned seat was always the last seat in the row during the first through sixth grades, although I usually was one of the best students with the highest marks in every class.

This is what it was like for me to be Indian when Dwight Eisenhower, the American war hero, was president of the United States and Oklahoma was a provincial state. I also remember the ring of the bell that started those all too common drills in elementary school. I remember hiding in the school's basement or in hallways. In case of a nuclear attack, we were to sit in rows against the wall, ducking our heads. The imminence of it seemed real, and I was taught to understand the serious threat Communism posed to democracy in the world. Despite this, I continued to go to stomp dances in my tribal community, and that seemed right. Our ground was Gar Creek. My family's connection to that place was through the Ceyvha band of Seminoles. They started the ceremonial fire for their community after removal to Oklahoma from northern Florida in the late 1830s.

Only later did I begin to comprehend just how detrimental the 1950s were for tribal communities. The government tried to dismantle tribal leadership across Indian Country, and with a firm, paternalistic hand it attempted to suppress any leadership movement among tribes. I remember feeling frustrated about this helpless situation, and it contributed to my decision to study termination and relocation as my doctoral dissertation topic. I kept thinking, what could be more important than writing about the termination policy? It seemed so ultimate, so final. If termination had been carried out to its full, logical conclusion—and in some cases it was—it would have brought an absolute end to treaties and the complete nullification of trust responsibilities that the federal government really did not want to live up to anyway. Through my studies, I came to learn that the Eisenhower administration's view on Indian affairs derived from a small group of Western congressmen—Arthur Watkins, Patrick McCarren, Hugh Butler, and Richard Neuberger—whose constituents' interests conflicted with tribal resources on reservation lands in states such as Utah, Nevada, Wisconsin, and Oregon.

As I naively began research into this enormous national topic (which I do not recommend to Ph.D. students), I was questioned more than once by people who were put off by the fact that I was paying critical attention to their "favorite sons." They were the relatives of terminationists or, in some cases, archivists who did not want me to see these congressmen's papers. I also remember that during one visit to a regional National Archives center, the archivists did not even believe that I was a doctoral student. I was an

Indian, and an Indian had never been there to conduct manuscript research in federal documents.

After the 1986 publication of my book *Termination and Relocation*, which was essentially a policy study, I began to explore more deeply the idea that one must comprehend not only what happened in Washington DC but also the nature and complexity of tribal and Indian politics.[3] Moreover, with time I further concluded that tribal and Indian politics should not be taken as synonymous. In my mind, tribal politics involves the internal dynamics of communities, whereas Indian politics consists of tribal relationships with outsiders, including local, state, and federal governments, as well as other tribes.

My increased sensitivity to these complexities derived, in part, from a surge of activism during the 1960s and 1970s. There were fishing rights protests at rivers in the Northwest throughout the 1960s and then, during the next decade, the even more audacious occupations of abandoned government facilities, the Bureau of Indian Affairs headquarters in DC, and a place called Wounded Knee in South Dakota. Defiant calls for change surrounded all of us. At the University of Oklahoma, I watched with other students as a part of the south campus consisting of military barracks burned down. On another cool night, we were called out of our twelve-story dorm by campus police because someone had started a fire on the other end of it. Outside, in pajamas and bathrobes, we watched firefighters and policemen working hastily, trying to control the flames and prevent students from needlessly breaking more windows. These events became the norm, a part of daily life in those unpredictable times.

The rise of the American Indian Movement (AIM) was important to those of us who were coming of age during the late 1960s and 1970s (see tables 4 and 5). I was seventeen in 1969 and getting ready to enter Bacone Junior College in Bacone, Oklahoma. AIM had been founded in Minneapolis, Minnesota, the year before. At first, it was primarily a grassroots effort to stop police brutality against Indian people. George Mitchell, Clyde Bellecourt, and Dennis Banks—all of them Ojibwes—co-founded the organization with other Native people to stop their friends and relatives from being beaten. Eventually, the organization grew to include more than forty chapters in the United States and Canada. Russell Means (Lakota), Dennis Banks, and their compatriots soon connected with reservation-based elders and spiritual leaders. They articulated and showed the rest of the nation a new kind of militant leadership that was founded on a respect for tribal traditions. They said that they were willing to die for their people. AIM grew quickly, and their protests seemed to occur everywhere. Red was one of AIM's principal colors, and I recall that any Indian wearing something of that color

Figure 2. Vine Deloria Jr. (1933–2005) authored more than twenty books on topics ranging from theology to law. He is seen here in a photo taken during the late 1970s. From the Miami University Archives, Oxford, Ohio.

would likely catch a second glance. The 1970s were high times for militant activism.

I began my master's work at the University of Oklahoma in 1974. I remember being affected not only by the activism of AIM but also by the explosion of American Indian Studies programs on various college campuses. For me, Indian intellectualism was a critical part of activism. At that time, three books served as particularly powerful expressions of this kind of Red Power. Vine Deloria Jr., a Standing Rock Sioux lawyer, published *Custer Died for Your Sins: An Indian Manifesto* in 1969 (figure 2). It was a blazing criticism of the United States and white society and remains essential reading today. That same year, Kiowa scholar N. Scott Momaday won the Pulitzer Prize for his novel *House Made of Dawn*. Then, in 1970, Dee Brown's famed *Bury My Heart at Wounded Knee* challenged Americans to entertain the views of American Indians on the history of Indian–white relations. Even now, when asked about the most read book about Indians, many people cite *Bury My Heart at Wounded Knee*.[4]

These pivotal works aroused and shook America's conscience. But what did Indians want? For one, many of us felt passionately about the importance of ensuring a place in the academy so that our own perspectives on our own histories could be heard. When I began studying twentieth-century American Indian history as a graduate student in the late 1970s, I found that I could talk to only a few scholars who knew much about it. I am grateful to Francis Paul Prucha for discussing research sources with me during those confusing years and to scholars like Floyd O'Neil, who actually worked with tribes. For the most part, though, Indian politics was considered a part of tribal histories. Some graduate students selected these topics to write about, but very few scholars ventured to study the twentieth century—until it was almost over. In retrospect, I suspect that part of the reason was that ignoring modern Indians and writing about dead ones was much easier than facing possible criticism from people who might still be alive. Red Power had had a major impact.

In addition to Deloria, a few brave, early scholars wrote about Indians and their concerns. This group included Angie Debo, who focused on Oklahoma tribal politics in her classic *And Still the Waters Run: The Betrayal of the Five Civilized Tribes*; Wilcomb Washburn, who edited a volume on federal–Indian relations, *The American Indian and the United States*, as well as *Red Man's Land/White Man's Law: A Study of the Past and Present Status of the American Indian*; Alvin Josephy Jr., who edited *Red Power: The American Indians' Fight for Freedom*; Edgar Cahn, *Our Brother's Keeper: The Indian in White America*; Stan Steiner, *The New Indians*; and Hazel Hertzberg, *The Search for an American Indian Identity: Modern Pan-Indian Movements*.[5]

In most works, however, the general story was victimization, or how a tribe was usurped by a federal government that suppressed Indian initiative of any kind. As a doctoral student, I began to ask whether scholars were asking the right questions, whether they were even looking for Indian agency or exploring the internal logic of political activism. Salish Kootenai intellectual D'Arcy McNickle insightfully suggested this approach in his *Native American Tribalism: Indian Survivals and Renewals*, but most did not.[6] So I began to think about my own growing up experiences again, about my family, and my own communities.

This introspection affected the way I conceptualized politics in my books *The Invasion of Indian Country in the Twentieth Century* and *The Urban Indian Experience in America*. Both of these explored tribal politics (how individuals and families adapted to changes and confronted challenges inside their own communities) and Indian politics (how formal organizations related these concerns to outsiders).[7] I found that within tribes and communities, internal politics witnessed a new rise in leadership as more mainstream-educated individuals assumed important positions, especially in tribal business areas. In addition to the constant political struggle within, tribes persisted in their political dealings with other Indian groups and state governments. At the national level, tribes maintained a political relationship with the federal government. Pantribal organizations, such as the National Congress for American Indians (NCAI), the National Indian Youth Council (NIYC), AIM, and the Council of Energy Resource Tribes (CERT), gained ground as well. In each instance, leaders representing a large constituency of Native peoples that transcended tribal boundaries came to the forefront. And they became recognized by the United States.

It was not always this way. During the first fifty years of the twentieth century, Native people had limited influence. The Bureau of Indian Affairs controlled their lives. As we say, *BIA* stood for "Boss Indians Around." This is not to suggest that Indian people did not control their own communities within. Tribal communities continued old ways on reservations and in rural areas like the Seminole stomp ground where I grew up. My grandfather was a leader among our people at Gar Creek. He took care of the dance ground as the medicine maker, and as a child I watched him sprinkle the ground and give instructions to men who helped him. He was not the leader of the stomp ground or *Mikko*, who was in charge of political matters. In his role, my grandfather was an adviser to the Mikko about medicinal issues, and he had the respect of the community. Many years later, my uncle would fill the same role as the medicine maker and adviser to the Mikko. Among Indians, a real leader has the respect of the people, and he or she is more like a servant to them. This is the role that Indian leaders accept in life—to help their people.

My grandfather, like Native elders in many other communities, led his people in the internal way of tribal politics. Beyond the gaze of the dominant society, Native culture remained strong as devoted individuals continued to sing and dance traditional songs. This is what I remember so well. There seemed to be two worlds when I was growing up. Inside the communities, Indian women were also important leaders. My grandmother was the matriarch. Her daughters and their families and my family were under her protection. She played an even more important role after my grandfather died, and her word was final because she made decisions based on the wisdom gained from a long life of experiences. She had all our interests at heart. She was a strong woman.

When I wrote *The American Indian Mind in a Linear World*, I reflected on this personal dimension of politics in the context of stompdancing. The dance begins about midnight, usually after, and continues until dawn to welcome the cycle of night into day, the rebirth of life, coming from the dark into the light. Throughout the dances, invited singers lead the dances, one at a time, as people dance around the ceremonial fire. Women shake shells or cans nowadays, with the men responding in chants to the leader. The dance itself takes on a reality of its own as the present and the past merge into one. At times, I look at other dancers across the fire, and sometimes I see an elderly person dancing and I think that I see my grandmother, grandfather, or an aunt or uncle who has passed away. In the dark and by firelight, people resemble other people. Or are they actually there, singing and dancing to ancient songs that have been and always will be carried down through the generations? Past and present are confused, and the only thing important is that you are dancing. Sometimes when I am alone, especially late at night, I hear these ancient songs, the shells shaking, and can smell the smoke of burning wood that feeds *toca*, the fire. These kinds of "unseen forces" that shape individuals, collective action, and, by extension, history are intriguing.[8]

It is also true that, although federal paternalism controlled our communities externally, educated Indian individuals engaged the government and mainstream with early organizations such as the Society of American Indians (SAI). By and large, these were people who had been educated in either federal boarding schools or in the dominant society. They encountered education in the context of mainstream standards, but they utilized the knowledge acquired from this experience to speak for justice and better conditions for tribal communities. The General Citizenship Act of 1924 allowed the remainder of Indians to become American citizens, but my grandparents, like other elderly Indians, were not citizens of this country for most of their lives. So how does one survive in a colonial system as a minority? How do indigenous communities survive? Why do they persist? The Society of American Indians asked these questions; so did the NCAI, AIM, and CERT. And so did my grandparents. We Indian people have been asking these questions for a long time.

Many of the chapters in this volume explore how Indian people answered these questions, and much more work needs to be done. I am heartened to see that, increasingly, the ones doing it are Indian scholars trained in Indian schools. In the Twin Cities in Minnesota, AIM introduced the alter-Native elementary school when it created the Heart of the Earth School in 1972. Since the 1960s, sustained attention has been devoted to restoring Indian control over higher education. Navajo Community College began in 1969 as an experiment in this arena, and many more tribes have formed their own institutions within the boundaries of their homelands.

Today the American Indian Higher Education Consortium represents thirty-four tribal colleges and Haskell Indian Nations University, and the *Tribal College Journal* disseminates news of curricular innovations across Indian Country.

As I mentioned earlier, my own higher education began at Bacone Junior College. Located just outside Muskogee, Oklahoma, it was founded in 1880 as a missionary school called Indian University. It was later renamed to honor Baptist missionary Almon C. Bacone and is now a four-year college. I attended Bacone for a year and a half and learned much about many tribes from many parts of Indian Country. One fond memory is playing intramural basketball against other tribal teams, such as the Navajos, who preferred a fast running game up and down the court, and the Sioux, who liked to muscle you under the basket inside. Every team had its Indian name: "Cheyenne Dog Soldiers," "Bad Medicine," "Five Tribes." I also remember that I never saw an Indian professor, except for Dick West, a Cheyenne who was in charge of the art department. During the 1960s there were few Indian instructors. As I recall, I had two Indian teachers in the public schools, one in seventh grade and the other in ninth. My point is that you rarely saw a brown face at the front of the classroom.

The late 1960s and the 1970s saw the emergence of nationally recognized Indian intellectuals, such as Vine Deloria Jr., Alfonso Ortiz (Pueblo), Bea Medicine (Lakota), and N. Scott Momaday. They burst onto the scene with their books, and they had something important to say. Along with their predecessors D'Arcy McNickle, Edward Dozier (Pueblo), and Charles Eastman (Dakota), they cleared the academic way for the rest of us. Now Vine, Alfonso, and Bea are gone. But they were, all of them were, leaders. They helped start an Indian renaissance. They gave reliable if sometimes discomforting information to a public that wanted to learn more about American Indians. Their publications captured the interest of academicians too. I credit them with providing much of the momentum that led to the creation of Native studies programs during the rest of the twentieth century. The results were remarkable. One study done in the 1990s indicated that there were nearly one hundred American Indian studies programs, departments, and centers in the United States and Canada.

Despite the growth of studies programs, being an Indian in the academe was not easy during the 1980s. My first faculty position was at the University of Wisconsin–Milwaukee. At that time, Ojibwe people were asserting their treaty-protected, reserved rights to spearfish in waters outside their reservations. Non-Indians met them with violent resistance. On one afternoon during my second year, I received a call in my office. An unfamiliar male voice said that "they" were going to kill my wife that night. To this day, I remember calling her at home. I tried not to sound nervous as I announced that I would be home very soon and suggested that she lock the doors and windows. She asked why, and I said that I would explain as soon as I got there. After I hung up, I immediately called the campus police and my department chairman. I drove home quickly, the threat repeating again and again in my head. I had never been directly involved with the American Indian Movement, but members of that organization came through for me on that occasion. They heard about the threat, and for the next few days I had a bodyguard from AIM sitting in my classes and watching my house, making sure that my wife and I were safe. To this day, I wonder what I did. I cannot think of anything that would provoke such a threat. This was Indian–white politics at its worst as the spearfishing controversy heated up in northern Wisconsin (see tables 5 and 6).

I also remember when an organization called PARR (Protect Americans' Rights and Responsibilities) invited me and another professor from UW-Milwaukee to attend one of its first meetings in northern Wisconsin. Apparently, they wanted the academic community to know what they were about. I accepted without knowing what I was getting into, but it became quite clear early on that they were anti-Indian and firmly against Ojibwe fishing rights. They, too, must have been taken aback. At one point, the organizer of the meeting came up to me and whispered, "You didn't tell me that you were Indian." They proceeded to question my academic credentials until I showed them my faculty identification.

My colleague and I took our seats in a special reserved section of the second row. With the American and Wisconsin state flags prominently displayed, PARR blasted away at Ojibwes, arguing that Indians received unfair advantages and that the legal rights of non-Native fishermen were being violated. I was very glad to leave that meeting when it ended. That night the state police patrolled, with dogs, the halls of the motel where the conference was held—something I had never seen before. By more than happenstance, it turns out, Ojibwes and their supporters were planning to hold a meeting at the same motel the next day. News companies sent in their television cameras and reporters, fully expecting a fight. This was one occasion when one never broke out. But I remember being right in the middle of things as I checked out the next day. You could feel the tension as people on both sides showed up to make their presence felt at the meeting.

In Wisconsin and elsewhere, the 1980s and 1990s saw a new generation of sophisticated Indian leaders make changes to both tribal and Indian politics. They developed new techniques and responded to new issues and concerns under a new federal Indian policy called "Indian self-determination." College-educated, urbane, and articulate, tribal leaders and directors of

Indian organizations have bicultural backgrounds and operate in both the tribal and mainstream worlds. People often think of a dichotomy between Indian traditionalism and the white mainstream. These leaders revealed the simplicity of that way of thinking by moving comfortably between those two poles. Many were boarding school educated, like my current colleague Peterson Zah (Diné) at Arizona State University and my good friend Karen Gayton Swisher (Standing Rock Sioux), the first woman to serve as president of Haskell Indian Nations University.

In the same sophisticated ways, distant relative Mary McCormack has served as the chief of the Sac and Fox and presently Kelly Enoch Haney, also a distant relative, serves as the chief of the Seminole Nation in Oklahoma. They are intelligent and talented, they possess foresight, and they are very articulate. They are tremendous leaders with determined personalities to advance tribal causes. Mary and Kelly are good people. Their hearts are good. Their mannerism is simultaneously old and new, traditional and mainstream, cultural and modern. Mary comes from an educated family that gets involved and does things for the tribe. Kelly is very wise and always has a plan in mind to get things done.

They lead our tribes, and other tribal leaders lead their people during these difficult and exciting times. The booming explosion of unregulated Indian bingo that has led to a twenty-billion-dollar Indian gaming industry today demands the sophisticated and heads-up leaders of American Indian tribes. In the age of economics of the late twentieth century and early twenty-first century, Indian leadership is filled with pressure and instant national attention. This calls for effective Indian business leadership at the highest level of economically sound management. In an extraordinary way, Indian gaming has created a new arena of Indian–white gaming politics involving gaming tribes, other gaming operations, state governments, and the federal government. Although Indian gaming has been around since the late 1970s, today it is still in its early stages. Tribal leaders must negotiate conflicts with local and state governments, from California to Florida, as well as with other gaming interests, including other tribes.

But Indian leaders cannot do it alone, and they need the help of non-Indians. In my current study of American Indian leadership, I have observed that any great changes on a national scale necessarily require the involvement of people in powerful positions. In the recent past, this has included figures such as former United States senators James Abourezk from South Dakota and Fred Harris from Oklahoma. Colorado's Ben Nighthorse Campbell (Northern Cheyenne) and Senator Daniel Inouye of Hawaii have served as especially major players over the past few decades. All these men like to get things done; they are believers in good causes and they hate injustice. When you are around them, you can sense their strength. They are forceful leaders who introduced and pursued the passage of milestone Indian legislation during the 1970s and 1980s (see tables 4–6).

Meanwhile, internal tribal histories can help others to discover the nature of Indian politics and activism and to understand the origins of modern Indian sovereignty, tribal self-determination, decision making, communal sustainability, importance of place, leadership, and modern Indian ethos. This is where much of modern scholarship in Indian history is presently being directed—at the tribal roots level, inside communities. Ethnohistorians, anthropologists, political scientists, and historians increasingly realize the importance of visiting Native communities and their places of government. Moreover, scholars have begun reciprocating by sharing their research, defining projects according to the needs of tribal communities, and writing truer accounts of Indian activism and tribal politics. All of this makes clear that if you are afraid to talk to Indians, you are afraid to do what it takes to understand us.

We need continued emphasis on the internal dynamics of Indian persistence, on how tribal people have continued to function as separate communities against sometimes overwhelming odds. The exploration of the complex, internal nature of Indian politics requires combining anthropology, history, sociology, and other disciplinary approaches. These new perspectives should engage Indian activism at various analytical levels that will help us account for the success of Indian politics and today's prosperity of tribal governments in the twenty-first century.

Looking at the inside of tribal communities and Indian organizations is not so easy, but we must if we are going to learn more about the reality of Native politics. Knowing how and why a centuries-old or new community works enables us to understand Indian people. As we look back over the years, the Indian world has become more complex, with sophisticated, modern tribal governments and dynamic leadership in organizations. As an enrolled Sac and Fox, I have watched endless tribal council discussions dealing with issues that outsiders have brought into our communities. And I have seen how fundamental Indian values persist in and through them. These moments remind me of childhood days when Creek and Seminole elders sat during summer days under the Green Corn arbors. They spoke Muscogee as one or two held sticks and drew on the ground, making important decisions for their people. And they still do this today.

Having witnessed the past fifty years of federal–Indian relations and Indian politics from the vantage points of scholarship and personal experience, I find it remarkable how much things have changed. Yet in general, it seems that things occur in cycles. Indian life does. Perhaps Indian progress does too. On one hand, the twentieth century was not entirely good for Indians. There were decades when being Indian or looking dark skinned was a curse and light-skinned Indians denied being Native at all. On the other hand, the late 1960s and the 1970s were proud times—with the advent of hippies, New Agers, and the early environmental movement, it seemed as though even white people wanted to be Indian. It is often hard to be Indian, especially having been Christianized, Americanized, "citizenized," urbanized, boarding-schooled, allotted, terminated, relocated, and assimilated. What does this feel like? What does it feel like inside? Like tribal politics, what is happening inside is where you learn about leadership, clan influence, kinship blocs, community, nepotism, and medicine. It is where you learn about continuity and survival. Tribal leaders change, but the politics stays much the same. Too often we do not look inside. But that is exactly where we should turn our gaze, because the heart of tribal politics and Indian activism resides within.

Notes

1. These changes can be traced through time in Calvin Martin, ed., *The American Indian and the Problem of History* (Oxford: Oxford University Press, 1987); Donald Fixico, ed., *Rethinking American Indian History* (Albuquerque: University of New Mexico Press, 1997); Devon Mihesuah, ed., *Natives and Academics: Researching and Writing about American Indians* (Lincoln: University of Nebraska Press, 1998); Russell Thornton, ed., *Studying Native America: Problems and Prospects* (Madison: University of Wisconsin Press, 1998); Linda Tuhiwai Smith, *Decolonizing Methodologies: Research and Indigenous Peoples* (New York: Zed Books, 1999); Philip Deloria and Neal Salisbury, eds., *A Companion to American Indian History,* Blackwell Companions to American History (Malden, MA: Blackwell Publishing, 2002); Nancy Shoemaker, ed., *Clearing a Path: Theorizing the Past in Native American Studies* (New York: Routledge, 2002); Thomas Biolsi, ed., *A Companion to the Anthropology of American Indians,* Blackwell Companions to Anthropology (Malden, MA: Blackwell Publishing, 2004); and Clara Sue Kidwell and Alan Velie, *Native American Studies* (Lincoln: University of Nebraska Press, 2005).

2. Waziyatawin Angela Wilson and Michael Yellow Bird, eds., *For Indigenous Eyes Only: A Decolonization Handbook* (Santa Fe, NM: SAR Press, 2005).

3. Donald Fixico, ed., *Termination and Relocation: Federal Indian Policy, 1945–1960* (Albuquerque: University of New Mexico Press, 1986).

4. N. Scott Momaday, *House Made of Dawn* (New York: Harper and Row Publishers, 1968); Vine Deloria Jr., *Custer Died for Your Sins: An Indian Manifesto* (New York: Macmillan, 1969; reprinted with a new preface, Norman: University of Oklahoma Press, 1988); and Dee Brown, *Bury My Heart at Wounded Knee: An Indian History of the American West* (New York: Holt, Rinehart, and Winston, 1970–1971).

5. Angie Debo, *And Still the Waters Run: The Betrayal of the Five Civilized Tribes* (1940; Princeton, NJ: Princeton University Press, 1968); Stan Steiner, *The New Indians* (New York, Evanston, IL, and London: Harper and Row Publishers, 1968); Edgar Cahn, ed., *Our Brother's Keeper: The Indian in White America* (New York: A New Community Press Book, 1969); Hazel

Hertzberg, *The Search for an American Indian Identity: Modern Pan-Indian Movements* (Syracuse, NY: Syracuse University Press, 1971); Alvin Josephy Jr., ed., *Red Power: The American Indians' Fight for Freedom* (New York: American Heritage Press, 1971); Wilcomb Washburn, *Red Man's Land/White Man's Law: A Study of the Past and Present Status of the American Indian* (New York: Scribner, 1971); and Wilcomb Washburn, ed., *The American Indian and the United States: A Documentary History* (New York: Random House, 1973).

6. D'Arcy McNickle, *Native American Tribalism: Indian Survivals and Renewals* (1973; New York: Oxford University Press, 1993).

7. Donald Fixico, *The Invasion of Indian Country in the Twentieth Century: American Capitalism and Tribal Natural Resources* (Niwot: University Press of Colorado, 1998); *The Urban Indian Experience in America* (Albuquerque: University of New Mexico Press, 2000).

8. Donald Fixico, *The American Indian Mind in a Linear World: American Indian Studies and Traditional Knowledge* (New York: Routledge, 2003).

2 Missing the Point
Academic Experts and American Indian Politics

Frederick E. Hoxie

For the past several decades, the Smithsonian Institution's *Handbook of North American Indians* has been considered the authoritative source for information about the history and culture of Native peoples. The latest volumes incorporate the most recent innovations in the field, but some of the older publications have come under close scrutiny in recent years. In this chapter, which adds to Fixico's personal narrative in chapter 1, Fred Hoxie uses the fourth volume of the handbook, *History of Indian–White Relations*, as a springboard into a historiographical discussion of how scholars represent—and often misrepresent—American Indian politics. He raises important questions about the construction of historical knowledge and shows why the way we think about the past carries serious consequences for the present and future.

At first glance, "American Indian Politics" would seem a self-evident category. Obviously, "Indian politics" would entail the activities of American Indian community leaders (and their followers), the operations of the decision-making institutions within which they operate, and their relationships with other political bodies, particularly the institutions of outsiders such as state and federal agencies. But, as with many aspects of Native American life, what is obvious is not always what gets written down. Just as "Indian education" rarely involves descriptions of Native learning and "Indian religion" does not always focus on what people believe, what experts call "Indian politics" rarely describes the reality of indigenous peoples' experiences with national and state governments and their laws.[1] Perhaps the situation would be different if the subject were brand new, but experts have written about

"American Indian Politics" for more than a century, and, unfortunately, their efforts have often limited and distorted the meaning of the term.[2]

Perhaps the easiest way to describe how academic experts have captured and altered the meaning of "Indian politics" is to examine a major scholarly document. Published in 1988, the *History of Indian–White Relations*, volume 4 of the Smithsonian Institution's *Handbook of North American Indians*, marked a significant achievement in academic writing about Native Americans.[3] Edited by historian Wilcomb Washburn and bringing together the work of scholars from several disciplines, the volume seemed to signify that Indian people had finally gained recognition as historical actors.

The 1988 volume was part of the Smithsonian Institution's effort to produce a new edition of the original 1907 handbook, edited by anthropologist Frederick Webb Hodge. The original contains no entries on "Politics" or "Diplomacy" and has little to say about decision making and political thinking within tribes. For example, an entry on "Government" comments, in passing, that "for most of the tribes of North America, a close study and analysis of the social and political organization are wanting...."[4] Happily, the 1988 project devotes significant space to diplomatic encounters between indigenous tribes and European powers and to the multiple political relationships between Indians and the United States government. The volume also includes chapters on a variety of contemporary topics such as Indian hobbyists, Indians in literature, and Indians in popular American culture. Unusual among the modern handbook's projected twenty volumes, the *History of Indian–White Relations* volume defines itself by history rather than by culture. Volume 4 appeared to be a fitting capstone to a generation of new scholarship that collectively had brought indigenous peoples into academic consciousness.

Identifying academic generations with great precision is difficult, but the era of American Indian scholarship that culminated in the publication of the *History of Indian–White Relations* probably began four decades earlier with D'Arcy McNickle's *They Came Here First* in 1949. The first general history of indigenous peoples written by an Indian scholar, McNickle's book emphasized the ability of Native communities to adapt to new circumstances and to survive the consequences of American conquest and colonization. McNickle believed that Indian history should not be seen as the story of "the vanquished and vanishing American."[5] When it came to their political relations with outsiders, McNickle pointed out that Indian people had not been passive objects of government policy. Modern Indian communities were continuous with the independent peoples who had first encountered Europeans in the sixteenth and seventeenth centuries. "Indian tribes have rights under United States law," McNickle reminded his readers. "They have a place in our society as functioning units of political and social content. They cannot be destroyed without leaving a vacuum." As a former Indian Office employee, McNickle had traveled extensively across North America and had learned firsthand about Native political aspirations. He noted that "the white man might be ignorant of the existence of social organization, but it was alive and operating, sometimes in plain view, sometimes beneath the surface. Probably there was not a tribe anywhere in the United States...which did not continue some form...of native organization."[6]

Ten years later, McNickle and Harold E. Fey produced a popular volume focused on the indigenous experience in the United States: *Indians and Other Americans*. Like *They Came Here First*, it argues that non-Indians were, by deliberate custom and policy, disinterested in the humanity and inventiveness of tribal people. But reflecting the optimism of his mentor, John Collier, former commissioner of Indian Affairs (to whom *They Came Here First* is dedicated), McNickle and his co-author wrote that with proper support tribal communities could shape productive futures in the United States. "The unfulfilled dream of the Indians of this country," they wrote, "is that they will be permitted at last to make the primary decisions affecting their lives and property."[7]

McNickle's passion and optimism were evident in much of the new scholarship on Indian people that the American public began to read and buy in the 1960s. His views were also shared by the activists who began to grab the nation's headlines as the decade unfolded. The 1961 American Indian Chicago Conference embraced a "Declaration of Indian Purpose," drafted in part by McNickle, that equates Native Americans with other colonized peoples. It insists that Indians meant to defend their reservation homelands "as earnestly as any small nation or ethnic group was ever determined to hold to identity and survival." Later that same year, the National Indian Youth Council was founded by a group of impatient young leaders "to preserve and establish the rights of Indian people." Also in 1961, Alvin Josephy published *The Patriot Chiefs*, a collection of profiles of famous tribal leaders.[8] Josephy's book presents familiar figures—Tecumseh, Black Hawk, Crazy Horse, Joseph—but reverses the traditional view that these noble individuals had defended doomed and backward ways of life. Echoing the themes of McNickle's earlier histories, Josephy argued that these warriors had been pushed into battle by the inability of US leaders to find a place for them within the American nation. They were not "renegades," but patriots defending their nations.

At the end of the 1960s, Josephy's proposal that the general public needed to reorient its thinking about Native Americans was amplified eloquently by Vine Deloria Jr., the son of a renowned Sioux Anglican priest who had recently stepped down as executive director of the National Congress of American Indians. In *Custer Died for Your Sins*, Deloria argued that the chief problem confronting Indians was their invisibility. Outsiders, from well-meaning anthropologists to hostile politicians, all believed that they knew Indians and could speak and make decisions for them. "Other groups have difficulties, predicaments, quandaries, problems, or troubles," Deloria wrote. "Traditionally we Indians have had a 'plight.'" He added, "Our foremost plight is our transparency. People can tell just by looking at us what we want, what should be done to help us, how we feel, and what a 'real' Indian is really like."[9] Along with N. Scott Momaday's *House Made of Dawn*, this "Indian manifesto" marked a new high-water level in the campaign of American Indians to be heard and recognized by a national audience.

The articles for the *History of Indian–White Relations* were commissioned in the 1970s, just as this recognition seemingly was about to become widespread. Deloria and Momaday's emergence coincided with a rise in political activism—symbolized by Indian occupations of Alcatraz in 1969 and Wounded Knee in South Dakota four years later—and in public interest in Indian affairs (see table 4). (Recall that *Bury My Heart at Wounded Knee*, Dee Brown's scathing indictment of American treatment of Indians in the nineteenth century, topped the best seller lists following its publication in 1970.)[10] Scholarship in the field also expanded as colleges and universities established courses and academic programs in American Indian studies. D'Arcy McNickle served on the volume 4 planning committee (though he died in 1977 and did not live to see the book in print), and essays were solicited from a number of scholars who had recently published major monographs in the field. Among these were Francis Paul Prucha, Reginald Horsman, Robert Utley, Hazel Hertzberg, Robert Winston Mardock, and Wilbur Jacobs.

The *History of Indian–White Relations* emphasizes Indians' persistent efforts to defend their homelands and to adapt to the presence of intruders on their lands. It focuses on the actions of Indian diplomats and reformers, and by appearing as part of the Smithsonian's definitive *Handbook* series, it recognizes in an unprecedented way the prominent place Indian people and their cultures had long maintained in the national imagination.

But picking up volume 4 nearly two decades after its publication is a shock. Created with great sincerity and devotion, it nonetheless has more in common with the histories of the nineteenth century than with what modern scholars hope to produce in the twenty-first. Despite the book's worthy intentions and ongoing value as a reference work, it fails to fulfill the aspirations of McNickle, Deloria, and other Native scholars who had inspired and encouraged the academic authors who produced it. The *History of Indian–White Relations* demonstrates the power of traditional views of the Indian past to capture and compress these intellectuals' original vision. As a consequence, it perpetuates the invisibility Vine Deloria had identified as the Indians' "foremost plight."

The volume is divided into six sections, each devoted to a different aspect of American Indian relationships to the outside world. The largest number of essays—thirteen—focus on "Political Relations," largely with the United States (treaties, land transfers, legal status, government agencies, and education). Twelve essays describe the "National Policies" of countries who maintained relations with Native Americans, and eleven additional pieces address "Economic Relations" (trade, slavery, and ecological change). Smaller sections (eight and nine essays, respectively) focus on "Religious Relations" (separate essays on different sectarian mission efforts) and "Conceptual Relations" (white images of Indians, Indians in literature, and so on). In keeping with the volume's gentle tone, only three essays make up the smallest section, on the "Military Situation."

The editors assumed (perhaps not surprisingly, given its title and sponsor) that Indian "Relations" began and ended with white people and their institutions. Moreover, the book's organization implies that these various "Relations" occurred in separate and discrete compartments of Native American life. Education was separate from religion, and law did not spill over into trade. Moreover, in the editors' hands, "Relations" were formal and public: they did not appear to involve intermarriage, migration, or other dimensions of personal life, such as clothing, music, popular beliefs, or childrearing. These shortcomings are partially attributable to the handbook's encyclopedic format and academic style, but the collective effect of its structure and approach is to transform the Indian people whose prominence in American history is surely one of the book's implicit themes into passive objects of governments, missionaries, and educators.

In volume 4, Indians are the people whom the missionaries sought to convert; they are the students in the government schools; they are the trade partners who become players in the new economy; they are the pitiful victims who call forth the benevolence of reformers, policymakers, and artists. In each instance, the essays' narratives begin with external actors and institutions rather than with Native reality. A focus on Indian actors—central to the books by McNickle, Josephy, and Deloria—disappears as the handbook's authors struggle to identify an Indian "role" in the operation of European and American institutions.[11] And, in the process, "Indian politics" is reduced to the responses of Native leaders to the actions of outsiders.

The most striking evidence that the inventiveness, persistence, and dynamism of American Indian political leaders is being ignored in volume 4 comes in its final section, a compilation of 294 "Non-Indian Biographies." This admittedly valuable list of missionaries, scholars, reformers, and government officials underscores the book's not-so-subtle message: "Indian–White Relations" were (and presumably continue to be) initiated and shaped by non-Indian actors, the people who control the Indian Office, direct government agencies, organize the missions, and chart the course of academic scholarship. (Stated more baldly, the volume seems to suggest that white people control history and that the Indians' role is to react.) Native people might be prominent in their resistance—or even their contribution—to one or another aspect of their "Relations" with the outside world (as educators, treaty negotiators, or missionaries), but they neither shaped their relationships with external actors nor developed an intellectual apparatus for tutoring their communities or their neighbors in how best to proceed into the modern era.

Taken as a whole, the *History of Indian–White Relations* is a sobering document. On the one hand, it is a laudable attempt to frame a pluralistic view of the North American past. Indians are located in every arena and era. Their presence cannot be denied. In addition, the volume's organization and tone are comprehensive, benign, and optimistic. On the other hand, Indians appear as figures who have ultimately reconciled themselves with the American state and its institutions. Whether the topic is education, religion, or the law, this reconciliation (and the cultural sensitivity it required) was clearly equated in the editors' minds with "success." Alternatively, arbitrary authority and violence were thought to undermine "good" Indian–white relations. There seems to be no place in the volume for Indian agency, for Indian creativity, or for an American Indian intellectual tradition that might have shaped the national narrative. And nowhere is the absence of Indian agency and foresight more evident than in the volume's treatment of Native politics.

In volume 4, all politics are national, and all political initiatives occur outside Indian communities. Essays on national policies and congressional policy making dominate the section "Political Relations." No essays address political activity at the state or regional level, and no essays focus on the relationship between tribal communities and other-than-federal agencies such as state governments, private relief groups, lawyers, and political parties. No essay takes an Indian idea or initiative as a point of departure. The two essays on policy making (called "The Indian Rights Movement" before and after 1887—when Congress approved the Dawes Severalty Act) focus almost exclusively on white ideas and white actors. In Robert Winston Mardock's essay on the pre-1887 rights movement, he discusses the tradition of white critics of national policy but ignores the Indian activists who were often their contemporaries, such as Samson Occum (Mohegan), William Apess (Pequot), John Ross (Cherokee), and Sarah Winnemucca (Paiute). Hazel Hertzberg followed a similar approach in her essay on the Indian Rights Movement after 1887. She focused on white officials and ignored Susette LaFlesche (Omaha), Charles Eastman (Dakota), Arthur Parker (Seneca), and Carlos Montezuma (Yavapai). This myopia led her to assert that it was "difficult to ascertain Indian opinion of allotment policy" and to pronounce that "not until the progressive era was well underway did an Indian wing of the rights movement emerge."[12]

Paul Prucha was less dismissive of Indian activists, but readers of his essay "Presents and Delegations" learned no more from him about Indian political ideas than they did from Mardock and Hertzberg. Prucha wrote that Indian leaders who visited Washington DC on official business "were much impressed by the power of the Whites and returned to their tribes with stories of wonder they had seen. But," he added, "the total effect of the visits...is difficult to assess."[13] Devoting no space to the many unofficial visitors who traveled (and continue to travel) to Washington on behalf of their tribes—or to the legions of lobbyists and lawyers whom tribes have employed to promote their interests over the past 150 years—Prucha left his readers with little sense of Indian attitudes beyond "wonder" and apparent confusion.

Viewed from the perspective of Capitol Hill, the effect of visits to Washington DC may be difficult to assess, but from the perspective of an individual group such as the Cherokees, Lakotas, or Navajos, this assessment might not be so hard to deduce. After all, the Cherokees hired their first lawyers in Washington in the 1830s; the Lakotas struggled for a century to win a legal reversal of the government's seizure of the Black Hills; and the Navajos—with their own full-time lobbyists on site for most of the past generation—have long been effective players in bureaucratic struggles over policy and budget allocations. Within the past few years, two separate monographs have appeared, based almost entirely on petitions submitted to the US government by, respectively, Navajos and Cherokees.[14]

Confined to bureaucratic straitjackets and measured by reactions to white initiatives, the Indian political actors in volume 4 are unrecognizable as members of historically engaged, rapidly evolving, articulate, adaptive communities. It seems that the Indians' role in "history" was to react—along predictable and marginal pathways—or keep to themselves. Despite good intentions, by 1988 the term *Indian politics* had become the captive of several incorrect assumptions. Volume 4 demonstrates that two decades ago many academic scholars still assumed that political activism occurred within the confined spaces of national institutions and along the simple track of external initiative and Native response. Moreover, Indian political actors were assumed to be reactors who emerged episodically to defend local interests. They were portrayed as marginal, derivative individuals who seemed to lack ability to think or debate with colleagues in other tribes or with allies in the bar or political establishment.[15] Most of these assumptions were artifacts of an earlier tradition of historical writing.

Public debate over "the Indian question" began in earnest after the Civil War. Before that time, missionaries and politicians had debated US policy toward the continent's indigenous peoples, but those earlier discussions had taken place when imagining a separate existence for Indians and whites was possible. White experts before 1865, regardless of their point of view, shared some version of Thomas Jefferson's idea that, in the short term, the two groups should live apart. Over time, perhaps, integration could occur in isolated locations and among select groups, but few commentators argued that the rapid incorporation of Indians into the American body politic should be national policy. After the war, there seemed no other option—as a national bureaucracy took shape, the pace of western settlement picked up, and national rail lines framed an integrated national economy. The atmosphere of crisis in the late nineteenth century inspired a number of historians and academic writers to examine the Indians' potential for participating in national politics (see table 1).[16]

Among the earliest of these commentators was George E. Ellis, a clergyman from Charlestown, Massachusetts, who published *The Red Man and the White Man in North America, from Its Discovery to the Present* in Boston in 1882. Ellis professed great sympathy for Indian people but saw no alternative to their becoming the objects of white charity. He admitted that there had been a few Indian leaders who were "able, gifted, great" but all of them (from Pontiac to Black Hawk) "stood and fought for savagery." They understood civilization, Ellis wrote, "but they...loathed it, despised it, rejected it." In the future, it would be essential for groups to produce their own leaders ("furnishing masters and guides from its stock"), but for Ellis there was little chance that this would occur. Given the backwardness of Indian leadership, there was no alternative to white control and tutelage. In short, "a race that cannot itself contribute its redeemers will never be redeemed."[17]

Others shared Ellis's pessimistic view of the Indians' adaptive ability. Elbridge S. Brooks, a popular historian, published *The Story of the American Indian* in 1887. Like Ellis, he argued that Indians deserved public pity but that they were incapable of providing their own political leadership. The Indians' history, he wrote, "is indeed but that of similar subject races who have been antagonized and absorbed by the resistless and more vigorous civilizations that have conquered them." Indians made small adaptations, but this "pseudo civilization...fell because of its own inherent unworthiness." Eventually, there was no alternative for Indians: "[T]hey dropped their weapons...and fell at last into a condition of vassalage, pupilage and involuntary concession in which it became the duty of the civilization that had forced them there to protect, educate and develop them."[18]

According to these commentators, because Indians were "backward" and Americans were "civilized," it was inconceivable that Native people could initiate significant historical change. White people stood with history; Indians, with the past and therefore could only resist. They could not win. This pious view expressed sympathy for the Indians' regrettable predicament but could not imagine a coherent Indian analysis of events. Because Indians could merely respond, they could not observe, plan, and communicate among themselves. They could only suffer or, like Pontiac and Tecumseh, "conspire."

This pessimistic view of Native ability continued as a central theme among academic authors of commentaries on "Indian–White Relations" in the early twentieth century. In 1903, for example, Cyrus Thomas, one of the first self-taught anthropologists whom John Wesley Powell had recruited to staff the Smithsonian's Bureau of American Ethnology, published *The Indians of North America in Historic Times*, another discussion of recent history. Like his predecessors Ellis and Brooks, Thomas was quick to concede the cruelty of American actions. The United States had been "unjust and in some cases even cruel," he wrote. But the sins of white Americans did not erase what Thomas believed was the reality of "the childhood state of the race. That they were children," Thomas continued, "is shown in their ceremonies, plays and amusements."[19]

Fellow anthropologist Warren K. Moorehead took a similar approach a decade later in *The American Indians in the United States, 1850–1914*. Shifting from the language of racial backwardness to an evolutionary view of cultural development, Moorehead noted that even though the Indians' "sun has rapidly declined," their communities would not become extinct. Instead, they were "becoming merged into our larger body of citizens.... [T]he great majority of Indians," he added, "belong to the body politic." Active in Indian reform circles, Moorehead was an advocate of Indian citizenship and civil rights, but his position did not lead him to value Indian political leadership or to imagine an autonomous Indian political philosophy. Instead, it reinforced his view that white people and their institutions would deliver progress to Native America: "A helpless, a trusting and a dependent people look to us to keep the final one of all our promises."[20] Indian political life had little significance for Moorehead. After all, he wrote, "the entire West has been transformed from an Indian country to a white man's country."[21]

In the 1920s and 1930s, writers on Indian affairs expressed growing sympathy for tribal cultures and occasional interest in Native American political leadership. The rise of cultural anthropology, the early opposition to segregation and lynching, and the initial stirrings of cultural pluralism among the leaders of recent immigrants had fueled the belief that conformity to Anglo-American ideals was not the only pathway to civilized life. But the assumption remained that, when compared with Europeans and white Americans, Indian culture was deficient, incapable of adapting to modern conditions, and poorly suited to producing either leaders or ideas that could improve Native life. William Christie Macleod, for example, an academic dissenter from the University of Pennsylvania who attacked the popular orthodoxy of Frederick Jackson Turner, attributed the innovative political life of Indian Territory not to Indian traditions, but to the presence of black and white intruders. This phenomenon, he argued, made "the Indians not only in culture but in blood, more white than Indian." Writing in 1928, Macleod predicted that the forthcoming conclusion of the allotment process would eliminate Indians from American life, reducing their lot "to the utmost shabbiness."[22]

A few years later, Jennings C. Wise, also an academic outlier, produced another volume deeply sympathetic to the cause of the tribes. But even here, the language of pity and helplessness was inescapable. Although he rejected "the smug conclusion that these things were inevitable," he could not resist describing a past in which "the Indian fatherland has been saturated with the blood of a helpless race." He called on his readers to counter this history with "good conscience and reason," but he expressed no curiosity about the content of Indian political life. History, action, initiative—all of these were white monopolies.[23]

This line of sympathetic paternalism extended to mid-century and beyond the borders of the United States. A. Greenfell Price, an Australian historian, had published laudatory volumes on Captain Cook and nineteenth-century Australian settlers before turning to the comparative study of white settlement at the end of his career. Price published *White Settlers and Native Peoples*, a comparative study of Canada, New Zealand, Australia, and the United States, in 1950. When he discussed Americans, Price concentrated on federal policymakers and praised both nineteenth- and twentieth-century reformers for their belief that "the Indian was a worthwhile factor in American life." He concluded with a warm endorsement of John Collier and the benevolent policies of the modern nations (see table 2). "From the broad point of view," Price wrote, "there can be no regret that the invasions took place. Without them the natives would have lost some of the most valuable and healthy English-speaking influences."[24]

The thematic linkage between the Smithsonian's *History of Indian–White Relations* and this earlier scholarly tradition illuminates the remarkably narrow definition of American Indian politics that had come to exist among American academics. Confining Native actors to discrete bureaucratic categories—their participation in treaty negotiations or their role as respondents to Indian Office policy—obscures from view an arena of Native life where tribal members might discuss their predicaments, assess the alternatives offered by both traditional and innovative political structures, and chart a course of action for the future. Limiting American Indian political participation to reactive moments when they confronted or resisted federal officials shields us, as well, from the conversations that occurred among Indians and between Indians and sympathetic whites, therefore preventing us from identifying any organizing principles in the Native conduct of their political lives. Without any sense of the principles Indian people employed to evaluate the political alternatives before them, we have no sense of the intellectual traditions connecting them to one another and to the past.

By contrast, a view of Indian politics that would lift the cloak covering political debate and discussions regarding politics within and among tribal communities can reveal a tradition of disagreement and strategic thinking in a national community of Native actors. When politics is confined to purely internal community debates or to a simple version of "relations" between individual agencies or bureaucrats and individual tribal groups, American Indian political ideas are little more than responses to authority in which Native people speak back to initiatives from beyond the horizon. When the definition of politics is expanded, a new universe of discussion and activism comes sharply into view. Religious leaders may debate politics with elder women who might, in turn, communicate their judgments to newly returned boarding school students for transmission to tribal lawyers or lobbyists. The range of possibilities is far wider than the government transcripts of a treaty proceeding or congressional hearing might suggest.[25]

What are the outlines of a new, wider view of American Indian politics? Of course, Indian political leaders existed for centuries before the arrival of Europeans, and Indian diplomats were engaged with representatives of European powers in North America from the sixteenth century forward. These two eras of political life—the precontact and the colonial—each deserve their own history. The creation of the United States as a sovereign entity marks a third era that had several unique features. Founded as a political democracy, the United States was committed to rule by consent. With the exception of African slaves, the citizens of the republic—even nonvoting women—were believed to have agreed to membership in a representative state whose borders were defined by law, not by ethnicity or geography.

Because their voices were heard, these citizens agreed to obey the nation's institutions. Because Indians were not citizens, the US Constitution declared that they would engage with the United States through diplomatic channels supervised by Congress. When the new nation adopted treaty making as the instrument for this diplomacy, it was assumed that formal agreements would structure relations between the groups. This arrangement would preserve both the authority of the American state and the autonomy of Native people through mutual consent.

But that arrangement did not last. The distinctive flavor of this third era of American Indian political history was set in the first decades of the nineteenth century when white settlers became convinced that their nation should expand to the West and that they—and not the continent's indigenous peoples—deserved the title "Americans." US leaders then determined to displace indigenous peoples from their homelands. This decision disrupted the consent that had underlain the treaty process and produced the forced removal of entire Native communities from territories previously guaranteed to them by treaty. This effort of elimination—called "removal" by modern historians—defined the central paradox of American Indian political life in the United States: Native people were participants in a political system that had become an instrument for a new form of colonization. The American settler state was now engaged simultaneously in conquest and democratization. The pressures unleashed during the removal era set off a struggle by tribal leaders to use the tools of democracy to oppose their dispossession. Their struggle was not limited to a specific institution, organization, or tribe. It was evident in a variety of arenas and among a wide range of leaders, both in eastern areas where tribes were removed by force and in the territory west of the Mississippi where the arrival of easterners disrupted existing patterns of trade and diplomacy.

Later in the nineteenth century, as the destructive ambitions of US settlers multiplied, the veterans of the removal struggle—together with their non-Indian allies and the Indian leaders they encountered in the West—developed a series of principles and tactics to challenge the power of the American state. Their knowledge of US political culture was communicated from tribe to tribe across the continent with accelerating speed. Over time, those who held and added to this knowledge developed ever more articulate challenges to settler authority and to the rhetoric surrounding the Americans' violent westward expansion. Leaders in Indian Territory (modern Oklahoma), for example, called for the recognition of tribal sovereignty within the framework of the US Constitution. They argued that tribal communities could be affiliated with the American state and that they could form progressive political and economic institutions. Elsewhere, outspoken

Indian women like Sarah Winnemucca adopted the language of domesticity to defend their role within their communities and to challenge national efforts to undermine Indian control over the private lives of their children and families. Still others—including leaders from Indian Territory to Minnesota and beyond—turned to tort law and the US Court of Claims in an effort to hold American officials accountable for damages they had inflicted or treaty pledges they had broken or ignored. The Lakotas were the most famous of those who adopted this tactic, but by the early twentieth century it had become a universally acknowledged weapon in the tribal arsenal (see table 1).

By the twentieth century, this tradition of American Indian political activism had expanded to include challenges to the majority's definition of American citizenship, as well as to white people's widely shared assumption about the Indian community's inability to embrace modern economic and cultural life. As a consequence, the congressional grant of citizenship to Indians in 1924 was accompanied by an equally strong statement that the new law would not undermine an individual's right to participate in tribal affairs. In the aftermath of World War II, Native American activists were beginning to articulate a wide-ranging challenge to American power and the hegemony of the nation state (see tables 2 and 3). What is more, Indians began to pose an alternative to the current arrangement, noting that America would be more properly labeled a *plural* rather than a *homogeneous* nation. (It was this attitude that inspired D'Arcy McNickle's defense of tribal governments in *They Came Here First.*)

During American Indians' interactions with one another and with the United States over the past two centuries, they have created a new American political language of rights for themselves and their communities. In the process, this language and the ideas it inspired created an anticolonial critique of the American settler state that was employed by leaders across the country. This critique emerged first in the era of removal when southeastern tribal leaders like James McDonald, a young Choctaw lawyer, argued that American law should provide a curb to arbitrary power. Over time, this argument was elaborated to articulate a defense of tribal sovereignty (developed most fully by Cherokee and Choctaw leaders in the decades following the Civil War) and in a wholesale demand for the reform of the often corrupt federal agencies charged with Indian "uplift." These challenges—which emerged from articulate community leaders such as Sarah Winnemucca and Susette LaFlesche, as well as more traditional figures such as Susette's brother Francis and the Dakota physician Charles Eastman—produced new ideas that were communicated broadly across the continent. Treaty rights, tribal rights, the right to compensation for damages, water and land rights, individual rights to religion, political freedom, and access to cultural traditions—all of these unprecedented ideas were articulated by Native Americans in their ongoing encounter with the expansive pretensions of the American settler state (see table 1).[26]

For the past two centuries, Native leaders have argued that US sovereignty is neither natural nor all-embracing; although ever present, it cannot override treaty obligations to indigenous peoples or deny Indian people the rights that flow from those agreements. To do so, they have argued, would be to deny their communities' participation in a consensual society. By overriding treaty commitments and tribal rights, American officials would be admitting that the United States had become (and would continue to be) an imperial power willing to discard its democratic principles when these become politically unpopular or financially costly. Using the language of democracy to counter their own dispossession, Indian political activists insisted that a consensual state cannot function if legal processes are abandoned and that American citizenship has no meaning if their communities' humanity is ignored. By embracing an imperial position, they warned, American leaders would be subverting their own democratic heritage. These Native activists avoided having their political agendas captured either by white reformers or by Indian traditionalists. They sought neither to assimilate into the American mainstream nor to restore tribal regimes from the precontact era.

American Indians argued that democracies cannot retain their claim to legitimacy if they function outside the arena of consent. This argument lay at the heart of Native peoples' anticolonial critique of the United States. It was a powerful weapon, for the settlers' nation could not deny permanently the Indians' human rights nor could it prohibit forever the participation of Native community leaders in a broad, national discussion of Indian rights. At the same time, American Indian leaders could not avoid acting within the boundaries of American political life. Their campaigns were waged to support the interests of indigenous communities, but their successes were won through interaction with the legal institutions of the United States. The history of this struggle is complex, and it reveals how intertwined Native people became in the institutions of the United States. Also, this history bears out anthropologist James Clifford's assertion that "entanglement is not necessarily cooptation."[27]

Over the past two centuries, American Indian political activists have participated in a variety of widely separate settings but have rarely held official public office. If one looks only at government documents, these activists appear to be scattered, marginal actors, surfacing occasionally to oppose this or that federal action. Nevertheless, their careers and ideas had a coherence that thus far has eluded most scholars. These activists touched one another in ways that allowed the lessons learned in one corner of the continent to be passed on to another for refinement and elaboration. The language and tactical arsenal they created was a collection of words, ideas, and strategies that enabled Native Americans to survive and to articulate a new relationship with the American settler colonizers. Their story remains largely invisible to academic scholars; it challenges those who view American Indian politics in the narrow containers of nation, culture, or race. As it comes into view, this narrative will also undermine the neat but wildly inaccurate assumptions that underlay the Smithsonian's *History of Indian–White Relations* and the paternalistic scholarly literature it represents.

The ambition of the chapters in this volume represents a new chapter in the history of American Indian politics. Specifically, this ambition is to understand Native communities as active nodes in a network of assessment, thought, and action. Of course, that network was rooted in an ancient, indigenous past, but it was also constantly involved with, and responding to, a variety of new conditions, some created by external forces generated nationally or locally and some produced by an internal dynamic of change and innovation. For much of this network's history, the border between the "Indian" and "white" worlds—and the nature of the "relationship" between them—was neither clear nor simple. In the political arena, this network of Indian communities was acutely aware of shifts in power and of the arrival of new tools for community mobilization and new instruments for altering the calculus of influence between groups. In a rapidly shifting national political environment, new conditions, opportunities, and tools were constantly appearing over every horizon.

To aspire to write the political history of this indigenous network—or of individual nodes within it—is to turn aside from the paternalistic Victorian assumption that Indian and non-Indian histories occupy separate spheres and to acknowledge the deeply intertwined nature of these histories, particularly in an expanding imperial democracy such as the United States. Determining exactly how these histories evolved and intersected with each other—where they diverged and where they overlapped—is a task historians have ignored for too long. The aspiration of this volume is to begin work on that task.

Notes

1. There is a large literature—produced mostly by anthropologists—on the inner workings of tribal societies and on political struggles within Native communities. This literature rarely speaks

to the relationship between American Indians and state or federal authorities, and it generally explains Native behavior in terms of cultural traditions and resistance. See, for example, Loretta Fowler, *Arapahoe Politics: Symbols of Crisis and Authority, 1851–1978* (Lincoln: University of Nebraska Press, 1982); and my own *Parading through History: The Making of the Crow Nation in America, 1805–1935* (New York: Cambridge University Press, 1995).

2. Certainly, insightful authors from Angie Debo to Alan Taylor have taught us much about political relationships between outside powers and Indian people, but few have made Indian political ideas and activism on a regional or national level the central focus of their narratives. One such attempt, published many years ago but not yet surpassed, is Russell Lawrence Barsh and James Youngblood Henderson, *The Road: Indian Tribes and Political Liberty* (Berkeley: University of California Press, 1980). See Angie Debo, *And Still the Waters Run: The Betrayal of the Five Civilized Tribes* (1940; Princeton, NJ: Princeton University Press, 1968); and Alan Taylor, *The Divided Ground: Indians, Settlers, and the Northern Borderland of the American Revolution* (New York: Knopf, 2006).

3. *Handbook of North American Indians*, vol. 4, *History of Indian–White Relations*, ed. William Sturtevant (Washington DC: Government Printing Office, 1988).

4. *Handbook of American Indians North of Mexico*, Smithsonian Institution, Bureau of American Ethnology, Bulletin 30, 1907, vol. 1, 498 (from the entry "Government" by J. N. B. Hewitt).

5. D'Arcy McNickle, *They Came Here First: The Epic of the American Indian* (Philadelphia: J. P. Lippincott, 1949), 9.

6. McNickle, *They Came Here First*, 293.

7. Harold Fey and D'Arcy McNickle, *Indians and Other Americans: Two Ways of Life Meet* (New York: Harper and Brothers, 1959), 200.

8. Alvin Josephy Jr., *The Patriot Chiefs: A Chronicle of American Indian Leadership* (New York: Viking, 1961).

9. Vine Deloria Jr., *Custer Died for Your Sins: An Indian Manifesto* (New York: Macmillan, 1969), 1. Deloria's book has become such an icon of academic life that essays on it are now for sale on many student-oriented websites. See, for example, http://www.academon.com/lib/paper/48216.html (accessed February 16, 2007).

10. Dee Brown, *Bury My Heart at Wounded Knee: An Indian History of the American West* (New York: Holt, Rinehart and Winston, 1970–1971).

11. McNickle, Josephy, and Deloria did not hold Ph.D. degrees. In addition, although McNickle and Deloria held university appointments at various times in their careers, all three men's first writing in American Indian studies came when they held nonacademic positions.

12. *Indian–White Relations*, 306.

13. *Indian–White Relations*, 244.

14. Peter Iverson, *"For Our Navajo People": Diné Letters, Speeches and Petitions, 1900–1960* (Albuquerque: University of New Mexico Press, 2002); and Andrew Denson, *Demanding the Cherokee State: Indian Autonomy and American Culture, 1830–1900* (Lincoln: University of Nebraska Press, 2004).

15. The history of people (both Native and non-Native) who practiced "Indian law" is another topic the volume's editors ignored.

16. For a general discussion of this era and the rise of a new version of "the Indian question," see Frederick Hoxie, *A Final Promise: The Campaign to Assimilate the Indians, 1880–1920*

(Cambridge: Cambridge University Press, 1984; Lincoln: University of Nebraska Press, 2001).

17. George Ellis, *The Red Man and the White Man in North America, from Its Discovery to the Present* (Boston: Little Brown, 1882), 629, 630.

18. Elbridge Brooks, *The Story of the American Indian: His Origin, Development, Decline and Destiny* (Boston: Lothrop, 1887), 281.

19. Cyrus Thomas, *The History of North America*, vol. 2, *The Indians of North America in Historic Times* (Philadelphia: George Barrie and Sons, 1903), 412, 417. Thomas also wrote, "The history of America has no dawn—it burst upon the world as the risen sun. It is at this time and place [October, 1492, when Columbus stepped ashore] that the history of the natives of America begins," lx.

20. Warren Moorehead, *The American Indians in the United States, Period 1850–1914* (Andover, MA: The Andover Press, 1914), 18, 171.

21. Moorehead, *Indians*, 31.

22. William Christie Macleod, *The American Indian Frontier* (London: Kagan Paul, Trench, Tribner and Co., 1928), 534, 544.

23. Jennings Wise, *The Red Man in the New World Drama: A Politico-Legal Study with a Pageantry of American Indian History* (Washington DC: W. F. Roberts, 1931), vi, 583.

24. A. Greenfell Price, *White Settlers and Native Peoples* (Melbourne: Cambridge University Press, 1950).

25. This discussion begs the question of how dramatically the scholarly literature has changed since 1989. Although promising studies of individuals and tribes have emerged, the general definition of *Indian Politics* remains fixed in the framework the handbook established. Among the new generation of monographs are Joy Porter, *To Be an Indian: The Life of Iroquois-Seneca Arthur Caswell Parker* (Norman: University of Oklahoma Press, 2001); Paul Rosier, *The Rebirth of the Blackfeet Nation, 1912–1954* (Lincoln: University of Nebraska Press, 2001); Sally Zanjani, *Sarah Winnemucca* (Lincoln: University of Nebraska Press, 2001); and the studies of Cherokee and Navajo petitions cited above. This activism is also a central theme of my *Talking Back to Civilization: Indian Voices from the Progressive Era* (Boston: Bedford/St. Martin's, 2001).

26. See works by Zanjani and Denson cited in notes 25 and 14, respectively.

27. James Clifford, *Routes: Travel and Translation in the Late Twentieth Century* (Cambridge, MA: Harvard University Press, 1996), 276.

3 The Foundations of Federal Indian Law and Its Application in the Twentieth Century

Taiawagi Helton and Lindsay G. Robertson

Taiawagi Helton and Lindsay Robertson, faculty members of the University of Oklahoma's College of Law, explain how federal law and policy reflect changing American attitudes toward Indians and show inconsistency over time. This inconsistency complicates Indian political strategies and contributes to a recent effort on the part of American Indians to participate in international forums and institutions. Helton and Robertson's discussion also makes clear why American Indians are not merely another American minority but, rather, have "special status" and sovereign powers under the law. They show that law structures but does not determine the space in which Native political actors move.

When the United States was founded, it adopted the practice of its European predecessors, recognizing tribal nations as separate, self-governing sovereigns, entering into treaties for peace and land acquisition with tribal states, and establishing centralized, national authority over foreign and Indian relations. Responding to the destabilizing effects of an ambiguity within the failed Articles of Confederation, the US Constitution implicitly divested states of power to relate with foreign and tribal sovereigns alike, investing

Congress with "the powers of war and peace; of making treaties, and of regulating commerce with foreign nations, and among the several States, and with the Indian tribes."[1] In three opinions delivered between 1823 and 1832, Chief Justice John Marshall effectively assessed the scope of these powers.[2] Through the Marshall Trilogy, the US Supreme Court determined that (1) upon discovery by Europeans, tribes lost to the discovering European sovereign full ownership of their lands, retaining a right to occupy those lands, which right to occupy they might convey, but only to the same European sovereign;[3] (2) tribes are neither domestic states nor foreign nations, at least for purposes of Article III of the US Constitution original jurisdiction,[4] but are "domestic dependent nations,"[5] their relationship to the United States "resembl[ing] that of a ward to his guardian";[6] and (3) any attempt by a tribe to enter into relations with a foreign sovereign would be considered an act of war. The Marshall Trilogy provided the legal framework though which tribal governments could be integrated into the political fabric of the United States. Upon these principles, subsequent US–Indian relations were founded.

Given the central role of the federal legislative branch in relating with tribal governments, federal law and policy dominate the history of US–Indian relations. Congressional policy has generally embodied two competing principles—separation of Indian cultural and political entities from non-Indians, on the one hand, and assimilation of Indians into the Anglo-American cultural and political frameworks, on the other. Reflecting changing attitudes of the American electorate toward Native Americans and their resources, congressional policy has shifted in order to advance the prevailing sense of the solution to the "Indian problem." Therefore, the prevalence of one principle over the other has varied across time. Scholars have divided the history of US–Indian relations into "eras" of federal Indian law and policy, identifying each by its dominant policy (see tables 1–7).

As law and policy changed, however, Congress rarely repealed earlier statutes, even when new laws and policies expressly repudiated earlier attitudes and eras. Consequently, marked by "inconstancy, indeterminacy, and variability," federal Indian law is a remarkably complex web of treaties, statutes, and cases—fascinatingly complex to scholars and frustratingly complex to advocates for Native Americans and to Indians themselves.[7]

The twentieth century included four major eras of federal Indian law and policy, opening at the height of the assimilation and allotment era (table 1), then transitioning in 1934 to the reorganization era (table 2). The termination era (table 3) began at the end of World War II but gave way to an era of self-determination policy in the early 1960s, which persisted through the close of the century (tables 4–7). In the establishment and maintenance of

US–Indian policy, Congress remained the principal organ of the federal government. Arguably, the Supreme Court opened a contrary legal era in 1978, however, by introducing the common law doctrine of "implicit divestiture" and actively expanding the authority of state governments in Indian Country while significantly constraining tribal power and jurisdiction.

The twentieth century was a century of shifting policy. As the following chapters describe, Native American activism often focused not only on proactively meeting the needs of Indian communities but also on reacting to the changing legal and political landscape. They fought to preserve cultural values and institutions and, especially, the capacity for self-determination— for the right to live in accordance with their own cultural, spiritual, political, and economic norms and aspirations. Indeed, Indian activism has always been about self-determination. As Chief Justice Marshall observed two centuries ago, "so long as their actual independence was untouched, and their right to self-government acknowledged, [Indians] were willing to profess dependence on the power which furnished supplies of which they were in absolute need, and restrained dangerous intruders from entering their country." However, "[t]he extravagant and absurd idea, that the feeble settlements on the sea coast…acquired legitimate power…to govern the people, or occupy the lands from sea to sea, did not enter the mind of any man."[8]

Before describing the specific, major Indian law-and-policy eras of the twentieth century, we offer one additional contextual observation to advance an understanding of Indian activism and responses to it. As a consequence of the legal and political nature of American Indian rights claims, Native American activists were uniquely situated relative to domestic civil rights movements and post–World War II decolonialist movements abroad. Inherent in struggles for social, political, and legal equality is acquiescence to the authority and legitimacy of the national sovereign—a request to be equally included within the civil society from which such rights are demanded. Non-Indian civil rights movements undoubtedly threatened short-term cultural and societal upheaval, uncertainty, or unrest, particularly when they affected significant numbers of people residing in urban population centers (for example, adult female citizens and citizens of African descent). Their request for equal rights within the US system, however, posed no challenge to the United States as the sole vessel of state authority. Conversely, American Indian movements urging for the recognition of their sovereign (as opposed to civil) rights manifested a rejection of the authority—or, minimally, a challenge to the exclusive legitimacy—of the national government. They were not requesting rights arising from within the United States, but asserting external or supranational rights that constrained it. Even though the geographic remoteness and relatively small numbers of people involved in American Indian political movements vis-à-vis other domestic rights movements threatened substantially less cultural and societal upheaval, the nature of their legal and political claims posed a challenge to US dominion in North America that proved a theoretical affront much more difficult to countenance.[9]

The post–World War II decolonialist movements in Africa and South Asia presented a similar challenge to European sovereigns, but geographic separation from the respective imperial home made those movements less structurally troubling to the colonial power than did American Indian rights claims. When those colonies insisted that the European colonists "go home," there existed a European home to which they could return. After the American Revolution, however, American colonists and their descendants retained no such trans-Atlantic abode. Whereas a successful decolonialist movement threatened the loss of national pride and of assets on the fringe of an empire, aboriginal rights movements triggered fears of autonomous regions and national disintegration within the heart of the American homeland.

Assimilation and Allotment

The first era of federal Indian policy of the twentieth century, the assimilation and allotment era, began in approximately 1871 and continued until 1934 (see table 1). The era fundamentally altered the relationship between the United States and tribal nations. Indian affairs came to be viewed as an increasingly domestic, rather than international, matter, particularly following the "Indian wars." At the outset of the era, Congress ended the practice of treating formally with tribes, although it continued to negotiate agreements ratified as statutes.[10] Giving unprecedented deference to Congress, the Supreme Court dramatically expanded congressional authority over Indians, empowering it to pursue the central goals of the era: the dissolution of tribal governments, the involuntary assimilation of Native Americans into the dominant culture, and the allotment and acquisition of communally owned land.[11]

In 1885 Congress passed the Major Crimes Act, extending federal jurisdiction over seven felonies, a theretofore unseen effort to govern tribal internal relations and extend Anglo-American legal norms in Indian Country.[12] Reviewing a challenge to the statute, the Supreme Court held in *United States v. Kagama* (1886) that, even though no constitutional provision authorized the statute, the guardian-ward relationship established an extra-constitutional source of plenary authority:

> The power of the General Government over these remnants of a race
> once powerful, now weak and diminished in numbers, is necessary to

their protection, as well as to the safety of those among whom they dwell. It must exist in that government, because it never existed anywhere else, because the theatre of its exercise is within the geographical limits of the United States, because it has never been denied, and because it alone can enforce its laws on all the tribes.[13]

Shortly thereafter, Congress passed the General Allotment Act of 1887, by which communally owned land was allotted to individual tribal members in parcels of 40, 80, or 160 acres.[14] The federal government was to hold legal title to the land in trust for a period of twenty-five years, during which time the land could not be encumbered or alienated. At the end of twenty-five years or upon proof of "competency," the encumbrances were to be removed.[15] The remainder of the land, deemed "surplus," was then opened to white settlement. Similarly, Congress promoted non-Indian acquisition of Indian mineral resources through several mineral-leasing acts that provided a narrowly confined role for tribal or individual Indian owners to prohibit or participate in mineral development.[16]

The General Allotment Act was applied on a tribally specific basis, so its level of implementation varied across Indian Country. Its overall impact, however, was devastating. Described by President Theodore Roosevelt as "a mighty pulverizing engine to break up the tribal land mass," the act resulted in the loss of two-thirds of Indian lands between 1887 and 1934, from 138 million acres to 48 million acres.[17]

In *Lone Wolf v. Hitchcock* (1903), the Supreme Court rejected a challenge to the allotment and expropriation of Kiowa, Comanche, and Apache lands in violation of the Treaty of Medicine Lodge of 1867, article twelve of which required approval by vote of three-fourths of the adult male population.[18] The *Lone Wolf* Court held challenges to the assertion of congressional plenary power, recently expanded in *Kagama*, to raise political questions not subject to judicial review.[19] *Lone Wolf* characterized the trust relationship as a power-conferring doctrine, rather than a limitation on federal authority, and allowed the federal trustee to transfer the Indian beneficiaries' land assets to cash, despite accusations of fraud and misrepresentation. Described by one federal judge as "the Indians' Dred Scott decision," the *Lone Wolf* Court confirmed congressional authority to abrogate Indian treaties, just as treaties with foreign nations, effectively unbridled by any trust responsibilities.[20] After *Lone Wolf* and *Kagama*, subsequent decisions found that "Congress has plenary authority to limit, modify or eliminate the powers of local self-government which the tribes otherwise possess" and "[t]he sovereignty that the Indian tribes retain...exists only at the sufferance of Congress and is subject to complete defeasance."[21]

Complementing the General Allotment Act's promotion of dominant culture norms, private property, and individual participation in the agricultural economy, Indian education received particularized attention during the assimilation and allotment era. The government contracted with faith-based boarding schools to educate Native American children far from tribal cultural influences.[22] Finally, Congress passed the Citizenship Act of 1924. Before this, Native American Indians had been generally citizens of their tribal nations and not of the United States or its constituent states.[23] The Citizenship Act granted US citizenship to all Indians born within its territorial limits, though the Supreme Court held in *United States v. Nice* (1916) that dual citizenship remained possible.[24]

Reorganization

By the mid-twenties, the negative consequences of allotment, including poverty and disease, had become evident. The now famous *Meriam Report* of 1928, a two-year, nongovernmental study of the Indian Bureau, sparked a policy shift toward the rejuvenation of tribal governments and communities, from 1934 until 1946 (see table 2).[25] Consistent with the programs of President Franklin D. Roosevelt's New Deal, Congress passed the Johnson-O'Malley Act of 1934 to allow state and local governments (later, also public and private institutions) to receive federal funds for Native American education, medical care, agricultural assistance, and social welfare programs.[26] That same year, Congress expressly repudiated the allotment policy when it passed the Indian Reorganization Act of 1934 (IRA); its purpose was to "encourage economic development, self-determination, cultural plurality, and the revival of tribalism."[27]

The IRA indefinitely extended the trust period for remaining trust allotments, limited transfers of Indian lands to Indians or tribes, and authorized the secretary of the interior to acquire land in trust on behalf of tribes to expand the dwindled land mass. To promote economic development in tribal communities, the legislation established a revolving fund; it also provided for the establishment of tribal corporations and the preservation of certain claims against the United States. The IRA also reaffirmed tribal governmental authority and permitted tribes to organize under a constitution and establish their own courts; approximately 181 tribes did so. Though not required by the act, the model constitution offered by Commissioner of Indian Affairs John Collier included a provision requiring approval of amendments by the secretary of the interior.[28]

To further economic development and revitalization of tribal governments, Congress expanded the role of tribes in resource extraction activities through the Indian Mineral Leasing Act of 1938 (IMLA).[29] The IMLA required tribal consent for mineral leases, encouraged competitive bidding for leasing contracts, and allowed for tribal inspections of leased lands. The act was only moderately successful because its tribal consent provision applied only to the option of whether to lease, but did not affirm regulatory authority, and the secretary of the interior retained broad authority and discretion. Throughout the twentieth century, mineral development on Indian lands was vital to US economic and military interests. Ironically, the barren lands thought worthless, to which tribes had been relocated in the nineteenth century, were inordinately rich in mineral resources.

Termination

After World War II, economic pressures to lessen federal spending and increase non-Indian access to Indian resources converged with sentiments favoring individual equality over social group rights, bringing a close to the reorganization era. Congress implemented two significant changes in policy during the termination era, 1946–1961 (see table 3). First, to address conclusively and extinguish existing Indian legal claims against the United States, Congress established an administrative tribunal, the Indian Claims Commission (ICC). Second, Congress declared its intention to end federal supervision of American Indians "as rapidly as possible" and instituted a policy of promoting the "complete integration" of Indians.[30] Unfortunately, the Indian Claims Commission proved to be a frustrating and unfulfilled promise, and the termination policy, a devastating, albeit short-lived, experiment.

The Indian Claims Commission was established with much promise, lauded as "the most constructive piece of Indian legislation…during the past quarter of a century" and "the dawn of a new era for the American Indian."[31] As President Harry S. Truman signed the Indian Claims Commission Act of 1946 (ICCA), he proudly proclaimed:

> This bill makes perfectly clear what many men and women, here and abroad, have failed to recognize, that in our transaction with the Indian tribes we have at least since the Northwest Ordinance of 1787 set for ourselves the standard of fair and honorable dealings, pledging respect for all Indian property rights. Instead of confiscating Indian lands, we have purchased from the tribes that once owned this continent more than 90 percent of our public domain, paying them approximately 800 million dollars in the process.[32]

The statute was intended to remedy the long-standing denial of court access to American Indians, but its primary aim was to extinguish ancient Indian grievances and to quiet title to lands taken from them in preparation for the termination of the federal–tribal relationship.[33]

Before the passage of the Indian Claims Commission Act, tribes had virtually no access to federal courts.[34] The holding in *Cherokee Nation v. Georgia* that tribes, as domestic dependent nations, lacked standing to sue in federal court on their own behalf established a common law rule preventing tribes from protecting their own rights in court and rendering them dependent on their federal trustee, in its discretion, to bring suit against state and even private defendants.[35] The doctrine of sovereign immunity developed more recently as a bar to suits against states by tribes in federal court, and that doctrine had historically prohibited tribes from suing the United States without its permission.[36] Congress had created the Court of Claims to hear monetary suits brought against the national government in 1855, but in 1863, as a punishment for some tribes' allying with the Confederacy, Congress amended the statute to prohibit claims by all Indians.[37] Consequently, tribes could bring only lawsuits based on specific jurisdictional grants from Congress, and those statutes were narrowly construed. The executive branch, which possessed most of the documents relevant to such suits, often delayed the process significantly by withholding them.[38]

The ICCA created the Indian Claims Commission, an administrative tribunal with jurisdiction to hear not only typical tribal land and tort claims but also a new cause of action "based upon fair and honorable dealings that are not recognized by any existing rule of law or equity."[39] Although the statute required claims to be filed within five years of its passage, the act protected ancient claims from statutes of limitations or time-based equitable defenses. Finally, commission decisions were subject to judicial review by the Court of Claims and the Supreme Court.

Numerous structural issues assured that the promises of the ICCA would remain unfulfilled.[40] First, Commissioner of Indian Affairs Dillon S. Myer reinvigorated an 1872 statute that required tribes to obtain the approval of the secretary of the interior for the expenditure of any funds to hire an attorney and for any contracts for attorney services.[41] Myer applied the statute strictly and often withheld permission for as long as possible without expressly denying it.[42] Second, though the ICCA permitted a cooperative model for investigating and compensating Indian claims, the commission adopted an adversarial system with "a minefield of liability-limiting rules."[43] Third, despite having a trust responsibility to its Indian wards, the US Department of Justice viewed the United States as defendant only, aggressively defending each suit, resisting settlement, and even requesting that Congress overturn commission rulings that favored tribes. Fourth, the commissioners themselves were generally adverse to Indians' needs or ignorant of Indian history, resulting in the forum's favoring US interests.[44] Finally, of great significance, the commission had the power to grant only monetary relief. At best, then, the commission could require payments for wrongs—effectuating a forced sale long after a land taking—but could not grant equitable relief or return the land to the Indians.[45]

Given long delays inherent in the commission's procedure, the ICC was extended repeatedly, finally terminating in 1978 and transferring active cases to the Court of Federal Claims. In the end, historian Francis Paul Prucha argues, "the Indian Claims Commission did not fulfill its purpose, for it did not bring the finality in the settlement of all claims that its framers had wanted. In some ways Indian grievances seemed to be heightened instead of diffused as the commission went about its work."[46]

The termination policy was intended "to make the Indians...subject to the same laws and entitled to the same privileges and responsibilities as are applicable to other citizens of the United States, and to grant them all the rights and prerogatives pertaining to American citizenship."[47] Pursuant to that policy, Congress passed a number of statutes that provided for the rapid assimilation of individual Indians into the dominant culture and for the diminishment of tribal rights. For example, early in the era Congress extended state civil and criminal jurisdiction into certain Indian lands for specific tribes and, in response to state lobbying, for the states of New York and Kansas.[48] In 1953 Congress expanded the policy by passing Public Law 280, which extended state jurisdiction in California, Minnesota, Nebraska, Oregon, and Wisconsin without Indian consent. It authorized other states to do so as well, but in response to Indian activism, that provision was limited to require tribal consent in the next legislative session.[49] Public Law 280 also transferred certain Indian health, education, and welfare programs to states, and individual "Termination Acts" ended federal supervision and the government-to-government relationship with approximately 110 tribes and bands, most famously with the Menominee Tribe.[50] Through the Bureau of Indian Affairs, the federal government implemented programs to promote assimilation, including relocation of entire families into distant urban settings, and established the Indian Adoption Project in 1958, promoting the adoption of Indian children by non-Indian parents.[51]

Termination era policies were expanded with approval in the Supreme Court in cases involving Indian land claims and state jurisdiction. Though courts had described the aboriginal right of occupancy, even when unacknowledged by Congress, to be "as sacred as the fee simple of the whites," the Court held in *United States ex rel. Hualapai Indians v. Santa Fe Pacific Railroad Co.* (1941) that such "aboriginal title," though a secure property right, was more easily terminable than "recognized title," that is, land rights recognized by the federal government in a treaty, statute, or executive order.[52] Remarkably, in 1955 the Court defined the aboriginal title of Alaskan Natives, who had never been subjects of conquest, to be a mere right to use that was not a compensable property interest pursuant to the Takings Clause of the US Constitution. The Court articulated its reasoning in a now famous passage: "Every American schoolboy knows that the savage tribes of this continent were deprived of their ancestral ranges by force and that, even when the Indians ceded millions of acres by treaty in return for blankets, food and trinkets, it was not a sale but the conquerors' will that deprived them of their land."[53]

To a lesser degree, the Court departed from the foundational principles regarding state jurisdiction in Indian Country in *Williams v. Lee* (1959).[54] Based on the inherent sovereignty of tribes, *Worcester v. Georgia* had established a bright-line rule that had been little changed for more than a century: on Indian lands, the laws of a state can have no effect.[55] The *Williams* Court reframed that absolute prohibition into an "infringement test": "Essentially, absent governing Acts of Congress, the question has always been whether the state action infringed on the right of reservation Indians to make their own laws and be ruled by them."[56] The infringement test created the potential for state law to be applied within Indian Country, subject to challenge on a case-by-case basis. Though the Court applied the test so as to prohibit state jurisdiction over a suit arising between a non-Indian creditor and a Navajo on the reservation, *Williams* provided the basis for more significant shifts by subsequent courts.

Most tribes resisted the termination policy from the outset, and opposition in Congress appeared as early as 1956.[57] As scholar David Getches and others have noted, the termination era invigorated Indian activism and tribalism. "Ironically, termination, which was originally designed as an effort once and for all to detribalize the American Indian, worked precisely the opposite effect," they found. "The policy awakened Indians to the historical realization that more often than not, federal policy had been directed toward the destruction of tribalism, and that only tribal control of Indian policy and lasting guarantees of sovereignty could assure tribal survival in the United States."[58]

Self-Determination

President Richard Nixon formally announced the policy of self-determination without termination in 1970, but its roots trace to the Kennedy administration (see table 4).[59] Throughout the 1960s and 70s, each administration encouraged tribal "self-determination."[60] Likewise, Congress passed numerous statutes promoting tribal autonomy and economic development. The Menominee Restoration Act of 1973 was an important expression of the new policy; it repealed the act that had terminated the tribe and that had come to symbolize the negative consequences of termination.[61] Numerous, similar restoration acts were passed for other tribes. In 1966 Congress allowed tribes to bring suit in federal courts on their own behalf, without representation by their governmental trustee.[62] At the same time, a resurgence of Native American activism developed, and treaty rights and natural resources claims reached a new prominence. Finally, Indians were able to access the courts to protect their own rights. Tribal litigation increased dramatically, as did the number of appeals to the Supreme Court.[63]

In the mid-1960s, under President Lyndon B. Johnson's Great Society programs, agencies outside the Bureau of Indian Affairs provided grants to tribal entities that demonstrated competence at service provision.[64] Congress expanded and formalized that practice through a variety of statutes. The Indian Education Act of 1972 established a comprehensive federal program for Indian education with grants administered by tribes, the Indian Self-Determination and Education Assistance Act of 1975 further empowered tribes to accept federal funds for and administer a variety of education and social service programs, and the Tribally Controlled Community College Act of 1978 promoted tribal control of higher education.[65]

In addition to the education acts, Congress enacted statutes to preserve and promote tribal families, cultural practices, and resources. Perhaps most significant among these was the Indian Child Welfare Act of 1978, which redefined the "best interests of the child" standard in proceedings governing the placement of Indian children in foster and adoptive homes so as to better reflect and preserve Indian cultural values.[66] The ICWA established a preference for placement with the child's extended family and tribe and required notice of state court proceedings to tribal governments, which may, under certain circumstances, claim exclusive jurisdiction over the matter. Though the Supreme Court's decision in *Lyng v. Northwest Indian Cemetery Protective Association* (1988) confirmed that the American Indian Religious Freedom Act of 1978 was a statute without teeth, the act constituted an important policy statement that Congress intended to end historic discrimination against Native American religious practices.[67]

Perhaps the most controversial statute of the self-determination era, the Indian Civil Rights Act of 1968 (ICRA) earned both praise for promoting individual rights in Indian Country and strong criticism as a federal intrusion into self-governance that constrained tribal power.[68] As nonsignatory, preconstitutional sovereigns, tribal governments were never constrained by the Constitution or the Bill of Rights.[69] The ICRA imposed on tribal authority statutory analogues to certain provisions in the Bill of Rights. Although it did not include limitations on government structure based on the Separation of Powers Doctrine or the Establishment Clause, the ICRA required the equal protection of laws and limited tribal criminal-sentencing authority to $5,000 and a one-year term of incarceration. As the Court held in *Santa Clara Pueblo v. Martinez*, the act did not create an individual cause of action for other than habeas corpus relief.[70]

The Equal Protection Clause of the US Constitution subjects laws that discriminate on the basis of race to strict judicial scrutiny, requiring that they be justified by a compelling state interest and be narrowly tailored to advance that interest. In *Morton v. Mancari* (1974), the Supreme Court noted that Indian status is not a racial, but a political classification.[71] Therefore, statutes and regulations providing for different treatment of Indians as a consequence of tribal membership are subject to a lesser standard of review: "As long as the special treatment can be tied rationally to the fulfillment of Congress' unique obligation toward the Indians, such legislative judgments will not be disturbed."[72] By reviewing the federal action, the *Mancari* Court rejected the political question doctrine established in *Lone Wolf* and preserved an Indian hiring preference within the Bureau of Indian Affairs, so it is generally deemed a favorable case for Native Americans.[73] Nevertheless, *Mancari's* standard was a double-edged sword, also including the potential for deference to discriminatory treatment of Indians to which other racial minorities could not be subjected.[74]

As during earlier policy eras, tribes pursued their rights through all available avenues. Empowered to sue on their own behalf, tribes during the self-determination era instituted numerous lawsuits alleging violations of their treaty rights and raising land and natural resource claims. For example, the Oneida Indian Nation established that the State of New York had acquired its land in violation of federal law. The Sioux Nation won monetary damages for the uncompensated taking of the Black Hills, though the tribes have insisted on the return of the land and refused the award, which remains in a federal trust fund.[75] Indian fishing rights returned to prominence in 1974 after the Boldt decision in *United States v. Washington*, in which the tribes were awarded the opportunity to take up to one-half the harvestable catch (see table 5).[76]

As the 1970s came to a close, executive administrations continued to profess the importance of tribal empowerment but emphasized language of self-governance over self-determination, describing "government-to-government" relationships with tribal sovereigns.[77] Likewise, Congress continued to pass numerous acts promoting tribal self-governance but demonstrated increased attention to state and non-Indian interests. Those relatively slight shifts may not signify a new law-and-policy era, but Professor David H. Getches identified a significant change in US–Indian relations. Beginning in approximately 1979 and lasting to the present, federal policy has been influenced more by the Supreme Court (see tables 6–7).[78]

Throughout the era, Congress continued to pass statutes that empowered tribes to accept federal funds for and administer a variety of health, education, economic development, and social service programs. These include the Tribally Controlled Schools Act of 1988, the Indian Tribal Government Tax Status Act of 1982, the Native American Housing and Self-Determination Act, and the Tribal Self-Governance Act of 1994.[79]

Congress significantly enhanced tribal control of natural resources within tribes' jurisdiction in a variety of acts, such as the Indian Mineral Development Act of 1982, allowing for tribes to participate in mineral development as regulators, in joint ventures, and in negotiating mineral leases.[80] The National Indian Forest Management Act of 1990 promoted tribal revenue and management of timber resources. The Clean Air Act and Clean Water Act were amended to allow tribal governments to participate in the system of cooperative federalism for environmental protection by being treated as a state (TAS).[81] TAS status allows tribes to accept the federal delegation of authority to set and enforce clean water and air standards. The Indian Land Consolidation Act of 1983 was intended to lessen fractionalization of tribal land and return meaningful ownership to tribes.[82]

Indian tribes, the federal government, and states began an increasingly important dialogue over the scope of authority and jurisdiction. A major arena for such discussions involved games of chance in Indian Country. In certain traditional forms, gambling had existed in numerous tribes, but gaming as an industry appeared in the 1970s. The Cabazon Band of Mission Indians established such an operation, and California, a PL 280 state, sought to prohibit the tribe from continuing its operation. Despite the Supreme Court's authority under that statute, it held that the state lacked jurisdiction in *California v. Cabazon Band of Mission Indians* (1987).[83] Tribes across the nation then established or expanded gaming operations while states complained vociferously.

In response, Congress passed the Indian Gaming Regulatory Act of 1988 (IGRA), which divided games into three classes: (1) traditional tribal games with awards of nominal value, (2) bingo and similar games, and (3) other games, including slot machines, horse racing, and Vegas-style card games.[84] The act prohibited Class III games unless the tribe entered into a compact with the state regarding terms of operation, such as infrastructure and law enforcement. The act required states to negotiate in good faith and waived the sovereign immunity of both states and tribes, balancing the act's limitation of the important tribal right and the expansion of state power. The Supreme Court upset that balance in *Seminole Tribe v. Florida* (1996), in which it held that the act unconstitutionally waived state sovereign immunity from suit, thus foreclosing the tribes' judicial remedy in the event states refused to negotiate in good faith.[85] The act also established a federal regulatory agency, the National Indian Gaming Commission. Though a relatively small number of tribes have benefited from flourishing gaming operations, the industry has created significant income for public works.

The Indian Arts and Crafts Act of 1990 reflected an interest in promoting economic opportunity for Native American artists. By providing a uniform definition of "Indian" artists, it aimed to protect Native American artists from unfair non-Indian competition and protect consumers from imitated works.[86] The act was also intended to protect Indian cultural expression through the arts. It was received with mixed reactions—appreciation of its aims but concern that it excluded artists identified by their communities as Indian by descent and cultural affiliation, albeit not meeting the statute's tribal enrollment requirements.

The Native American Graves Protection and Repatriation Act of 1990 (NAGPRA), as its name suggests, provided for the in situ preservation of Native American graves and sacred sites, as did the Archaeological Resources Protection Act.[87] Acknowledging the history of the wrongful taking of sacred objects and objects of cultural patrimony, NAGPRA also required most museums to identify Indian remains and cultural artifacts within their collections for the return to lineal descendants or the culturally affiliated tribe, unless the museum could demonstrate that its possession was obtained through "voluntary consent."

Before 1975 the trust doctrine had generally created more federal powers than duties. In two decisions arising from the same litigation, known as *Mitchell I* (1980) and *Mitchell II* (1983), the Court established tiers of trust that included some enforceable duties on the federal government.[88] In order for a tribe to have a cause of action against the United States for breach of trust, the federal government must have expressed its intent to assume either specific or full fiduciary trust obligations.[89] This intent may be expressed in a treaty or statute or may be implicit in a comprehensive federal management scheme for tribal resources.[90] As manager of individual Indian trust accounts, the Bureau of Indian Affairs was shown to have egregiously failed in its duties, unable to account for billions of dollars in Indian assets. Although not a complete solution, Congress responded to the bureau's failure by passing the American Indian Trust Management Reform Act of 1994.[91]

During the last few decades of the self-determination era, Congress and the executive branch received less deference from the Court, which, instead, revitalized former policies of forced assimilation that had long since been repudiated.[92] The Rehnquist Court issued a number of decisions that limited tribal autonomy and expanded state jurisdiction in Indian Country. Regarding the Indian canons of construction, the Rehnquist Court developed a practice of either opining with no reference to them at all or reciting them but finding them inapplicable to the case at bar.[93]

The judicial shift began with *Oliphant v. Suquamish Indian Tribe* (1978), an opinion written by then justice William H. Rehnquist, holding that, as a result of the subordinating effect of conquest, tribes lacked criminal jurisdiction over non-Indians.[94] The conclusion "came as a surprise to many" and was widely criticized.[95] The *Oliphant* Court conceded that no act of Congress had removed tribal criminal authority over non-Indians; neither did it offer any precedent describing an inherent limitation on such criminal jurisdiction.[96] The Court expressed concern at the prospect that tribes could prosecute non-Indians, even in accordance with the civil rights guarantees of the Indian Civil Rights Act and tribal law and order codes. Consequently, it invented a third inherent limitation on tribal authority, based on a "shared assumption" among the three branches of government.[97] "Nowhere," explains David Getches, "does the Court explain why popular assumptions about tribes' criminal jurisdiction should override the foundation principles' guarantee that Indian autonomy will be curbed only at the direction of Congress."[98]

Three years after *Oliphant*, its ruling was extended to limit tribal civil jurisdiction as well, in *Montana v. United States* (1981).[99] *Montana* held that tribes lacked authority over non-Indians on fee lands within Indian Country unless the non-Indian had some commercial relationship with the tribe or the activities directly affected the tribe's political integrity, economic security, or health or welfare. In the following two decades, the Court further limited tribal jurisdiction and land holdings and narrowed the *Montana* exceptions substantially.[100]

In response to the Rehnquist Court's new practice, Congress moved to restore recognition of inherent tribal sovereignty in certain areas. For example, in *Duro v. Reina* (1990), the Court expanded its holding in *Oliphant* to deny tribes' jurisdiction over Indians from other tribes, and Congress legislated an override, the "*Duro* fix."[101] In *United States v. Lara* (2004), the Court acknowledged Congress's power to do so. In response to the Court's limitation on religious freedom in *Employment Division v. Smith* (1990), Congress passed the Religious Freedom Restoration Act of 1993, which was successfully challenged as unconstitutional, in part.[102] As the Court granted states additional powers within Indian Country, state and tribal governments began entering into agreements over jurisdiction and other matters through compacts. Such tribal-state compacts address gaming, transboundary criminal enforcement, and tobacco and motor fuel taxation.

The federal courts and, to a lesser extent, Congress became decreasingly accommodating to Indian rights. At the same time, concern for the well-being of indigenous peoples became increasingly important within the international community. Beginning in the 1970s but particularly in the 1980s and 1990s, indigenous groups, including American Indian tribes, became active nonstate participants in international institutions. International legal norms favoring self-determination, land and resource rights, and the preservation of cultural integrity began crystallizing. These norms are reflected in documents such as the International Labour Organization Convention on Indigenous and Tribal Peoples, Convention No. 169 of 1989, the United Nations Draft Declaration on the Rights of Indigenous Peoples, and the Organization of American States Draft Declaration on the Rights of Indigenous Peoples of 1995.

The experience of the self-determination era generally confirmed John Marshall's early observation that, so long as assured sufficient autonomy for self- and community actualization through economic opportunity, as well as cultural and political choice, tribal peoples would find means of maintaining the peaceful coexistence they had promised in numerous treaties. Even as domestic dependent nations integrated into the political fabric of the United States, Native peoples during the self-determination era experienced improved economic, health, and social well-being, and conflicts with non-Indians found some resolution in negotiated compacts and an affirmation of shared interests. The events of the twentieth century demonstrated to Congress and the executive branch that earlier fears of tribal autonomy posing a threat to US political stability were misplaced and avoidable and that the people of the United States also experienced economic, moral, and political benefit from tribal autonomy.

Notes

1. *Worcester v. Georgia*, 31 US (6 Pet.) 515, 559 (1832) (quoting US Const., art. I, § 8, cl. 3). Exclusive federal authority over Indian relations was further secured by one of the first acts of the first Congress, the Indian Trade and Intercourse Act, 1 Stat. 137 (1790), which prohibited the acceptance of title to Indian lands "unless…made by treaty or convention entered into pursuant to the Constitution" and criminalized "attempts to negotiate such a treaty or convention" without the permission of the federal government. The current version of the act, passed in 1834, contains the same provisions without significant amendments.

2. The cases are *Johnson v. M'Intosh*, 21 US (8 Wheat.) 543 (1823); *Cherokee Nation v. Georgia*, 30 US (5 Pet.) 1, 17 (1831); and *Worcester v. Georgia*, 31 US (6 Pet.) 515 (1832).

3. *Johnson*, 21 US 574; *Cherokee Nation*, 30 US 17; *Mitchel v. United States*, 34 US (9 Pet.) 711, 748 (1835).

4. *Cherokee Nation*, 30 US at 18.

5. *Cherokee Nation v. Georgia*, 30 US (5 Pet.) 1, 17 (1831).

6. *Cherokee Nation*, 30 US at 17. This statement provided the basis for canons of Indian treaty construction, under which courts interpret treaties as Indians would have understood them and resolve ambiguities in their favor. See *Worcester*, 31 US 582. See also *Carpenter v. Shaw*, 280 US 363, 367 (1930) ("Doubtful expressions are to be resolved in favor of the weak and defenseless people who are wards of the nation, dependent upon its protection and good faith").

7. David Wilkins and K. Tsianina Lomawaima, *Uneven Ground: American Indian Sovereignty and Federal Law* (Norman: University of Oklahoma Press, 2001), 6.

8. *Worcester*, 31 US 548, 544–545.

9. The "Black Separatist" movement differed from the African American civil rights movement in means and ends, contemplating "by any means" the establishment of an autonomous region in North America. Though posing a challenge to the United States' exclusive jurisdiction (similar to Native American rights movements), that nationalist movement was not founded on the notions of first-in-time and long-standing political recognition.

10. Appropriations Act of Mar. 3, 1871, ch. 120, 16 Stat. 544, 566 (codified, in part, at 25 USC § 71 [2000]).

11. See Janet McDonnell, *The Dispossession of the American Indian, 1887–1934* (Bloomington: University of Indiana Press, 1991), and C. Blue Clark, *Lone Wolf v. Hitchcock: Treaty Rights and Indian Law at the End of the Nineteenth Century* (Lincoln: University of Nebraska Press, 1994).

12. Appropriations Act of Mar. 3, 1885, ch. 341, 23 Stat. 362, 385 (codified as amended as the Federal Major Crimes Act, 25 USC § 1153 [2000]).

13. 118 US 375, 384–385 (1886).

14. General Allotment Act of 1887, ch. 119, 24 Stat. 388 (codified as amended at 25 USC §§ 331–333 [2000]).

15. The trust period for allotments not yet held in fee was indefinitely extended by the Indian Reorganization Act of 1934, ch. 576, § 2, 48 Stat. 984 (1934) (codified as amended at 25 USC § 462 [2000]).

16. See Judith Royster, "Mineral Development in Indian Country: The Evolution of Tribal Control over Mineral Resources," *Tulsa Law Journal* 29, no. 3–4 (1994): 541, 552–557.

17. Quoted in President Theodore Roosevelt, "First Annual Message" (December 3, 1901), in *A Compilation of the Messages and Papers of the Presidents*, vol. 15, ed. James Richardson (Washington DC: Bureau of National Literature and Art, 1917), 6, 672; and Wilcomb Washburn, *Red Man's Land/White Man's Law: A Study of the Past and Present Status of the American Indian* (New York: Scribner, 1971), 145.

18. 187 US 553, 565 (1903); Treaty with the Kiowa, Comanche, and Apache, October 21, 1867, 15 Stat. 581; Charles Kappler, ed., *Indian Affairs: Laws and Treaties* (Washington DC: GPO, 1904), 982–984.

19. The plenary power doctrine has been condemned from virtually all perspectives. See Robert Williams Jr., "The Algebra of Federal Indian Law: The Hard Trail of Decolonizing and Americanizing the White Man's Indian Jurisprudence," *Wisconsin Law Review* 1986, no. 2 (1986): 219, 260–265 (noting the racist foundation of the doctrine and oppressive consequences);

Milner Ball, "Constitution, Court, Indian Tribes," *American Bar Foundation Research Journal* 135, no. 1 (1987): 1, 46–59 (assessing the doctrine as unconstitutional); Robert Clinton, "There Is No Federal Supremacy Clause for Indian Tribes," *Arizona State Law Journal* 34 (Spring 2002): 113 (criticizing the doctrine as founded in conquest); Natsu Taylor Saito, "The Plenary Power Doctrine: Subverting Human Rights in the Name of Sovereignty," *Catholic University Law Review* 51, no. 4 (2002), 1115 (criticizing the doctrine as legal rationale for denying international human rights); and William Bradford, "Another Such Victory and We Are Undone": A Call to an American Indian Declaration of Independence, *Tulsa Law Review* 40, no. 1 (2004): 71, 73 (describing the doctrine as "the thinnest of veneers for de facto rule over both tribes and individual Indians without restraint and across all manner of human affairs").

20. *Sioux Nation of Indians v. United States*, 601 F. 2d 1157, 1173 (Ct. Cl. 1979).

21. *Santa Clara Pueblo v. Martinez*, 436 US 49, 56 (1978); *United States v. Wheeler*, 435 US 313, 323 (1978). Ironically, five years later, in *Winters v. United States*, 207 US 564 (1908), the Court held that the reservation of land implicitly included the reservation of sufficient water to fulfill the purposes of the land reservation. The Fort Belknap Reservation at issue in *Winters* was intended, in part, to promote Indian agricultural activity, and the decision established a basis for Indian water rights of continuing importance. Applying the canons of treaty construction and tribal sovereignty doctrine, the Supreme Court held that, from an expressly reserved fishing right, a right to water may also be implied, even if on non-Indian, off-reservation lands. *United States v. Winans*, 198 US 371 (1905).

22. See Frederick Hoxie, *A Final Promise: The Campaign to Assimilate the Indians, 1880–1920* (Cambridge: Cambridge University Press, 1984; Lincoln: University of Nebraska Press, 2001). The broad efforts to "civilize" the Indians during this period were perhaps best articulated by Captain Richard Henry Pratt's infamous instructional method at the Carlisle Indian Boarding School in Pennsylvania: "All the Indian there is in the race should be dead. Kill the Indian in him and save the man." Francis Paul Prucha, ed., *Americanizing the American Indians: Writings by the "Friends of the Indian"* (Cambridge, MA: Harvard University Press, 1973), 260–261.

23. Act of June 2, 1924, 43 Stat. 253 (codified as amended at 25 USC § 13 [2000]).

24. 241 US 591 (1916).

25. Lewis Meriam, ed., *Institute for Government Research Studies in Administration: The Problem of Indian Administration* (Baltimore, MD: Johns Hopkins University Press, 1928).

26. 48 Stat. 596 (1934) (codified as amended at 25 USC §§ 452–454 [2000]).

27. Also known as the Wheeler-Howard Act, 48 Stat. 984–988 (1934) (codified as amended at 25 USC §§ 461–479 [2000]). For quote, see Rennard Strickland, editor-in-chief, *Felix S. Cohen's Handbook of Federal Indian Law* (Charlottesville, VA: Michie Bobbs-Merrill, 1982), 147.

28. *Kerr-McGee Corp. v. Navajo Tribe of Indians*, 471 US 195, 198 (1985).

29. 25 USC §§ 396a–396g (2000). For a general discussion of the evolution of mineral development in Indian Country, see Royster, supra, note 16.

30. According to the Alaska Native Claims Settlement Act, 43 USC § 1601(b) (2000), this was part of the effort to avoid "any permanent racially defined institutions, rights, privileges, or obligations." *Alaska v. Native Village of Venetie Tribal Government*, 522 US 520, 521 (1998).

31. Statement of Representative Robertson, *Congressional Record*, vol. 92 (July 29, 1946), p. 10403, quoted in Michael Lieder and Jake Page, *Wild Justice: The People of Geronimo v. The United States* (Norman: University of Oklahoma Press, 1999), 64.

32. Pub. L. No. 726, ch. 959, § 2, 60 Stat. 1049, 1050 (codified at 25 USC § 70 until the commission's termination on September 30, 1978). For quote, see David Wilkins, *American Indian Sovereignty and the US Supreme Court: The Masking of Justice* (Austin: University of Texas Press, 1997), 178.

33. Nell Jessup Newton, "Indian Claims in the Courts of the Conqueror," *American University Law Review* 41, no. 3 (1992): 753, 771, and n96. For causes of action arising after August 13, 1946, Congress amended the Tucker Act, Act of Mar. 3, 1887, ch. 359, 24 Stat. 505, to remove the discriminatory prohibition and granted jurisdiction to the Court of Claims. See 28 USC § 1505 (2000). "It became obvious that the commission broke no new ground and was really a government measure to enhance its own efficiency by disposing of the old claims and terminating Indian tribes." Harvey Rosenthal, "Indian Claims and the American Conscience: A Brief History of the Indian Claims Commission," in *Irredeemable America: The Indians' Estate and Land Claims*, ed. Imre Sutton (Albuquerque: University of New Mexico Press, 1985), 63. See also Francis Paul Prucha, *The Great Father: The United States Government and the American Indian*, 2 vols. (Lincoln: University of Nebraska Press, 1984).

34. Newton, "Indian Claims," 769. Indeed, even after statutes denying the right to testify in court on the basis of race were declared unconstitutional, see generally *McCormick on Evidence* §§ 61, 63, 64, 66, at 155–162 (Edward Cleary, ed., 1984) (discussing the early common law rules of witness incompetency such as interested parties, spouses, race, religion, and prior conviction); Gerard Magliocca, "The Cherokee Removal and the Fourteenth Amendment," *Duke Law Journal* 53, no. 3 (2003): 875, 940 (federal regulations were necessary to allow Indians to testify, and those regulations were limited to allowing the incompetent wards to provide evidence furthering the prevention of their access to alcohol). See Revised Statutes, tit. 28, ch. 4, §§ 2140 (2d ed., 1878), cited in Regulations of the Indian Department § 491, at 85 (GPO 1884). See also Regulations of the Indian Office § 571 at 103 (1894).

35. Newton, "Indian Claims," 769.

36. See *Seminole Tribe v. Florida*, 517 US 44 (1996); *Idaho v. Coeur d'Alene Tribe*, 521 US 261 (1997); and Lieder and Page, *Wild Justice*, 52.

37. Act of Feb. 24, 1855, ch. 122, 10 Stat. 612; Act of Mar. 3, 1863, ch. 92, § 9, 12 Stat. 765, 767.

38. Glen Wilkinson, "Indian Tribal Claims before the Court of Claims," *Georgetown Law Journal* 55 (1966): 511–512. Assuming that a tribe successfully retained an attorney to investigate the ancient claim, draft a proposed jurisdictional statute, and solicit a sponsoring legislator, such a bill, if proposed, encountered a number of often insurmountable obstacles. Upon reaching the relevant Senate and House committees, the bills were held, pending "a report and recommendation" from the executive branch as to "whether the bill should be passed. A negative report almost always doomed the bill." Those few bills favorably reported by the committees to the entire legislative house were placed on the consent calendar, so an objection from a single legislator postponed its consideration and three objections led to its cancellation. Such objections were offered as a matter of course. See Lieder and Page, *Wild Justice*, 53–57; and Newton, "Indian Claims," 771.

39. 25 USC § 70a (2) (2000).

40. For an expanded discussion of obstacles in the Indian Claims Commission, from which much of this section is derived, see Lieder and Page, *Wild Justice*, 69–96, and Newton's "Indian Claims."

41. Before being appointed as Indian commissioner, Myer, a friend of anti-Indian legislators, had administered the concentration camps at which people of Japanese descent were interned during World War II. See Richard Drinnon, *Keeper of Concentration Camps: Dillon S. Myer and American Racism* (Berkeley: University of California Press, 1987). After investigating Myer's work for seven months, a special committee established by the American Bar Association found that Myer exceeded his statutory authority and, without justification, "rever[ted] to the doctrine that the 'Indian has no rights except those extended as privileges through rules and regulations and through mere sufferance'" (Drinnon, *Keeper*, 196). "At the end of Myer's first year, Harold Ickes publicly called him 'a Hitler and Mussolini rolled into one.'" Quoted in Prucha, *The Great Father*, 1030; Act of May 21, 1872, 17 Stat. 136.

42. Drinnon, *Keeper*, 189.

43. Newton, "Indian Claims," 772, quote at 819. See Tanner, chapter 10, this volume.

44. Lieder and Page, *Wild Justice*, 86, 92–94, 122–125, 138–139.

45. Newton, "Indian Claims," 773, and Steven Paul McSloy, "Revisiting the 'Courts of the Conqueror': American Indian Claims against the United States," *American University Law Review* 44, no. 2 (1994): 537, 584.

46. *United States Indian Claims Commission, Final Report* (1978), 20; for quote, see Prucha, *The Great Father*, 1022.

47. HR Con. Res. 108, 83d Cong., 1st Sess. (1953), 67 Stat. B132. On termination, see Donald Fixico, *Termination and Relocation: Federal Indian Policy, 1945–1960* (Albuquerque: University of New Mexico Press, 1986).

48. Carole Goldberg, "Public Law 280: The Limits of State Jurisdiction over Reservation Indians," *UCLA Law Review* 22, no. 3 (1975): 535. See Act of June 30, 1948, ch. 759, 62 Stat. 1161 (granting Iowa civil and criminal jurisdiction over the Sac and Fox Reservation); Act of May 31, 1946, ch. 279, 60 Stat. 229 (granting North Dakota jurisdiction over the Devil's Lake Reservation); Act of June 8, 1940, ch. 276, 54 Stat. 249 (Kansas); and Act of Sept. 13, 1950, ch. 947, § 1, 64 Stat. 845 (New York).

49. Act of Aug. 15, 1953, HR 1063, ch. 505, 67 Stat. 588 (codified, in part, at 18 USC § 1162 [2000] and 25 USC § 1360 [2000]).

50. David Getches, Charles Wilkinson, and Robert Williams, *Cases and Materials on Federal Indian Law* (St. Paul, MN: West Publishing Co., 2005), 204; Act of June 17, 1954, ch. 303, 68 Stat. 250 (Menominee); and *Menominee Tribe v. United States*, 391 US 404 (1968). See also Charles Wilkinson and Eric Biggs, "The Evolution of the Termination Policy," *American Indian Law Review* 5, no. 1 (1977): 139.

51. Prucha, *The Great Father*, 1059–1084, 1153.

52. *Mitchel v. United States*, 34 US (9 Pet.) 711, 746 (1835); 314 US 339 (1941).

53. *Tee-Hit-Ton v. United States*, 348 US 272, 289 (1955).

54. 358 US 217 (1959).

55. *Worcester*, 31 US, p. 520.

56. *Williams*, 358 US, p. 220.

57. *Williams*, 358 US, pp. 1056–1057.

58. Getches, *Cases and Materials*, 216.

59. See "Message from the President of the United States Transmitting Recommendations for Indian Policy," HR Doc. No. 91-363, at 3 (1970); Angie Debo, *A History of the Indians of the*

United States (Norman: University of Oklahoma Press, 1970), 405.

60. See "Special Message to Congress on the Problems of the American Indian: The Forgotten American," *Pub. Papers of Lyndon B. Johnson, 1968–69*, at 335–344 (1970) (proposing "a new goal for our Indian programs: a goal that ends the old debate about 'termination' of Indian programs and stresses self-determination"); and "Message from the President of the United States Transmitting Recommendations for Indian Policy," HR Doc. No. 91-363, at 3 (1970) (President Richard M. Nixon). "President Gerald R. Ford also stressed tribal self-determination, [but] [u]nlike Nixon, Ford issued no sweeping statement on Native American concerns...." Dean Kotlowski, "Alcatraz, Wounded Knee, and Beyond: The Nixon and Ford Administrations Respond to Native American Protest," *Pacific Historical Review* 72, no. 2 (2003): 217–218.

61. Act of June 17, 1954, ch. 303, 68 Stat. 250.

62. Act of Oct. 10, 1966, Pub. L. No. 89-635, § 1, 80 Stat. 880, codified at 28 USC § 1362 (2000).

63. See Newton, "Indian Claims," 769–770.

64. See D'Arcy McNickle, *Native American Tribalism: Indian Survivals and Renewals* (1973; reprint, New York: Oxford University Press, 1993).

65. Pub. L. No. 92-318, 86 Stat. 335; Pub. L. No. 93-638, 88 Stat. 2203 (1975) (codified as amended at 25 USC § 450a [2000]); Pub. L. No. 95-471, 92 Stat. 1325–1327 (1978).

66. 25 USC § 1901.

67. 485 US 439 (1988); 42 USC § 1996.

68. 25 USC §§ 1301–1341 (2000).

69. See *Talton v. Mayes*, 163 US 376 (1896).

70. 436 US 49 (1978).

71. 417 US 535 (1974).

72. 417 US 554 (1974).

73. See *Delaware Tribal Business Committee v. Weeks*, 430 US 73, 85 (1977) (noting that plenary power is no longer "absolute"). The Supreme Court further limited the scope of *Lone Wolf* in *Menominee*, 391 US 143, requiring that treaty abrogation must be explicit.

74. Deference to Congress remains quite broad. Indeed, "the Court has never struck down a federal statute directly regulating tribes on the grounds that Congress exceeded its authority to govern Indian affairs." Philip Frickey, "Congressional Intent, Practical Reasoning, and the Dynamic Nature of Federal Indian Law," *California Law Review* 78, no. 5 (1990): 1137, 1139.

75. *Oneida Indian Nation of NY v. County of Oneida, NY*, 414 US 661 (1974); *United States v. Sioux Nation of Indians*, 448 US 371 (1980).

76. 384 F. Supp. 312 (WD Wash. 1974), affirmed in part, 520 F. 2d 676 (9th Cir., 1975), cert. denied, 423 US 1086 (1976).

77. See "Annual Message to Congress" (Jan. 25, 1979), 1 Pub. Papers of Jimmy Carter, Jan. 1–June 22, 1979; Statement on Indian Policy, Pub. Papers of Ronald Reagan 96 (Jan. 24, 1983); Statement Reaffirming the Government-to-Government Relationship between the Federal Government and Indian Tribal Governments, 27 Weekly Comp. Pres. Doc. 783 (June 14, 1991) (President George H. W. Bush); 59 Fed. Reg. 22951 (1994) (President William J. Clinton); Exec. Order No. 13,084, 63 Fed. Reg. 27, 655 (May 19, 1998) (same); Proclamation No. 7500, 66 Fed. Reg. 221 (Nov. 15, 2001) (President George W. Bush). See also Department of Energy, Working with Indian Tribal Nations 3 (2000), available at http://homer.ornl.gov/oepa/guidance/

cultural/em_guide.pdf (accessed September 30, 2005). See also Debo, *A History*, 405, and Getches, *Cases and Materials*, 218.

78. See David Getches, "Conquering the Cultural Frontier: The New Subjectivism of the Supreme Court in Indian Law," *California Law Review* 84, no. 6 (1996): 1573, 1594–1595.

79. See Indian Health Care Amendments of 1990, 25 USC §§ 1613–1682; 25 USC § 2501; 26 USC § 7871 (2000); 25 USC § 4101; Pub. L. No. 103-413, tit. III, 108 Stat. 4270 (1994) (codified at 25 USC § 458aa).

80. 25 USC §§ 2101–2108 (2000).

81. 25 USC § 3101; 42 USC § 7401; 33 USC § 1251.

82. 25 USC § 2201.

83. 480 US 202 (1987).

84. Pub. L. No. 100-497, 102 Stat. 2467 (1988) (codified at 25 USC §§ 2701–2721).

85. *Seminole Tribe v. Florida*, 517 US 44 (1996).

86. 25 USC § 305; *Native American Arts, Inc. v. Bundy Howard, Inc.*, 168 F. Supp. 2d 905, 914 (ND Ill 2001).

87. 25 USC §§ 3001–3013; 16 USC § 470aa.

88. See *Cape Fox Corp. v. United States*, 4 Cl. Ct. 223, 232 (1983). Likewise, this general trust responsibility does not necessarily require the United States to reveal or address conflicts of interest stemming from its concurrent representation of tribes and other entities. See *Nevada v. United States*, 463 US 110 (1983); *Navajo Tribe v. United States*, 9 Cl. Ct. 227, 244 (1985). *United States v. Mitchell*, 445 US 535 (1980) (*Mitchell I*); *United States v. Mitchell*, 463 US 206 (1983) (*Mitchell II*).

89. *Mitchell II*, 463 US 206.

90. On express intent, see *Cheyenne-Arapaho Tribes v. United States*, 512 F. 2d 1390 (Ct. Cl. 1975). See 25 USC §§ 161(a), 161(b) (2000) (establishing federal trust management of tribal funds). On the implicit dimension, see *United States v. Navajo Nation*, 123 S. Ct. 1079, 1091 (2003):

> To state a claim cognizable under the Indian Tucker Act [28 USC § 1505 (2000)], *Mitchell I* and *Mitchell II* thus instruct, a Tribe must identify a substantive source of law that establishes specific fiduciary or other duties, and allege that the Government has failed faithfully to perform those duties. See 463 US at 216–217, 219, 103 S. Ct. 2961. If that threshold is passed, the court must then determine whether the substantive law "can fairly be interpreted as mandating compensation for damages sustained as a result of a breach of the duties [the governing law] impose[s]. Id., at 219, 103 S. Ct. 2961. Although "the undisputed existence of a general trust relationship between the United States and the Indian people" can "reinforc[e]" the conclusion that the relevant statute or regulation imposes fiduciary duties, id., at 225, 103 S. Ct. 2961, that relationship alone is insufficient to support jurisdiction under the Indian Tucker Act. Instead, the analysis must train on specific rights-creating or duty-imposing statutory or regulatory prescriptions. Those prescriptions need not, however, expressly provide for money damages; the availability of such damages may be inferred.

Despite an accurate statement of the holdings in the *Mitchell* cases, five members of the Court appeared to state a preference for a specific, express textual source for the "substantive duty." See id., at 1010. If this strict interpretation is followed, it will allow the federal government to rely on nontextual sources to exert power over tribes (see *Board of County Comm'rs v. Seber*, 318 US 705, 715 [1943]; *United States v. Kagama*, 118 US 375, 384–385 [1886]), while requiring tribes to point to a specific textual source in order to enforce the government's trust responsibility.

91. 25 USC § 4001.

92. 25 USC § 4001. See *South Dakota v. Yankton Sioux Tribe*, 522 US 329 (1998).

93. See Getches, "Conquering," 1620–1621.

94. 435 US 191, 195 (1978).

95. For quote, see Getches, "Conquering," 1597. For criticisms, see Russell Barsh and James Henderson, "The Betrayal: *Oliphant v. Suquamish Indian Tribe* and the Hunting of the Snark," *Minnesota Law Review* 63, no. 4 (1979): 609, 616–635; Catherine Stetson, "Decriminalizing Tribal Codes: A Response to Oliphant," *American Indian Law Review* 9, no. 1 (1981): 51, 54; Williams, "Algebra," 267–274; Kevin Meisner, "Comment: Modern Problems of Criminal Jurisdiction in Indian Country," *American Indian Law Review* 17, no. 1 (1992): 175, 191–193; Peter Maxfield, "*Oliphant v. Suquamish*: The Whole Is Greater Than the Sum of Its Parts," *Journal of Contemporary Law* 19, no. 2 (1993): 391; N. Bruce Duthu, "Implicit Divestiture of Tribal Powers: Locating Legitimate Sources of Authority on Indian Country," *American Indian Law Review* 19, no. 2 (1994): 353; Judith Royster, "The Legacy of Allotment," *Arizona State Law Journal* 27, no. 1 (1995): 1, 43–48; Getches, "Conquering," 1597; Philip Frickey, "Adjudication and Its Discontents: Coherence and Conciliation in Federal Indian Law," *Harvard Law Review* 110, no. 8 (1997): 1754, 1769 ("The modern decline of tribal geographical sovereignty can be traced from *Oliphant*…"); and David Getches, "Beyond Indian Law: The Rehnquist Court's Pursuit of States' Rights, Color-Blind Justice and Mainstream Values," *Minnesota Law Review* 86, no. 2 (2001): 267, 274 (describing the rule in *Oliphant* as "aberrant").

96. 435 US at 204 ("Congress never expressly forbade Indian tribes to impose criminal penalties on non-Indians,…"); see 435 US 208 (holding the Treaty of Point Elliott, 12 Stat. 927 [1855] was insufficient to remove criminal jurisdiction over non-Indians) and 198.

97. 25 USC §§ 1301–1341 (2000); 25 USC §§ 193. The Court further conceded that "Indian tribal court systems have become increasingly sophisticated and resembled in many respects their state counterparts." 25 USC §§ 211–212. See also Maxfield, "*Oliphant v. Suquamish*," 402.

98. Getches, "Conquering," 1597.

99. 450 US 544 (1981).

100. See *Brendale v. Confederated Tribes and Bands of the Yakima Indian Nation*, 492 US 408 (1989); *South Dakota v. Bourland*, 508 US 679 (1993); *Strate v. A-1 Contractors*, 520 US 438 (1997); *Nevada v. Hicks*, 533 US 353 (2001); *Atkinson Trading Co., Inc. v. Shirley*, 532 US 645 (2001).

101. 495 US 676 (1990).

102. 494 US 872 (1990); 541 US 193 (2004); 42 USCA § 2000bb; *City of Boerne v. Flores*, 521 US 507 (1997).

Part II
Continuing Encounters: Historical Perspectives

Daniel M. Cobb

At the end of the twentieth century, a generation of scholars completely revised our understanding of the nature of the first 350 years of contact between Natives and newcomers. Eventually, they took as their interpretive framework for this revisionist approach the idea of *encounters*, which historian James Axtell richly described as "mutual, reciprocal—two-way rather than one-way streets," "generally capacious," and "temporally and spatially fluid."[1] Emphases on diplomacy, negotiation, treaty making, cultural brokerage, ethnogenesis, and exchange supplanted worn-out narratives based on ethnocentric notions such as discovery and conquest. Although this perspective put Native people at the center of the history of the North American colonies and Early Republic, it did not lead to new interpretations of the nineteenth or twentieth centuries. Indeed, historians typically imagine twentieth-century American Indian history as being fundamentally different in nature from the more distant past, despite the fact that, from the perspective of Native America, the colonial period has not ended.

Historian James Merrell once argued that because Indians no longer "intrude on contemporary consciousness," it was difficult enough simply to convince people today of how central Indians were to politics during the seventeenth and eighteenth centuries. "We need to remember," he countered, "that things were different two or three centuries ago."[2] If things were in many ways different two or three centuries ago, the chapters in Part II demonstrate that the sharp distinctions we draw between the political histories of the distant past and the more recent past need to be scrutinized. To

57

be sure, the balance of power shifted dramatically through the eighteenth, nineteenth, and twentieth centuries as federal policies, congressional legislation, and Supreme Court decisions increasingly shaped the world in which Native peoples lived (Helton and Robertson, chapter 3, this volume). But this shift amounted primarily to a change of context. Political encounters within indigenous communities and between Natives and newcomers have continued.

To underscore this point and to provide an interpretive framework for the chapters in Part II, this introduction recasts the policy eras typically used to structure American Indian history between the 1880s and early 1970s, by viewing them through the lens of historian James Axtell's definition of encounters. This recontextualization is important because it significantly changes the storyline. For instance, the policy narrative tells of dramatic shifts—first, from assimilation to self-government and then from termination to self-determination—whereas in the political activism narrative, continuity prevails as Native people consistently take steps within their communities and in outside relations with local, state, and federal governments to innovate, resist, and accommodate (see the juxtapositions in tables 1–7).[3] In addition, this vantage point clearly reveals that the advent of Red Power during the late 1960s and 1970s was not an aberrant moment when Indians suddenly became politically active. Instead, it can be recognized as an episode in an ancient, multifaceted, and ongoing American Indian political tradition.

Assimilation and Allotment as a Two-Way rather than One-Way Street

The late nineteenth century represents a dark period in which the federal government consolidated its power over tribal communities and exerted enormous pressure to destroy them through laws, the courts, support for mission work, and an imposed educational system. Yet it was not a one-way street. In the face of allotment and assimilation, Native people forged local, regional, and national organizations—such as the Alaska Native Brotherhood (1912), the Alaska Native Sisterhood (1915), the Northwest Federation of American Indians (1914), the Black Hills Treaty Council (1911), and the Society of American Indians (1911)—to secure citizenship and voting rights and to compel the federal government to live up to its treaties and legal obligations (Clark, chapter 4, this volume). Meanwhile, at the local level, Redbird Smith (Cherokee) and Chitto Harjo (Creek) served as the driving forces behind the formation of the Four Mothers Society

(1912), a community-centered political and religious movement in north-eastern Oklahoma that resisted allotment, preserved sacred practices, and reasserted indigenous notions of peoplehood.[4]

As Native people openly challenged the federal government's policies, Congress and the courts became sites of contestation. Chitto Harjo hired lawyers to take the fight to Washington and made the trip himself on more than one occasion. On the Plains, Lakotas challenged the illegal taking of the Black Hills. In the Southwest, Pueblos unified locally and then allied themselves with non-Indian advocacy organizations to defeat legislation that would have led to massive land loss during the 1920s. In Oklahoma, Lone Wolf (Kiowa) challenged the allotment of the Kiowa, Comanche, and Apache reservation through litigation, arguing that it violated the Treaty of Medicine Lodge. Worth noting, too, is that his nephew, Delos Lone Wolf, a student of the assimilationist Carlisle Indian Industrial School, played a crucial role in the case—something advocates of "Indian civilization" certainly did not have in mind when they established off-reservation boarding schools.[5]

Resistance and accommodation manifested in still other, subtler forms within and beyond reservation borders. Native people often turned federal policy on its head in order to protect their tribal identities, by choosing contiguous allotments so that kin groups could continue residing together. In later years, holding land privately afforded protection to carry on dances and ritual practices the Bureau of Indian Affairs (BIA) sought to extinguish (Troutman, chapter 5, this volume). Tribal leader Quanah Parker (Comanche) and others like him further set about indigenizing externally imposed institutions, such as the BIA's Courts of Indian Offenses. At the same time, leaders of the Native American Church consciously wove elements of Christianity into their use of peyote and, amidst intense persecution, adopted articles of incorporation in the state of Oklahoma in order to gain constitutional protection for free exercise of religion. Throughout Indian Country, Native people accommodated themselves to new ways of making a living, including wage labor, farming, ranching, playing professional sports, and carving out careers as actors, writers, artists, singers, and white collar professionals.[6]

All of these purposeful acts carried with them profoundly political messages, at times overt and at times disguised, about indigenous survival. Through bold acts of resistance and subtle accommodationist techniques, Native people defied the assumption that they were innately inferior and the expectation that they must inevitably disappear. They demonstrated that the persistence and flexibility of both individual concepts of identity and collective notions of peoplehood could knock the so-called "pulverizing engine of progress" off its tracks. In so doing, to change metaphors slightly, they transformed allotment and assimilation from a one-way to a two-way street.

Without question, the use of intertribal alliances, the courts, creative personal and collective adaptations, and religious syncretism, no less than the indigenization of external institutions and the rise of intermediaries that could operate between cultures, were old phenomena taking place in dramatically transformed contexts.

Indian Reorganization as a Mutual and Reciprocal Process

This multifaceted political tradition carried into the 1930s. Commissioner of Indian Affairs John Collier was undoubtedly driven by a romantic depiction of Indians. The legislation he originally proposed to replace allotment with a commitment to self-government invested his own office with the authority to approve the decisions made by tribes. Be that as it may, his attempt to secure support for the Indian Reorganization Act (IRA) in 1934 revealed that the politics of federal policy reform would be a mutual and reciprocal process, another critical component of Axtell's definition of encounters that links this era to the past.

The mutual and reciprocal character of these encounters could be seen in particular repose during the spring of 1934, as Collier and his staff held a series of congresses with tribal leaders across the West. During the meetings, many Native people—who could aptly be considered diplomats—made clear their preference for either their traditional forms of government or business committees and tribal courts established before the 1930s. Others had become comfortable with their individual allotments and criticized the philosophical underpinnings of Collier's landmark legislation as communistic—particularly his idea of mandating the tribalization of land ownership. The more general concern elicited in the various congresses centered on whether Collier's ideas were in accordance with tribes' rights to self-determination or were simply meant to impose a system of indirect control.[7]

In the end, more than two-thirds of the tribes voted to accept the Indian Reorganization Act, ninety-two wrote new constitutions, and seventy-two drafted charters to form business corporations. In each instance, they had their own motivations quite apart from realizing Collier's utopian vision of the "Red Atlantis." LaDonna Harris memorably described her tribe's approach this way: "The Comanche said, 'Well, we are going to pass this constitution to get white people off our back. Who needs it? We will not use it anyway.'"[8] In other parts of Indian Country, tribes did use the IRA to great effect. The Stockbridge Munsee reclaimed their tribal land base in Wisconsin. On the Wind River Reservation in Wyoming, the Indian Division of the Civilian

Conservation Corps provided critically important employment opportunities. Elsewhere, unrecognized tribes adopted constitutions under the IRA to secure federal acknowledgment (Osburn, chapter 6, this volume).[9] By openly engaging in a dialogue regarding Collier's reform agenda, then by taking purposeful action to invest it with their own meanings, Native people transformed the Indian reorganization era into a mutual and reciprocal process.[10]

The Temporal and Spatial Fluidity
of the Termination and Relocation Era

The onset of World War II seriously undermined the Indian New Deal and eventually contributed to the rise of the termination era, but the federal government's desire to end its legal obligations to tribes certainly did not begin in the late 1940s and early 1950s, as the policy era might be taken to suggest. The United States had always endeavored to find a way to solve the so-called Indian problem; disputes over land, water, and natural resources that drove termination had been in existence for generations. Congress merely breathed new life into the effort to "get out of the Indian business" during and after the war. From a Native-centered encounter perspective, the termination and relocation period might better be understood as an integral part of a constant struggle to protect and enhance tribal sovereignty, as well as another moment in which indigenous peoples redefined what it means to be Indian in places outside their homelands.

During the Second World War, tribes initiated a cultural and political renaissance. More than twenty-five thousand Native men and women served in the armed forces. Tribal communities revived dances, songs, and rituals to prepare young men for battle and to heal them upon their return, to celebrate valorous achievements, and to mourn the dead. After the war, veterans used newly gained skills and stature to reinvigorate traditional soldier societies and vault themselves into leadership positions—as the World War I generation had done before them. These new leaders proved instrumental to the growth of the National Congress of American Indians (NCAI). Founded in 1944, the NCAI carried on the tradition of organizing across tribal lines to act in concert at the national level. From the first, it took as its purpose the aggressive defense of treaty rights, the promotion of self-determination, and the creation of a formal legal mechanism through which tribes could settle outstanding claims against the federal government.[11]

The threat of termination during the 1950s actually energized the National Congress of American Indians; throughout the decade, it met the challenge to tribal nationhood head on. Meanwhile, individual tribes sent delegations to Washington DC to protest specific legislation. But the contest should not be oversimplified in such a way that it pits "the government" against "the Indians." The Choctaws, Klamaths, Menominees, Colvilles, and Utes experienced bitter internal divisions as they debated whether to continue the federal trust relationship. A local perspective shows that the politics of termination certainly involved issues such as federal services, the distribution of claims settlement money, control over tribal resources, and treaty rights, but it also involved matters of identity, class, legitimacy, and community (Kidwell, chapter 7, this volume).[12]

Understood in terms of political encounters, termination had greater temporal fluidity than the policy era period suggests. Congressional acts terminating several tribes continued to be proposed and passed well into the mid-1960s. Moreover, the communities that were slated for termination during the late 1950s and early 1960s immediately launched efforts to delay it from taking effect or to restore their tribes' relationships with the federal government. Menominee activist Ada Deer spearheaded a community-based campaign that gained momentum during the 1960s and ultimately ended in restoration in 1973; the Klamaths continued their own pursuits into the 1980s (see tables 4 and 6). For the Mixed-Blood Utes, however, the termination era has yet to end. They retain their sense of peoplehood, despite a federal district court's dismissal of a lawsuit they initiated to restore their rights in January 2006.[13]

The Indian Claims Commission (Helton and Robertson, chapter 3, and Tanner, chapter 10, this volume) and relocation, two additional features of the termination era, have equally complex political histories. Relocation provided incentives to Indian individuals and families to leave their reservation communities for urban centers such as Denver, Chicago, Los Angeles, and Minneapolis. There, policymakers imagined, Indian people would shed their tribal identities and lose their connections to their homelands. At the individual level, Native people often moved fluidly between reservation and city. They also banded together to form urban centers that cultivated a pantribal Indian identity—furthering yet another process that earlier generations had already begun.[14] Rather than melt into the dominant society, they mobilized to demand that the Bureau of Indian Affairs and state, county, and municipal agencies extend services to urban communities. In time, urban Indians pressed their home communities to recognize them as vital members through the extension of services, the creation of technologies that enabled them to vote in elections and participate in meetings, and periodic visits from tribal leaders. They also established community schools, business cooperatives, intertribal powwows, institutions of higher learning, and a host of advocacy organizations.[15]

Termination, claims cases, and relocation, of course, were not the only political issues on the minds of Native people. Alaska Natives, Mississippi Choctaws, and Lumbees in North Carolina fought against racial discrimination and segregation. Tribes in New Mexico mounted a successful campaign to secure the right to vote in state elections. When the United States Army Corps of Engineers began planning for the construction of the Kinzua Dam, the Senecas orchestrated a concerted effort to prevent it from being built. A similar process unfolded along the Missouri River, where Northern Plains tribes attempted to forestall the construction of a series of dams under the Pick-Sloan Plan.[16] These represent but a few examples of the termination era's spatial and temporal fluidity.

The Capaciousness of the Early Tribal Self-Determination Era

Historians often refer to the 1960s as the "beginning" of the tribal self-determination era, but Native and non-Native people were, in fact, in the midst of a tremendous diversity of ongoing struggles. Indeed, as Helton and Robertson argue in chapter 3, Indian activism has *always* been about self-determination. One of this particular period's hallmarks, the fish-in movement, actually represented a new twist in an old fight (Smith, chapter 8, this volume). Although states such as Washington, Wisconsin, and Oklahoma extended de facto jurisdiction over hunting and fishing in lands ceded by tribes through treaties or opened via allotment, they did so without the consent of Indian people. Throughout the nineteenth and early twentieth centuries, this transformed the treaty-protected practice of fishing and hunting in these ceded lands into everyday acts of defiance. Consequently, when Native people in states such as Washington, Oregon, Oklahoma, Minnesota, and Wisconsin risked arrest and harassment to exercise these rights during the late 1950s and early 1960s, they were participating in long-standing family and community traditions.[17]

The same can be said of activists engaged in national politics during the 1960s. To advocate for tribal nationalism, Indian people situated their struggles in the context of international politics throughout the twentieth century. The practice of drawing upon the language of decolonization and the Cold War, then, was not a new phenomenon (Cobb, chapter 9, this volume). In the wake of World War I, tribal leaders and reformers such as Robert Yellowtail (Crow) and Carlos Montezuma (Yavapai) called upon President Woodrow Wilson to extend elements of his Fourteen Points to

Native peoples. During the early 1920s, Oneida-Cayuga chief Deskaheh traveled to Europe with a passport issued by the Iroquois Confederacy in order to condemn Canada's Indian policies before the League of Nations. In an equally strident move, Iroquois and Miccosukee Seminole delegates met with Fidel Castro to forge friendly relations with Cuba during the late 1950s.[18] The advent of the American Indian Movement in 1968, the increase in militancy through the 1970s, and the formation of the International Indian Treaty Council (IITC) in 1974 occurred in this rich context of Native politics and activism. It is notable that the IITC, which became the first organization of indigenous peoples to be recognized as a nongovernment organization with consultative status to the United Nations, began with the issuance of a "Declaration of Continuing Independence."[19]

Native people articulated an expansive definition of self-determination during the 1960s. Through the Community Action Program, a central component of the War on Poverty, men and women, youths and elders, found an open door into more active involvement in the political life of their communities (Kidwell, chapter 7, and Cobb, chapter 9, this volume).[20] An infusion of federal money also realized long-standing efforts to create tribally controlled educational institutions, such as the founding of the Rough Rock Demonstration School and Navajo Community College.[21] The War on Poverty's Legal Services program served as a vehicle for challenging discrimination, provided a stepping stone for some Native people to assume leadership positions, and contributed to the establishment of the Native American Rights Fund (1970)—the most effective national legal organization advocating for tribal sovereignty today.[22] As innovative artists such as Oscar Howe (Dakota) and Fritz Scholder (Luiseño) joined the faculties at the University of South Dakota and the Institute of American Indian Arts in Santa Fe, respectively, an artistic renaissance that contributed to the rise of the "esthetic sovereignty" movement gained momentum (Warrior, chapter 16, this volume).[23]

Meanwhile, concern for the future of Indian youths served as an impetus for the creation of the Workshop on American Indian Affairs and the Southwest Regional Indian Youth Council during the 1950s. Both organizations provided training grounds and opportunities to network with other young Native college students, eventually giving birth to the National Indian Youth Council (NIYC) in 1961 (Warrior, chapter 16, this volume). At the workshops and in the activism of the NIYC, Native youths made potent connections between their own struggle for self-determination and the movements for decolonization among indigenous peoples across the globe (Cobb, chapter 9, this volume). And finally, predominantly non-Native entities, such as the Association on American Indian Affairs, the

Indian Rights Association, and the American Friends Service Committee, provided support for tribal rights even as they engaged in competitions with the emergence of Indian-controlled organizations, such as the NCAI, NIYC, and Survival of American Indians Association (Smith, chapter 8, this volume). If these few examples merely scratch the surface of Indian political activism during the 1960s, they at least give an indication of the capaciousness of the movement for self-determination.

Why Do Continuing Encounters Matter?

To return to where this chapter begins, James Merrell certainly argued correctly that things were different two or three centuries ago and that the dominant society consistently proves unwilling or unable to acknowledge the reality of Native people's presence in contemporary times. This introduction, the tables, and the chapters in Part II demonstrate, however, that the more things change, the more they stay the same. Looking through the lens of encounters, we discern strong connections between the politics and activism during the twentieth century and during earlier periods. The recent past and the more distant past no longer seem as fundamentally different as they might at first appear. The political, social, economic, and cultural contexts may have changed over time, in other words, but the encounters have continued unabated. They are no less mutual, reciprocal, temporally and spatially fluid, and capacious than the ones that preceded them.

Acknowledging this point matters because it challenges the idea that the era in which Native peoples were central actors in their own history is over. Wittingly or unwittingly, this stance is connected to the notion that tribal sovereignty has been lost or, at the very least, irrevocably diminished. This myth has served and will continue to serve as a countervailing force to the economic and political resurgence of tribes during the twentieth and twenty-first centuries—a process that has altered the balance of power in many parts of the country. Even as Native people increasingly "intrude on contemporary consciousness," to draw once again on Merrell's language, the dominant society remains largely ignorant. In large measure, this ignorance is due to the fact that it requires less thought and is somehow less discomfiting to believe that Indian history ended in late December 1890, when the Seventh Cavalry massacred hundreds of Lakota people at Wounded Knee. Indeed, the argument that the colonial era—a period most Americans typically confine to the seventeenth and eighteenth centuries—has not ended for Native people is often met with either disbelief or resistance.

Given this reality, it is all the more important for scholars to write histories that acknowledge the endurance of a multifaceted political tradition.

It is a tradition that has, for centuries, countered the expectation that Native people will inevitably disappear—and it will continue to do so in the future.[24] The chapters in Part II and, more generally, the interpretive framework of continuing encounters demonstrate that to look at federal policies as anything other than contexts for Native action is to create the false impression that indigenous peoples are no longer makers of their own histories. They underscore the point, powerfully articulated by Donald Fixico and Frederick Hoxie in chapters 1 and 2, respectively, that to confuse policies with politics is to obscure the reality of American Indians' lived experiences within and outside their communities.[25]

Notes

1. James Axtell, "Colonial Encounters: Beyond 1992," *William and Mary Quarterly* 3rd series, 49, no. 2 (1992): 336.

2. James Merrell, "Some Thoughts on Colonial Historians and American Indians," *William and Mary Quarterly* 3rd series, 46, no. 1 (1989): 116.

3. Donald Fixico, "Federal and State Policies and American Indians," in *A Companion to American Indian History,* Blackwell Companions to American History, ed. Philip Deloria and Neal Salisbury (Malden, MA: Blackwell Publishing, 2004), 379–396.

4. Frederick Hoxie, "Exploring a Cultural Borderland: Native American Journeys of Discovery in the Early Twentieth Century," *Journal of American History* 79, no. 3 (1992): 969–995; Kenneth Tollefson, "The Political Survival of Landless Puget Sound Indians," *American Indian Quarterly* 16, no. 2 (1992): 227–230; Alexandra Harmon, *Indians in the Making: Ethnic Relations and Indian Identities around Puget Sound* (Berkeley: University of California Press, 1998), 178–185; and Tom Holm, *The Great Confusion in Indian Affairs: Native Americans and Whites in the Progressive Era* (Austin: University of Texas Press, 2005). On the idea of peoplehood, see Tom Holm, Diane Pearson, and Ben Chavez, "Peoplehood: A Model for the Extension of Sovereignty in American Indian Studies," *Wicazo Sa Review* 18, no. 1 (2003): 7–24.

5. Kenneth Philp, *John Collier's Crusade for Indian Reform, 1920–1954* (Tucson: University of Arizona Press, 1977); Frederick Hoxie, "Exploring a Cultural Borderland"; Edward Lazarus, *Black Hills/White Justice: The Sioux Nation versus the United States, 1775 to the Present* (New York: Harper Collins, 1991); C. Blue Clark, Lone Wolf v. Hitchcock: *Treaty Rights and Indian Law at the End of the Nineteenth Century* (Lincoln: University of Nebraska Press, 1994); David Wallace Adams, "More Than a Game: The Carlisle Indians Take to the Gridiron," *Western Historical Quarterly* 32, no. 1 (2001): 25–53; and Clifford Trafzer, Jean Keller, and Lorene Sisquoc, eds., *Boarding School Blues: Revisiting American Indian Educational Experiences* (Lincoln: University of Nebraska Press, 2006).

6. Omer Stewart, *Peyote Religion: A History* (Norman: University of Oklahoma Press, 1987); William Hagan, *Quanah Parker: Comanche Chief* (Norman: University of Oklahoma Press, 1993); Peter Iverson, *When Indians Became Cowboys: Native Peoples and Cattle Ranching in the American West* (Norman: University of Oklahoma Press, 1994); Brian Hosmer, *American Indians in the Marketplace: Persistence and Innovation among the Menominees and Metlakatlans, 1870–1920* (Lawrence: University Press of Kansas, 1999); Emily Greenwald, *Reconfiguring the Reservation:*

The Nez Perces, Jicarilla Apaches, and the Dawes Act (Albuquerque: University of New Mexico Press, 2002); Philip Deloria, *Indians in Unexpected Places* (Lawrence: University Press of Kansas, 2004); and Colleen O'Neill, *Working the Navajo Way: Labor and Culture in the Twentieth Century* (Lawrence: University Press of Kansas, 2005).

7. Vine Deloria Jr. and Clifford Lytle, *The Nations Within: The Past and Future of American Indian Sovereignty* (New York: Pantheon, 1984); Thomas Biolsi, *Organizing the Lakota: The Political Economy of the New Deal on the Pine Ridge and Rosebud Reservations* (Tucson: University of Arizona Press, 1992); and Vine Deloria Jr., ed., *The Indian Reorganization Act: Congresses and Bills* (Norman: University of Oklahoma Press, 2002).

8. LaDonna Harris, quoted in Kenneth Philp, ed., *Indian Self-Rule: First-Hand Accounts of Indian–White Relations from Roosevelt to Reagan* (Salt Lake City: Howe Brothers, 1988; Logan: Utah State University, 1995), 108.

9. John Savagian, "The Tribal Reorganization of the Stockbridge Munsee: Essential Conditions in the Re-creation of a Native American Community, 1930–1942," *Wisconsin Magazine of History* 77, no. 1 (1993): 39–62; and Brian Hosmer, "'Dollar a Day and Glad to Have It': Work Relief on the Wind River Reservation as Memory," in *Native Pathways: American Indian Culture and Economic Development in the Twentieth Century*, ed. Brian Hosmer and Colleen O'Neill (Boulder: University of Colorado Press, 2004), 283–307.

10. Vine Deloria Jr. underscored this point regarding continuity in his introduction to the transcriptions of the congresses: "When the old chiefs speak at the congresses we find that some of them remember the days of freedom prior to the establishment of the reservations, and they speak of treaties as a present reality that, for them, still endured…. Above all…these meetings demonstrate the strong continuity of Indian life and values over many generations and continuing today." Deloria, ed., *Indian Reorganization Act*, xvi.

11. Stephen Cornell, *The Return of the Native: American Indian Political Resurgence* (New York: Oxford University Press, 1988); Alison Bernstein, *American Indians and World War II: Toward a New Era in Indian Affairs* (Norman: University of Oklahoma Press, 1991); Thomas Britten, *American Indians in World War I: At Home and at War* (Albuquerque: University of New Mexico Press, 1997); Thomas Cowger, *The National Congress of American Indians: The Founding Years* (Lincoln: University of Nebraska Press, 1999); and Clyde Ellis, "'We Don't Want Your Rations, We Want This Dance': The Changing Use of Song and Dance on the Southern Plains," *Western Historical Quarterly* 30, no. 2 (1999): 133–154. Local politics among the Iroquois took a different form. Even though many Iroquois enlisted to serve, the Six Nations rejected the arbitrary imposition of US citizenship and initially protested the draft as an infringement of their national sovereignty. A select group of Iroquois, without formal approval of the Six Nations Leadership, proceeded to issue their own declaration of war on the Axis powers in 1942. Laurence Hauptman, *The Iroquois Struggle for Survival: World War II to Red Power* (Syracuse, NY: Syracuse University Press, 1986), 2–9.

12. Nicholas Peroff, *Menominee DRUMS: Tribal Termination and Restoration, 1954–1974* (Norman: University of Oklahoma Press, 1982); and R. Warren Metcalf, "Lambs of Sacrifice: Termination, the Mixed Blood Utes, and the Problem of Indian Identity," *Utah Historical Quarterly* 64, no. 4 (1996): 322–343.

13. Donald Fixico, *Termination and Relocation: Federal Indian Policy, 1945–1960* (Albuquerque: University of New Mexico Press, 1986); R. Warren Metcalf, *Termination's Legacy: The Discarded Indians of Utah* (Lincoln: University of Nebraska Press, 2002); and "Mixed-Blood Utes Lose

Termination Lawsuit," February 8, 2006, www.indiancountry.com (accessed October 3, 2006).

14. David Beck, "Developing a Voice: The Evolution of Self-Determination in an Urban Indian Community," *Wicazo Sa Review* 17, no. 2 (2002): 117–141; and James LaGrand, *Indian Metropolis: Native Americans in Chicago* (Urbana: University of Illinois Press, 2002).

15. Peter Iverson, "Building toward Self-Determination: Plains and Southwestern Indians in the 1940s and 1950s," *Western Historical Quarterly* 16, no. 2 (1985): 163–173; Joan Weibel-Orlando, *Indian Country, LA: Maintaining Ethnic Community in Complex Society* (Urbana: University of Illinois Press, 1999); Donald Fixico, *The Urban Indian Experience in America* (Albuquerque: University of New Mexico Press, 2000); and Terry Straus, ed., *Native Chicago*, 2nd ed. (Chicago: McNaughton and Gunn, Inc., 2002).

16. Karen Blu, *The Lumbee Problem: The Making of an American Indian People*, with a new preface by the author (Cambridge: Cambridge University Press, 1980; Lincoln: University of Nebraska Press, 2001); Michael Lawson, *Dammed Indians: The Pick-Sloan Plan and the Missouri River Sioux, 1944–1980* (Norman: University of Oklahoma Press, 1982); Hauptman, *Iroquois Struggle*, 105–122; and Terrence Cole, "Jim Crow in Alaska: The Passage of the Alaska Equal Rights Act of 1945," *Western Historical Quarterly* 23, no. 4 (1992): 429–449.

17. Daniel Boxberger, *To Fish in Common: The Ethnohistory of Lummi Indian Salmon Fishing*, with a new afterword by the author (Lincoln: University of Nebraska Press, 1989; Seattle: University of Washington Press, 2000); Charles Wilkinson, *Messages from Frank's Landing: A Story of Salmon, Treaties, and the Indian Way* (Seattle: University of Washington Press, 2000); Larry Nesper, *The 'Valleye War: The Struggle for Ojibwe Spearfishing and Treaty Rights* (Lincoln: University of Nebraska Press, 2002); Donna Hightower-Langston, "American Indian Women's Activism in the 1960s and 1970s," *Hypatia* 18, no. 2 (2003): 114–132; and Charles Wilkinson, *Blood Struggle: The Rise of Modern Indian Nations* (New York: W. W. Norton, 2005).

18. Hauptman, *Iroquois Struggle*, 163, 206–207; Frederick Hoxie, ed., *Talking Back to Civilization: Indian Voices from the Progressive Era* (Boston: Bedford/St. Martin's, 2001); and Harry Kersey Jr., "The Havana Connection: Buffalo Tiger, Fidel Castro, and the Origin of Miccosukee Tribal Sovereignty, 1959–1962," *American Indian Quarterly* 25, no. 4 (2001): 491–507.

19. "Declaration of Continuing Independence by the First International Indian Treaty Council at Standing Rock Indian Country June 1974," www.treatycouncil.org/PDFs/DECLARATION_OF_CONTINUING_INDEPENDENCE.pdf (accessed November 15, 2006). By the 1980s, the movement for a statement addressing the global dimensions of the struggle culminated in the formation of the Working Group on Indigenous Peoples. The "Draft Declaration on the Rights of Indigenous Peoples" was finally approved by the UN's Commission on Human Rights in the summer of 2006 and went before the UN General Assembly in November 2006. Valerie Taliman, "UN Human Rights Council Adopts Declaration on Indigenous Rights," *Indian Country Today*, July 10, 2006; and Charmaine White Face, "Indigenous Peoples Still Lack Human Rights," *Indian Country Today*, July 21, 2006.

20. Päivi Hoikkala, "Mothers and Community Builders: Salt River Pima and Maricopa Women in Community Action," in *Negotiators of Change: Historical Perspective on Native American Women*, ed. Nancy Shoemaker (New York: Routledge, 1995), 213–234; Daniel Cobb, "Philosophy of an Indian War: Indian Community Action in the Johnson Administration's War on Indian Poverty, 1964–1968," *American Indian Culture and Research Journal* 22, no. 2 (1998): 71–102; and Daniel Cobb, "'Us Indians understand the basics': Oklahoma Indians and the Politics of Community Action, 1964–1970," *Western Historical Quarterly* XXXIII, no. 1 (2002): 41–66.

21. Peter Iverson, *The Navajo Nation* (Albuquerque: University of New Mexico Press, 1983), and *Diné: A History of the Navajos* (Albuquerque: University of New Mexico Press, 2002).

22. Cobb, "Philosophy." For more on NARF's history, see http://www.narf.org/about/about_whatwedo_mission.html (accessed February 16, 2007).

23. Lucy Lippard, "Esthetic Sovereignty, or, Going Places with Cultural Baggage," in *Path Breakers: The Eiteljorg Fellowship for Native American Fine Art, 2003* (Seattle: University of Washington Press, 2003), 1–10.

24. On expectations and framing, see Deloria, *Indians in Unexpected Places*, 4, 7.

25. The attempt to expand the meaning of political history has deep roots. In a seminal essay published in 1971, Robert F. Berkhofer argued for Native-centered studies of communities, leadership, and reform organizations. He made this call amidst a more general effort on the part of social historians to write history "from the bottom up." Robert Berkhofer, "The Political Context of a New Indian History," *Pacific Historical Review* 40, no. 3 (1971): 357–382. Also see D'Arcy McNickle Center for the History of the American Indian, *The Struggle for Political Autonomy: Papers and Comments from the Second Newberry Library Conference on Themes in American Indian History*, Indian Occasional Papers in Curriculum Series, no. 11 (Chicago: The Newberry Library, 1989).

4. At the Headwaters of a Twentieth-Century "Indian" Political Agenda

Rethinking the Origins of the Society of American Indians

D. Anthony Tyeeme Clark

In 1900 most Americans thought that Native peoples had become a "Vanishing Race." The American Indian population had reached an all-time low, tribal lands had been reduced to only a few million acres, and the US government had embraced allotment and assimilation policies devoted to exterminating tribal cultures (see table 1).[1] Not until the 1970s did scholars begin to take seriously Native peoples' perspectives on how they survived this harrowing period.[2] D. Anthony Tyeeme Clark adds still greater complexity to this body of literature, which is centered on the era's foremost intellectuals and the organization they founded in 1911, the Society of American Indians (SAI).[3] Rather than center his focus on an individual or accept the founding of the SAI as the "beginning" of Indian activism, he turns his gaze toward a series of networks that had been in the making since at least the 1880s. Speaking to Don Fixico's call for internally oriented approaches and Fred Hoxie's argument for studies of Native activist networks, Clark's essay offers one example of how the history of local, regional, and national reform organizations can be reconceptualized.

The Society of American Indians (the Society) emerged over a period of twenty years from extensive webs of relationship and from prior efforts at organization that joined tribally connected American Indian women and men. From the "inaugural national Indian conference," as organizers advertised the October 1911 meeting in Columbus, Ohio, through its final meeting in Chicago, the Society for twelve years served as a critical alternative for Indian peoples to the non-Indians who, until that time, had done most of the talking for them. It provided a meeting ground for individual Indian advocates of race progress to develop a leadership (a sort of indigenous "Talented Tenth") and promote the autonomy of Indian nations.[4] At the Society's twelve annual meetings in places with opportunities for important media attention, Indians from reservation communities, rural locations, small towns and growing cities, and government service gathered to discuss solutions to their shared concerns (figure 3).

Defining characteristics of the Society were the diversity of and disagreements among its participants. The 103 Society charter active members—the founders—represented relationships to at least fifty-one Indian nations located in, or surrounded by, nineteen states. Among this group were graduates of English-language schools, as well as bilingual and multilingual individuals who had nothing to do with these schools. There were among them adults dealing with the lingering effects of child removal and adoption. There were people who infrequently left the homes in which they had been born. There were Christians and non-Christians, employees of the government Indian service, attorneys and doctors, laborers, and tribal leaders. The diversity of the participants, the open debates, the unguarded yearly election of officers, and the locations for annual meetings combined to offer opportunities for a variety of Indian people to develop already emerging political strategies for negotiating with representatives of an occupation government.

The Society's origins were rooted in various efforts among Indians to launch local, regional, and national issue-based bodies to represent their political interests and problems on their terms. Using the Carlos Montezuma papers and other surviving correspondence between colleagues and friends, what comes into unmistakable view is a twenty-year effort (1891–1911) involving many individuals to assemble Indian-led political organizations such as the Indian Memorial Association, the Society, and the Brotherhood of North American Indians. Also unambiguous in their correspondence—in the webs of relationship the correspondence represents—is powerful indication that political organizations did not define activism but, instead, were material expressions of it. Thus, the case of the Society's origins is just one instance of a larger pattern for how we need to recast the twentieth-century history of American Indian activism.

Figure 3. Society of American Indians members outside the Engineering Building of Haskell Institute in Lawrence, Kansas. Fifth Annual Meeting, October 1, 1915. This image originally appeared in the *Quarterly Journal of the Society of American Indians* 3, no. 4 (October–December 1915), 280–281. Photo courtesy of D. Anthony Tyeeme Clark.

Carlos Montezuma and Webs of Relationship

Carlos Montezuma was one person among many in growing webs of relationship who advocated for a national organization of Indian people after 1892.[5] Montezuma was born around 1866 among the Yavapai—one of the thirteen bands of Pai, or Pa'a (the People)—in what would become central Arizona. He was raised by the pastor of the First Baptist Church in Urbana, Illinois. After taking his doctorate in medicine from the Chicago Medical College in 1889, he entered the government Indian service in September as agency clerk and physician at Fort Stevenson, North Dakota. In July 1890, six months after the massacre at Wounded Knee, he transferred to the Western Shoshone Agency in Nevada, where he remained until December 1892 before spending a few months in Nespelem, Colville Agency, Washington, and three years at the government Indian school in Carlisle, Pennsylvania (see table 1, 1879). He resigned in January 1896 to enter private practice in Chicago. There Montezuma assumed a role that followed a tradition of leadership among many Indian peoples—that of caring for less fortunate citizens, hosting Indian visitors to his community, and, eventually, advocating for the rights of Indian nations. These experiences, along with living in Chicago, prepared him to contribute in important ways to the formation of a national organization.

At Western Shoshone in September 1892, Montezuma mounted what proved to be an ineffective letter-writing campaign. He tried to mobilize government Indian school students who had returned to their reservation homelands and other English-reading and -speaking persons living on reservations.[6] His strategy for mustering "educated" Indians was an unsophisticated, if not ill-conceived, reaction to the government-sponsored "Indian Congress" at the approaching World's Fair in Chicago.[7] Rather than support those tribally connected Indians he labeled (in ignorance) "the old grumblers," he decided to launch a campaign that would convince decision makers in the government Indian service to "gather the educated [Indians]," an act he assumed would be, in his words, "rational, cheapest, and most beneficial."[8]

Montezuma was not alone in advocating for a national organization of "educated" Indians during the closing decade of the nineteenth century. Charles Eastman reported in *The Indian To-Day: The Past and Future of the First American*, "The idea of a national organization was discussed at some length by Reverend Sherman Coolidge, my brother, John Eastman, and myself" (probably around 1900, or earlier).[9] After 1911 the Eastman brothers had little to do with the Society. (Although Charles Alexander Eastman was Society president in 1919 and paid membership dues, for the preceding eight years he boycotted the Society after failing to convince others at the inaugural meeting in Columbus to exclude government Indian service employees from holding office.) The Reverend Coolidge, on the other hand, was a central Society figure until 1920, when the organization turned toward unambiguous advocacy for the autonomy of Indian nations. He was Society president from 1912 to 1916, member of the board for the quarterly publication from 1913 to 1918, and Advisory Board member for five terms. Although his birth parents were Arapahos, as a young boy he was adopted by a US military family in 1870. The Reverend Coolidge received his bachelor of divinity degree in 1884 from Seabury Divinity School in Faribault, Minnesota, after which he was ordained an Episcopalian deacon. His first assignment in 1884 was to the Wind River Agency in Wyoming, where he was reunited with his mother during a period when Shoshone and Arapaho families literally were starving and increasingly forced to give up much of their reservation lands in order to survive.

These Indian men came to know one another in the closing decade of the nineteenth century, joining a gathering stream of Indian women and men in webs of relationship that connected them in attempts at national organization. Charles Alexander Eastman, as early as 1888, and Montezuma at about the same time, like Coolidge after 1894, lectured throughout the

Midwest and the northeast United States to earn money or draw attention to what non-Indians already had determined were the needs of Indian peoples. Eastman should have included Montezuma in the group he later credited with discussing a national organization of Indians in his book *The Indian To-Day.* All four—Coolidge, the Eastman brothers, and Montezuma —came to know one another from public speaking. They also supported one another. In 1903, for instance, Charles Alexander asked Montezuma to help market his forthcoming "lectures," as he called them, to the doctor's friends in Chicago.[10]

During the opening decade of the twentieth century, Montezuma both guided and joined efforts to organize Indians politically. He followed the lead of Luzena Choteau, for instance, when she launched the National Indian Republican Association. Choteau was a Wyandotte woman from Indian Territory and graduate of the government Indian school at Carlisle. After completing her studies at Carlisle in 1892, Choteau worked as an accountant in the Office of Indian Affairs at its Chicago warehouse before moving in 1899 to the nation's capital to work for the Department of Treasury and the Department of War. Through her connection to particular places—Carlisle, Chicago, and the District of Columbia—and their growing, mobile Indian populations, Choteau participated in an emerging, and expanding, national network of rural and urban Indian people. From this network, she recruited Montezuma and also Vincent Natalish, an 1899 Carlisle graduate and Indian service employee at the Anadarko Indian Agency.[11]

In July 1901 Montezuma circulated an outline for a national organization to contacts such as Richard Henry Pratt, founder in 1879 of the government Indian school at Carlisle. Pratt told his friend that he could not "undertake to endorse a scheme of this kind." He mentioned two objections. First, he suggested that the document placed too much financial responsibility on Indians and that it needed "the backing of a very strong man with substantial means." Second, he told Montezuma that he did not

> think a body of people congregating together in any cause, good or indifferent, has the force and effect of individual effort. Of course if the society is dominated by one individual and he can control and direct it in one line, it may work very well; but even then there is danger, because the head may become arrogant, useless, or dishonest.12

The difficult work of national organization, in this example dismissed by Pratt, followed from efforts to organize at the grass roots among reservation communities. Probably known to both Montezuma and Eastman, the Standing Bear brothers, Luther and Henry, labored with others to organize

English-speaking returned students and their allies on the Pine Ridge and Rosebud reservations.

In 1891, just months after the massacre at Wounded Knee and twelve years after leaving home to attend the first class at the government Indian school in Carlisle, Luther Standing Bear and Clarence Three Stars clandestinely joined with others to form a group of government Indian school graduates in the Allen Issue Station District of the Pine Ridge Agency. For almost thirty years, Three Stars was an employee in schools on the Pine Ridge Reservation, as well as a member of the Oglala Council and the Sioux Black Hills Council in 1911. Representing the Oglala Council and working as interpreter for Red Cloud, he testified before Congress in 1897. He was states attorney for Bennett County, South Dakota, in 1912–1913.[13]

As Standing Bear recalled his efforts with Three Stars and his brother in his first book, their earliest hard work led to the formation of an issue-oriented body, the Oglala Council. Through the Oglala Council, these Lakota men labored to counter unwanted aspects of government Indian administration, provided for less advantaged persons in their communities, and located their authority in the diplomacy of their predecessors. Luther Standing Bear later recalled that, as council president, Henry "explain[ed] things which were incorporated into the different treaties which many did not thoroughly understand."[14]

The Oglala Council is just one of many examples of a gathering momentum among reservation-based Indian peoples toward new forms of organization through which they negotiated with the power of the United States. Earlier, in 1874 on the Yankton Reservation, Philip Joseph Deloria and other leaders at Standing Rock formed the Planting Society, renamed the Brotherhood of Christian Unity in 1893, an organization of prominent men able to perform charitable work. They also were first-responders to emergencies and family tragedies.[15] All four—the Standing Bear brothers, Three Stars, and Deloria—later participated in the Society.[16]

Montezuma was, for six months in 1901, engaged to Gertrude Simmons. Over the duration of their relationship, Montezuma and Simmons exchanged ideas through correspondence regarding national organization. Simmons, who would be an elected Society officer in 1916 and editor of the quarterly publication in 1918, was home-schooled by her mother and extended Yankton family until age eight and then, after 1884, studied mostly at Quaker schools in Indiana. She was an employee of the government Indian service for fourteen years, first at Standing Rock Agency, North Dakota, and until 1916 at the Uintah and Ouray Reservation, Utah.

From her first publication in *Atlantic Monthly* in 1900, Simmons (later Bonnin) demonstrated that she had many talents. She distinguished herself in no small way as a critic of government administration of Indian affairs and as an advocate for Indian peoples. After 1920 she worked with a number of non-Indian organizations, including the General Federation of Women's Clubs and the American Indian Defense Association. In 1926, with her husband, she founded the National Council of American Indians and the *Indian Newsletter*, in which until 1938 she tenaciously advocated what she called "home rule" for Indian nations, better educational opportunities for Indian children, economic self-determination, and improved access to health care for all Indian peoples. Throughout her public life, she was a relentless critic of forced assimilation and made strategic accommodations to what she believed would be long-term colonial relationships with the United States.[17]

In 1901 Simmons chastised Montezuma for not including women in his thinking about a national organization. She told him that his "idea for an organization seems a plausible project" but teased:

> *Why do you think the men are able alone to do it—and in a queer afterthought—suggest the Indian women should have theirs too? I feel like putting my hand forward and simply wiping the Indian men's committee into no where!!! No—I should not really do such a thing. Only I do not understand why your organization does not include Indian women. Am I not an Indian woman as capable in...serious matters and as thoroughly interested in the race—as any one or two of you men put together? Why do you dare to leave us out? Why? Sometimes as I ponder the...actions of men—which are so tremendously out of proportion with the small results—I laugh.18*

Two weeks later, after visiting her fiancé in Chicago, she shared in person her ideas with Montezuma and Roland Nichols, a Potawatomi who would be elected to the Society's General Council in 1912.[19] In a letter, Simmons reflected on the conversation: "I was very much interested in what you both said yesterday regarding the organization to be." Except, she declared, "[L]et us not think of asking money of any white man. Let us have nothing to do with charity from others."[20] In June 1901, after returning to the Uintah and Ouray Reservation in Utah, Simmons wrote again that she had been "pondering" the question of organizing. "Sometimes I think the times are not ripe enough." She mused, "Then again by the day that there are more educated individuals—old arts will be partially if not wholly lost!"[21]

The Indian Memorial Association

We know from Montezuma's published correspondence that a group of Indian women and men formed the Indian Memorial Association (IMA).

Thomas L. Sloan, its president, would later be elected Society president for three terms, from 1920 to 1923. Raised by his grandmother and extended family on the Omaha Reservation after 1863, Sloan graduated from Hampton Institute in Virginia. There he was editor of the monthly journal *Talks and Thoughts* and valedictorian of the 1889 Indian Program class. He then studied law with Hiram Chase, who also was Omaha and a Society participant. The pair opened a law practice together on the Omaha Reservation in Nebraska when Sloan was admitted to the bar in April 1891. Both Sloan and Chase advocated the fundamental significance of using the Omaha language, a core component to the idea and sustainability of a distinct Omaha people. The two were concerned that the younger people in the community at Pender, Nebraska, were losing their first language. To preserve, in writing, traditional Omaha knowledge, in 1897 the two attorneys published a system of reading and recording their first language so that, in their own words, "Indians may be able to record their thoughts, a subject of importance to the class known as the Indian population."[22] In 1904 the bilingual Sloan practiced law for the first of three times before the US Supreme Court. Within his Omaha extended family, he remains a troublesome figure, but in 1890 he was elected surveyor of Thurston County and, later, mayor of Pender (both of which were within Omaha Reservation lands).[23]

The IMA also included, among others, the Reverend John Eastman —Charles Eastman's older brother—and Walter Battice.[24] The Reverend Eastman, who was at least fifty in 1909 and fluent in the Dakota dialect, had been ordained as pastor of the Presbyterian Indian Church in Flandreau, South Dakota, in 1876.[25] Walter Battice had graduated from Hampton Indian Normal and Agricultural Institute in 1887 and the government Indian school in Lawrence, Kansas, ten years later. He was Sac and Fox from Cushing, Oklahoma, was an employee of the Indian services, and served in various capacities on his tribal council (beginning as early as 1885 at age twenty-two).[26]

Information about the IMA circulated through letters and telegrams in a network of mobile professionals—clergy, attorneys, tribal leaders, and government Indian service employees. From Washington DC, these professionals disseminated a plan for Indians to gather in June for a meeting in Lawrence, Kansas. Among their objectives, driven by changing administrations in Washington, was the removal of Commissioner of Indian Affairs Francis Ellington Leupp.[27] Responding to a letter in May from Thomas Saul, a Dakota from Crow Creek Reservation in South Dakota studying illustration and interior decoration at the Philadelphia School of Industrial Art, Montezuma enthusiastically embraced what he termed "our opportunity to act at once." Eighteen years after his first attempt to forge a national organization of "educated" Indians, Montezuma wrote Saul, "We should not wait for someone to speak for us. There are enough educated Indians in [the] United States to express their desires for the best interest of their people."[28] Montezuma immediately wrote letters to others, in which he pleaded, "*You must* come and be one of us."[29]

Those who participated in the IMA—from Oklahoma, Nebraska, South Dakota, and Wisconsin—represent a wide variety of Indians who, two years later, provided the vast majority of Society founders. The participants overwhelmingly were tribally connected Indian people who conducted business in English and through translators, individual Indians who had trust relationships with the US government, and Indian people who wanted to end their status as wards of the state. The organizing efforts of the letter writers suggest a core constituency that worked through webs of relationship on the matter of national organization well before 1911.[30]

In Lawrence, women and men gathered on June 15, 1909, from reservations and towns in Michigan, Wisconsin, Minnesota, Nebraska, and Kansas, from a number of the Lakota and Dakota peoples in South Dakota, and from at least four northeastern Oklahoma tribes and the Quapaw Agency. In addition to electing Sloan president and Battice secretary, they adopted thirteen resolutions. In a hastily written letter to Montezuma two weeks later, Battice noted that he was "satisfied our...powers are being felt by our palefaced brethren," suggesting the enthusiasm at least some of the attendees must have felt.[31]

Battice circulated the thirteen resolutions by mail, with help from Montezuma and Fayette Avery McKenzie, a non-Indian professor at Ohio State University who has been credited with founding the Society in 1911. McKenzie was a government Indian day school teacher on the Wind River Reservation in Wyoming, where in 1904 he met Charles Kealear, a Yankton from near Plain Center Township. Kealear earlier had graduated from the Indian Program at Hampton Industrial and Agricultural Institute in Virginia in 1889 and was a ten-year employee at the United States Indian Industrial School in Genoa, Nebraska. According to Kealear's own account in May 1912, he and his wife, Minnie O'Neal, had persuaded McKenzie (while he was in the Wind River community) "to take up the work of the Indians.... The Conference [in 1911] at Columbus was the result."[32]

Henry Standing Bear responded to Montezuma in August with a single line, "I want to join the organization you wrote me about."[33] In September 1909 McKenzie wrote Montezuma that he was sending the resolutions to people on a mailing list Montezuma had provided. Included were Charles Eastman, the Reverend Frank Hall Wright (a Choctaw from Old Boggy Depot and Reformed Church minister and missionary), and the musician, composer, and bandleader Dennison Wheelock, an Oneida from Wisconsin who led both the Carlisle and Haskell Institute bands (converting the latter in 1904 into the US Indian Band, a fifty-piece ensemble that presented programs well into the 1920s). "The die is cast," McKenzie wrote. "The venture is great."[34]

Addressing "My Dear Sirs and Friends," Battice suggested that his fellow organizers "outline in a general way the present status of the Indian question from the viewpoint of the educated Indians who have given the matter considerable study in the interest of their race." On Sac and Fox Agency, Oklahoma, letterhead, Battice wrote that the wide circulation of the resolutions was intended to generate a grassroots momentum among "all Indians throughout the country." He proposed that they later meet in Philadelphia "or some other place convenient to all interested" to inaugurate a "movement for the betterment of Indians...where the Indian himself will be the moving spirit."[35]

The June 1909 resolutions themselves suggest not only a struggle over who should represent Indian nations and how, but also that debates over the value of the Office of Indian Affairs, US citizenship, and the proper future of Indian nations preceded the Society's existence. Attacking congressmen and presidents but affirming their reading of the US Constitution as a legal document that empowers the self-government of Indian nations, resolution one characterized current Indian policies as "contrary to justice" and as "violations of the principles upon which the Republic itself was established." The second resolution proposed "[t]hat there is no valid authority for confining the Indians upon reservations" and, citing Indian policy, argued that "the Government's action in this respect is a repudiation of the underlying principle of the Constitution that the hand of the Government must rest equally upon all its subjects irrespective of race, color or previous condition." Resolutions three and four laid out grievances against functionaries of the Office of Indian Affairs. The fifth resolution called on Congress to change the arrangement of managing Indian affairs. Removing the process of appointing guardians to administer one-size-fits-all policies directed at Indians, according to the authors of the document, "is indispensable to the work of bringing the Indians into the full enjoyment of the rights and privileges to which they are entitled as men under the Constitution and Laws of this country."[36]

Resolutions six through eight and eleven and twelve articulated both explicit and coded demands for self-determination and self-representation in the education of Indian children and in managing individual economic matters. The final three resolutions declared:

> [O]urselves as hereby pledged to do our utmost as individuals, and collectively, if necessary, to bring about a change in the Government's

relations with the Indians on the Reservations, and to do what lies in our power to our several localities to present to the public the Indian's side of the question as exigencies may suggest through actual experience, to the end that public sentiment may be turned to his aid.

We declare it also to be our purpose to do what we can to combat and show the falsity of the theory advanced by individuals, societies, associations, leagues, and by government officials to-wit: that the work of aiding the Indian consists in doing what you can to make him a "better Indian," as though there were something about the Indian as an Indian that distinguished him as a man from the rest of mankind, while the fact is that the name is nothing; whereas, the true theory is that you can only aid the Indian by developing and making better the man that is in him, thus leaving whatever of the Indian as such there may be in him to take its departure as the man makes itself manifest.

We believe the permanent advancement of the Indian can only be brought about by action taken in accordance with the recognized fact that the word "Indian" as a name signifies nothing worthy of attention, but that the man is everything, and that in seeking a way to promote the interests of the men called Indians, we should view them from the same standpoint as other men are viewed when their welfare is being considered.[37]

Within months after the meeting in Lawrence, the "we" and "our" that emerged in the language of these thirteen resolutions divided into those who placed community above individual well-being and those who placed themselves above community. The lines distinguishing the two blended and often were crossed; they should not be interpreted simply as "Indian" factionalism that separated so-called moderates from militants, apparent progressives from separatists. Evidence of this point about a splitting yet synthesizing constituency also was apparent in a second expression of national Indian politics that emerged in 1911, the Brotherhood of North American Indians (the Brotherhood).

The Brotherhood of North American Indians

Since 1882 the Indian Rights Association (IRA), an organization controlled by non-Native philanthropists, had been the most politically powerful group in a network of local and national organizations mobilized to influence public opinion and change policy. The Society of American Indians is often thought of as the most important Indian-centered advocacy organization to have emerged during the twentieth century. The Brotherhood, however, after its founding in December 1911, competed with both the Society and IRA to gain the broader attention of tribally connected Indian peoples. Indeed, in 1914 the Brotherhood was active still in Minnesota, Montana, Oklahoma, Wisconsin, and the District of Columbia.[38]

Signifying the threat posed to the influence of particular Society members, self-serving condemnation of the Brotherhood from Society critics was relentless. In December 1911 Charles Dagenett suggested that the Brotherhood was an organized effort to weaken the Society.[39] After graduating from Carlisle in 1891 with Henry Standing Bear, Dagenett returned home to his Peoria family in Northeast Indian Territory for three years. There, he edited the *Miami Chieftain*. Accompanied by his wife, the Miami woman Esther Miller (also a Society active member after 1911), for the next five years (1894 to 1899) he taught at government Indian schools at Fort Thompson, South Dakota, in Arizona, and at the Chilocco Indian Agricultural School. He worked at Carlisle until 1900, when he was appointed head clerk at the Quapaw Agency. He served as special agent for the Indian services for two one-year appointments in 1907 and 1908 and for a term that ended in 1911. He also worked for the Indian employment office in Denver and Washington DC, where he was responsible for providing labor from reservations and government Indian schools for white farmers and businesses.[40]

Dagenett was not alone in his scathing criticism of the Brotherhood. Arthur Parker characterized the Brotherhood as "secret" and "reactionary," as well as selfish and intent on appealing to "the blanket Indian."[41] Parker, an adopted Seneca and an employee of the New York state government, turned over the names of Haudenosaunee men who spoke unfavorably about Six Nations involvement in World War I. Representing the Indian Rights Association in 1913, Samuel Brosius promised the amateur historian, linguist, and anthropologist Lucullus V. McWhorter information that would equip him "to attack the reputation of the Brotherhood."[42] An unidentified journalist writing in the *New Republic*, a short-lived periodical concerned with temperance and prohibition, published a vicious attack on several of the Brotherhood's members, including Richard C. Adams, a Delaware from Oklahoma and the Brotherhood's founder and president.[43] Other Society participants endorsed the Brotherhood. Gustave H. Beaulieu, for instance, defended the Brotherhood and its officers in his newspaper, *The Tomahawk*.[44]

Among the 1911 organizers of the Brotherhood were persons who were involved earlier with the Indian Memorial Association and simultaneously the Society but were devoted to political strategies and calculated accommodations to US rule that returned self-government to Indian nations.[45]

Gustave H. Beaulieu and Richard Calmit Adams represent, in profoundly differing ways, both the dividing and the blending of an emergent Indian identity influenced, in part, by organizational activism as it intersected with and was constituted by US law. In addition to Beaulieu and Adams, I have exhumed from archives six others who participated in the Brotherhood between 1911 and 1913: August Breuninger, John Carl, Louis Joseph Carpenter, Joseph Craig, John Doherty, and Perry Kennerly. Breuninger, an unenrolled Menominee from Shawano and secretary of the Progressive Indian Association of Wisconsin, was involved in planning for the IMA and the American Indian Association. Carl, from White Earth, who attended Haskell, the University of Minnesota, and law school at the University of Kansas, was elected vice president of membership by active members of the Society in 1919. Carpenter, also from White Earth and a student in the Indian Program at Hampton from 1903 to 1905, was treasurer of the organization. Craig was secretary. Doherty was Anishinaabe from Bad River on the La Pointe Agency, Wisconsin. Kennerly was Pikuni Blackfeet from Montana.[46]

Beaulieu was a longtime critic of the government administration of Indian affairs and, since 1899, a frequent witness before congressional committees and fact finders. Twenty-five years before he participated in both the Brotherhood and the Society, in 1886, he was a controversial leader from the White Earth Reservation in Minnesota. As "the most influential (and notorious) métis cultural broker at the White Earth Reservation," according to Melissa L. Meyer, he owned, edited, and/or influenced what was published in the two English-language newspapers that voiced the concerns of the métis (mixed-blood) elite.[47] In the inaugural issue of *The Progress*, the first newspaper published on the White Earth Reservation, Beaulieu announced:

> We shall aim to advocate constantly and withhold reserve, what in our view, and in the view of the leading minds upon this reservation, is the best for the interests of its residents. And not only for their interests, but those of the tribe wherever they now are residing. The main consideration in this advocacy will be the political interests, that is, in matters relative to us and to the Government of the United States.... We intend that this journal shall be the mouth-piece of the community in making known abroad and at home what is for the best interests of the tribe.[48]

Following the publication of *The Progress* on March 25, 1886, according to Gerald Vizenor, federal agents confiscated the press and ordered Beaulieu to leave the reservation. "The second issue of the first newspaper on the reservation was circulated about six months later, when a federal district

court ruled that *The Progress* could be 'published without government interference.'"[49] Beaulieu was participating in both organized bodies, the Brotherhood and the Society, when his legitimacy as a leader at White Earth
suffered a blistering attack from conservatives at Pine Point (among whom
were Society participants) who had strategically aligned themselves with
representatives of the government Indian service.

Adams embodied a different sort of tribally connected "Indian" leadership. In his published work and in his correspondence, he often added to
his signature the words "Representing the Delaware Indians." He represented the Delaware Tribe and individuals in many ways. After 1897 he did
so for twenty-four years in Washington DC as the author of five books—the
first published in 1899 and two that remain in print still today—as an
archivist of documents important to Delaware (Lenape) political history, as
knowledge keeper and poet, and as a political activist.[50] He was born in
Wyandotte County, Kansas, in 1864, thirty-five years after a forced removal
into what would become Kansas Territory and three years before what
Delawares today refer to as the "last removal." By his own account, his family reluctantly moved to Cherokee Nation, Indian Territory, in 1869, where
they lived near Alluwe in the center of Delaware political activity, in what
became Nowata and Washington counties, Oklahoma. In 1896 the allotment of Cherokee Nation lands surfaced as an issue that divided families;
many Cherokee persons questioned Delaware claims to allotments. Adams
moved his family to Washington DC in 1897 under a contract with the
Delaware Tribe. For the next twenty-four years, he remained in the US capital as legal and legislative representative of the Delaware Tribal Business
Committee.[51]

Adams introduced the Brotherhood in a memorial to Congress in 1912.
The House was considering legislation offered by Charles David Carter that
would allow the citizens of Indian nations to nominate their local agents.
Adams recognized that Congress, except when wrongfully applying its laws
or exceeding its rightful powers, in his words, "is the lawmaking power for
the Indians."[52] Carter, a Chickasaw who represented the Fourth District of
Oklahoma in Congress (and who, like Frank Hall Wright, was born in Old
Boggy Depot, Choctaw Nation), was a Society member when he introduced
the legislation in 1911 with the explicit support of the Society's Temporary
Committee.

In a section of the memorial titled "Declaration of Indian Policy by the
Brotherhood of North American Indians," a sort of prototype for broad
agreement between Indian nations and the representatives of the United
States, Adams championed ten "Indian rights" and detailed a legislative

agenda. "The Brotherhood of North American Indians favors and advocates," he wrote, "[t]he right to have Indian delegates on the floor of the Congress of the United States" and "the right to ratify or reject by vote of the tribe or tribes affected, after 60 days notice, any legislation of the Congress of the United States...in all cases where there has not been an agreement with the Indians." Adams further recommended specific appropriations for the Indian services, as well as the creation of advisory boards of Indians "for each Indian school or agency" and "greater cooperation between the Federal Government and State governments in matters of education for all Indian youth." He called on Congress to grant Indians "the right of petition and assembly without restriction or restraint, and the right to come and go at will without the permission of any superintendent or agent." He argued for what would become a policy of "Indian preference," asking that "Indians by blood...be given preference in the Indian Service as superintendents, financial clerks, teachers, farmers, and mechanics." Finally, Adams called on Congress to grant "[p]rotection as persons under the Constitution of the United States, for all Indians, whether as tribes or individuals, of life, liberty, and property, and the right to enforce such protection in the courts." Further, he pleaded,

> Surely our interests are vast enough, our people intelligent enough and our personal training of more than 100 years under Government control and tutorship good enough to entitle us now to have a voice in the making and administering of the laws that affect our people and control our property.... If after 100 years of Government wardship, we are not in a position to attend to our own affairs and our own business, then there must be something wrong with the training and civilization administered to us by the government.[53]

Thus, Adams, representing both the Brotherhood and the Delaware Tribe in Oklahoma, offered a vision for future relationships between Indian and non-Indian peoples living in the United States, with Indian nations as, at least, semisovereign entities.

Some Conclusions

The Society was neither the first nor the only (so-called) "national" organization of Indians that emerged as a response to the development and administration of government policies. Montezuma's correspondence and Eastman's recollections, numerous exchanges between colleagues, friends, and lovers, and the emergence of national Indian organizations through webs of relationship before 1911 represented at least twenty years (and probably longer) of shared labor among tribally connected Indian people.

Whether this collective struggle for national community succeeded in the short term may not be as important as the networks—the webs of relationship—that outlived the organizations. To the extent that we can recover them through correspondence (and perhaps other forms of memory keeping too), these relationships suggest, first, that tribally connected individuals have a sort of shared agency within the constraints of the homogenizing, sometimes debilitating, at other times empowering, "Indian" sign.[54] After all, it was as "Indians" in wide-ranging conversations over at least a twenty-year period that women and men discussed, formulated, negotiated, positioned, and repositioned the "Indian" sign in ways that tribal peoples could, in moments, connect with as an emergent intertribal identity (sometimes abhorrently expressed as "pan-Indian"). The Society and the Brotherhood are but two substantive expressions (signs) of this national (or, better, transnational) community and identity.

Notes

1. On the logic behind these policies, see Frederick Hoxie, *A Final Promise: The Campaign to Assimilate the Indians, 1880–1920* (Lincoln: University of Nebraska Press, 1984, 2001), and David Wallace Adams, *Education for Extinction: American Indians and the Boarding School Experience, 1875–1928* (Lawrence: University Press of Kansas, 1995).

2. Hazel Hertzberg, *The Search for an American Indian Identity: Modern Pan-Indian Movements* (Syracuse, NY: Syracuse University Press, 1971); Margot Liberty, ed., *American Indian Intellectuals of the Nineteenth and Early Twentieth Centuries* (Norman: University of Oklahoma Press, 1978); Peter Iverson, *Carlos Montezuma and the Changing World of American Indians* (1982; Albuquerque: University of New Mexico Press, 2001); Raymond Wilson, *Ohiyesa: Charles Eastman, Santee Sioux* (Urbana: University of Illinois Press, 1983); Frederick Hoxie, ed., *Talking Back to Civilization: Indian Voices from the Progressive Era* (Boston: Bedford/St. Martin's, 2001); and Joy Porter, *To Be an Indian: The Life of Iroquois-Seneca Arthur Caswell Parker* (Norman: University of Oklahoma Press, 2001).

3. In *Indians in Unexpected Places*, Phil Deloria identifies "a recognizable cohort of Indian people" at the turn of the twentieth century to make the case that these individuals and groups—this cohort—"figured [out] ways to move with[in] the institutions that did, in fact, constrain, dominate, and transform them." Their daily actions, in Deloria's telling, "took concrete shape around struggles over representation." They "inevitably confronted prevailing expectations" that "tend to assume a status quo defined around failure." In doing so, in Deloria's words, this cohort "offered a foundational narrative for a kind of cultural politics that would be constantly rediscovered and renewed by Indian people throughout the twentieth century." See Philip Deloria, *Indians in Unexpected Places* (Lawrence: University Press of Kansas, 2004), 229, 230, 231, 233. For other views, see also Tom Holm, *The Great Confusion in Indian Affairs: Native Americans and Whites in the Progressive Era* (Austin: University of Texas Press, 2005), and Lucy Maddox, *Citizen*

Indians: Native American Intellectuals, Race, and Reform (Ithaca, NY: Cornell University Press, 2005).

4. During this same period, African American intellectual and activist W. E. B. DuBois, a dues-paying associate member of the Society of American Indians, called upon elite members of the black community, to whom he referred collectively as the "Talented Tenth," to take responsibility for leading the masses. See William E. B. DuBois, "The Talented Tenth," in *The Negro Problem: A Series of Articles by Representative Negroes of To-day* (New York: James Pott and Company, 1903), 33–75. For a later rearticulation of his views, see William E. B. DuBois, "The Talented Tenth Memorial Address," *Boulé Journal* 15 (October 1948): 3–13.

5. For more on Montezuma, see Iverson, *Carlos Montezuma*, and Leon Speroff, *Carlos Montezuma, MD: A Yavapai American Hero* (Portland, OR: Arnica Publishing, Inc., 2003).

6. Carlos Montezuma to Horatio Rush, 5 September 1892, *The Carlos Montezuma Papers, 1871–1952 (CM Papers)*, ed. John W. Larner Jr. (Wilmington, DE: Scholarly Resources, 1984), microfilm.

7. In many ways, the phrase "educated Indians" is offensive, as well as profoundly misleading. Its descriptive power rests upon the assumption that, before coming into contact with the settler-colonizers' English-language schools, human beings are uneducated and illiterate. Of course, Indian peoples have long had autonomous languages (that do not rely on English for meaning) and our own ways of education.

8. Carlos Montezuma to Richard Henry Pratt, 21 June 1892, box 6, folder, 213, *Richard Henry Pratt Papers*, Yale Collection of Western Americana, Beinecke Rare Book and Manuscript Library, Yale University, New Haven, CT; Pratt to Montezuma, 8 July 1892, transcription, *CM Papers*; Montezuma to Pratt, 20 July 1892, *CM Papers*.

9. Charles Eastman (Ohiyesa), *The Indian To-Day: The Past and Future of the First American* (Garden City, NY: Doubleday, Page and Company, 1915), 130–131. The conversation to which Eastman referred was more likely a number of conversations through which the idea for a national organization of Indians was circulating after 1890. See, for instance, Dennison Wheelock to Carlos Montezuma, 10 October 1898, *CM Papers*.

10. Charles Eastman to Carlos Montezuma, 16 June 1903, *CM Papers*. See also Eastman to Montezuma, 9 February 1911, TS, *CM Papers*.

11. D. Anthony Tyeeme Clark, "Representing Indians: Indigenous Fugitives and the Society of American Indians in the Making of Common Culture" (Ph.D. diss., University of Kansas, 2004), 15.

12. Richard Henry Pratt to Carlos Montezuma, 1 July 1901, *CM Papers*. Neither the Montezuma nor the Pratt papers include the document. I have been unable to locate a copy.

13. See *Indian Helper*, June 8, 1888, 2; *Indian Helper*, July 20, 1888, 2; *James H. Red Cloud Papers*, folder 2: Sioux Black Hills Council, file 60, Jean Smith Collection, Part 2, SC 245-317, Special Collections and Manuscripts, Oglala Lakota College, Kyle, SD; "Concerning Ex-Students and Graduates," *Red Man* 6 (February 1914): 241. Thomas Andrews, "Turning the Tables on Assimilation: Oglala Lakotas and the Pine Ridge Day Schools, 1889–1920s," *Western Historical Quarterly* 33 (Winter 2002): 421, characterizes Three Stars as "a voracious learner, superb teacher, and tireless advocate for his people."

14. Luther Standing Bear, *My People the Sioux*, ed. E. A. Brininstool (1928; reprint, Lincoln: University of Nebraska Press, 1975), 235–237.

15. See Virginia Driving Hawk Sneve, *That They May Have Life: The Episcopal Church in South Dakota, 1859–1976* (New York: Seabury Press, 1977), 13–16, and Vine Deloria Sr., "The Establishment of Christianity among the Sioux," in *Sioux Indian Religion: Tradition and Innovation*, ed. Raymond DeMallie and Douglas Parks (Norman: University of Oklahoma Press, 1987), 91–111. Philip Joseph Deloria was born among the northernmost and westernmost of the Yanktonais bands of the Dakota-dialect-speaking peoples in 1853. By 1911, when participating in the Society, he had been a chief for thirty-seven years. He was a member of the tribal business committee that resolved the dispute over ownership of the Red Pipestone Quarry in Minnesota. See Vine Deloria Jr., *Singing for a Spirit: A Portrait of the Dakota Sioux* (Santa Fe, NM: Clear Light Publishers, 2000), 49–54, 61–66, 72–75.

16. Henry Standing Bear, Three Stars, and Deloria were among the 103 Society charter active members. The list of members published in the *Quarterly Journal of the Society of American Indians* 1, no. 2 (1913), 247, includes Luther Standing Bear as an active member.

17. See P. Jane Hafen, "Gertrude Simmons Bonnin: For the Indian Cause," in *Sifters: Native American Women's Lives*, ed. Theda Perdue (New York: Oxford University Press, 2001), 127–140.

18. Gertrude Simmons to Carlos Montezuma, 2 May 1901, *CM Papers*.

19. For more on Nichols, see *American Indian Magazine*, 6, no. 1 (1918), 47–48.

20. Gertrude Simmons to Carlos Montezuma, 13 May 1901, *CM Papers*.

21. Simmons to Montezuma, 1 June 1901, *CM Papers*.

22. Hiram Chase, *O Mu Hu W B GRa Za: The Chase System of Reading and Recording the Omaha and Other Indian Languages* (Pender, NE: Republic Press, 1897).

23. See Nebraska State Gazetteer, *Business Directory and Farmers List for 1890–91* (Omaha, NE: J. M. Wolfe and Co., 1890), 31, and Pender Centennial Book Committee, *Pender, Nebraska: The First 100 Years, 1885–1985* (Dallas: Curtis Media Corporation, 1984). Sloan, one of the six initial organizers of the American Indian Association in 1911, subsequently held several Society positions, including vice president for legislation. At the Minneapolis meeting in 1919, he was elected president, a position to which he was re-elected annually for the next four years. Hubert Work, who succeeded Albert B. Fall as secretary of the interior after the Teapot Dome scandal, appointed Sloan and other Society members to the Committee of One Hundred in December 1923.

24. Helen Grey to Carlos Montezuma, 24 May 1909, *CM Papers*.

25. Amy Lyn Rogel, *"Mastering the Secret of White Man's Power": Indian Students at Beloit College, 1871 to 1884* (Beloit, WI: Beloit College, Archives Publication Number One, 1990), 31.

26. "An act to ratify and confirm agreements with the Sac and Fox Nation of Indians, and the Iowa tribe of Indians, of Oklahoma Territory, and to make appropriations for carrying out the same," *Statutes at Large*, 26, 393 (1890); Helen Baldwin Herring, "History of Lincoln County" (master's thesis, University of Oklahoma, 1943).

27. Richard Henry Pratt to Carlos Montezuma, 22 May 1909, and Montezuma to Ernest Robetail, 29 May 1909, *CM Papers*.

28. Carlos Montezuma to Thomas Saul, 25 May 1909, *CM Papers*. At age twenty-four, in September 1900 Saul left his Isanti (or Dakota) family at Crow Creek for the government Indian school at Carlisle.

29. Montezuma to Robetail, 29 May 1909, *CM Papers*.

30. Montezuma and others, including Charles Eastman, earlier had labored in the courts and in the Indian bureau to secure access to allotments of tribal lands for themselves (in Eastman's case, for his children). See Iverson, *Carlos Montezuma*, 10–11, and Wilson, *Ohiyesa*, 94–95.

31. Walter Battice to Carlos Montezuma, 30 June 1909, LS, *CM Papers*.

32. Charles Kealear to Arthur Parker, 5 May 1912, *SAI Papers*.

33. Henry Standing Bear to Carlos Montezuma, 2 August 1909, *CM Papers*.

34. Fayette McKenzie to Carlos Montezuma, 14 September 1909, *CM Papers*.

35. Walter Battice to My Dear Sirs and Friends, n.d., *CM Papers*.

36. Battice, "Resolutions Adopted by the Indian Memorial Association of the Educated Indians of the United States," June 15, 1909, *CM Papers*.

37. Battice, "Resolutions," *CM Papers*. These resolutions strategically are antiracist (or antiracialist); they suggest the presence of a liminal moment when persons who subscribed to them continued to hold out hope that like-minded men, as different in many ways as men can be, could nonetheless organize around shared principles. Yet the gendered male speaking "our" identifies with "Indian" in at least the dimensions of what Battice and his co-authors named "experience" and "the Indian's side of the question." It is the meaning invoked by "individuals, societies, associations, leagues, and by government officials," as well as the debilitating manifestations of these meanings in the administration of government policies directed at "the Indian" (understood as a pathology), that, authors of the resolutions argued, should not exist outside the sign, outside the unjust culture of power that labored to limit the Indian to a form of amusement for those who found "him" interesting.

38. See, for instance, We-uk-sau-at to L. V. McWhorter, 19 March 1914, box 22, folder 188, *Lucullus V. McWhorter Papers, 1848–1945*, Manuscripts, Archives, and Special Collections, Washington State University Libraries, Pullman. Nonetheless, Parker continued to malign the Brotherhood's elected officers. In 1916 he wrote that "most of the officers were either in jail or under indictment." Parker to Max Barnaby, 11 May 1916, *SAI Papers*.

39. Charles Dagenett to Arthur Parker, 3 December 1911, *SAI Papers*.

40. See *Red Man* 4, no. 3 (November 1911): 127; Moses Friedman, "Indians Who Have 'Made Good': Charles E. Dagenett, National Supervisor of Indian Employment," *Red Man* 2, no. 8 (1910): 39–45; and Louise Houghton, *Our Debt to the Red Man: The French-Indians in the Development of the United States* (Boston: Stratford Company, 1918), 153–156.

41. Parker to Laura Cornelius, 29 December 1911, *SAI Papers*. Publicly, Parker urged others to be cautious and careful about negatively and publicly characterizing the Brotherhood, its officers, and its members. See Parker to Charles Dagenett, 14 December 1911, *SAI Papers*. "Blanket Indian" often meant an Indian individual who refused to assimilate into white selfish individualism.

42. S. M. Brosius to L. V. McWhorter, 19 February 1913, box 35, folder 342, *McWhorter Papers*.

43. "Perry Kennerly, Cow Thief, Forger, and Ex-Convict, Now 'Special Attorney' for Brotherhood of North American Indians," *New Republic*, March 21, 1913, and "Another Indian Grafter in Jail," *New Republic*, May 30, 1913.

44. Gus Beaulieu, "A Strong Arraignment," *Tomahawk*, April 10, 1913.

45. Steven Crum suggests that Brotherhood members "were largely poor, had limited formal education, and lived primarily on reservations." See Steven Crum, "Almost Invisible: The

Brotherhood of North American Indians (1911) and the League of North American Indians (1935)," *Wicazo Sa Review* 21 (Spring 2006): 45–46.

46. See Louis Carpenter, Deer River, Minnesota, to M. N. Koll, Cass Lake, Minnesota, 20 November 1912, LS, box 2, *Mathias Koll Papers, 1874–1934,* Manuscript Collections, Minnesota Historical Society, Minneapolis, and J. B. Monroe to L. V. McWhorter, 26 February 1913, box 35, folder 342, LS, *McWhorter Papers.* The Reverend George Waters, a Yakima and Methodist minister, has also been identified. See Crum, "Almost Invisible," 47.

47. Melissa Meyer, *The White Earth Tragedy: Ethnicity and Dispossession at a Minnesota Anishinaabe Reservation, 1889–1920* (Lincoln: University of Nebraska Press, 1994), 102; see also 101–104.

48. *The Progress,* March 25, 1866, quoted in Gerald Vizenor, *The People Named the Chippewa: Narrative Histories* (Minneapolis: University of Minnesota Press, 1984), 78.

49. Vizenor, *The People,* 78; see also 92–94.

50. Senate Committee on Indian Affairs, *Reinstatement of Suits by Delaware Indians: Hearings on S. 1979,* 61st Cong., 2d Sess., 1910, 11, 13.

51. Between 1901 and 1912 Adams testified at least five times before congressional committees; in the published proceedings, he is identified as an oil land owner, an attorney representing the Delaware Indians, and a hereditary chief. See Deborah Nichols, "Richard C. Adams: 'Representing the Delaware Indians,'" in *Legends of the Delaware Indians and Picture Writing,* ed. Deborah Nichols (Syracuse, NY: Syracuse University Press, 1997), xv–xlv.

52. HR 25242; reprinted in Vine Deloria Jr., ed., *The Indian Reorganization Act: Congresses and Bills* (Norman: University of Oklahoma Press, 2002), 3–5. See also House Committee on Indian Affairs, Subcommittee Report on HR 25242, 62d Cong., 2d Sess., 1912, Committee Print; ibid., *Right of Indians to Nominate Their Agent,* 62d Cong., 2d Sess., 1912; and Senate Committee on Indian Affairs, *Granting Indians the Right to Select Agents and Superintendents,* 64th Cong., 1st Sess., 1916. For quote, see Senate Committee on Indian Affairs, *Memorial of the Brotherhood of North American Indians,* 62d Cong., 2d Sess., S. Doc. 489, 6.

53. Senate Committee on Indian Affairs, *Memorial,* 6–7.

54. In plain language, a "sign," whether an object, a word, or a picture, has particular meaning to individuals who come to identify with—and as—a group of people named and who name themselves _____ (in this case, *Indian*). Thus, a sign is neither the thing nor the meaning alone. What matters are the two (the thing and the meaning) working together—when and where associative meaning is made. For instance, to illustrate the tremendous power of the sign, Roland Barthes uses a rose, which widely is recognized as a symbol of passion. In this understanding, a rose is not passion by itself, but rather a rose (signifier) + the concept of passion (signified) = roses (sign). Before the association of the thing (signifier) and meaning (signified), according to Barthes, "the signifier is empty," but when the sign is signified, it "is full, it is a meaning." See Roland Barthes, *Mythologies* (New York: Noonday Press, 1972), 112, 113. Thus, we can understand that "Indian" is a sign that has no autonomous meaning, until objects, words, and/or pictures (signifiers) and concepts (signifieds) are linked (until meaning is made) in ways that make sense to individuals who either apply the "Indian" sign to an Other (foreigners, outsiders) or to themselves and those they identify as relatives. At points, when a critical mass identifies as Indians, they are Indians. These points are particularly powerful when human beings are moved to consent spontaneously to being Indians, when meaning-construction no longer requires active

reflection before consent. It also is possible, however, that human beings strategically deploy the Indian sign, attaching it to themselves even though they may not personally identify with it (except for political purposes), because they recognize its persuasive force in the culture of the settler-colonizer.

5 The Citizenship of Dance
Politics of Music among the Lakota, 1900–1924

John Troutman

Native people resisted the federal government's allotment and assimilation policies in manifold ways (see table 1). Individuals, including boarding school graduates, tried to influence public opinion or filed suit to prevent allotment.[1] Revitalization movements, such as the Ghost Dance, the Redbird Smith and Chitto Harjo movements, and the peyote religion, offered hope for a future in which Indians could live life on their own terms.[2] Within communities, much of the resistance took the form of dissemblance as Native leaders indigenized American institutions of Christianity, fairs, and rodeos and camouflaged traditional rituals.[3] John Troutman contributes to the discussion of Native resistance to assimilation by focusing on returned Lakota students, many of whom served in World War I. While older Lakotas used direct tactics, such as delegations to Washington DC, these young men employed dancing activity as a vehicle to assert Lakota values. Drawing upon symbols of American patriotism, they defied oppressive regulations against dancing and articulated their own definition of what it meant to be a citizen.[4]

During the late nineteenth and early twentieth centuries, US citizenship for American Indians was generally conceived as a reward based on the completion of a set of specific cultural, economic, and political requirements.[5] The reformers who backed the allotment and assimilation era legislation believed that American Indian survival necessitated their undergoing perhaps the greatest of personal salvations: they would have to shed their "savage" cultural traits of Indianness and transform, under the reformers' terms and definitions, into members of a "proper," Christian, civilized American citizenry. This belief served as the cornerstone of an assimilation philosophy that rushed Native children to off-reservation boarding schools, where they fell under intense pressure to replace their stories, languages, political and military allegiances, economic and subsistence practices, clothes, religions, dances, and songs with those deemed suitably "American." Meanwhile, the liquidation of tribal landholdings via allotment endeavored to "break up the tribal mass" by providing individuals with the most cherished of American ideals, that of private property. To facilitate the citizenship agenda, local Office of Indian Affairs (OIA) employees attempted to control the resources, the cultural practices, and the very meaning of citizenship for Native people.

Although OIA officials went to great lengths to dictate the economic and cultural practices of American Indians, Native people disillusioned with or disgusted by the directives of the allotment and assimilation policies challenged them through a series of inventive political acts of revitalization and resistance. For reservation-based peoples, protesting on the public or national level proved nearly impossible. The Indian Affairs office controlled the resources necessary for subsistence, and local agents could and frequently did retaliate by withholding rations for such "trouble." Even though Indians on reservations often found traditional avenues of expressing dissent in the American political system closed to them, many did effectively challenge the economic and cultural mandates of the allotment and assimilation policy, as well as the meaning of American citizenship. Rather than present speeches before the American public, testify in congressional hearings, or use mass media, they engaged in local-level struggles that revealed the adaptability of alternative methods of resistance.[6]

Musical performance represents one, often overlooked example. Like fairs, rodeos, and syncretistic spiritual movements, music acted as a form of everyday resistance that contained, in the words of political scientist James C. Scott, "hidden transcripts" that were often disguised and located "behind the scenes." For the Lakota, as well as many other American Indian people, the dance ground became "a social space in which offstage dissent to the official transcript of power relations [could] be voiced."[7] Musical performance, then, served as an unexpected and highly political medium of political engagement that combined the subterfuge of "hidden" acts of resistance with blatant and effective challenges to federal Indian policy. In the first three decades of the twentieth century, many Lakotas used drumming, singing, and dancing to engage in the cultural politics of American citizenship and, in so doing, to disarm the more culturally insidious, local manifestations of federal Indian policy.

It should be recognized, however, that dancing, singing, and drumming are extremely powerful, important, and complex acts. In addition to being transformed into methods of protest against the presence of oppressive outside forces in daily life, these continued to function internally as ways of articulating individual, clan, and community identities, communing with the sacred, and, in some cases, providing entertainment. As it continues to do today, musical performance fostered intense competition at intertribal powwows, mediated tensions, and healed or reconstituted individuals and communities. No less than in the present, the practice of music within Native communities, in other words, simultaneously took on many layers of meaning that derived from multiple sacred and secular systems of knowledge. Acknowledging the profound complexity of music, this chapter focuses on one aspect of the political function of dance, specifically, on how Lakotas recognized in music a means of shaping the local implementation of federal Indian policy.

In many ways, dance lay at the heart of the matter for employees of the Office of Indian Affairs as they set about implementing federal policy prerogatives among the Lakota. These officials, as well as missionaries, generally considered all "Indian" dances "heathenish" and antithetical to their assimilation and citizenship campaign and struggled feverishly to eradicate them. Despite the collective horror they expressed at "Indian dancing," they never really established a list of characteristics that differentiated an "Indian" from a "white" dance—primarily because they had assumed that anyone who witnessed these could tell them apart. Furthermore, they rarely distinguished between specific so-called Indian dances, such as side-step dances, grass dances, war dances, or others, or even between secular and sacred dances.

Correspondence between OIA reservation superintendents and the commissioner's office, however, suggests some of the basic organizational principles through which they racialized performative practices. The OIA maintained a polarized view of Native performance in this period: "Indian" dances were typically organized by Native people, usually those considered the "traditionals" or "conservatives" least prone to accepting the tenets of the federal government's assimilationist citizenship agenda. These dances were deemed either completely heathen or plainly problematic because they incorporated purportedly "non-Christian" elements. Sometimes the participants would wear feathers and/or paints and would sing unrecognizable phrases in unrecognizable melodies—certainly not the acceptable melodies or modes of European or white American composers. The dances would also typically feature drums and voices as the primary instruments, and dance gatherings could last for days or sometimes weeks. All of these characteristics directed the OIA to conclude, time and time again, that any tolerance for such dancing would hinder the "uplift" of Native people.

OIA officials and missionaries, though repelled by Lakota dance, were more than aware of its central role in sustaining Lakota society, and for both reasons they went to great ends to destroy the practice of Lakota music. Since the 1880s the federal government had nearly, but not completely, suppressed the public performance of dances such as the Sun Dance and the Ghost Dance.[8] Deeming "all similar dances and so-called religious ceremonies...'Indian Offenses,'" the OIA established punishment by "incarceration in the agency prison for a period not exceeding thirty days" (see table 1, 1883).[9] On the Lakota reservations, OIA personnel forbade and "vigorously repressed" dances through insidious penalties of withholding due rations and making arrests.[10] On the Standing Rock Reservation, missionary Father Barnard reported that dancing was "universal" until "the Messiah craze came on and Sitting Bull and some of his followers had been killed on December 15, 1890," at which point the dances were "entirely annihilated."[11] The massacre of Ghost Dancers and their families two weeks later at Wounded Knee crippled the Lakota's ability to hold large dances or gatherings of any sort.

In addition to the assimilation mandate and the enforced suppression of Indian dances by the Indian Affairs office, a vision of the utter economic and agricultural fiasco of allotment surrounded the Lakota in the fields and prairies of their lands. Through the late nineteenth century, the Lakota became increasingly destitute; starvation due to the lack of rations, because local agents withheld them or were unable to secure sufficient amounts of them, was partially responsible for the uprising that culminated in the Ghost Dance and the massacre at Wounded Knee. The Lakota, by necessity, became dangerously dependent on an exceedingly undependable distribution of rations. In addition, the OIA did not provide enough tools or supplies for farming.[12] To make things worse, what land remained in the hands of Native people, particularly the Lakota, was practically useless for farming.[13]

By the early twentieth century, most agency officials maintained the view that the only hope economically for Indians lay in training them, especially the young men, in low-wage labor and agricultural skills.[14] This was due, in part, to the failures of the allotment and assimilation policy to produce self-sufficient farmers or even harvestable crops, usually blamed on the Indians' lack of abilities rather than on the real obstacles that doomed the outmoded agrarian policy from the start. The OIA's plan to deliver "civilization" through ranching and seasonal wage labor failed before it could even begin: ranching required more capital than the Lakota could raise, the amount of land allotted to individuals was vastly insufficient for the enterprise, and few jobs existed on or near the reservations.[15]

The Lakota were thus led into a misguided agricultural economy and philosophy that could not sustain them or foster self-sufficiency. Rather, in practice, the allotment policy established and reinforced an economy of dependence by necessity, leaving the Lakota with no effective means in the legal system to defend themselves or articulate their opposition. Along with the honing of menial skills, the Office of Indian Affairs continually maintained that the fulfillment of its conception of the cultural requirements for American citizenship was the key to solving the economic crises of the reservations. It did not acknowledge that the very policies of allotment and assimilation had exacerbated if not entirely created them.

The early twentieth century found Lakota people in dire circumstances. Yet despite the concerted assimilationist efforts of agents, white farmers, missionaries, and even some tribal members, Lakota teens and young adults began dancing and singing with an urgency and a determination not witnessed in decades. The Indian Affairs office became quite concerned and grew convinced that the performance of these "heathen" Indian dances signified unabashed resistance to the official assimilation policy and citizenship agenda. Believing that Native youths represented the future and the potential success of allotment and assimilation, the OIA had sent them to distant boarding schools. Far removed from the cultural influence of home, they were to become "proper" American citizens. But when they came back to the reservation, these so-called returned students seemed to adopt a cultural agenda of their own—they began to use dance as a means of reincorporating themselves into the families and communities that assimilationists had hoped they would abandon.

How did a renaissance of Lakota dance become possible in the face of such tremendous physical and philosophical opposition? Confronted with local superintendents and missionaries who fought vigorously to dismantle any cultural practice emblematic of Lakota identity, residents of many reservations developed strategies to maintain certain dances and teach these to their younger community members. This often began with the older generations' disarming their local agents by making promises to exclude the youth from participating. Although the Sun Dance, War Dance, Scalp Dance, Horse Dance, Kiss Dance, Mothers of the Brave Sons Dance, and Ghost Dance had been forcefully suppressed since 1883, older Lakotas in the Hunkpati camp and the Lower Yaktonai camp in North Dakota convinced their local agents to allow periodically a dance that had recently swept the Lakota reservations, called *peji wacipi* (Grass Dance), under the stipulation that "no returned students or pupils of the reservation schools" could participate.[16] Indian Affairs agents typically succumbed to the repeated requests by older Lakotas to hold dances, particularly because they tended to see the elders as "lost causes" when it came to assimilation. However, Standing Rock Agency superintendent James McLaughlin observed a steady increase in dance participation between 1902 and 1922 and reported that it had begun to include "nearly every male adult of the reservation."[17]

Despite OIA agents' efforts to the contrary, American Indian youth began publicly dancing en masse on several reservations. Bishop Burleson noted among the Lakota that the revival of the dances in the early twentieth century was not a continuation of old customs or traditions, but rather a particularly new creation fostered by the Native youth. "My own observation is that the majority of the dancers are not over thirty and in some cases are under sixteen," he added. "The old people are on the outside and the young people are in there dancing."[18] Noting that "dancing is on the increase" at the Sisseton Reservation, Superintendent Whillihan witnessed "one small boy some three or four years of age keeping step just as nicely as the elder Indians."[19] Although the grass dances before 1901 at the Standing Rock Reservation were held mostly by the older Indians, since that time young men had taken up the dance and given Superintendent Mossman the most "trouble."[20]

It seems that a cultural renaissance taking place on the Lakota reservations was designed, in large part, to oppose the imposition of the assimilation policy and that it was led not by the older generation, but by youths. Teenagers and other Lakotas who had left the reservations for boarding school returned with a desire to rejuvenate pride in Lakota performative practices. The participation of the students also demonstrated to OIA officials and missionaries the very failure of the "civilization" program. The curriculum of the boarding schools—designed to break tribal and communal ties, eradicate Native religious beliefs and languages, and foster Christianity, individualism, and economic independence through instruction in the arts of industry and thrift—was having unexpected results.

Native missionary Dallas Shaw keenly observed the consequences. "A good many of my brothers and friends have been to school. I teach them that they must not go back to the blanket but on the Rosebud Reservation all the returned Carlyle [sic] students have returned to blankets. They are the cause of a great deal of this trouble…," he reported. "[I went to a dance at Black Pike] and saw a number of men who had on war bonets [sic] and there was one young man there dressed just like the old men and this man came near and I seen that this young man had a mustache on—it looked so funny. And I was ashamed of myself. I felt so ashamed of myself. He talked better English than I do and I was ashamed. The outward look of him was more like a white man. He spoke the English language and yet he was all painted up. And so there is a great problem."[21]

Shaw's comments at once reveal the complex meaning and at times the seemingly contradictory signals sent by the young dancers. These returned students brought an array of cultural influences from the schools—for example, they read and wrote English as well as they danced. The schools, often filled with Native students from reservations all across the country, inadvertently served as a "hotbed" of new and foreign Native customs, songs, dances, and traditions that the students could adapt and bring back to their reservations. Also, dance offered a way for returned students to gain the acceptance of their older peers and elders. For these reasons, the off-reservation boarding schools, ironically, fostered the on-reservation dancing renaissance of the early twentieth century. Furthermore, as the students developed increasingly sophisticated understandings of the English language and American culture, so too did Lakota dance take on political meanings in entirely new and expanded contexts.

The Lakota's victories in the local cultural politics of an oppressive federal Indian policy were due, in part, to their growing participation in and adaptive interpretation of national and global events such as World War I. Indeed, war and the intensified tropes of patriotism and nationalism that followed factored heavily into their growing cultural and performative vocabulary. Indian Affairs agents and missionaries believed that proper American citizenship rested upon the acceptance of a singular political allegiance to the United States—not to tribes, bands, or customs. However, much to the consternation of many an OIA agent, the language of cultural citizenship was not univocal and could not be contained or controlled. In other words, Lakota dancers and singers began to appropriate the language and the monikers of what the OIA would consider "proper" Americanism, such as national holidays and service in the armed forces, to foster and legitimate their own dance in terms beyond the challenge of the OIA. They used tenets of the federal government's citizenship agenda to enhance their own cultural agenda. Indeed, by the end of World War I, it was unclear on the Lakota reservations just who was on which "side" and who had succeeded and who had failed in controlling the language of American cultural citizenship.

Because Native students and their parents were quite cognizant of the OIA officials' desire to inculcate a patriotic spirit within reservation communities, they effectively used these tropes for the express purpose of establishing and maintaining Native song and dance traditions. Throughout the country, organizers of Native dances made requests to their local superintendents for permission to hold particularly important and well-attended

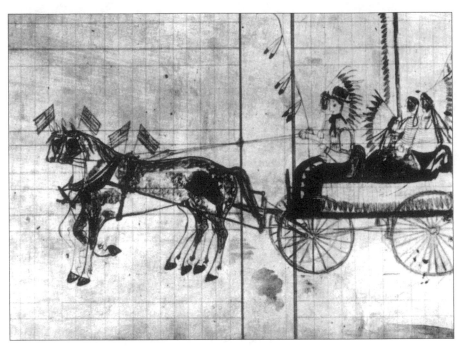

Figure 4. This ledger drawing depicts men traveling to one of the first Oglala Fourth of July giveaways in 1898. The giveaways featured modern buggies, as well as beadwork and feathers, and the participants were sure to place American flags in prominent places. Reproduced from *A Pictographic History of the Oglala Sioux*, by Amos Bad Heart Bull, text by Helen H. Blish, by permission of the University of Nebraska Press. Copyright © 1967 renewed 1995 by the University of Nebraska Press.

dances on American holidays such as the Fourth of July, the days before and following Lent, Christmas, even New Year's Eve (figure 4).[22] Held ostensibly to celebrate the American holidays, Indians ably convinced their agents to allow dances on behalf of their patriotism, their apparent desire for integration into American society, and because such requests would represent the agent's own success in assimilating "his" Indians.

In 1922, for example, a group of Lakota on the Rosebud Reservation asked Superintendent McGregor and the local missionaries for permission to hold dances on several national holidays, including Washington's Birthday, Indian Day, and Armistice Day.[23] They recognized that a dance honoring the republic's founding would be perceived as less threatening to the agent's control and the "civilizing process." Severt Young Bear, noting that the Lakota in the Porcupine district petitioned for dances on "New Year's, and Washington's and Lincoln's birthdays, Memorial Day, Flag Day, July Fourth and Veterans Day," reiterated the success of their strategy. "I guess the BIA agents thought those weren't dangerous occasions, so we got to dance. We also were allowed to dance at fairs in late summer or early fall because there would be displays of vegetables, rodeos, and other signs that we were becoming good modern citizens instead of sticking to all that old ceremonial and warrior stuff," he recalled. "But we still got to dance."[24]

These acts of appropriation and resistance called the very ownership of concepts like patriotism and Americanness into question. Furthermore, they quite possibly indicated that the cultural agenda of the dancers was gaining more headway than that of the OIA. Of course, many agents recognized that the Fourth of July was more of an excuse than a reason to dance. In 1922 Dean Ashley, a missionary of the Cheyenne River Reservation, reported that since 1916 the Independence Day dances had grown larger and larger and were led by the Teton Lakota for reasons other than the celebration of the United States. "The 4th of July celebration in the Indian Country and the 4th of July celebration by the whites are two totally different things," he fumed. "It is proper and eminently fitting that our Indians should be called together and impressed with the ideals of our government, but I am going to ask how many of you present here have ever heard the ideals of our government set forth at a 4th of July celebration? Have heard the principles for which our government was founded? The Indians celebrate the 4th of July with a regular Indian Pow wow [sic] with all its frills and fixings that go with it."[25]

Ashley's abhorrence of the dances, even when held on a national holiday, was shared by many of his peers. One white visitor to a dance at Little Eagle on the Grand River in 1920 was horrified at the sight of a dancer "dressed in imitation of the American flag!"[26] A celebration conducted under the rubric of nationalism became threatening in the minds of these officials only when they realized that they could not contain the symbolism of the holiday they wanted the Indians to observe. This symbolic appropriation by the Lakota demonstrated their ability to wield the politics of dance in very creative ways, succeeding even when the agents questioned the sincerity of the dancers' patriotism.

However unpatriotic these dances may have seemed to some, the missionaries and federal officials could not deny the fact that an estimated seventeen thousand American Indians served in World War I: "Indians volunteered and...inducted at a rate nearly twice as high as the rest of the American population."[27] The war provided the chance for many Indians to fight for the United States, perhaps to demonstrate their value and patriotism to the country. More significantly, they fought to gain status within their own communities. Commissioner of Indian Affairs Cato Sells (1913–1921), who originally thought that Indian military service would demonstrate their preparedness for eventual US citizenship, was discouraged when he heard that recently returned Indian veterans "had counted coup, taken part in victory dances, watched as their sisters, mothers, and wives performed Scalp Dances, and had been ritually cleansed of the taint of combat by medicine people."[28] Cherokee scholar Tom Holm argues that the military "Indianized" more than Americanized these veterans, that Native participation in World War I prompted a rejuvenation of warrior societies, and that these veterans received the honor and status granted warriors "one hundred years before.... In short, he was a warrior and, whether clad in traditional dress or in olive drab, he had reaffirmed his tribal identity."[29]

The World War was a transformative event for Indian soldiers and reservation communities. As service in the armed forces contributed to the increase of Native dances on reservations across the country, the young returning soldiers became both the subjects of and the participants in dances. Around the Pine Ridge Agency, Indians held the Crow Dance "on the order of a victory dance, the words of the song being exultation over victory, real and supposed, over [their] late enemies in the World War." This was one of the most popular dances at Pine Ridge by 1923.[30] Although the Sun Dance had been strenuously suppressed on the reservations by government officials and missionaries, the Lakota held at least three Sun Dances at Kyle between 1917 and 1919, the first two in dedication of the war, the last to the Allied victory.[31] The veterans who danced the Grass Dance at the Standing Rock Agency were "among the more enthusiastic participants of the dance, which ex-soldier element gives it increased prestige."[32]

During the war, entire communities on reservations gathered together and held "giveaway" dances to honor the local men who had enlisted and to raise money for the war effort. Superintendent Mossman, of the Standing Rock Agency, stated that the Indians "gave a large amount of money to the Red Cross and other kindred causes but as a rule this money was raised at Indian Dances." He continued:

> Had it been given outright or raised in any other way the volume of patriotism would have been wonderfully diminished. The method of raising this money is as follows: The Indians are congregated in the dance hall, the women and children on one side, the men on the other. The master of ceremonies makes a speech in Indian in which he depicts the German army being destroyed by the valiant Indian soldiers. An old man rises and says, "I give ten cents in honor of my grandson." The grand son [sic] rises and goes to the old man and shakes his hand and probably puts the ten cent piece on the drum. The six or more men sitting around the drum then sing in a loud voice the merits of the donor,

or as they express it "honor him." When the song is done every one [sic] dances chanting and making motions of killing Germans. By the time the entire crowd has worked itself into a frenzy of excitement, horses, cattle, machinery and all kinds of property are given away.... That is the way the war funds were raised.

It did not matter to Mossman that they were raising money for the war effort. Because they did so through a medium that pooled community resources, he defined them as communistic and recommended that Commissioner Burke forbid the Indians from raising funds for "fairs, [the] Red Cross, and any other proper purpose at heathen dances."[33]

The irony of the government's precluding the raising of relief funds through dances was not lost on the Lakota. They took full advantage of arguing the politics of such "patriotic" dance before the higher-ups within the Office of Indian Affairs. In 1919 a group of Standing Rock Sioux urged Commissioner of Indian Affairs Cato Sells to reprimand school superintendent James Kitch and the local missionaries for banning the giveaways. "The only time that we do give anything at dances is when there are donations to be made to the Red Cross, War Work Fund and Liberty Loans," they wrote, "and we feel that it is our duty to do so." They felt that the missionaries who complained about the giveaways would not have done so if they had given the dance proceeds to the churches and not the war effort and that they were therefore considered "German sympathizers."[34]

The Standing Rock Sioux were particularly proud of their participation in World War I, on the home front and abroad. They believed, however, that Superintendent Kitch, a man who truly despised all forms of Native dance, impeded their efforts to serve in the war effort and to honor local veterans. Kitch imposed a laundry list of bans, rules, and prohibitions regarding dances. Although he claimed to have reduced Indian dance on "his" reservation to a bare minimum, his correspondence indicates that he was constantly thwarted, if not outmaneuvered, by Lakota people determined to have their dance. Thomas Frosted and John Brown of Standing Rock also protested Kitch's dance prohibition by petitioning Commissioner Sells.[35] They held Red Cross giveaway dances, they argued, because Lakotas wanted to "do [their] part and be true Americans in every way."[36]

The side-step giveaway dances, which were only occasionally approved by Kitch, were absolutely necessary, according to Frosted and Brown, to "do [their] part as true Americans in helping get the kaiser." They reminded the commissioner that 150 Standing Rock Sioux were soldiers at the time, "doing their part in patriotism." To maintain optimism and hope throughout the war, they argued, the Lakota needed these dances—which they made a point of calling Christian instead of heathen. Finally, they stressed to the commissioner that "the persons opposing these simple dancrs [sic] are unconsciously opposing a good work and without intending it, are pro-German to the extent that they are hindering the full efficiency with which we must all work together to win the war."[37] Whether or not we take the seemingly pro-American pleas of Frosted and Brown at face value, their arguments demonstrate a sophisticated understanding and use of the contested language of American cultural citizenship.

"It's funny," Severt Young Bear wrote, "when you think of the Christian principle of charity, that once we were put on reservations, both the missionaries and the [Bureau of Indian Affairs] opposed the sharing of material goods because it kept us from becoming modern, self-supporting American citizens."[38] Indeed, Mossman and Kitch abhorred giveaways because they believed that the patriotic purpose was undermined by the way in which the funds were raised. After all, they were giving away the very commodities that the Office of Indian Affairs had been using to teach Indians how to accumulate and cherish as individuals. For the Lakota, these giveaways represented a modern adaptation of a long-standing tradition by which communities could honor their warrior soldiers, as well as their commitment to helping one another through difficult times and maintaining an expressive sense of pride in their Lakota identity. The struggle over the giveaway dances and their meaning vibrantly demonstrates the political nature and evocative power of performance.

The Lakota became increasingly creative and focused on their use of dance, which seemed a particularly adaptive tool to engage the local implementation of the assimilation policy. In 1908, for example, a group of men from the Oak Creek district of Standing Rock formed a singing association for the ostensible purpose of raising money to buy a threshing machine. Forbidden to sing by their local agent, association member Ignatius White Cloud directly petitioned the commissioner of Indian Affairs. The Standing Rock agent refused to believe the singers or acknowledge the hardship of farming without a threshing machine. Instead, he informed the commissioner that he believed they were raising money for more song meetings and feasts that subsequently interfered with their tending of crops. Consequently, the agent took away their drum.[39] Regardless of the association's intentions, this correspondence provides still another example of the way dance and music had become enmeshed within the implementation of federal Indian policy, particularly in the wake of allotment.

White Cloud and his group did not succeed in gaining permission to sing, but other Lakotas persistently thwarted their agents' efforts to ban giveaways. Just a few years later, Standing Rock superintendent Kitch, who was clearly outmaneuvered on many occasions, expressed frustration at the defiance of Lakotas who held giveaways so that they could send delegations to Washington DC to petition for the return of the Black Hills.[40] The give-away dances, sharply politicized and narrowly focused, prompted Lakota participants to amass hundreds and even thousands of dollars to fund these diplomatic meetings. The political and economic adaptability of dance proved for the Standing Rock Sioux to be the most effective mechanism for raising material goods or money, not only to feed themselves when the allotment policy's agrarian economy failed them but also to challenge the federal government's theft of the Black Hills.

Likewise, the Lakota, and particularly the returned students and veterans, utilized their education in myriad ways to assault the assimilation policy further. Those granted US citizenship through the assumption of allotments in fee simple title realized that their activities on the land were not as restricted as these had been when their legal status was that of a ward. Some Lakotas, understanding the new limitations of this control, exercised their prerogative of holding public dances under the newfound status that private property and US citizenship granted. Others even hired attorneys to defend their right to hold these dances when the local superintendents forbade them.[41] Superintendent Kitch reported in 1920 that the dance "trouble" was "caused mainly by fee patent or citizen Indians, who claim that they are not under the jurisdiction [wardship] of the United States and that they have the right to dance or costume themselves as they deem advisable."[42] In 1922 Commissioner Burke lamented that his officials could not legally prevent citizen Indians from dancing on allotments, acknowledging that citizenship, one of the most lauded goals of the assimilation and allotment policy, had actually provided the Lakota with the capability to defy the Office of Indian Affairs legally.[43]

The Lakota people's struggle continued to shape their modern political vision in many ways. After the General Citizenship Act of 1924 bestowed US citizenship on the remaining one-third of Indians who had not yet assumed it, the implications of this new legal status for dances was foremost on many Lakota people's minds. Superintendent Mossman reported that at a meeting of the Standing Rock Business Council following the act, "the new citizenship proposition was discussed vigorously." With distress, he noted, "the only thing about it which seemed to interest the larger portion of the council was its effect upon the regulations against the dance and the giving away."[44] The daily hardships confronted by Lakotas, as well as their acts of resistance, found expression in performance. To be sure, dancing and singing contained complex, multifaceted internal meanings for Lakota communities. But these also served as political weapons that could be wielded against local agency superintendents and their policies of cultural destruction. Through musical performance, Lakotas subverted the meanings the federal government and its agents assigned to a host of assimilative concepts such as allotment, empropertiment, education, civilization, acquisitiveness, and even citizenship.

A consideration of cultural performance as an everyday form of resistance reveals the simultaneous expression of overt political action and hidden transcripts. Sometimes obvious and sometimes well disguised, this technique fits neatly within a much more expansive array of tactics that Native people utilized to engage in and often combat the cultural and geographic dispossession embodied in the US government's vision of (Indian) American citizenship. Of course, the political message of music represents only one of many possible layers of meaning Lakotas attributed to each performance, and they were not the only people to utilize performance in such a manner. Indeed, indigenous peoples across North America, and beyond, experienced similar challenges in this period, and dance represented one avenue of resistance among many.

Dance may have operated particularly well as a catalyst for change on the reservations of the Northern Plains. Faced with policies of assimilation on all fronts, Native peoples used dance to redistribute food and other resources to those in need, to reincorporate boarding school students into their reservation communities, and to honor and recognize their soldiers and veterans—their warriors—of World War I. Ironically, Native dancing became more prevalent on reservations in the early 1900s as a direct result of the increased deployment of boarding school education and the recruitment of young men into the armed forces. The meanings of the dance transformed, as well, to reflect an expanded incorporation of shifting cultural, social, and economic influences. Dance became an arena of selective, cultural brokerage that fostered the community understanding, meaning, and healing needed in the wake of the dire social and economic toll of the citizenship agenda. A medium of resistance, adaptation, and incorporation, dance was imbued with political resonance and meaning that sparked a series of culture wars on reservations throughout the country. The tools of assimilation—boarding schools, the legal status of citizenship, service in the armed forces—became, through dance, tools of Lakota revitalization and celebration.

Notes

1. Frederick Hoxie, "Exploring a Cultural Borderland: Native American Journeys of Discovery in the Early Twentieth Century," *Journal of American History* 79 (December 1992): 969–995; C.

Blue Clark, *Lone Wolf v. Hitchcock: Treaty Rights and Indian Law at the End of the Nineteenth Century* (Lincoln: University of Nebraska Press, 1994); and Alexandra Harmon, "American Indians and Land Monopolies in the Gilded Age," *Journal of American History* 90 (June 2003): 106–133.

2. James Mooney, *The Ghost Dance and the Sioux Outbreak of 1890*, Part 2, 14th Annual Report of the Bureau of Ethnology, 1892–1893 (Washington DC: GPO, 1896); Omer Stewart, *Peyote Religion: A History* (Norman: University of Oklahoma Press, 1987); and Tom Holm, *The Great Confusion in Indian Affairs: Native Americans and Whites in the Progressive* Era (Austin: University of Texas Press, 2005).

3. Loretta Fowler, *Arapahoe Politics: Symbols of Crises and Authority, 1851–1978* (Lincoln: University of Nebraska Press, 1982); Loretta Fowler, *Shared Symbols, Contested Meanings: Gros Ventre Culture and History, 1778–1984* (New York: Cornell University Press, 1987); William Meadows, *Kiowa, Comanche, and Apache Military Societies: Enduring Veterans, 1800 to the Present* (Austin: University of Texas Press, 1999); Luke Lassiter, Clyde Ellis, and Ralph Kotay, *The Jesus Road: Kiowas, Christianity, and Indian Hymns* (Lincoln: University of Nebraska Press, 2002); and Allison Fuss Mellis, *Riding Buffaloes and Broncos: Rodeos and Native Traditions in the Northern Great Plains* (Norman: University of Oklahoma Press, 2003).

4. See also Clyde Ellis, Luke Lassiter, and Gary Dunham, eds., *Powwow: Native American Performance, Identity, and Meaning* (Lincoln: University of Nebraska Press, 2002).

5. Citizenship was granted to American Indians in a haphazard, case-by-case manner from the 1870s through 1924. An exception to the general rule of a case-by-case bestowal of citizenship before 1924 was the Citizenship for World War I Veterans Act of 1919, which permitted those Indian veterans to receive it because of their patriotic service overseas.

6. There are, of course, important exceptions, the most prominent being the output of Native writers such as Charles Eastman or Carlos Montezuma and the development of organizations such as the Society of American Indians. Certainly, such opportunities were fewer and farther between for reservation-based, non-urban Indians.

7. These hidden transcripts represent "a critique of power spoken behind the back of the dominant." Scott goes on to suggest that such transcripts are "typically expressed openly—albeit in disguised form." James Scott, *Domination and the Arts of Resistance: Hidden Transcripts* (New Haven, CT: Yale University Press, 1990), xi–xiii.

8. Clyde Holler, *Black Elk's Religion: The Sun Dance and Lakota Catholicism* (Syracuse, NY: Syracuse University Press, 1995), 110.

9. Quoted in Harry James, *Pages from Hopi History* (Tucson: University of Arizona Press, 1974), 186. These efforts continued through the 1920s with the dissemination of circulars 1665 in 1921 and a supplement circular in 1923 that maintained a prohibition of dance.

10. Holler, *Black Elk's Religion*, 130.

11. Transcript of proceedings, Investigation into the Practices of the Sioux Indians on the Dakota Reservations with Particular Reference to the Indian Dance, conducted by Commissioner Charles H. Burke, Pierre, SD, October 24, 1922, p. 18, file 10429-1922-063, general service, central classified files (CCF), record group 75, National Archives, Washington DC. Hereafter cited as *Transcript of proceedings*. Barnard is referring to the murders, committed by Lt. Bull Head and 2nd Sgt. Red Tomahawk, of Sitting Bull and eight others from his camp in front of his house. Six policemen were also killed, including Bull Head. Sitting Bull was heavily involved with the Ghost Dance movement that had taken form within many Sioux communities. The Wounded Knee massacre occurred shortly thereafter, on December 29, 1890. See Mooney, *The*

Ghost Dance (North Dighton, MA: JG Press, 1996), 218–220. Forced underground during the ban and significantly reduced in occurrence, the dance lost its central relevance among the people. Holler, *Black Elk's Religion*, 135–136.

12. Guy Gibbon, *The Sioux: The Dakota and Lakota Nations* (Malden, MA: Blackwell Publishing, 2003), 136.

13. Thomas Biolsi, *Organizing the Lakota: The Political Economy of the New Deal on the Pine Ridge and Rosebud Reservations* (Tucson: University of Arizona Press, 1992), 24.

14. Frederick Hoxie, *A Final Promise: The Campaign to Assimilate the Indians, 1880–1920* (Cambridge: Cambridge University Press, 1984; Lincoln: University of Nebraska Press, 2001); and K. Tsianina Lomawaima, *They Called It Prairie Light: The Story of the Chilocco Indian School* (Lincoln: University of Nebraska Press, 1994).

15. Biolsi, *Organizing the Lakota*, 24.

16. This dance, by the late nineteenth century, was very closely related to the *Omaha wacipi* (Omaha Dance). According to one scholar, the Grass Dance was originally, and for many communities still remains, a "war dance." The dance is believed to have originated among the "Inloshka and Hethuska societies of the Kansa (Kaw), Omaha, and Ponca, and in the Iruska of the Pawnee." It spread in the nineteenth century to reservations across the Northern and Southern Plains. Like most dances, its meaning for the various groups who practice it has changed and is continually redefined. Among the Ponca, Pawnee, Omaha, and Osage, for example, the dance began to resonate with "revitalization features similar to the Ghost Dance" around the late nineteenth and early twentieth centuries. See Thomas Kavanagh, "Southern Plains Dance: Tradition and Dynamism," in *Native American Dance: Ceremonies and Social Traditions*, ed. Charlotte Heth (Washington DC: National Museum of the American Indian, Smithsonian Institution, with Starwood Publishing, Inc., 1992), 105–123. According to Severt Young Bear, the Grass Dancers "would go out and pick some tall grass, tie it together, and put it on their backs at the waist. Some even braided the grass and wore it like a sash across the chest. They have their own set of songs and their dancers do a lot of fancy footwork. They dance backwards, cross their legs, and go in circles. By comparison, the *Omaha* and *tokala* dancers were straight dancers. They might go down low, but not like these grass dance guys, who were a little bit fancier and somehow identified with grass. Some say it represents scalps and others say it symbolizes generosity. Originally, Omaha dance and grass dance were two different dance customs. Later on, I think in the 1880s and 1890s, they came together in their songs and their costuming." Severt Young Bear and R. D. Theisz, *Standing in the Light: A Lakota Way of Seeing* (Lincoln: University of Nebraska Press, 1994), 55–56. See also Tara Browner, *Heartbeat of the People: Music and Dance of the Northern Pow-wow* (Urbana: University of Illinois Press, 2002), 20–21.

17. "Memorandum on Reports of Superintendents of Sioux Reservations in North Dakota and South Dakota Relative to Dancing among the Indians of Their Respective Reservations," James McLaughlin, inspector, Office of Indian Affairs, to Burke, 27 February 1922, file 10429-1922-063, general service, CCF. McLaughlin, the Standing Rock agent during the manifestation of the Ghost Dance movement in the Dakotas, was responsible for arranging the arrest of Sitting Bull that resulted in Sitting Bull's murder. Mooney, *Ghost Dance*, 216.

18. Transcript of proceedings, p. 15, file 10429-1922-063, general service file, CCF.

19. Transcript of proceedings, p. 50, file 10429-1922-063, general service file, CCF.

20. Transcript of proceedings, p. 51, file 10429-1922-063, general service file, CCF.

21. Transcript of proceedings, pp. 29–30, file 10429-1922-063, general service file, CCF.

22. Superintendent of the Pine Ridge Agency to Burke, 5 April 1923, file 10429-1922-063, general service file, CCF; James B. Kitch to the Commissioner of Indian Affairs, 6 March 1919, file 109123-17-063, Standing Rock Agency, CCF. For an excellent history of the Fourth of July dances that took place in the late nineteenth and early twentieth centuries, see Adriana Greci Green, "Performances and Celebrations: Displaying Lakota Identity, 1880–1915" (Ph.D. diss., Rutgers: The State University of New Jersey, 2001).

23. James H. McGregor to the Commissioner of Indian Affairs, 20 January 1923, file 7141-23-063, Rosebud Agency, CCF.

24. Young Bear and Thiesz, *Standing*, 55.

25. Transcript of proceedings, p. 11, file 10429-1922-063, general service file, CCF.

26. Mary Patterson Lord to John Barton Payne, secretary of the interior, 5 October 1920, file 109123-17-063, Standing Rock Agency, CCF.

27. Tom Holm, *Strong Hearts, Wounded Souls: Native American Veterans of the Vietnam War* (Austin: University of Texas Press, 1996), 99; and Thomas Britten, *American Indians in World War I: At Home and at War* (Albuquerque: University of New Mexico Press, 1997).

28. Quoted in Holm, *Strong Hearts*, 99, 101. Here Holm also states that "there can be little doubt that the veterans' separation pay or their pensions helped finance these rituals."

29. Holm, *Strong Hearts*, 101.

30. Superintendent of the Pine Ridge Indian Agency to Burke, 5 April 1923, file 10429-1922-063, general service file, CCF.

31. Holler, *Black Elk's Religion*, 136.

32. "Memorandum on Reports of Superintendents of Sioux Reservations in North Dakota and South Dakota Relative to Dancing among the Indians of Their Respective Reservations," James McLaughlin, inspector, Office of Indian Affairs, to Burke, 27 February 1922, file 10429-1922-063, general service file, CCF. Standing Rock Indian School superintendent James Kitch stated that about 130 boys from this school alone served in the army during World War I. Britten, *American Indians*, 65.

33. Mossman to Burke, 10 February 1922, file 10429-1922-063, general service file, CCF.

34. No Heart et al. to Cato Sells, 7 June 1919, file 109123-17-063, Standing Rock Agency, CCF.

35. James B. Kitch to the Commissioner of Indian Affairs, 8 September 1919, file 75420-19-063, Standing Rock Agency, CCF.

36. Thomas Frosted and John Brown to the Commissioner of Indian Affairs, 7 October 1918, file 109123-17-063, Standing Rock Agency, CCF.

37. Thomas Frosted and John Brown to the Commissioner of Indian Affairs, 7 October 1918, file 109123-17-063, Standing Rock Agency, CCF.

38. Young Bear and Theisz, *Standing*, 58.

39. File 71473-08-751, Standing Rock Agency, CCF. Stealing, destroying, or otherwise mishandling a drum is practically unthinkable among Lakota singers and would almost certainly devastate the singers, which was probably what the agent intended.

40. James B. Kitch to the Commissioner of Indian Affairs, 9 January 1920, file 109123-17-063, Standing Rock Agency, CCF.

41. Transcript of proceedings, pp. 50, 55, file 10429-1922-063, general service file, CCF.

42. James B. Kitch to the Commissioner of Indian Affairs, 9 January 1920, file 109123-17-063, Standing Rock Agency, CCF.

43. Transcript of proceedings, pp. 56–57, file 10429-1922-063, general service file, CCF.

44. Mossman to Farmers, 1 July 1924, file 60373-24-062, Standing Rock Agency, CCF; Mossman to the Commissioner of Indian Affairs, 12 August 1924, ibid.

6 "In a name of justice and fairness"

The Mississippi Choctaw Indian Federation versus the BIA, 1934

Katherine M. B. Osburn

Congress responded to critics of Indian policy by enacting the Wheeler-Howard Act, or Indian Reorganization Act (IRA), in June 1934, which effectively reversed allotment (see table 2). Now the Bureau of Indian Affairs (BIA) encouraged tribes to "reorganize" to accept constitutional government and to incorporate to take full advantage of new economic opportunities. Research on the new governments showed that where Native peoples recognized potential for more control over local affairs or where they were desperate for economic assistance, acceptance of an IRA government was part of a larger strategy. Elsewhere, where tribes were involved in disputes over federal intervention, rejection of the IRA government was part of a pattern of resistance.[1] In many cases, an elected government was (or over time became) compatible with traditional political values. In others, the introduction of an IRA council led to an intensification of political conflict.[2] Until the late 1960s, historians generally viewed the New Deal as a positive change for Indians; recently, the assessments have been more qualified.[3] Katherine Osburn's chapter contributes to this discussion of the IRA's consequences by offering a rare examination of the implementation process in the South. Osburn describes the Mississippi Choctaws' effort to respond to the IRA by constructing a tribal government without direct supervision by BIA personnel. This struggle drew on older strategies of activism in which Choctaws cultivated alliances with local, non-Choctaw politicians.

On May 12, 1934, a Mississippi Choctaw man named Joe Chitto attended a meeting in Union, Mississippi, that several observers called "the largest assemblage of Indians that had gathered in Mississippi since 1895." At this gathering, the Mississippi Choctaw, citing their approval of the 1934 Indian Reorganization Act, constructed a tribal government called the Mississippi Choctaw Indian Federation (MCIF) and approved a constitution drafted by state senator Earl Richardson. Chitto was elected secretary-treasurer, and Choctaw Baptist minister E. W. Willis was elected chief.[4] Simultaneously, Senator Richardson and E. T. Winston—a newspaper editor and close associate of Governor Theodore Bilbo—founded the Mississippi Choctaw Welfare Association (MCWA), an "affiliate" of the federation, which existed to "assist the Indians in their very laudable undertaking toward self-government and self-expression."[5] Chief Willis then informed Choctaw superintendent Archie C. Hector of these actions.[6] Superintendent Hector was not impressed, however, for he had already created a Tribal Business Committee (TBC) to consider the Indian Reorganization Act.[7] Ironically, two-thirds of the committee had attended the Union meeting and voted in favor of the federation.

In the following years, the Mississippi Choctaw Indian Federation and its allies engaged Agent Hector and Commissioner of Indian Affairs John Collier in a passionate debate over who had the authority to construct a tribal government for the Mississippi Choctaw under the IRA. The process of hammering out a tribal government took eleven years, during which time the MCIF demanded recognition by using strikes, boycotts, and petitions. They did not prevail, however, and the federation's leadership was absorbed into an officially sanctioned tribal council in 1945.

At first glance, this story appears to be simply a tale of failed political initiative. Yet the campaign raised several significant questions. Why did these Choctaws agree to join the superintendent's Tribal Business Committee and then create their own government behind his back? Why did the federation's leadership continue to serve on the TBC, even as they claimed their federation as the real tribal government? Why did the federation leadership fight so fiercely for recognition, only to be "co-opted" into a third governing body? The answers to these questions suggest that the Mississippi Choctaw Indian Federation's campaign should not be understood by reference to a dichotomous political model in which two organi-zations compete for legitimacy and one "wins." Rather, the federation's activities reveal a Choctaw political strategy deeply rooted in historical patterns of activism and an indigenous view of politics as multifaceted.

The Choctaw example is also instructive because it highlights how one tribe used the policy of Indian reorganization for purposes other than those designed by the Office of Indian Affairs (OIA). The struggle to create a tribal government in the 1930s was merely the latest assertion of Choctaw sovereignty in a century of political activism. Article 14 of the 1830 Treaty of Dancing Rabbit Creek had promised that the Choctaws who remained in Mississippi would be given land; if they resided on these lands for five years, they would hold the political status of free white citizens.[8] The allotment process was hopelessly corrupt, however, and the majority of the remnant band became squatters and sharecroppers without political standing. In response, Choctaws retreated into ethnic enclaves where they could preserve their cultural distinctiveness.

Despite the laws proclaiming the dissolution of the Choctaw Nation in Mississippi, the remnant band conflated its ethnic identity with a continuing juridical status under which it claimed treaty rights to land. The band campaigned for these rights in a variety of venues over the late nineteenth and early twentieth centuries, building up a network of political allies. In 1918 the Choctaws won the establishment of an Office of Indian Affairs agency in Mississippi, which provided schools, reimbursable farm allotments, and vocational training. Choctaws used these government services to maintain a third racial identity in the biracial South—one that could help them to overcome poverty and racism. The battle over the Mississippi Choctaw Indian Federation ultimately strengthened the Choctaws' relationships with local politicians who could advance this strategy. Thus, the shaping of this national policy was deeply rooted in the Choctaws' local context.

In the 1930s most Choctaws who remained in Mississippi lived in seven communities of extended families that had clustered around churches and mission schools in eastern-central Mississippi during the late nineteenth century (figure 5).[9] Despite the assistance of the Office of Indian Affairs agency, the majority of the Mississippi Choctaws were desperately poor sharecroppers living far below the poverty line.[10] Politically, Choctaws kept to their own communities, which had rudimentary political structures. At the Tucker community, where they lived on lands of the Holy Rosary Catholic Mission, the Indians elected a chief to conduct community business with the priest. The other six communities were mostly Baptist and held meetings in government day schools according to parliamentary procedures used in their churches.[11] Farm clubs and their ladies' auxiliaries also provided opportunities for community leadership. At the agency level, the Choctaw had a police force—with one Indian policeman—but no other centralized institutions.[12] The tribe's political organizations were mostly informal and localized at the time that agency superintendent Archie Hector introduced the Indian New Deal.

In February 1934 Superintendent Hector appointed the Tribal Business Committee to consider the Indian Reorganization Act. This task was the

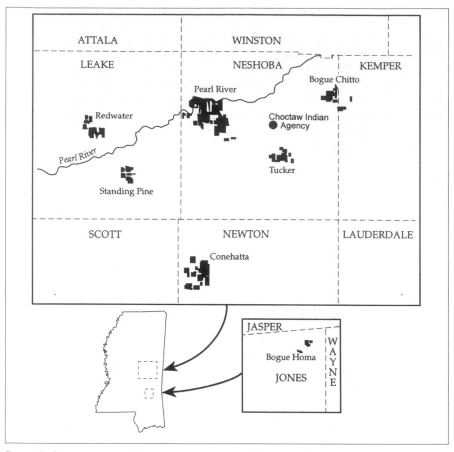

Figure 5. Contemporary Choctaw communities in Mississippi. Map from *Choctaws and Missionaries in Mississippi, 1818–1918,* by Clara Sue Kidwell. Copyright © 1995 by the University of Oklahoma Press, Norman. Reprinted by permission.

committee's only responsibility, and it met only when called. Seventeen people composed this council: three each from the communities of Conehatta, Tucker, and Pearl River and two each from the smaller districts of Red Water, Standing Pine, Bogue Chitto, and Bogue Homa. The delegates held office until OIA officials decided to make reappointments.[13] In March, Hector reported to Commissioner of Indian Affairs John Collier that the Tribal Business Committee had approved of the IRA but some Choctaws feared that they lacked sufficient education to create a tribal government. Others were concerned that "there were a considerable number of Indians who had received practically no help and…they believed that such Indians should be helped first."[14]

In April, Joe Chitto, a Tribal Business Committee representative from the Standing Pine community, wrote to Collier, asking him to clarify the powers of this body and questioning whether Collier indeed wanted them to form a tribal government. Chitto believed that they should wait until the Indian Reorganization Act was approved.[15] Collier replied that Chitto should draft a constitution so that they would be ready to institute their new government when the bill passed.[16] Taking Collier at his word, Chitto and his friends created the Mississippi Choctaw Indian Federation.

Agency superintendent Hector immediately denigrated the organization and asked for Collier's backing.[17] Collier wrote to the Tribal Business Committee, explaining that the drafting of a constitution was a matter "in which the Indians will need careful guidance" and instructing them to wait for further instructions. He also disavowed the preceding letter to Chitto, explaining that it had been composed by a member of his staff who was unaware of the proper procedures. Although Collier supported "the right of Indians of any community or reservation to meet as and when they please without reference to a Superintendent," he could not endorse the federation because he had already approved the TBC as the legitimate government.[18]

Collier also addressed a petition that the federation had sent him. Two hundred and fifty-two Choctaws, including two-thirds of the Tribal Business Committee, had demanded Hector's removal: he was "trying to make us believe that our organization is not legal unless whatever business we do [is] done through him.... In a name of justice and fairness we ask that you remove him at once." The entire leadership of Red Water and Standing Pine and two-thirds of the leaders of Conehatta, both male and female, signed the petition. Additionally, the petition requested that the commissioner transfer various personnel.[19] Collier assumed full blame for the mistake that had allowed the two groups to emerge, but he declined to act on the petition. Instead, he sanctioned the federation as an organization of salvage anthropology, encouraging it to work with the welfare association to promote "historical research and endeavor to keep alive the traditions of the inhabitants," and reiterated that only one organization could officially represent the tribe.[20]

Joe Chitto responded with a sharp assertion of Choctaw autonomy. He informed Superintendent Hector that, in support of the federation, "most of the committee" would boycott the upcoming committee meeting. He further stated that the federation did not exist "just to fight [the Tribal Business] Committee" but rather the majority of Choctaws preferred "the organization and we are going to stand by it regardless whether you or [the] commissioner recognize [it or] not." According to Chitto, the Choctaw did not organize this government to defy the Office of Indian Affairs agency but rather to assert their political autonomy. "We are not fighting the government or you," he wrote, "but it is time we did something for our own welfare. It is over one hundred years since we lost our right of organization but we are making up [for it]."[21]

It is clear that Chitto viewed his actions as the embodiment of the Indian Reorganization Act. In boycotting the Tribal Business Committee meeting, the Choctaws were holding the government to the promises of the IRA. "We believe in [the] government's intention and their policies," he wrote, "but it [sic] are not carried out as the[y] should [be]."[22] According to the members of the Mississippi Choctaw Indian Federation, these policies recognized the rights of the Choctaw to organize whatever political bodies they chose. Even though the petition for agency superintendent Hector's removal was a direct challenge to the Office of Indian Affairs, Chitto seemed to view this step as a means to gain recognition of the federation as the true incarnation of the IRA, not necessarily as a way to replace the Tribal Business Committee, in which he retained membership.

Given that the majority of the committee's leaders held membership in both organizations, it is reasonable to conclude that they saw the two as complementary. The Choctaw did not conceive of the world in binary opposites but rather incorporated seemingly contradictory ideas into a complex ideology that held supposed incongruities in creative tension. This worldview had been manifested for more than a century in the Choctaws' use of Christianity to carry Choctaw culture through white encroachment and removal. Similarly, in Choctaw thinking, if one political organization did not meet all their needs, they could create another one.[23]

Joe Chitto also wrote to Commissioner John Collier, criticizing the IRA process as undemocratic, for the committee was not "approve[d] by vote or otherwise, just named."[24] Yet in an apparent irony, he claimed legitimacy for the federation by appealing to the authority of the committee, noting that all but one member of that body had attended the meeting in Union and all but three voted for the federation. Instead of being a "faction," the Mississippi Choctaw Indian Federation was a vehicle to carry out grassroots political actions. The petition, he noted, was written on federation letterhead but "was started and signed by the Indians [as] individuals [sic] citizens," not by the organization.[25] Consequently, he concluded, "there was not any faction or division or any feeling among the Choctaws as you seem to think."[26] Rather, there was a universal desire for democracy.

The federation's allies echoed Chitto's charge of faux democracy in the IRA process. Senator Earl Richardson, president of the Mississippi Choctaw Welfare Association, wrote Collier that Choctaw headmen had approached him "several months ago with a view of organizing a federation." He acknowledged Archie Hector's Tribal Business Committee, stressing that the

Choctaws did not intend to interfere with it. Nonetheless, the majority of the Indians felt that the superintendent's group neglected "the ancient customs, rules, and regulations. They wanted a more democratic and larger organization, one that would embody all the Indians and one that all the Indians would have an opportunity to have a voice in." Although indigenous Choctaw politics were ranked, all Choctaw had input into political decisions.[27] In Hector's plan, however, Indians living outside the seven "official" communities had no representation.[28] In contrast, the federation granted membership to "any Mississippi Choctaw Indian of twenty-one years of age or more, or who is the head of a family as husband, wife, or guardian, and whose degree of blood is more than one-half."[29] Richardson also insisted that the Choctaw were not fighting the Office of Indian Affairs but were "carrying out the personal wishes of the Commissioner in this matter, as revealed in the Howard Wheeler [sic] Indian Act."[30]

In Chitto's next letter to Collier, he drew upon the Choctaws' activist history. He cited an 1842 speech by Choctaw leader Samuel Cobb to government agents investigating the failures of Article 14. The vocabulary of this speech suggests that even twelve years after removal, Cobb still had a sense of Choctaw sovereignty. Cobb's speech was a classic example of Native American treaty language, a rhetorical style that built understanding between treaty partners by reference to a common humanity.[31] Significantly, rather than use the term *father*, implying a hierarchical relationship, Cobb repeatedly used the term *brother*, indicating an association between equals. He also appealed to an emotion common to all people—a love for ancestors and homeland: "Brother: Our hearts are full. Twelve winters ago our chief sold our country. Every warrior that you see here was opposed to that treaty. If the dead could have been counted, it never would have been made; but alas, though they stood around they could not be seen or heard. Their tears came in the rain-drops and their voices in the wailing wind, but the pale faces knew it not, and our land was taken away."[32]

In Cobb's closing remarks, he also invoked religious sanction, again in keeping with traditional diplomatic protocols between sovereign nations.[33] "When you took our country, you promised us land," he observed. "There is your promise in the book. Twelve times the trees have dropped their leaves, and yet we have received no land." Building upon Cobb's words, Joe Chitto concluded his letter to John Collier by emphasizing what he considered to be the obvious parallels. "You see how the government treated our fathers, and now after more than one hundred years, the remnant of the once powerful Choctaws took Mr. Collier at his word [only] to be told by you that you would not recognize our federation," he wrote. "It makes us Choctaws wonder if the government ever makes its promises good to the

Indians."[34] Chitto's reference to the "remnant of the once powerful Choctaw" declared his people's desire to reassert their historical juridical identity in Mississippi under the Indian Reorganization Act.

To celebrate their tribal rebirth, the federation and its allies performed a ceremony to install federation officials on September 27—the 104th anniversary of the signing of the Treaty of Dancing Rabbit Creek. The festivities were preceded by a stickball game, and George H. Ethridge, assistant justice of the state supreme court, swore in the new government. The Mississippi congressional delegation was invited, and the new representative from Pontotoc attended.[35]

A close analysis of the press clippings about this ritual illuminates the Choctaws' strategies for political renaissance. When first posed with the prospect of a tribal government, Choctaw leaders had raised several concerns. They feared their lack of education. Aligning themselves with Judge Richardson and newspaper editor Winston, who was "considered the best read student of Indian history and lore in the state," provided them with political expertise.[36] Several committee members had also noted the Choctaws' dire need for financial assistance.[37] The Mississippi Choctaw Welfare Association addressed that anxiety as well, for it planned to seek federal funds for various projects—a tradition long practiced by Mississippi officials allied with the Choctaws.[38]

The tribe's work with these political leaders reflected a long-standing strategy of activism. Because Jim Crow laws requiring literacy and poll taxes disenfranchised them, Choctaws did not represent a constituency in Mississippi politics.[39] Nonetheless, state and local politicians had rallied to assert Indian interests since the early twentieth century, when Representative Pat Harrison attempted to open the tribal rolls of the Oklahoma Choctaw Nation to the Mississippi remnant.[40] Harrison's agitation led to the establishment of the Office of Indian Affairs agency, for which Mississippi politicians then continually sought greater funding. Accordingly, the federation appealed to its elected officials to support the Indian Reorganization Act in return for "the deep gratitude and sincere appreciation of all the Mississippi Choctaw Indians."[41] Whether these officials lobbied on behalf of the IRA is unclear, but several members of the state's congressional delegation contacted Collier on behalf of the Mississippi Choctaw Indian Federation over the next year.

It appears, then, that state and local politicians took the concerns of "their Indians" seriously—but why? E. T. Winston's newspaper articles and correspondence with John Collier intimate economic motives rooted in the Great Depression, a cataclysmic event that reached its nadir by the time of the conflict over tribal self-governance in Mississippi. "Present economic conditions create a new order," Winston wrote. Both Indians and whites were "engaged in a struggle for mere existence, and hence the strong arm of government is besought to stay the impending calamity that threatens both civilizations."[42] The federation and welfare associations were born at this moment: "A 'new deal' has been promised the white man and the Indians from Washington."[43] Mississippi politicians, understanding the economic benefits of the Indian New Deal—the revolving credit fund and the land purchase program—saw an opportunity to fatten state coffers.[44] The welfare association also planned to seek compensation for lost lands and funding to turn the nearby Nanih Waiya mound into a national park, which would "be a great help to our Indians and to our county."[45]

Because the Tribal Business Committee assembled by Superintendent Archie Hector was the federally recognized organization and therefore the only one that could access New Deal monies, the seemingly overwhelming preference for the Mississippi Choctaw Indian Federation seems counterintuitive. The alliance between non-Indian congressional representatives, the governor's office, and tribal leaders, however, allowed the Choctaws to request federal funds while simultaneously asserting state's rights. Newspaper editor E. T. Winston implied as much when he claimed that the supreme authority on the issue of Choctaw sovereignty came not from the Office of Indian Affairs but from the 1830 state laws that abolished all tribal governments in the state, revoked all tribal laws save marriage, and instituted a fine of $1,000 for anyone exercising the office of "chief."[46] The installation ceremony would rescind these laws and reestablish federally recognized Choctaw political institutions under state authority.[47]

This pursuit of federal funding while asserting local authority in administration also reflected larger patterns of Southern interactions with the New Deal. For example, despite provisions protecting tenants in the Agricultural Adjustment Act (AAA), Southern landlords often evicted their tenants when "downsizing" their farms and frequently failed to distribute parity funds designed to mitigate these hardships. These actions, in turn, threw the remaining tenants onto the relief roles. Thus, Southern landlords shifted their old paternal duties to their tenants to the federal government.[48] Similarly, the federal government could now relieve the Choctaws' neighbors of their charitable obligations, which, according to E. T. Winston, they had graciously embraced.[49] Winston's creation of the tribal government that would institute this transaction would buttress state's rights even as the federal government insinuated itself into Mississippi's political domain. The Choctaws exhibited similar ambivalence, embracing the Office of Indian Affairs agency while skillfully using their allies to advance their own agenda of asserting more power over its policies.

The Choctaws' appeals to their allies seem to have affected some of the decisions the Office of Indian Affairs made regarding local agency matters. In August, an anonymous OIA memo argued that one particular employee should be transferred because he dragged "the local citizenry" into agency matters. The author of the memo also added: "Hector should also be moved.... He has had other personnel difficulties but they have been accentuated by local politics and politicians. He has not the support of the local congressmen."[50] Around the same time, the Indian Affairs office decided to transfer the individual named on the federation's petition. Hector warned Collier that if they did, "certain Indians will feel that they had something to do with this and that they can tell the Agency what to do."[51] Even though there is no specific evidence that pressure from "the local congressmen" was directly responsible for this change, it is plausible that the Office of Indian Affairs considered the opinions of Mississippi political leaders in these matters. The Choctaws counted on that in their campaign.

Over the summer and fall of 1934, federation leaders pressed the Office of Indian Affairs for federal recognition. Joe Chitto challenged agency superintendent Archie Hector openly in a Tribal Business Committee meeting, preventing a vote on its leadership. A two-hour argument ensued, and the committee finally delayed the vote.[52] When Hector called another meeting, on August 16, Chitto announced his boycott.[53] This meeting was two members shy of a quorum, but Hector was uncertain whether that was Chitto's doing. He complained that the one thing Choctaws agreed on was that "they did not want to comply with the rules laid down in you [sic] letter for holding meetings." They again adjourned without electing officers.[54] In response, Superintendent Hector blamed the situation on "the local politicians."[55] Nonetheless, he continued his preparations for the vote on the Indian Reorganization Act. Even as parents held a strike against the Standing Pine School in solidarity with the Mississippi Choctaw Indian Federation, Hector claimed that support for the IRA was building.[56]

Despite the strike at Standing Pine, the majority of Choctaws approved the IRA on March 19, 1935. The Conehatta, Tucker, Pearl River, Red Water, and Bogue Homa communities all voted affirmatively, Bogue Chitto turned in only three votes, and Standing Pine cast a majority negative vote.[57] The vote appeared to support Hector's contention that he had triumphed over the federation, but a close analysis suggests a more nuanced interpretation. Those who voted for the Indian Reorganization Act may not have viewed this action as a repudiation of the federation, as Hector claimed. Instead, the federation's agitation may well have shaped the vote.

Archie Hector addressed some of the concerns Joe Chitto had raised nearly a year before. In this election, he arranged for the "scattered Indians to vote in the school districts with which they should be affiliated."[58]

Perhaps his willingness to include these Indians made the election process more acceptable to federation members. Also, rather than appoint the new Tribal Business Committee, Hector called for elections during the vote on the Indian Reorganization Act.[59] Hector assumed that this new committee would put an end to the Mississippi Choctaw Indian Federation. It did not.

The Choctaws' actions following the election suggest that they countenanced two governments, for the federation continued to function and the new Tribal Business Committee did not assert its power over it.[60] In the new committee's first meeting, it discussed the strike at Standing Pine, and "someone" suggested closing the school. The members voted unanimously, however, to keep the school open until the "parents of the district could discuss the matter."[61] Over several months, parents at the Standing Pine School began gradually to return their children to the classroom.[62] Perhaps the Tribal Business Committee's light touch in the matter mitigated some of the frictions between the Standing Pine community and the local OIA agency.

Tensions persisted with other communities, nonetheless. In June, the Bogue Homa School went on strike. Strike leader Henry Jim belonged to both the Mississippi Choctaw Indian Federation and the Tribal Business Committee. Using federation letterhead, he petitioned the Mississippi congressional delegation to transfer the teacher and close the school.[63] Congressmen Bill Colmer and Albert Dunn asked Commissioner of Indian Affairs John Collier to look into Jim's grievances.[64] As with the earlier petition, these complaints led to an investigation that resulted in the teacher's transfer.[65] Thus, even though the majority of Choctaws embraced the TBC, the federation continued to serve as a vehicle to protest the agency establishment through appeals to the Choctaws' political allies. The committee's refusal to disband the "rival" federation government or punish its actions suggested that the committee viewed this organization as another method to protect Choctaw interests.

In June 1936 Joe Jennings, a special agent for the Office of Indian Affairs, went to Mississippi to establish the official IRA government. He noted the existence of two political organizations and proposed "to bring both groups together in a new constitution and bylaws." He instructed Superintendent Hector to include delegates of the Mississippi Choctaw Indian Federation in all meetings of the Tribal Business Committee; Hector claimed to comply.[66] References to the federation fade out of the records about this time, so it is conceivable that a hybrid council operated. A few months later, however, Joe Jennings decided that the Choctaw were not eligible for the IRA, because they were not a tribe and did not live on trust lands.[67] Ultimately, neither the federation nor the committee prevailed, and the Choctaws had to begin the organizing process anew.

Searching for solutions, the Office of Indian Affairs debated various proposals. One plan allowed the Choctaws to organize at the local level and eschew a tribal council. Another suggested that the OIA simply declare the Choctaws' reimbursable lands as an Indian reservation and let them form a tribal government. Both suggestions included plans for purchasing lands under IRA provisions for "full-blooded" Indians.[68] Choctaw leaders refused to choose one plan. They voted to form councils at the local level but also to keep the central business committee for "negotiation with the government." This committee would operate under an unofficial constitution; how the two groups would function together was unclear.[69] Again, the Choctaws opted for the most flexible plan and for more than one governing organization.

The matter of a tribal government lay dormant over the next few years, although the Office of Indian Affairs directed the local agency to begin purchasing lands. When the Interior Department solicitor authorized these purchases, he also ruled that the Choctaws were still not a recognized tribe and could not access the revolving credit funds that would enable economic development.[70] Agency superintendent Archie Hector pushed for an official IRA council through the end of his term in 1938, but to no avail.[71] Then, in 1944 the Shell Oil Company became interested in oil leases on Choctaw lands in the Pearl River district. After much legal wrangling, the reimbursable lands were reclassified as a reservation and the Choctaws declared a "tribe" so that a tribal council could negotiate oil leases.[72]

The second TBC disbanded, and the Choctaws elected a tribal council. Following the example of the all-inclusive Mississippi Choctaw Indian Federation, these representatives then called meetings in their communities to gather input for the new constitution. On April 20, 1945, the Choctaws approved this council and constitution, 346 to 71, and the Mississippi Choctaw became a "tribe" under the Indian Reorganization Act.[73] The new council consisted of four members of the original Tribal Business Committee and five men who had not previously held leadership positions beyond their communities.[74] Joe Chitto remained a prominent figure in Choctaw politics, serving as tribal council chairman in the 1950s.[75]

Although Chitto could not keep alive his dream of the Mississippi Choctaw Indian Federation, the campaign demonstrated the Choctaws' continuing political acumen. The interactions of the Choctaws with their political allies and elected officials reinforced their position as constituents within Mississippi political networks. What happened to the Mississippi Choctaw Welfare Association is unclear from official records, but over the next decades the Choctaws would continue to work with their elected officials to bring federal funds into the state. The Choctaws' political allies were true to promises to mitigate "the industrial disadvantage incidental to their racial and educational disadvantages," helping them cope with rural poverty and discrimination. In upholding the federation as one means of asserting their interests, the Mississippi Choctaws maneuvered around the Office of Indian Affairs and used the implementation of the Indian Reorganization Act to strengthen their relationship with Mississippi's elected officials.

Acknowledgments

For their assistance in formulating this analysis, I would like to thank the editors of and contributors to this volume, Kathryn Abbott, Brian Hosmer, the students in History 4440 in spring 2005 at Tennessee Tech, and the members of the Newberry Library Lannan Summer Seminar in Indian Political Activism, with special thanks to Fred Hoxie and Mike Tsosie. I would also like to acknowledge the support of the American Philosophical Society, which awarded me a Phillips Fund Grant for Native American Research.

Notes

1. Loretta Fowler, "Politics," in *A Companion to the Anthropology of American Indians*, Blackwell Companions to Anthropology (Malden, MA: Blackwell Publishing, 2004), 69–94.

2. For example, see Thomas Biolsi, *Organizing the Lakota: The Political Economy of the New Deal on the Pine Ridge and Rosebud Reservations* (Tucson: University of Arizona Press, 1992).

3. Lawrence Kelly, *The Navajo Indians and Federal Indian Policy, 1900–1935* (Tucson: University of Arizona Press, 1968); Donald Parman, *The Navajos and the New Deal* (New Haven, CT: Yale University Press, 1976); Kenneth Philp, *John Collier's Crusade for Indian Reform, 1920–1954* (Tucson: University of Arizona Press, 1977); Graham Taylor, *The New Deal and American Indian Tribalism: The Administration of the Indian Reorganization Act, 1934–1945* (Lincoln: University of Nebraska Press, 1980); Lawrence Hauptman, *The Iroquois and the New Deal* (Syracuse, NY: Syracuse University Press, 1981); Vine Deloria Jr. and Clifford Lytle, *The Nations Within: The Past and Future of American Indian Sovereignty* (New York: Pantheon Books, 1984); and Kenneth Philp, *Termination Revisited: American Indians on the Trail to Self-Determination, 1933–1953* (Lincoln: University of Nebraska Press, 1999).

4. E. T. Winston, vice president of the MS Choctaw Indian Welfare Association (MCWA), to Commissioner of Indian Affairs (CIA) John Collier, 24 July 1936, record group 75 (RG 75): records of the Bureau of Indian Affairs, central classified files (CCF), Choctaw: 150-54948-1933, National Archives and Records Administration (NARA), Washington DC.

5. CCF: 068-9544A-1936: 19 May 1934, The Mississippi Choctaw Indian Federation (MCIF) to The Honorable Senators Pat Harrison and Hubert D. Stevens and Congressmen Ross Collins, Wall Doxey, W. M. Whittington, John E. Rankin, Jeff Busby, William M. Colmer, and Russell Elizey (hereafter cited as the *Mississippi congressional delegation*); CCF: 150-54948-1933: 31 July 1934, Winston to CIA; CCF: 150-54948-1933: 21 August 1934, Choctaw superintendent Archie C. Hector to CIA; quotation from E. T. Winston, "Choctaws Turn to Friends among Pale Faces in Effort to Recapture Old Glories," *The Memphis Commercial Appeal*, August 21, 1934, no page number, clipping with the file.

6. CCF: 068-9544A-1936: 19 May 1934, MCIF to the Mississippi congressional delegation.

7. MCIF to the Mississippi congressional delegation. For a listing of the council members, see CCF: 150-54948-1933: 13 February 1934, Hector to CIA.

8. The Treaty of Dancing Rabbit Creek, Article 14, in Charles Kappler, ed., *Indian Affairs: Laws and Treaties*, vol. 2 (Washington DC, 1892), 222. Also see John Williams Wade, "The Removal of the Mississippi Choctaws," *Publications of the Mississippi Historical Society* 8 (1904): 397–426; and Ronald Satz, "From the Removal Treaty Onward," in *After Removal: The Choctaw in Mississippi*, ed. Samuel Wells and Roseanna Tubby (Jackson: University of Mississippi Press, 1986), 3.

9. The seven Choctaw communities are Pearl River, Standing Pine, Red Water, Bogue Homo, Bogue Chitto, Conehatta, and Tucker.

10. "Condition of the Mississippi Choctaws," hearings at Union, MS, March 16, 1917; *Congress, House, Hearings before the Committee on Investigation of the Indian Service, March 12–14, 1917*, vol. I (Washington DC: Government Printing Office [GPO], 1917), 117–178; CCF: 806-38014: *A Study of the Social and Economic Condition of the Choctaw Indians in Mississippi in Relation to the Educational Programs*, May 1935, by Joe Jennings, superintendent of Indian schools, eastern area, Vernon L. Beggs, supervisor of Indian education, and A. B. Caldwell, superintendent of Indian education, Lake states area; Clara Sue Kidwell, *Choctaws and Missionaries in Mississippi, 1818–1918* (Norman: University of Oklahoma Press, 1995), chapter 8–epilogue; Clara Sue Kidwell, "Choctaw Women and Cultural Persistence in Mississippi," in *Negotiators of Change: Historical Perspectives on Native American Women*, ed. Nancy Shoemaker (New York: Routledge, Inc., 1995), 115–134.

11. CCF: 068-9544A-1936: summer 1934, *Questionnaire on Tribal Organization*.

12. CCF: 100-98178-1922: 14 May 1927, Choctaw superintendent R. J. Enochs to CIA.

13. CCF: 100-98178-1922: 14 May 1927, Enochs to CIA.

14. CCF: 150-54948-1933: 10 June 1934, Hector to Collier.

15. CCF: 150-54948-1933: 30 April 1934, Joe Chitto to Collier.

16. CCF: 150-54948-1933: 7 June 1934, Collier to Chitto.

17. CCF: 150-54948-1933: 10 June 1934, Hector to Collier.

18. CCF: 150-54948-1933: 30 July 1934, Collier to the Choctaw Tribal Business Committee.

19. CCF: 150-54948-1933: 30 July 1934, Collier to Chitto. The petition of July 14, 1934, was filed with the letter to Chitto.

20. CCF: 150-54948-1933: 30 July 1934, Collier to Choctaw Tribal Business Committee, Collier to Hector, and Collier to Chitto.

21. CCF: 150-54948-1933: 14 August 1934, Chitto to Hector; 16 August 1934, Chitto to Collier.

22. CCF: 150-54948-1933: 14 August 1934, Chitto to Hector.

23. Kidwell, *Choctaws and Missionaries*, passim. The Choctaws' fluid conceptions of power are skillfully analyzed in Greg O'Brien's *Choctaws in a Revolutionary Age, 1750–1830* (Lincoln: University of Nebraska Press, 2002).

24. CCF: 150-54948-1933: 16 August 1934, Chitto to Collier.

25. CCF: 150-54948-1933: 16 August 1934, Chitto to Collier.

26. CCF: 150-54948-1933: 16 August 1934, Chitto to Collier.

27. John Swanton, *Source Material for the Social and Ceremonial Life of the Choctaw Indians*, Bureau of American Ethnology, Bulletin 103 (Washington DC: GPO, 1931), 96–102; Angie

Debo, *The Rise and Fall of the Choctaw Republic*, 2d ed. (Norman: University of Oklahoma Press, 1961), 21; and O'Brien, *Choctaws in a Revolutionary Age*, 31.

28. CCF: 800-4313-1951: 20 February–20 March 1936, report of Edna Groves, supervisor of home economics.

29. CCF: 068-9544A-36: *The Constitution of the Mississippi Choctaw Indian Federation, 1934.*

30. CCF: 150-54948-1933: 11 September 1934, Senator Earl Richardson to Collier.

31. For an analysis of Indian diplomacy and treaty language, see Robert Williams Jr., *Linking Arms Together: American Indian Treaty Visions of Law and Peace, 1600–1800* (New York and London: Routledge, 1999), chapter 2.

32. CCF: 150-54948-1933: 20 August 1934, Chitto to Collier. Chitto quoted Cobb's speech from Colonel John F. H. Claiborne, *Mississippi as a Province, Territory, and State*, vol. 1 (Jackson, MS: Power and Barksdale, Publishers and Printers, 1880; Baton Rouge: Louisiana State University Press, 1964), 512–513. The original speech may be found in *Niles Weekly Register* 64 (April 29, 1843): 131–132.

33. See Williams, *Linking Arms*, chapter 3.

34. CCF: 150-54948-1933: 20 August 1934, Chitto to Collier.

35. CCF: 150-54948-1933: 21 August 1934, Hector to Collier, including press clippings from the *Meridian Star*, July 30, 1934, the *Memphis Commercial Appeal*, August 21, 1934, and the *Daily Jackson News*, September, 10, 1934; 1 December 1934, Hector to A. J. Shippe, director of extension services, noting the congressman who attended the ceremony.

36. CCF: 150-54948-1933: 21 August 1934, Hector to Collier.

37. CCF: 150-54948-1933: 14 March 1934, Hector to Collier; CCF: 919-70945-38: 12 September 1934, Hector to Collier.

38. CCF: 150-54948-1933: clipping from the *Daily Jackson News*, "Choctaw Lovers of Land: Legend Surrounds Start," September 10, 1934; "The Story of Neshoba" by R. L. Breland, *The Neshoba County Democrat*, February 1, 1935, in vertical files: Indians, Neshoba County Library, Philadelphia, MS.

39. John Peterson Jr., "The Mississippi Band of Choctaw Indians: Their Recent History and Current Relations" (Ph.D. diss., University of Georgia, 1970), 13, 220.

40. See William Sidney Coker, "Pat Harrison's Efforts to Reopen the Choctaw Citizenship Rolls," *Southern Quarterly* 3 (October 1965): 36–61.

41. CCF: 068-9544A-36: 19 May 1934, the MCIF to the Mississippi congressional delegation.

42. CCF: 150-54948-1933: 31 July 1934, Winston to Collier.

43. Winston quotation from CCF: 150-54948-1933: clipping from the *Daily Jackson News*, "Choctaw Lovers of Land: Legend Surrounds Start," September 10, 1934.

44. For an analysis of the impact of the New Deal in the South, see James Cobb and Michael Namorato, eds., *The New Deal and the South* (Jackson: University Press of Mississippi, 1984).

45. CCF: 150-54948-1933: clipping from the *Daily Jackson News*, "Choctaw Lovers of Land: Legend Surrounds Start" September 10, 1934; "The Story of Neshoba" by R. L. Breland, *The Neshoba County Democrat*, February 1, 1935, in vertical files: Indians, Neshoba County Library, Philadelphia, MS.

46. Peterson, "The Mississippi Band of Choctaw Indians," 13–14.

47. CCF: 150-54948-1933: clipping from the *Daily Jackson News*, "Choctaw Lovers of Land:

Legend Surrounds Start," September 10, 1934.

48. See Pete Daniel, "Federal Farm Policy and the End of an Agrarian Way of Life," in *Major Problems in the History of the American South*, vol. 2, *The New South*, ed. Paul Escott and David Goldfield (Lexington, MA: D. C. Heath and Company, 1990), 397–406. For further information on the New Deal South, see the essays in Elna Green, ed., *The New Deal and Beyond: Social Welfare in the South since 1930* (Athens: University of Georgia Press, 2003).

49. CCF: 150-54948-1933: 31 July 1934, Winston to Collier.

50. CCF: 150-54948-1933: 29 August 1934, memorandum to extension, no signature.

51. CCF: 150-54948-1933: 7 August 1934, Hector to Collier.

52. CCF: 150-54948-1933: 20 August 1934, Hector to Collier.

53. CCF: 150-54948-1933: 14 August 1934, Chitto to Hector.

54. CCF: 150-54948-1933: 20 August 1934, Hector to Collier.

55. CCF: 150-54948-1933: 10 June, 7, 20, and 21 August, 25 September 1934, Hector to Collier; 1 December 1934, Hector to Shippe.

56. CCF: 150-54948-1933: 1 April 1935, Hector to Collier.

57. CCF: 150-54948-1933: 1 April 1935, Hector to CIA; 21 February 1936, Collier to Winston. If Chitto was behind the boycott of the vote at Bogue Chitto, he was unaware that abstaining from voting was registered as a yes vote.

58. CCF: 150-54948-1933: 29 December 1934, Hector to Collier.

59. CCF: 150-54948-1933: 29 December 1934, Hector to Collier.

60. On the continued activities of the MCIF, see CCF: 150-54948-1933: 13 November 1935 and 24 February 1936, Winston to CIA; 21 February 1936, Collier to Winston.

61. CCF: 057-21159-1935: 15 April 1934, memo of Byrd Issac, secretary, TBC.

62. For the gradual diminishment of the Pearl River strike, see CCF: 134-48712-33: 18 June 1935, Hector to Collier.

63. For the petition, see CCF: 134-48712-33: 4 June 1935, Henry Jim et al. to Senators Theodore Bilbo and Pat Harrison and Congressmen Bill Colmer and Albert Dunn. For the Bogue Homa school strike, see CCF: 134-48712-33: 11 June 1935, S. Keyzer, teacher at Bogue Homa Day School, to Hector.

64. CCF: 134-48712-33: 4 June 1935, Henry Jim et al. to Bilbo, Harrison, Colmer, and Dunn; 8 June 1935, Comer to Collier. Winston frequently copied his correspondence with the office to these individuals.

65. CCF: 150-54948-1933: 1 December 1934, Hector to Shippe.

66. CCF: 150-54948-1933: 26 June 1936, Joe Jennings to Collier.

67. CCF: 150-54948-1933: 21 September 1936, Jennings to Collier.

68. CCF: 150-54948-1933: 21 September 1936, Jennings to Collier.

69. CCF: 150-54948-1933: 21 September 1936, Jennings and Charlotte T. Westwood to Collier.

70. Nathan Margold, solicitor, Department of the Interior, memorandum for the Office of Indian Affairs, August 31, 1936, RG 279, ICC docket 52, box 620, entry 11UD.

71. CCF: 150-54984-1933: 4 November 1937, Hector to CIA; CCF: 068-9545-1936: 20 March 1940 and 3 June 1940, Stewart to CIA.

72. On oil interests, see CCF: 066-9545-1936: 18 April 1944, Walter V. Woehlke to Jennings;

24 April 1944, Mr. Reeves, for Joe Jennings; 21 August 1944, Jennings to Choctaw superintendent Archie H. McMullen; 4 May 1945, McMullen to CIA; 22 May 1945, Oscar Chapman, assistant secretary, to McMullen; 5 July 1973, Baxter York interview by the staff of *Nanih Waiyah*, Southeastern Indian Oral History Project, University of Florida, in vertical file: Choctaw Indians, Neshoba County Library, Philadelphia, MS.

73. CCF: 066-9545-1936: 15 February 1944, McMullen to CIA; CCF: 068-9544A-1936: 4 May 1945, McMullen to CIA.

74. CCF: 066-9544-1936: 5 January 1945, tribal council to CIA.

75. CCF: 066-9544-1936: 5 January 1945, tribal council to CIA; 14 November 1951, Chitto to W. O. Roberts, area director, Muskogee, OK, file: "Miss. Band of Choctaw Indians, 1951–53." Entry 327: Office of Tribal Operations, office files of Tribal Affairs officer, 1947–65, box 43, RG 75: Five Civilized Tribes Agency, National Archive and Records Administration, Southwest Region, Fort Worth, TX (NARA-SW).

7 Terminating the Choctaws

Clara Sue Kidwell (Choctaw)

After World War II, the federal government launched the termination policy (see table 3). Though couched in the rhetoric of liberation, it sought nothing less than the complete destruction of tribal sovereignty. Not until the 1960s, primarily because of pressure exerted by Indian and non-Indian advocacy organizations, did Congress begin to embrace self-determination. By the 1970s and 1980s, several locally orchestrated grassroots movements led to the restoration of many terminated tribes' legal relationships with the federal government (see Part II introduction). Clara Sue Kidwell's analysis of the Choctaw Nation of Oklahoma demonstrates that, for some communities, the threat posed by termination did not actually end there. By carrying the narrative into the mid-1970s, and into a region that has heretofore been neglected by scholars, she reveals that termination's reach extended beyond the conventional chronological and spatial boundaries that have been established for it. Moreover, Kidwell shows that, when viewed from within a community, resistance to termination can be seen as an impetus for tribal nationalism.[1]

When the Congress of the United States in 1953 announced its policy to terminate its relationships with Indian tribes (see table 3), Harry J. W. Belvin, the federally appointed chief of the Choctaw Nation in Oklahoma, was ready for the change.[2] The Choctaw Nation had endured the impact of Andrew Jackson's Indian Removal policy between 1831 and 1832, when the majority of its citizens made the long trek from their aboriginal homelands in Mississippi to the Indian Territory west of the Mississippi River. In 1897 its leaders had agreed to the allotment of the Choctaw Nation's land base under the congressional mandate to the Dawes Commission, culminating in the Curtis Act in 1898 (see table 1). Its courts were dissolved, and the federal government took control of its school system. In 1906 Congress delivered the ultimate coup de grâce in a law providing for the dissolution of the tribal governments of the Choctaws, Chickasaws, Cherokees, Creeks, and Seminoles as a prelude to Oklahoma statehood in 1907. The power to appoint Choctaw National chiefs now rested with the president of the United States.

This is all to say that after 1907 the Choctaw Nation existed politically only as a shadow government to oversee the final disposition of the remaining unallotted land and coal and asphalt deposits in tribal holdings.[3] Those assets, viewed by the federal government as mere remnants of property to be disposed of, would become the basis of Choctaw political identity and Harry Belvin's political agenda in the 1950s. The organic act establishing the state of Oklahoma specifically recognized that the remaining lands of the Five Tribes were still under federal supervision, not that of the state. Moreover, Congress never acted to dissolve the boundaries established by the original treaties with the Choctaws, and it has been argued that there are, indeed, still reservations in Oklahoma, despite widespread sentiment to the contrary.[4] Under the legislation of 1906, the appointed governors of the Five Tribes in eastern Oklahoma were subject to a congressionally mandated relationship with the Bureau of Indian Affairs (BIA).[5] That mandate maintained the paternalistic control exercised by the BIA over Indian people during the late nineteenth century. To Harry Belvin, the federal termination policy thus offered not a threat to tribal identity, but an opportunity to escape the control of the BIA.

In the 1950s the Choctaw Nation in Oklahoma persisted in the families, communities, language, and cultural identity that survived the assimilation policy embodied in the Curtis Act. In the early twentieth century, many Choctaws in southeastern Oklahoma lived in small rural enclaves, where they raised crops and some cattle. They could no longer be self-sufficient. They were now dependent on a market economy. Those who could raise cotton averaged $54.40 in yearly income, and those who grew corn averaged $20.10.[6] The Curtis Act had provided approximately 320 acres to each Choctaw citizen, 160 acres as a homestead protected in trust and the remainder as surplus land they could sell. Many Choctaws took those allotments far to the west in the rich farming and grazing lands of the Chickasaw Nation, where they leased the land to white ranchers and lived primarily off rental income.[7] In the southeastern part, those around the Durant area, mainly mixed bloods, raised crops of peanuts, cotton, and feed grains. Choctaw homesteads in this area were, for the most part, poorly suited for agriculture.

Full-blood Choctaws in the mountains clung to community and language, becoming a kind of backwash in the wave of post–World War II American prosperity. Communities continued a loosely knit structure of government in the form of councils in each Oklahoma county within the boundaries of the old Choctaw Nation.[8] Christianity was a pervasive influence in community life. In missionary churches, Choctaws often sang hymns and listened to preaching and Scripture reading in the Choctaw language. The churches became a last bastion of Choctaw language because many young people were not learning Choctaw in their own homes.[9]

By the early 1950s many Choctaw allottees had lost their lands to taxation or sale. Although one scholar described the lifestyle of Choctaws on allotted land as "a picture of appalling social and economic degradation," they represented a largely culturally intact, full-blood lifestyle of subsistence hunting and farming, albeit judged against the standards of 1950s American society.[10] The problem was that subsistence had given way to the market economy, within which families could not meet all their needs.

In typically bureaucratic fashion, the Bureau of Indian Affairs attempted in the 1940s to address problems of poverty among Choctaws in southeastern Oklahoma by devising a project whereby Choctaws would raise sheep. The women would weave cloth out of the wool, and the men could sell the excess. The project provided the occasion for social activity among women, but it did not develop into an economically viable cooperative enterprise and was abandoned.[11]

The failure of such projects inspired Congress to pursue its termination policy. If it could not assimilate Indians economically, the government would simply leave them to the forces of American society, to survive as they could with the resources they had. In preparation for the change, Congress in 1946 established the Indian Claims Commission as a way of settling outstanding Indian claims to clear the way for termination (see table 3).[12] The commission's decisions were to be based on matters of fact, as well as of law, thus opening the door to the doctrine of liberal interpretation that was unique to Indian treaty litigation. It was also Congress's way of settling Indian claims with payments that would finally enable it to terminate its relationship with Indian tribes. The Court of Indian Claims, by mandating money payments to satisfy Indian land claims, would divide communal assets on an individual basis and would give Indians individual payments. Per capita payments represented the ultimate goal of the United States government to foster individual interest among Indians.[13]

The Choctaw Nation had pursued its claims against the federal government for unfulfilled treaty provisions since the early 1830s (the Net Proceeds case). In 1881 it finally gained access to the US Court of Claims with its claims for the proceeds of the sale of its lands east of the Mississippi River, ultimately winning a favorable judgment. After the Civil War, the Choctaw pursued their claims for the value of the western lands they had ceded for the settlement of western Indian tribes (the Leased District case).[14] The Indian Claims Commission gave the Choctaw Nation a new legal venue for its claims, but the length of the judgment process and the promise of per capita payments led some Choctaws to become disillusioned with the idea of a tribal government during the early twentieth century.

Choctaw political identity in the early twentieth century depended on the coal and asphalt deposits that had been reserved as communal resources both in the 1897 Atoka agreement and the 1902 supplementary agreement that was to expedite the allotment of land. The 1902 agreement called for the sale of the communally held coal and asphalt reserves within two years. The government alternately offered the lands for sale and rejected offers for it. In 1948, after lengthy debate, Congress finally carried out the terms of the 1902 agreement by agreeing to buy the Choctaw coal and asphalt for $8 million. The House appropriations bill authorized only $1.5 million, however, and Senator Elmer Thomas of Oklahoma had to wage a determined fight for the full amount.[15]

The Indian Claims Commission Act set the stage for per capita distributions of the proceeds of Indian land. The congressional purchase of Choctaw coal and asphalt seemed to indicate the ultimate demise of the Choctaw Nation in a flurry of claims for individual payments. Senator Elmer Thomas received a steady stream of letters inquiring about the progress of legislation concerning the sale of the coal and asphalt.[16] Some Choctaws who were aware of the 1902 agreement expressed their concerns. O. W. Folsom wrote to Thomas, asking him to do his "duty": "to cause them to pay the full amount we have waited for settlement 47 years."[17]

Some Choctaws had given up on the idea of a tribal government altogether. Kathleen Hunter, a Choctaw living in Oklahoma City, wrote to Elmer Thomas: "It was provided long ago that the tribal estate be wound up, and the residue of properties be converted into cash and paid out to the individual allottees.... We want the tribal government dissolved and such waste discontinued. I am a widow and have three children to support and need my proportionate share of these properties now." Victor Locke, who had been the first federally appointed chief in 1911, declared that "the Choctaw people regard the continuation of the tribal government as a useless ornament, costly to these Indian people and the sooner disposed of by the Government the better will be the outcome from a financial standpoint to all concerned."[18] To what extent Locke spoke for Choctaw people generally is questionable, but his views and Mrs. Hunter's, spanning the first half of the twentieth century, reflect a distinct sense of individualism and a basic distrust of any organized tribal government. When finally approved, the $8.5 million payment for the coal and asphalt in 1948, plus the more than $1 million in the Choctaw trust fund, would amount to a per capita payment of approximately $330 to each tribal member.[19]

The sale took place on the watch of Chief Harry Belvin. He had established his political credentials in southeastern Oklahoma as a county commissioner in Bryan County and had lobbied actively for the position of chief of the Choctaws.[20] The per capita distribution of the payment for the coal and asphalt took place between 1949 and 1952.[21] Ostensibly, then, the Choctaw claims on the federal government were settled.

Belvin, however, found new sources for Choctaw claims against the government. In 1951 he took a claim of $753,609.41 to the Indian Claims Commission. The claim was for charges that the federal government had levied against the Choctaw Nation in connection with the sale of its assets in the course of the Net Proceeds and Leased District claims, as well as $38,416.27 for expenses incurred with the sale of the coal and asphalt. The Indian Claims Commission rejected the suit because the US Court of Claims had already rejected it and the Choctaws' lawyers had no new evidence to present.[22]

For individual Choctaws, the failure of the tribe's suit against the government went largely unnoticed as they collected their per capita payments from the coal sale. For Belvin, political ambition to preserve the Choctaw Nation led him to create a democratically elected tribal council and Choctaw councils in each of ten counties in southeastern Oklahoma. Also, he had plans for a constitution to reestablish a functioning tribal government. But many Choctaws saw no need for a tribal government. Indeed, they felt that it was an unnecessary expense. Belvin maintained that the Bureau of Indian Affairs recognized his tribal council, and he sought its sanction for his recommendations. Ultimately, though, the director of the Bureau of Indian Affairs opposed his efforts as well. The coal sale seemingly ended the last reason to maintain any form of Choctaw government.[23]

The situation was complicated by Belvin's relationship, which was both ideologically and personally antagonistic, with the area director for the Muskogee area office. Belvin accused Paul Fickinger of being "very dilatory in pursuing his duty" with regard to sale of the Choctaw resources. Of particular concern to the Choctaw principal chief was the fact that Fickinger had not secured a final appraisal of the remaining Choctaw unallotted land so that it could be offered for sale.[24]

Harry Belvin then made a critical political move. He turned away from Fickinger and the Indian bureau and appealed to Oklahoma representative Carl Albert for a bill that would terminate BIA authority over the approximately 7,000 remaining acres of unallotted Choctaw land, the final remnant of Choctaw political identity. The bill would still allow individual Choctaws to be eligible for various federal services, primarily access to federal loan programs. Carl Albert presented his bill as a supplement to the original 1906 act for the disposition of the affairs of the Five Civilized Tribes. It would apply only to the remaining Choctaw assets: a paltry three-quarters interest in 7,731 acres of unallotted tribal land, 8,610 acres purchased for the tribe and held in trust by the federal government, and one-half of the mineral rights in these lands. These assets would be placed in a corporation to be organized under state law. Belvin held out hope to his constituency, remarking that "one never knows where oil might be found in Oklahoma."[25] He thus expressed an optimism common among Oklahoma state landowners, that wealth was right around the corner. The proceeds of the sale of this land, together with the approximately $433,000 in the tribal trust account, would be distributed in a per capita payment to the living tribal members on the Dawes rolls and to their heirs.[26] Albert's law would also terminate federal supervision over Belvin's appointed Choctaw government.[27]

It is important to note that Harry Belvin did not intend to cut off government services to the Choctaws. Nonetheless, his political strategy fit into federal policy in the 1950s, which sought to terminate relationships between the US government and Indian tribes.[28] Representative Carl Albert reassured his Choctaw constituents that "this was not a general termination bill."[29] The majority of tribal members who expressed any opinion on the matter were interested in the distribution of tribal funds on an individual basis, that is, per capita payments.[30] The transition from tribal to individual identity for Choctaws seemed to be virtually complete. Although Albert's bill reaffirmed the existence of a tribal entity, it was now based on a vestige of original tribal communal land holding, and it was a political one with decision-making powers over limited communal assets, instead of a governing body over a group of people.[31]

Belvin's termination scheme proved, however, to be a replay of the Atoka agreement of 1897 and its 1902 supplement. Then, issues of determining tribal membership slowed the process of allotment, and the government's failure to dispose of the coal and asphalt thwarted the final dissolution of the tribal government. After 1959 Belvin's plan would fail because of circumstances arising from the 1902 agreement. It proved almost impossible for the federal government to identify and locate the heirs of the original allottees and to clear title to land for the sale of the mineral reserves beneath it.

More important, the Bureau of Indian Affairs, contrary to Albert's assurances and Belvin's understanding, interpreted the act as a complete termination of the federal relationship, including Choctaw access to services provided by the BIA. The 1959 act negated the terms of the Oklahoma Indian Welfare Act and the Indian Reorganization Act (see table 2, 1934). If passed, it would mean that Choctaws would no longer be eligible for loans from the Bureau of Indian Affairs.[32] Suddenly, the termination that Belvin had seen as a move toward political freedom transformed into a threat to Choctaw access to economic resources.[33]

Further complicating matters, Harry Belvin confronted this ironic turn of events in the midst of a surge of political consciousness among American Indians throughout the United States (see tables 3 and 4). That consciousness grew with other concerns in American society, such as the civil rights movement, the growing awareness of the level of American involvement in the civil war in Vietnam, and an attempt to address the economic disparity between men and women. The American Indian Chicago Conference in June 1961 signaled the increased involvement of Native scholars, community leaders, anthropologists, and social scientists in the burgeoning reform movement.[34] In the general social turmoil of the 1960s, a new sense of Indian nationalism began to emerge. It expressed itself in the idea that grassroots people were capable of effecting change in American government and their own communities through organized political action. Moreover, as Robert K. Thomas, a Cherokee anthropologist, attested by likening Indian reservations to "internal colonies," it connected Native issues to larger global processes such as decolonization (Cobb, chapter 9, this volume).[35]

In Oklahoma, this heightened Indian political awareness manifested in a new organization, Oklahomans for Indian Opportunity (OIO). OIO grew out of President Lyndon Johnson's War on Poverty, a key component of which was the Office of Economic Opportunity (OEO), with its commitment to grassroots political activism to solve problems of poverty at the community level (see table 4, 1964). Community Action Programs (CAP) gave local people control over federally funded programs intended to improve the economic situation in their communities. Senator Fred Harris of Oklahoma, elected in 1964, was one of Johnson's strong supporters for the OEO program. Harris, son of a sharecropper, was born and raised in Walters, Oklahoma. His wife, LaDonna, was also born and raised in Walters, by her Comanche grandparents. She supported her husband through law school, campaigned with him as he ran for the senate, and used his office to advance their mutual commitment to promoting the access of American Indians in Oklahoma to the economic advantages of American society.[36]

In 1965 Fred and LaDonna Harris decided that the best way to accomplish their goals would be through the programs of the Office of Economic Opportunity. Convinced that the Bureau of Indian Affairs was not helping Indians, they used the resources of Senator Harris's Washington office and Mrs. Harris's position as a member of the executive board of the Southwest Center for Human Relations at the University of Oklahoma to convene a conference on the university campus.[37] They argued that federal programs administered by the Bureau of Indian Affairs were aimed primarily at reservation communities and that the unique status of Oklahoma tribes who did not have extensive land bases meant that they were not served by many of these programs. Also, the historic division between the Five Tribes in the eastern part of the state and the tribes in the western part, who had been settled there in the latter part of the nineteenth century, meant that no real basis for unified action existed among Oklahoma Indians.[38]

More than five hundred people gathered in Norman on August 14, 1965, and became the initial membership of the new organization. Among them was Harry J. W. Belvin, who was elected to a five-year term on the board of directors.[39] Other representatives included the directors of the Anadarko and Muskogee area offices of the Bureau of Indian Affairs. Although the Harrises used the Office of Economic Opportunity as their primary funding source, they saw the political advantages of cooperating with the bureau, not only to create a broad-based organization but also to be able to put pressure on the agency to carry out its responsibilities to Indians in areas such as housing and education. Oklahomans for Indian Opportunity also put a significant emphasis on youth programs, sponsoring community youth councils and statewide meetings that brought high school and college students together to hear speakers, hold elections, and, in general, practice skills of public speaking and political action.

The Harrises were a high-profile Washington political couple because of their youth, attractiveness, and vocal stand on Indian issues, but also because of their increasing criticism of American involvement in the Vietnam war and equally firm support of Lyndon Johnson's controversial antipoverty programs. LaDonna Harris became the first wife of a politician to appear before a congressional committee, when she testified against abolition of the Office of Economic Opportunity.[40] Suddenly, LaDonna and Fred Harris, not the tribal chairmen of the state, seemed to be the main spokespeople for Indian issues in Oklahoma, and inevitable tensions arose within the multifaceted leadership of Oklahomans for Indian Opportunity.[41]

The Harrises' outspokenness may have caused them to be perceived as threatening to established tribal leaders, but the actions taken by OIO at the local level exacerbated tensions. Iola Hayden, a Comanche tribal member and distant relative of LaDonna Harris, had become executive director of the organization in 1965, and she had invited Robert K. Thomas to speak at a summer OIO youth camp. Thomas was controversial because his work with a Cherokee literacy project in eastern Oklahoma had stirred up community opinions against the tribal government. Thomas's writings and growing reputation as an Indian activist threatened the status quo in Indian relationships with the federal government. Some Indian people viewed OIO as too "radical" for its own good and not responsive to direct community needs.[42]

In 1969 Oklahomans for Indian Opportunity received a grant from the Office of Economic Opportunity for a Rural Poverty Demonstration project. In the Choctaw area, it established community groups to buy groceries in bulk for discounted prices and funded a feeder pig cooperative organization. OIO used federal funds to encourage a sense of community activism during the time that Harry Belvin was committed to establishing a corporate form of Choctaw government with limited resources and the distribution of tribal assets on a per capita basis. OIO gave Choctaw communities new resources not tied to the Bureau of Indian Affairs. Now Oklahomans for Indian Opportunity and the Bureau of Indian Affairs were in competition for the attention and allegiance of Indian people, although OIO director Iola Hayden denied that there was any competition, "because we do not have that kind of money."[43]

Harry Belvin, as Choctaw chief, was a member of the OIO board of directors and soon realized that the organization threatened his own political agenda. Oklahomans for Indian Opportunity was having its own problems. By 1968 LaDonna Harris had left the organization to concentrate her energy in Washington DC. Belvin chaired a special personnel committee of the OIO board to investigate charges that Iola Taylor, executive director, had alienated staff members, causing significant staff turnover, and had ignored applications from community groups for funding. Belvin's report declared that Oklahomans for Indian Opportunity "was shot through and through with politics, favoritism, prejudice, and mismanagement." Equally clear was that OIO's activities in developing community groups and promoting Choctaw identity contradicted Belvin's vision of the Choctaw Nation as a simple corporate entity.[44]

Oklahomans for Indian Opportunity challenged Belvin's authority by creating community-level political activities, such as buying clubs that brought community members together to place bulk orders with grocers to get discount prices. OIO's educational activities with Indian students smacked of "militancy," a term that became shorthand for overt challenge to the American government, a stance that was anathema to Choctaws who had grown up in the assimilationist era of the late nineteenth and early twentieth centuries.[45] It was OIO's independence that irked Belvin the most.

He wrote a vituperative letter to William Bozman, accusing OIO officials of overstepping their bounds. What Belvin feared most was that OIO's program might be "designed to foster confusion among the people, to teach prejudice and hate, to fight the Government and its agencies, and the Tribal leadership."[46] Belvin, having found that his attempt at self-determination through termination would not produce the desired effects, was now trying to maintain a good relationship with the Bureau of Indian Affairs. This was a more likely scenario since Virgil Harrington, an Oklahoma Choctaw, had been appointed area director for the Eastern Area Office in Muskogee in 1965.[47]

By 1969 Belvin found himself under attack by members of his own council. Delos Wade asked pointed questions about the chief's salary and the tribe's landholdings and accused Belvin of withholding information from tribal members. Belvin promptly accused him of "disloyalty" and fired him from the council.[48] The termination issue was costing him political capital. Another attack came from outside the boundaries of the old nation in southeastern Oklahoma. Although the Choctaw population in Oklahoma City numbered only 119 (according to an OIO survey conducted in 1967), it was enough to give credence to the Oklahoma City Council of Choctaws.[49] This council published a mimeographed newsletter that became the medium of vigorous attacks on Belvin, on the expenses of maintaining a government, and on the fact of a federally appointed chief.[50] The council's leader was Charles Brown, who identified himself as a full blood. Politics and culture became intertwined in the power struggle over termination. The exchange provided a basis for a new Choctaw political identity, one especially important in light of President Richard Nixon's repudiation of the termination policy of the 1950s and Oklahoma senator Henry Bellmon's legislation giving the Five Tribes in Oklahoma the power to select their own leaders.[51]

As early as 1967 Belvin began asking Oklahoma congressman Ed Edmondson to sponsor legislation to repeal the termination legislation. The act was unworkable because heirs of original allottees could not be identified. Unless it was possible to establish a corporation by August 25, 1968, Choctaw mineral rights would be forfeit to owners of surface rights, and unclaimed funds would escheat to the United States Treasury. It was possible, as well, to dispose of tribal property under the terms of the original 1906 act. Also, "Repeal of the Act would be in accord with the majority opinions expressed in the 1966 and 1967 opinion polls."[52]

Opinion was building against the termination act. At a meeting at Camp Israel Folsom, near Bethel, on July 5, 1969, one speaker raised the issue of treaty rights, charging that past treaties between the Choctaw tribe and the federal government would have no effect because the Choctaw tribe would no longer exist in a legal sense.[53] Belvin defended the act, provided that it be significantly modified.

The original act had been set to expire in 1962 and had been twice amended to remain in effect so that there would be sufficient time for the sale of assets. The cumbersome processes of government, however, did not effect the liquidation of Choctaw assets, and the termination act severed government services to Choctaws. Belvin again sought to redefine the Choctaw relationship with the US government through the legislative process. He proposed to Oklahoma senator Mike Monroney that the 1959 act be amended to protect Choctaw tribal property but also to continue the office of principal chief and the tribe's tax exemption.[54]

Congress proceeded, instead, with the complete repeal of the termination legislation. The proposed sale of assets had created an administrative nightmare. Heirs of deceased allottees often proved difficult to find, contributing to the problems of clearing title to land. Many Choctaws expressed their desire to keep their tribal government. Retention of federal recognition was necessary for access to services for individual Choctaws, and repeal of the termination legislation was necessary for "the economic betterment of the tribe."[55]

Senator Fred Harris of Oklahoma also supported the repeal legislation. He noted that the 1959 act, as amended, would terminate the tribe as of August 25, 1970. His argument was premised on humanitarian grounds and a sense of the importance of tribal identity. He declared, "We now know that the actual results of termination are contrary to the well-being of the American Indian. The end of Federal assistance to the tribal entity destroys the Indian community and the Indian's sense of dignity."[56] Carl Albert, in his testimony before the House Committee on Interior and Insular Affairs, expressed a contrary opinion of the significance of the termination act—an economic one, that is, "that the Act will, when it becomes effective, terminate the eligibility of individual Choctaw members for certain federal services now provided Indians because of their status as Indians."[57]

The fallout of the proposed termination legislation for many individual Choctaws was a rise of political activism in the Choctaw Nation. An important source of the activism was the urban population in Oklahoma City. As early as the 1930s a number of Choctaws had moved from their rural homes to the major urban area in the state of Oklahoma. The Oklahoma City Council of Choctaws emerged under the leadership of Charles Brown, who became a vocal critic of Belvin and his Choctaw government. Brown portrayed his mimeographed newletter, "HELLO CHOCTAW," as the voice of the "Average Choctaw," to question Belvin's actions:

> For over 20 years...the Government has been appointing a "leader"
> for the Choctaw tribe.... For over 20 years the AVERAGE CHOCTAW
> has not known the NAMES of the people who actually got the money
> that was taken out of the AVERAGE CHOCTAW'S tribal funds.... For
> over 20 years the AVERAGE CHOCTAW has not known for sure how
> many thousands of dollars were taken out of his tribal funds in "annual
> budgets."... For over 20 years the AVERAGE CHOCTAW has not
> known how much of his tribal land was sold or how much it was sold
> for. Government "appointed" people had the power to sell the AVER-
> AGE CHOCTAW'S TRIBAL LANDS without the AVERAGE
> CHOCTAW even knowing his lands were being sold or how much they
> were being sold for.... The organization issued a challenge to Choctaws
> throughout the state to "organize YOUR OWN TRIBAL GROUP IN
> YOUR OWN COMMUNITY...."[58]

At issue in this new political climate was the Choctaws' ability to exercise their sovereignty through a popularly elected government. In the 1940s
tribal members demanded per capita payments and the complete dissolution of the tribal government. In 1959 the termination act eliminated popular election of tribal chiefs. Belvin, as the appointed chief, could retain
control over the political affairs of the nation. By the early 1970s, however,
an undated issue of Indian Affairs reported that "the Choctaws believe if
they can get rid of this rubber-stamp official they can voluntarily elect a
chief of their own...." The BIA's power to appoint the tribal chief was a
major infringement on the identity of the Choctaws as a self-governing people, and the newsletter urged Choctaws to organize their own clubs.[59] The
Oklahoma City council saw itself as a leader in initiating a tribal organization and enabling members to elect their own leader.[60]

This commitment to election was the major statement of a resurgent
sense of tribal self-government for the Choctaws. In the political foment
within the Choctaw Nation, a new statement for tribal identity emerged in
a constitution drafted by a young Choctaw man, Mike Charleston, whose
family was active in the Episcopal Church in Oklahoma City. The initial
paragraph expresses the hopes of a new generation of Choctaw leadership:

> The purpose of the Constitution of the Choctaw Nation is to provide
> unity and direction of efforts for the re-establishment of a traditional
> Choctaw Tribal Government. The constitution is the basis of a tribal
> government responsible to all of the Choctaw people and representative
> of their desires, interests, and needs; and it provides the structure and
> method necessary for the operation of the government. The writing and

> *distribution of this constitution is intended to act as a catalyst for the development of an acceptable tribal government resulting from the cooperation and actions of a great many Choctaw people.*[61]

Charleston's constitution was an eloquent statement for a generation of Choctaws who grew up in a period during which the federal policy was assimilation but who still retained a commitment to Choctaw tribal identity. Although financial advantage in the form of per capita payments drew many Choctaws away from tribal identity, in the 1970s the core of that tribal identity persisted, changed by political forces but still embedded in the lives of Choctaw communities in the old Choctaw territory and in the idealism of a younger generation.

The Choctaw Nation entered a market economy in the period after the Civil War and, as a result of the change, saw the transition of Choctaw identity to individualism and distribution of tribal resources in per capita payments. The communal land-holding pattern was destroyed, but a cultural sense of community remained. Economic poverty, in the American sense, represented a continuation of traditional Choctaw community ways of life. Political sovereignty and self-government emerged out of a conflict between the Bureau of Indian Affairs and its appointed leaders for the tribe and an emerging political activism rooted in rural community–based activity and an urban population that, although ostensibly acculturated, was vocally active in seeking Choctaw self-government in the form of popular elections.

Notes

1. Larry Burt, *Tribalism in Crisis: Federal Indian Policy, 1953–1961* (Albuquerque: University of New Mexico Press, 1982); Nicholas Peroff, *Menominee DRUMS: Tribal Termination and Restoration, 1954–1974* (Norman: University of Oklahoma Press, 1982); Donald Fixico, *Termination and Relocation: Federal Indian Policy, 1945–1960* (Albuquerque: University of New Mexico Press, 1986); Kenneth Philp, *Termination Revisited: American Indians on the Trail of Self-Determination, 1933–1953* (Lincoln: University of Nebraska Press, 1999); and R. Warren Metcalf, *Termination's Legacy: The Discarded Indians of Utah* (Lincoln: University of Nebraska Press, 2002).

2. Harry Belvin, *Choctaw Tribal Structure and Achievement, August 18, 1948, to August 25, 1975* (Durant, OK: Choctaw Bilingual Education Program, Southeastern Oklahoma State University, n.d.).

3. 30 Stat. L., 495, An Act for the protection of the people of the Indian Territory, and for other purposes, June 28, 1898 (The Curtis Act); 34 Stat. 137, 142, An Act to provide for the final disposition of the affairs of the Five Civilized Tribes in the Indian Territory, and for other purposes, April 26, 1906.

4. F. Browning Pipestem and G. William Rice, "The Mythology of the Oklahoma Indians: A Survey of the Legal Status of Indian Tribes in Oklahoma," *American Indian Law Review* 6, no. 2 (1978): 259–328.

5. An Act to enable the people of Oklahoma and of the Indian Territory to form a constitution and State government and be admitted into the Union on an equal footing with the original states; and to enable the people of New Mexico and of Arizona to form a constitution and State government and be admitted into the Union on an equal footing with the original states, 59th Congress, 1st Sess., cha. 3334, 1906.

6. Pierce Kelton Merrill, "The Social and Economic Status of the Choctaw Nation" (Ph.D. diss., University of Oklahoma, 1940), 49.

7. See E. Hastain, *Index to Choctaw-Chickasaw Deeds and Allottments* (Muskogee, OK: E. Hastain, 1908–1910), for the land descriptions of Choctaw allottees.

8. National Archives and Records Administration, Fort Worth, TX, record group (RG) 75, entry (E) 327, box 14, address of William Durant, June 3, 1938.

9. Bentley Beams interview, April 23, 1969, T-433, p. 17; Doris Duke Collection, vol. XXVI, American Indian Institute, University of Oklahoma, Norman, 1972, Western History Collections, University of Oklahoma.

10. Angie Debo, *The Five Civilized Tribes of Oklahoma: Report on Social and Economic Conditions* (Philadelphia: Indian Rights Association, 1951), 8, 15, 17, 34.

11. National Archives and Records Administration, Forth Worth Regional Archives, RG 75, E 327, box 13, Rehabilitation—Choctaw Program, Tuskahoma Project.

12. Harvey Rosenthal, "Their Day in Court: A History of the Indian Claims Commission" (Ph.D. diss., Kent State University, 1976).

13. Rosenthal, "Their Day in Court," 101, 137–138.

14. The Choctaw Nation was the first Indian tribe to gain access to the Indian Court of Claims, with the Net Proceeds case. The year was 1881. *Choctaw Nation and Chickasaw Nation v. United States and Wichita and Affiliated Bands of Indians*, 21 S. Ct. 149, argued March 7–9, 1900, December 1900; Glen Wilkinson, "Indian Tribal Claims before the Court of Claims," *Georgetown Law Journal* 55 (December 1966): 512.

15. Elmer Thomas Papers, subjects, box 11, folder 100, Carl Albert Center (CAC), University of Oklahoma, Norman.

16. Thomas Papers, subjects, box 11, folder 60, CAC.

17. O. W. Folsom, McCurtain County, to Elmer Thomas, 4 January 1949, Thomas Papers, subjects, box 11, folder 100, CAC.

18. Victor M. Locke Jr., Oklahoma City, to Clerk, Committee on Indian Affairs, 2 June 1941, "Leasing…," pp. 7, 8.

19. "Large Group Here Finds That Original Figure Still Intended," undated newspaper clipping from *Ada News*, Thomas Papers, subjects, box 11, folder 100, CAC.

20. J. H. Belvin, county superintendent, Bryan County, to William A. Brophy, 23 May 1946, National Archives, Fort Worth, RG 75, E 327, box 17, Choctaw Convention.

21. Harry J. W. Belvin to Ed Edmondson, Durant, OK, 28 December 1967, Carl Albert Papers, departmental series, box 63, folder 45, CAC.

22. *Choctaw v. United States*, 91 Ct. Cls. 320.

23. *History of the Intertribal Council of the Five Civilized Tribes*, n.d., n.p., 3; Belvin, *Choctaw Tribal Structure*, 8.

24. Harry J. W. Belvin to Congressman Carl Albert, 30 June 1961, Carl Albert Papers, legislative series, box 51, folder 29, CAC.

25. "Choctaws May Form Corporation," Indian Affairs, Carl Albert Papers, legislative series, box 40, folder 61, CAC.

26. "Department Supports Choctaw Termination Bill Introduced in Congress at Request of Tribal Representatives," Department of the Interior, Information Service, press release, Carl Albert Papers, April 23, 1959, CAC.

27. To supplement the Act of April 26, 1906 (34 Stat. 137), titled "An Act…," 73 Stat. 420, August 25, 1959.

28. See Fixico, *Termination and Relocation*, for a history and an assessment of the termination policy.

29. Carl Albert to Pete W. Cass, 16 July 1959, Carl Albert Papers, legislative series, box 40, folder 58, CAC.

30. O. W. Folsom, McCurtain, OK, RG 2, to Elmer Thomas, senator, Washington DC, 4 January 1949, Elmer Thomas Papers, subjects, box 11, folder 100, CAC.

31. John O. Crow to Carl Albert, 18 July 1961, Carl Albert Papers, legislative series, box 51, folder 29, CAC.

32. Harry J. W. Belvin to Carl Albert, 2 March 1964, Carl Albert Papers, departmental series, box 47, folder 53, CAC; area director, memorandum, Choctaw Fact Sheet and Questionnaire, Muskogee area office, July 21, 1966, Carl Albert Papers, departmental series, box 58, folder 4, CAC.

33. Statement of Harry J. Belvin, principal chief of the Choctaw Nation, on H.R. 18566, a Bill "To Repeal the Act of August 25, 1959, with respect to final disposition of the affairs of the Choctaw Tribe," before the Subcommittee on Indian Affairs of the United States Senate, Carl Albert Papers, departmental series, box 82, folder 36, CAC.

34. Alvin Josephy Jr., ed., *Red Power: The American Indian's Fight for Freedom* (New York: American Heritage Press, 1971).

35. Robert K. Thomas, "Colonialism: Classic and Internal" and "Powerless Politics," *New University Thought* 4, no. 4 (1966–1967): 37–53.

36. Daniel Cobb, "'Us Indians understand the basics': Oklahoma Indians and the Politics of Community Action, 1964–1970," *Western Historical Quarterly* XXXIII (Spring 2002): 41–66.

37. Memorandum, June 2, 1965, Fred Harris Papers, University of Oklahoma, box 282, folder 7, CAC; John B. O'Hara to Mrs. Fred R. Harris, Norman, OK, 16 September 1965, Fred Harris Papers, box 282, folder 7, CAC.

38. Memorandum, June 2, 1965, Fred Harris Papers, box 282, folder 7, CAC; Oklahoma Committee for Indian Opportunity, August 2, 3 [1965], Fred Harris Papers, box 282, folder 7, CAC; John B. O'Hara to Mrs. Fred R. Harris, Norman, OK, 16 September 1965, Fred Harris Papers, box 282, folder 7, CAC.

39. Constitution and By-Laws of Oklahomans for Indian Opportunity, Inc., Fred Harris Papers, box 282, folder 5, CAC.

40. Sarah Eppler Janda, *Beloved Women: The Political Lives of LaDonna Harris and Wilma Mankiller* (DeKalb, IL: Northern Illinois University Press, 2007).

41. Maynard Ungerman, chairman, Tulsa County Democratic Central Committee, to Senator and Mrs. Fred R. Harris, 2 August 1967, Fred Harris Papers, box 284, folder 16, CAC.

42. Neal McCaleb to LaDonna Harris, 24 July 1967, Fred Harris Papers, box 284, folder 16, CAC; Leon H. Ginsberg, School of Social Work, University of Oklahoma, to Senator Fred R. Harris, 2 August 1967, Fred Harris Papers, box 284, folder 16, CAC. On this point, see also

Cobb, "'Us Indians,'" 60–63. On the conflict involving Robert K. Thomas and the Cherokees in eastern Oklahoma, see Daniel Cobb, "Devils in Disguise: The Carnegie Project, the Cherokee Nation, & the 1960s," *American Indian Quarterly*, 31, no. 3 (2007): 201–37.

43. "Cherokee and Creek Chiefs Defend BIA," *Muskogee Times Democrat*, July 1, 1970.

44. Report of Special Personnel Committee, Muskogee area office, July 25, 1967, Fred Harris Papers, box 284, folder 16, CAC; Cobb, "'Us Indians,'" 60–63.

45. Indians—OIO, "Oklahomans for Indian Opportunity" folder, White House central files: staff member and office files: Leonard Garment, box 111, Richard M. Nixon Presidential Materials Staff at College Park, MD.

46. Harry J. W. Belvin to William H. Bozman, acting deputy director, Office of Program Development, Office of Economic Opportunity, 21 November 1969, Carl Albert Papers, departmental series, box 91, folder 37, CAC.

47. I would like to thank Dan Cobb for sharing with me the press clippings of Oklahomans for Indian Opportunity, which are currently in his possession.

48. "Choctaws Hold Firey Session," *Tahlina American*, May 1, 1969.

49. Oklahomans for Indian Opportunity, *A Socio-economic, Ecological Survey of Indians in Two Oklahoma Cities* (Norman, OK: n.p., 1967), unpaged.

50. Harry J. W. Belvin to Honorable Carl Albert, 16 February 1971, Carl Albert Papers, departmental series, box 91, folder 37, CAC; James J. Wilson, director, Indian Division, Office of Indian Operations, Executive Office of the President, Washington DC, to Honorable Harry J. W. Belvin, Durant, OK, n.d., Carl Albert Papers, departmental series, box 91, folder 37, CAC.

51. 84 Stat. 1091, An Act to authorize each of the Five Civilized Tribes of Oklahoma to popularly select their principal officer, and for other purposes, October 22, 1970.

52. Harry Belvin to Ed Edmondson, 28 December 1967, Carl Albert Papers, departmental series, box 63, folder 45, CAC.

53. "Local Indians Combat Termination Act," *McCurtain Weekly Gazette*, Idabel, OK, July 10, 1969, vol. 63, no. 37, departmental series, box 76, folder 61, CAC.

54. Harry J. W. Belvin to A. S. (Mike) Monroney, 14 March 1968, Carl Albert Papers, departmental series, box 70, folder 46, CAC.

55. Report no. 91-1151 of the House Committee on Interior and Insular Affairs, Carl Albert Papers, legislative series, box 128, folder 41, CAC.

56. Statement of Senator Fred R. Harris before the Subcommittee on Indian Affairs of the Committee of Interior and Insular Affairs, Carl Albert Papers, departmental series, box 82, folder 38, CAC.

57. Statement of Representative Carl Albert before the Subcommittee on Indian Affairs of the Committee on Interior and Insular Affairs, May 14, 1970, Carl Albert Papers, legislative series, box 118, folder 67, CAC.

58. HELLO CHOCTAW, Carl Albert Papers, departmental series, boxes 82, 39, 44, CAC.

59. HELLO CHOCTAW....HALITO CHAHTA, August 30, 1970, Carl Albert Papers, departmental series, box 82, folder 44, CAC.

60. HELLO CHOCTAW....HALITO CHAHTA, August 12, 1970, Carl Albert Papers, departmental series, box 82, folder 39, CAC.

61. G. Mike Charleston, Constitution of the Choctaw Nation, Page Belcher Collection, box 167, folder 14, CAC.

8 Indians, the Counterculture, and the New Left

Sherry L. Smith

When many of the Native peoples in the Pacific Northwest signed treaties with the United States during the nineteenth century, they reserved the right to hunt and fish in ceded or "non-reservation" areas. In Washington, however, the state government passed laws that forced Muckleshoots, Puyallups, Nisquallies, Lummis, and fifteen other treaty tribes to endure hostility and risk imprisonment in order to exercise those rights. During the 1960s the fish-in movement brought national attention to the controversy. It would take more than a decade for the landmark Boldt decision (*United States v. Washington*) to resolve it (see table 5, 1974). Past scholarship has focused particular attention on the legal arena, as well as on certain Indian families and communities central to the fishing rights struggle.[1] Sherry L. Smith's chapter offers a new perspective by critically assessing the roles played by members of the counterculture, the New Left, civil rights organizations, and churches.[2] Acknowledging their positive contributions, she also reveals tensions arising from their involvement. Her work reminds readers that non-Native participation in the Indian reform movement has a complex history that deserves closer scrutiny. She articulates an analytical model that could be applied to other facets of twentieth-century American Indian politics and activism.

Native Americans' demands for self-determination, observance of treaty rights, and tribal sovereignty have a long history. For many years, the United States and its citizens ignored their demands. Since the 1970s, however, these policies have become keystones of federal–Indian relations, with significant public support because of Indians' initiatives, determination, skills, and coalitions. The participation of sympathetic non-Indian supporters also played a part, as well as the gradual acceptance of such policies throughout the nation. The latter is especially noteworthy because these policies represent a fundamental reversal of centuries-long efforts (with the brief exception of the Indian New Deal years) to extinguish Indian cultures and polities. In particular, the termination policy, which lasted into the 1960s, set about destroying tribal governments, ending treaty rights, liquidating tribal assets, and eliminating reservations (see tables 3 and 4 and Kidwell, chapter 7, this volume). Why the dramatic shift in attitude among non-Indians in more recent decades, and what were the political consequences?

The turbulent period of reform identified as "the Sixties" is central to answering this question. Yet historians of Sixties social movements often slight Indian activism, and students of Native American history have not paid sufficient attention to the crucial interplay among Anglo-dominated, progressive religious organizations, civil rights advocates, counterculture/ Left groups, Mexican American activists, black nationalists, and Indians.[3] Out of this period of intense turmoil, experimentation, and barrier shattering came cross-fertilization of ideas, techniques, and partnerships. At a time when America was reflecting upon the shortcomings of its political and social system, Indian challenges to conformity and demands for acknowledgment of greater cultural diversity within the nation found allies. At a time when US involvement in the Vietnam War was eliciting criticism of American imperialism abroad, Indians were a domestic reminder of past aggressions and an opportunity to redress those wrongs. The particular confluence of contemporary issues, in fact, made Indians especially interesting and relevant (Cobb, chapter 9, this volume).

Native people, for their part, understood that they could not achieve treaty rights outside the US legal system, which gave those claims their meaning and power. Indians could not, therefore, ignore non-Indians. The non-Indians had to be reckoned with, educated, and enlisted. Given the political realities of the nation and the relative demographic insignificance of Indian people, the struggles required the interest and aid of non-Indians. In the process, Native activists gained allies who often demonstrated little genuine understanding of or deep commitment to treaty rights. Their presence, though, helped to bring Indians' issues to larger audiences and to broaden support for significant policy change. This argument might surprise those who see non-Indian sympathizers from the Left and the counterculture, in particular, as doing more harm than good in Indian communities or who see these non-Indians' interests as superficial, ephemeral, or exploitive.[4] But non-Indians supported Indian rights movements with their money, pens, talents, and skills (particularly the lawyers among them) and, in demonstrations, with their bodies. This interest and these actions mattered.

In the years following World War II, the nation began to confront its failure to ensure the civil rights of all its citizens. Interest in the concerns of all minorities followed. But the issues raised by Indian activists were about more than voting rights, and they did not seek integration. What they demanded was acknowledgment of difference. They called for realization of past promises that codified a separate and special status for tribal people. Instead of a rightful place within the mainstream, many Indians demanded their rightful place apart from it (see tables 3 and 4).

Americans who first understood and appreciated this distinction were those who were increasingly identified as counterculture. These people "discovered" Indians and found them appealing because they presumably offered an actual, living base for an alternative American identity. Challenging bourgeois culture's values and beliefs in progress, order, achievement, and established authority, the youthful counterculture advocated freedom from discipline and convention. They looked to drugs, sex, and music as vehicles for expression and liberation.[5] Many also looked to Indians as symbols of, and even models for, alternative ways of life. Native Americans seemed like perfect foils to all that these predominantly Anglo Americans disdained about their parents' lives. Indians supposedly were not only spiritual and ecological but also tribal and communal. Further, they were genuine holdouts against American conformity, the original American "long hairs." Counterculture iconography consequently became drenched in superficial images purporting to reflect "Indianness."

Inspired by these simplistic, romantic ideas, some young people began drifting to Native American Church ceremonies and eventually to reservations. Many Indians did not welcome the newcomers. Others proved more willing to interact and eventually enlisted non-Indians in their efforts to promote treaty rights and tribal sovereignty. The more politically oriented "hippies" and elements of the New Left formed the most visible alliances with elements of reservation-based and urban Indian communities. Likewise inspired, in part, by African American civil rights, black nationalism, Chicano-Chicana, and Vietnam antiwar movements, some Indians (particularly, young, student, and urban-based) sought partnerships with these other groups and patterned their strategies for change, tactics, and rhetoric on models from these groups, although for distinctively Indian goals.[6] By the late 1960s the boundaries among these identifiable groups and interests were porous. Influences spread in all directions. What activists shared was a deep discontent with conventional values, viewpoints, and politics. The tendency of historians and others, in retrospect, to separate them from one another does a disservice to the sometimes tenuous and temporary, but powerful, intersections that took place. It ignores the collaborations that occurred in a constellation of overlapping interests and issues.

The Pacific Northwest was one of the first places where such congruencies occurred and resulted in important successes regarding the reassertion of treaty rights. Interestingly, in the early 1960s no one seemed to be paying much attention to this region, let alone to the Indians of Washington State. In fact, Americans appeared inordinately concerned with the South and a struggle against racial hatred that was conceptualized as white against black. Indians remained well below the radar screen of national consciousness. Meanwhile, a non-Indian writer from Oregon and Native American activists in Washington were engaging in a radical rethinking of the cultural meaning and political place of Indians in contemporary America. The writer, Ken Kesey, articulated an Anglo American's sense of Indians' significance, particularly for the emerging youth culture that eventually spawned San Francisco's Haight-Ashbury hippies, Berkeley's New Leftists, and New Mexico's communitarians. At the same time, Nisquallies, Lummis, Puyallups, Makahs, and other tribes focused on their economic and political tribal interests, renewing their insistence that treaties matter and challenging state laws that ignored these.

Working apart, the author and activists never met. Yet their efforts related to each other. Moreover, other non-Indians *did* join Native activists' fish-ins and demonstrations, including actor Marlon Brando, comedian Dick Gregory, and hundreds of non-celebrity sympathizers. Indians pushed their cause onto newspaper front pages by borrowing, albeit altering, black civil rights tactics and by inviting Anglo and African American celebrities, as well as people of other races and ethnicities, to join them in acts of civil disobedience. The strategy worked.

Among the first non-Indians to signal an interest in things "Indian" were counterculture types. Among the first to define that difficult-to-define cultural movement and link it to Native Americans was Ken Kesey. By making an Indian the narrator and centerpiece of his first novel, *One Flew over the Cuckoo's Nest*, he placed his readers on the periphery of American society. As counterculture people careened across the landscape looking for alternatives to their parents' lifestyle, Kesey's Chief Broom, a half-blood member of a fictional and defunct Columbia River tribe, may have been their first engagement with a contemporary Indian figure and with contemporary Indian political issues.

The hero of *Cuckoo's Nest* is Randall McMurphy, a man who challenges the brutalizing power of authority in the form of Big Nurse and consequently serves as inspiration to the other inmates of the mental hospital where he has been incarcerated. He ends up lobotomized and eventually dies. The observer, interpreter, narrator, and ultimate survivor, however, is the supposedly silent and schizophrenic "Chief Broom" Bromden. Bromden is the novel's most fully developed character and the only one with a history. He is also the one who observes, interprets, understands, evolves, and takes positive action. Bromden's tribe has disintegrated, its village inundated by a federally financed Columbia River dam. For years, his father, a "full-blood" named Tee Ah Millatoona, fought the hydroelectric project, with its attendant pressures to give up ancestral fishing rights and retreat to government housing. Government agents beat Bromden's father and cut his hair. Still, Tee Ah Millatoona resisted until other members of the tribe sold out, some of them going to work on the dam construction with their "faces hypnotized by routine." Moreover, his own wife, a white woman from the Dalles, worked on him to submit, making him "too little to fight any more." Only then did he give up, turn to alcohol, and die.[7]

What remained, however, was the son—and his memories. McMurphy helps Bromden not only revive that history but also regain his voice: "I still hear the sound of the falls on the Columbia, always will...hear the slap of the fish in the water, laughing naked kids on the bank, the women at the racks." He begins to speak, telling McMurphy his family history, as both explanation and cautionary tale. The "Combine" beat his father, he said. "It'll beat you too." This proved prophetic for the red-haired Irishman, but in joining McMurphy's fistfight with the hospital attendants, in standing up for the patients' dignity, and in being subjected to one last shock treatment, Bromden concludes that he will never again be lost in the fog. This time he will beat *them*. Using the powers McMurphy helped him discover he still had, Bromden lifts the heavy control panel from the ward's tub room, heaves it through the window, and realizes his escape. His destination? Canada, eventually. But first he would go to the Dalles, seeking his Indian friends. "I'd like to see what they've been doing since the government tried to buy their right to be Indians. I've even heard that some of the tribe took to building their old ramshackle wood scaffolding all over that big million-dollar hydroelectric dam and are spearing salmon in the spillway. I'd give something to see that."[8] And so the story ends. The hope for the future rests with an Indian as he strides through the moonlit night—flying, free.

Given the novel's publication date of 1962, it might seem surprising that

Kesey chose a Native American narrator. Why use an Indian perspective—and a fishing tribe, to boot, complete with current political issues—to frame a novel populated otherwise by Anglo and African Americans? Kesey offered a light-hearted, playful explanation: peyote.[9] An alternative explanation for the inspiration and centrality of Chief Broom rests on two things: Kesey's Western background and orientation and a long-standing literary tradition. Born in Colorado but raised in Oregon, Kesey certainly knew that Indians still existed. Apparently, he had some familiarity with ongoing conflicts between Indians and the government over fishing rights in the wake of hydroelectric dam construction.[10] The details of Bromden's tribal life reveal a remarkable awareness of and sensitivity to Native politics in the twentieth-century West.

More than that, who could more appropriately represent the outsider who historically resists the omnipotence of expanding national power? What greater hope for this country than that supposedly offered by indige-nous people, whom Kesey (and many others before him) associated with the beauties of the natural world, genuine freedom, life apart from the machine, an organic community free of industrialization's alienation? For all his coun-tercultural inclinations, Kesey, in choosing an Indian narrator, was connect-ing with a time-honored tradition of associating Native Americans with resistance to modernity.[11]

In linking up, perhaps unconsciously, with this literary convention, Kesey provided his readers with a symbol that served the purposes of a new generation. Indianness proved to be a powerful concept that inspired the emerging counterculture from that point on. Moreover, it is a story with political implications. The novel's end promises Indian resistance, renewal, and renaissance in the erection of ramshackle wood scaffolding over the modern hydroelectric dam. If powerless Indians could fight the "Combine," surely others could too. It would be difficult to overstate Kesey's contribu-tion to the counterculture. He served as a bridge between the Beats and the hippies of Haight-Ashbury. He was the "Pied Piper of psychedelia" who, with the Merry Pranksters, "brewed the cultural mix that fermented every-thing from psychedelic art to acid-rock groups [and] in the process of his pilgrimage blew an entire generation's mind."[12] He was also among the first of his generation to turn to Indianness as inspiration for social criticism, political action, and cultural release.

The month President John F. Kennedy died in Dallas was the month Hank Adams dropped out of the University of Washington. A Sioux/Assiniboine who grew up on Washington's Quinault Reservation (his mother having married a member of that tribe), Adams decided to scrap the academic route. Instead, he wanted to engage in direct action and organize protests.

The most pressing issue at hand: fishing rights. More than a century had passed since territorial governor Isaac Stevens signed federal treaties with Northwest tribes in the 1850s, promising them, as they ceded huge swaths of property, the right to continue fishing in their "usual and accustomed places." Over time, Washington and Oregon ignored those rights, attempted to expand their jurisdiction over tribal members, and eroded sovereignty by harassing and sometimes arresting Indians who dropped nets on rivers outside reservation boundaries and beyond state-determined seasons. Indians maintained that their treaties allowed them to fish these spots, so they continued to do so, wherever and whenever they wanted. They believed that these nineteenth-century agreements provided immunity from state rules and regulations. Sports and commercial fishermen supported Washington State's efforts to prosecute, claiming that Indian fishing threatened the fisheries for everyone. In the early 1960s, with the lines now drawn, some Indians were continuing to challenge Washington State's interference with their fishing.[13]

Hank Adams attended his first National Indian Youth Council (NIYC) meeting in 1963, where he came into the orbit of Clyde Warrior, a Ponca from Oklahoma who helped found the group in 1961 (see table 4). The NIYC brought together young Indians inspired by the same impulse that was prompting other members of their generation to create new organizations with more activist agendas and aggressive strategies. When NIYC met at the Ute Reservation in Fort Duchesne, Utah, during the summer of 1963, Warrior invited Marlon Brando to join them. Brando had just participated in the March on Washington and had urged its leaders to participate in civil rights protests. Not all were interested, but Hank Adams and Bruce Wilkie (Makah), another NIYC founder, argued that black activists' methods, if not their goals, could be applied to Northwest Indian problems.

The following March, Adams and other NIYC members convinced Brando to participate in what the media would call a "fish-in." For several decades, Indians such as Billy Frank (Nisqually) and Bob Satiacum (Puyallup) had fished and endured arrest, assault, and imprisonment—with little media attention and no change in state policy. Now, Adams wanted to ratchet up the pressure. Not all local Indians welcomed NIYC's involvement, viewing its members as "college kids with sports jackets who showed up merely to make themselves look good."[14] Not all advocated direct action, preferring to resolve differences in courts of law.

Meanwhile, Brando, although not a counterculture figure, embraced the persona of a rebel *with* a cause. He spent several days in Washington in early March 1964 and stayed consistently "on message" regarding the legitimacy of treaty rights. He understood what was at stake, and the fish-ins marked the beginning of Brando's lifelong commitment to Indian issues. Joining him on the Puyallup River were Bob Satiacum and Episcopal priest John Yaryan of San Francisco's Grace Cathedral. Yaryan had formerly served at a church in Auburn, Washington. Working among the Muckleshoot tribe, he had learned about treaty rights. He returned to Puget Sound to participate in this action. "Once you get into this whole problem," Yaryan told a reporter, "you realize that the Indians' treaty has suffered complete abrogation." The decision to enlist Brando proved to be gold. The nation noticed, and the lessons were clear: to get widespread *white* attention, get white participation; to get widespread *media* attention, get celebrity participation.[15]

After Brando left, Pacific Northwest Indian activists continued their fish-ins. They also added marches and demonstrations to their repertoire. In May 1966 about fifty people participated in a "Treaty Trek" designed to bring attention to Muckleshoot fishing rights. About one-half of the marchers were University of Washington students who described themselves as "human rights advocates." Other protestors gathered on the capitol building steps in Olympia with signs reading "Ho Chi Minh: Beware of US Treaties" and "Custer Died for Your Sins." Still others established encampments on the capitol grounds and the Thurston County Courthouse grounds, complete with tipis, which were fast becoming the universal symbol of Indianness (although their use was not indigenous to the Northwest).[16]

Non-Indian celebrities, however, garnered the most media attention. In February 1966 Dick Gregory, a thirty-three-year-old black comedian and candidate for mayor of Chicago, arrived in Washington at the invitation of Adams and the Survival of American Indians Association (SAIA) to fish the Nisqually River. For the next two years, his activities dominated the news coverage of this issue.[17] That Gregory was neither an Indian nor a fisherman did not escape the attention of local law enforcement. For several days, they ignored him, even though news photographers showed up streamside to snap pictures of him holding dead fish. His motive, Gregory explained, was to see that the federal government live up to its treaties. But in a well-meaning statement that suggested a limited understanding of the distinction between treaty and civil rights, Gregory indicated that he preferred to see Indians receive full rights under the Constitution. Until then, their treaty rights should be honored.

Drawing a corollary between the fish-ins and the freedom rides on buses and sit-ins at lunch counters, Gregory thought that the Indians' "plight" had many of the earmarks of Southern blacks' position of earlier years. He also predicted that college kids and Easterners would join the cause. "It's about time the civil rights front shifted to this part of the country," he told reporters. Finally, after several days, state game officials arrested Gregory and his wife, Lillian, for setting illegal gill nets. Initially eschewing bail, Gregory began a publicity campaign from prison, eliciting supportive telegrams from British philosopher Bertrand Russell, Martin Luther King, and James Farmer, executive director of the Congress of Racial Equality. The Nisqually Tribal Council, however, disclaimed any connection with Gregory or the "renegade" Indians who participated in the fish-ins. Tribal chairman Elmer Kalama told reporters that the controversy should be settled in the courts, without any help from Gregory. "He is trying to turn this into a civil rights issue," Kalama said. "We are fighting for our fishing rights, and he is hurting our cause."[18]

By the fall of 1966 even Gregory's Indian allies had become critical, claiming that although they had invited him to join their efforts, they were now disappointed. According to Janet McCloud (Tulalip), his activities received publicity primarily in black magazines, which advanced his career but not their cause. Further, the publicity discouraged small, local donations.[19] In an attempt to undo some of this damage, SAIA invited Jay Silverheels, the television character Tonto from *The Lone Ranger*, to attend an Indian unity meeting. A Mohawk from Ontario, Canada, Silverheels arrived and posed for a photograph with Native American proponents and opponents of the fish-ins.[20]

When Gregory returned to Tacoma for sentencing, the judge slammed him with a six-month jail term, suspending only one-half of it. On June 7, 1968, he began serving time in the Thurston County jail. Gregory's attorney, Jack Tanner, warned that black power advocates H. Rap Brown and Stokely Carmichael, as well as the Reverend Ralph Abernathy, would show up to protest the sentence. He predicted that the Peace and Freedom Movement would demonstrate on behalf of Gregory, its candidate for president, and would boycott Washington State products such as apples and Olympia Beer. A group of Quakers, a Christian denomination formally known as the Society of Friends, paraded around the courthouse with "Set Dick Gregory Free" signs, having spent the preceding week discussing the Vietnam War and minorities' concerns. Some sported "Eugene McCarthy for President" buttons and sang "We Shall Overcome."[21]

Increasingly, the press coverage turned away from fishing rights and toward Gregory and African American issues. Gregory sent telegrams to President Lyndon Johnson, Secretary of State Dean Rusk, North Vietnam's Ho Chi Minh, China's Mao Zedong, and twenty-four other heads of state in order "to tell the Indians' and *his story* [my emphasis] to the world literally." According to one account, Gregory was particularly miffed that Johnson and Rusk had not included him in a meeting with six other presidential candidates, a slight he characterized as "a racial insult." He also decided to consume only distilled water and bread during his incarceration, describing the hunger strike as a protest against the denial of fishing rights, the war in Vietnam, and other issues. Consequently, newspapers regularly reported on his weight loss, and one journalist even mused on the political costs to Republican governor Dan Evans, should the activist die in custody. In the meantime, during a news conference called by Lillian Gregory and Jack Tanner, Janet McCloud tried to bring the focus back to the Indians' issues, reminding the state that she, as one reporter put it, "hasn't buried the hatchet." But the story's headline announcing "Gregory Tells World He's Alive, Hungry" indicated that the celebrity's health attracted most of the attention.[22]

Finally, on July 17, 1968, Judge Hewitt Henry released Gregory from prison. About twenty pounds lighter than when he had entered jail six weeks earlier, Gregory left the courthouse in the company of *I Spy* television star Robert Culp and his actress-wife, France Nuyen. Insisting that his purpose remained publicizing "the plight of the Indians," Gregory told reporters that he hoped Indians would not have to become "as militant and violent as black people are for America to wake up" and that Washington State would solve its black problems and become a model for the rest of the nation. For now, he intended to turn his attention to a "world fact-finding tour" that would take him to North Vietnam, China, and North Korea, where he hoped to talk with crew members from the recently captured US Navy vessel *The Pueblo*. With that, Gregory left the Northwest.[23] Without a doubt, Gregory's sympathies for Indian fishing rights were sincere. Yet this particular cross-racial partnership proved problematic and possibly counterproductive, diverting attention from treaty rights and diffusing it into a kaleidoscope of other issues.

About the same time Dick Gregory left the Pacific Northwest, a University of California, Santa Cruz, undergraduate named Richard White migrated into the region. White quit his summer job on Independence Day, 1968, and agreed to join a friend—Joseph Quinones, a Yaqui from California—on a road trip to the Democratic National Convention meeting in Chicago that summer. They never made it. Instead, the young men found their way up to the Sky River Rock Festival in Washington State. There, they met Rolling Thunder, a Cherokee medicine man who lived on the Shoshone Reservation in Nevada and had been making appearances at counterculture events at least since the 1967 San Francisco Be-In. Upon learning that Quinones was Yaqui, Rolling Thunder told him, "You have to go Frank's Landing. Your people need you." The next day, White and Quinones drove to Frank's Landing, a center of fish-in activity and an Indian settlement downriver from the Nisqually Reservation and outside Olympia. They ended up staying into the winter.[24]

What they found when they first arrived were members of the Billy Frank and Al Bridges (Nisqually/Puyallup/Duwamish) families and their Indian supporters. Also, there were non-Indian communists, Black Panthers, Students for a Democratic Society and Peace and Freedom Party members, unaffiliated radicals from the University of Washington and Portland's Reed College, alienated Indian and non-Indian Vietnam War veterans, Quakers from Seattle, and counterculture types passing through from all over the country—in short, "whoever [the Nisqually activists] could get." Sometimes several hundred non-Indians would be camping there; other times, only a core group of about thirty or forty. Their job was to "give bulk" to the demonstrations, help keep the cause in the public eye, and potentially reduce violence that might otherwise run rampant against Indian demonstrators. Law enforcement officials would presumably show more restraint with non-Indians. "We might be hippies and we might be worthless," as White put it, "but we still had the privilege of our whiteness and parents who might cause trouble [if we were beaten]."[25]

The camp dwellers also "ritually" guarded the fishing nets (although they proved hapless in protecting them from confiscation), drove members of the Bridges and Frank families to town and to meetings with other allies in their "hippie" vans and cars, collected firewood, fed people, took drugs, and experienced several raids on the Landing by state and county law enforcement officers. The newcomers to the Frank's Landing encampment lived as "they imagined Indian people lived," sleeping in tents, occasionally eating venison ("salmon was far too valuable to eat"), and waiting for the next demonstration. Of course, not all counterculture visitors joined the political fight. For some, Frank's Landing was just another place on the road—a temporary haven to use drugs (in spite of the Frank and Bridges families' best efforts to keep out drugs) and live beyond the boundaries of conventional life. Such passers-through were not committed to Indian treaty rights and just got in the way.[26]

Up to that point, White, who traveled in both counterculture and radical circles yet retained a distance from both, had thought little about Indians or their politics. His presence at Frank's Landing was completely accidental. But once there, he became drawn in by "the most interesting people [he] had ever met." Not that they fulfilled his romantic preconceptions of Indians. Expecting to find "spear-wielding Indians, leaping deftly from rock to rock, thrusting quickly to impale giant salmon who churned in the river's foam," he found instead men who fished with nets, drank beer, and risked police harassment, beatings, and imprisonment. They were, however, "incredibly rooted" to their place, had been fighting for something for one hundred years, and "didn't become distracted by the [counterculture] circus around them."[27] White was not privy to the strategy meetings or the inner circle of Hank Adams, Billy Frank, and Al Bridges, nor did he expect to be. The fundamental justice of their cause and, in particular, his personal commitment to the Bridges family kept him there.

While the Nisqually and Puyallup men endured harassment and arrest, the women kept camp and political activities going by raising bail, contacting sympathetic people to contribute food and supplies, selling any salmon caught to willing buyers, and occasionally getting arrested, beaten, and jailed themselves. Maiselle Bridges, Billy Frank's sister and Al Bridges' wife, "was the one you saw best and remembered," according to White. "She had calmness and a dignity that had seen outrages and survived intact."[28] Her daughters, Valerie, Suzette, and Alison, participated in all aspects of the camp's political activities. Hank Adams spent much of his time typing at the Bridges' kitchen table, strategizing, and negotiating complicated arrangements that often fell apart. He had escalated the nature of the conflict by bringing in non-Indians for large protest demonstrations as a way to make it more costly to the state. Adams himself was not a "radical," but he used radicals to buy time, get concessions, and garner publicity.[29]

In early September 1968, Students for a Democratic Society, the Peace and Freedom Party, and other leftist organizations announced an alliance with the "renegade" Nisqually fishermen. As Robby Stern, prominent member of the University of Washington SDS, saw it at the time, the state and federal governments had been systematically extinguishing Indians' cultures for years, and the "Red people are clearly among the most oppressed people in this society. They represent another important group that will join with other oppressed people of the society to destroy their oppressors." He also acknowledged the Vietnam War, a significant backdrop to all politics by the fall of 1968, noting that it was twice as deadly to be an Indian in America in 1965 to 1966 as a soldier in Vietnam. Others, too, noted parallels between Indian issues and those of the war in Vietnam. To Richard White, Frank's Landing represented "the backwater of Vietnam," another place where things had gone terribly wrong and the nation had committed grave injustices. Inclinations to join the issues found reinforcement from bitter Vietnam-era veterans in the camp and from Hank Adams, who identified a "commonality of historic and collective experience [which] established an affinity" between Indians and Vietnamese.[30]

Robby Stern, like White, understood that the fight was the Nisquallies', but he still believed that non-Indians could be of help. He attempted to impose order at Frank's Landing by creating committees for each fishing site and a master committee to coordinate them all. The committees, however, quickly fell apart. Outside the camp, an Indian Rights Commission formed to raise money, replace confiscated fishing equipment, and provide legal defense and bail. Further, it hoped to recruit people from all over the country to come to Frank's Landing. Suzette Bridges traveled to Denver to meet with Chicano activist Corky Gonzales, "The Guevara of the Rockies," who promised a busload of demonstrators for a mid-October demonstration.[31] After the Indian leaders decided on a demonstration date and site, Stern would call a meeting of non-Indians to decide whether any of them would be arrested—an "Alice and Wonderlandish" effort, because the police arrested whomever they chose. In the end, White concluded, the non-Indian camp was "ineffective, disorganized and tumultuous, but its weakness became its strength." Law enforcement officers and locals in Olympia were fearful of what might happen at Frank's Landing. Assuming that they were dealing with "unpredictable, drug-crazed maniacs, they gave the camp more power than it ever had in reality.... They feared hundreds of freaks and radicals in Olympia. This was Hank's success. It was one of the few things he had to bargain with."[32]

Most people, of course, had no idea what was happening at Frank's Landing. Their information came from newspaper accounts of the demonstrations. Just as Marlon Brando and Dick Gregory's participation had ensured front-page news coverage, the hundreds of people who supported Billy Frank and other fishermen as they strung their nets at the spillway from the Deschutes River and Capitol Lake on September 8, 1968, found their photo on *The Daily Olympian*'s front page the following day. The accompanying article claimed that the Indian fishermen's supporters were "goateed, long-haired, barefoot and bare-chested hippies from as far away as Los Angeles and Alabama, singing, swinging, and carrying signs protesting restrictions of civil rights and Indian rights." Police arrested only six people, however. Among them was Joseph Quinones, who, upon being booked on the fifth floor of the county courthouse, opened up a window, flung his hat into the crowd below, and shouted, "Freedom now!"[33]

One month later, state and county officers seized a net at Frank's Landing and subsequently confronted about thirty people camped there, "mostly non-Indians, long-haired, bearded youths and their girls." Officers arrested fisherman George Meskuotis, but the featured photo in the Olympia paper depicted not Meskuotis but non-Indian men and women "lecturing" Bruce Gruett, assistant chief of the Fisheries Patrol. The story focused on the "hippies'" verbal abuse of the lawmen. The same day, the *Seattle Post-Intelligencer* printed a photo of Quinones and Stern delivering a dead salmon to the Governor's Mansion and a photo of two hundred young people (again, mostly non-Indian) sitting in on the state's Temple of Justice in support of fishing rights.[34] Most news accounts, in fact, led with sentences noting the presence of Black Panthers, Socialist Worker Party members, and SDSers as a way to underscore the radicals' presence and, perhaps, discredit the Indians' position.

Such allies most assuredly carried costs. No doubt, many readers, including Native ones, found the hippies and political radicals quite distasteful. When the Seattle Liberation Front joined the Puyallups at their encampment along the Puyallup River, Bob Satiacum made a pointed comment in answer to a reporter's query about how he liked such volunteers: "Well, you don't see any of the good church people down here helping us, do you?"[35] Quite simply, supporters of any political stripe and race were welcome. Moreover, the presence of middle-class Anglo "kids" catapulted these events into people's consciousness. It brought home to people in the Northwest that challenges to the status quo regarding race relations and Indian politics were real, immediate, and gaining strength. The story was no longer about a handful of so-called renegade Indians demanding treaty rights. Non-Indians from across racial, ethnic, religious, geographic, and generational lines were joining them. Nothing quite like this had ever occurred in American history. Something big was happening here.

Simultaneously, behind the scenes other non-Indians, including "some good church people," were supporting the fish-ins in less public ways. Adams, Janet McCloud, Ramona Bennett (Puyallup), Guy McMinds (Quinault), and others had for years been establishing ongoing relationships with church groups and gathering support. Episcopal canon Yaryan's participation in the 1964 fish-in signaled an early response. In 1968, at the invitation of Olympia's Episcopal bishop, Adams and Bennett met with various Protestant leaders in seeking continuous, not just crisis, involvement. Bishop Ivol Curtis acknowledged that his denomination operated a church on Puyallup land and that it could become a political sanctuary for Indian fishermen, much as other Episcopal churches had been used by conscientious objectors to the Vietnam War. At the end of this particular meeting, the Indians received a check for $500 from an anonymous donor and a promise of $5,000 more.[36]

Even more impressive was Quaker support, particularly through the American Friends Service Committee (AFSC). In 1967 the committee completed an eighteen-month study of Muckleshoot, Puyallup, and Nisqually fishing rights. The National Congress of American Indians initially printed a mimeographed version of the report, and in 1970 the University of Washington published a book edition. The work, by a collection of authors, initially intended to sort out the complicated and emotional issues. Gradually, the writers determined that the Indians' side of things was not well understood and needed an outlet. The fishing rights cases attracted the Quaker organization's interest in the first place because of the ramifications beyond Washington State.

In a statement reminiscent of Kesey's Chief Bromden, the AFSC authors indicated that the Indians had come up against "the aggressive, development-oriented Western culture" and therefore shared much with other peoples' struggles around the globe. For too long, and to the Earth's detriment, Western civilization had imposed its values, religion, law, education, and technology on other cultures. Now, by recognizing the legitimacy of Native fishermen, people could also benefit "from the traditional conservation wisdom of Indians." The report explained that Indians integrated work, play, and religion with the environment and could consequently "serve as a model for the survival of man suffering now from too much fragmentation and not enough community feeling." If Robby Stern stressed the Indians' oppression, the AFSC stressed their "ecological awareness of kinship with environment." Indians were not the ones who built the Grand Coulee Dam and destroyed fisheries. They did not dump sewage and atomic waste into rivers.[37]

Yet conservation was not the core issue here. By adopting new values and attitudes, Americans not only could increase the number of salmon in their rivers but also could simultaneously cultivate diversity and cross-cultural respect. The hostility toward Indians and their legal rights reflected fear of difference. The larger concern, then, was to stop imposing conformity and to encourage the kind of diversity necessary for a healthy society and planet. In fact, the AFSC concluded, non-Indians needed to adopt a more Indian-like relationship with nature, based on harmony rather than on conquest. They also suggested that a commission made up of Indians, sportsmen, and commercial fishermen work on a fair allocation of fish. This was both the legally and the morally right thing to do.[38] How many people read this book is impossible to determine, but it went into multiple printings and certainly helped shape the outcome of the fishing rights controversy.[39]

Eventually, the controversy was resolved as activists turned away from demonstrations and the attendant publicity and looked to lawyers and the court system. They sought and received help from the Seattle Legal Services, the newly created Native American Rights Fund (NARF), and, most important, the United States Justice Department (see table 4). By September 1970 the Justice Department launched its case, *United States v. Washington*, and most of the state's tribes joined the litigation. This was a momentous turning point. The Indians now had the expertise of Indian lawyers, as well as the power and resources of the federal government, on their side. Finally, in February 1974 Judge George Boldt decided in favor of the tribes. It was a dramatic endorsement of treaty rights.

Indians, of course, deserve the lion's share of credit and responsibility for this impressive victory. They fought long and hard to sustain treaty rights. They were the ones who consistently risked life and limb and livelihood. But they also won because they operated in a national climate that was growing more conducive to acknowledgment of treaty rights and the justice of Indians' positions. Counterculture and radical types, celebrities and students, Quakers and Episcopalians, were no more than a "supporting cast" in all this—but an early, important, and perhaps even crucial element nevertheless. They did not represent a well-organized, disciplined, or regimented set of troops. Far from it. They wandered in and out of Frank's Landing and other sites of contention. Sometimes their attention and interest waned. But in their shared belief that the fishing rights issue represented America's legally sanctioned promises to a particular "minority" group, in their commitment to the validity, viability, and perpetuation of various cultures within the nation, and in their effort to redress America's imperialist past, as well as present foreign interventions, these allies helped to capture the eyes, ears, and hearts of fellow citizens, who, in the end, responded favorably to significant change. Hank Adams and others understood this at the time and used these groups for Indian purposes. To acknowledge the role of non-Indians reminds us that Indians and non-Indians were, and remain, deeply implicated in each other's cultures and politics.

Notes

1. American Friends Service Committee (AFSC), *Uncommon Controversy: Fishing Rights of the Muckleshoot, Puyallup, and Nisqually Indians* (Seattle: University of Washington Press, 1970); Fay Cohen, *Treaties on Trial: The Continuing Controversy over Northwest Indian Fishing Rights* (Seattle: University of Washington Press, 1986); Daniel Boxberger, *To Fish in Common: The Ethnohistory of Lummi Indian Salmon Fishing* (Lincoln: University of Nebraska Press, 1989; Seattle: University of Washington Press, 2000); Alexandra Harmon, *Indians in the Making: Ethnic Relations and Indian Identities around Puget Sound* (Berkeley: University of California Press, 1998); Roberta Ulrich, *Empty Nets: Indians, Dams, and the Columbia River* (Corvallis: Oregon State University Press, 1999); and Charles Wilkinson, *Messages from Frank's Landing: A Story of Salmon, Treaties, and the Indian Way* (Seattle: University of Washington Press, 2000).

2. Two discussions of how the counterculture appropriated its own particular constructions of "Indianness" are Stewart Brand, "Indians and the Counterculture, 1960's–1970's," in *The Handbook of North American Indians*, vol. 4, *History of Indian–White Relations*, ed. Wilcomb Washburn (Washington DC: Smithsonian Institution Press, 1988), 570–572; and Philip Deloria, *Playing Indian* (New Haven, CT: Yale University Press, 1998), 154–180. These, however, do not address how the counterculture constructively engaged in political issues.

3. For overviews of Indian activism during this period, see Paul Chaat Smith and Robert Allen Warrior, *Like a Hurricane: The Indian Movement from Alcatraz to Wounded Knee* (New York: The

New Press, 1996); and Charles Wilkinson, *Blood Struggle: The Rise of Modern Indian Nations* (New York: W. W. Norton, 2005).

4. Vine Deloria Jr., *Custer Died for Your Sins: An Indian Manifesto* (New York: Macmillan, 1969; Norman: University of Oklahoma Press, 1988), 159, 163–164.

5. The definition of counterculture remains imprecise. Theodore Roszak's *The Making of a Counterculture*, originally published in 1969, is a contemporary attempt to explain it. Braunstein and Doyle define counterculture as "an inherently unstable collection of attitudes, tendencies, postures, gestures, 'lifestyles,' ideals, visions, hedonistic pleasures, moralisms, negations, and affirmations. These roles were played by people who defined themselves first by what they were not, and then, only after having cleared that essential ground of identity, began to conceive anew what they were. What they were was what they might become—more a process than a product—and thus more a direction or a motion than a movement." Peter Braunstein and Michael William Doyle, eds., *Imagine Nation: The American Counterculture of the 1960s and 70s* (New York and London: Routledge, 2002), 10.

6. See Joanne Nagel, *American Indian Ethnic Renewal: Red Power and the Resurgence of Identity and Culture* (New York: Oxford University Press, 1996).

7. Ken Kesey, *One Flew over the Cuckoo's Nest* (1962; repr., New York: Signet, 1995), 186–187.

8. Kesey, *Cuckoo's Nest*, 73, 142–143.

9. No author, *Kesey's Garage Sale*, introduction by Arthur Miller (New York: The Viking Press and Intrepid Trips, 1973), 14–15. Tom Wolfe took Kesey at his word, indicating that drugs and even an experiment with shock treatment inspired and helped flesh out Chief Broom's character. See Tom Wolfe, *The Electric Kool-Aid Acid Test* (1968; repr., New York: Bantam Books, 1969), 44.

10. Stewart Brand, of *The Whole Earth Catalog* fame, indicated that Kesey first introduced him to Indians in the early 1960s, when Kesey took Brand to the Warm Springs (Oregon) Reservation. It seemed that Kesey had been there before. Stewart Brand, interview by author, February 12, 2002, Berkeley, CA.

11. Sherry Smith, *Reimagining Indians: Native Americans through Anglo Eyes, 1880–1940* (New York: Oxford University Press, 2000).

12. Christopher Lehmann-Haupt, "Ken Kesey," *New York Times*, November 11, 2001.

13. For details, see the works cited above in note 1.

14. Smith and Warrior, *Like a Hurricane*, 42–46.

15. For Brando's own account, see Lawrence Grobel, *Conversations with Brando* (New York: Hyperion, 1991), 43–47, 85, 105–125; and Marlon Brando with Robert Lindsey, *Brando: Songs My Mother Taught Me* (New York: Random House, 1994). For examples of local/regional media attention regarding Brando's fish-in activities, see *Daily Olympian* (hereafter *DO*), February 17, 1964; *Tacoma News Tribune* (hereafter *TNT*), March 2, 1964; *Seattle Times* (hereafter *ST*), March 2 and 3, 1964; and *Seattle Post-Intelligencer* (hereafter *PI*), March 3, 1964. For Indian disagreements about tactics, see Harmon, *Indians in the Making*, 233–234.

16. *ST*, May 13, 1966; *DO*, February 7, 1967; *ST*, June 30, 1968; and AFSC, *Uncommon Controversy*, 109–110. On June 30, 1968, Governor Evans ordered the dismantling of the three tipis and four tents that made up the encampment. See *DO* and *ST*, June 30, 1968.

17. According to an undated SAIA proposal for the "Inter-Community Organization and Cooperative Development Project," southern Puget Sound Indian fishermen organized the group in 1964: "to affirm, fight for and secure our treaty fishing rights by various means and

processes—on the riverbanks, in the courts, wherever." Hank Adams was the executive director. "General Correspondence, 1971" folder, box 80, Frederick T. Haley Papers, Special Collections, Suzzallo Library, University of Washington, Seattle, (hereafter FHUW).

18. See *DO*, February 7, 1966; *TNT*, February 7, 1966; *ST*, February 16 and 18, 1966; and *DO*, February 9, 10, 13, 15, and 16, 1966. For quote, see *ST*, February 17, 1966. See also Dick Gregory, *Up from Nigger* (New York: Stein and Day, 1976), 123–127, 173–176.

19. *ST*, March 2 and 30 and November 11, 1966; *DO*, March 3 and 29, April 29, and May 4, 1966.

20. *ST*, November 27, 1966.

21. *DO*, January 13, 1967, and June 8, 19, and 30, 1968; *Bremerton Sun*, June 18 and 19, 1968.

22. *PI*, July 4, 1968; *DO*, July 14, 1968; and "Gregory Booked at the 'Palace' for 90-Day Stay," *DO*, n.d., 1968, copy in "Indian-Fishing-Rights-1968," vertical file, Washington State Library, Olympia. This last article revealed that among the paperback books Gregory took with him to his cell were *Yoga Made Easy*, *American Astrology*, *Moon Sign Book*, *Horoscope*, and Alan Watts's *The Book: The Taboo against Knowing Who You Are*—all titles one might expect to find in a counterculture library. On Gregory's hospitalization, see *DO*, July 5 and 9, 1968.

23. *DO*, July 15, 16, and 17, 1968; *ST*, July 17, 1968; and *PI*, July 18, 1968. Robert Culp's arrival at the courthouse elicited a big photographic spread, including a full-body picture of France Nuyen in miniskirt and boots.

24. Information on the non-Indians' experiences at Frank's Landing comes from the author's interview with Richard White, April 9, 2004, in Palo Alto, CA, and from his unpublished, untitled, autobiographical account, written soon after his time there. For a non-Indian outsider's perspective, see Don Hannula, "Nisqually Fishing Confrontation Now 46 Days Old," *ST*, October 20, 1969. Housing for the encampment included a large tipi, plastic see-through shelters, and even a tree house. The landing, six acres of federal trust land, belonged to William Frank Sr., who at age eighty-nine was the oldest living Nisqually. He acquired this parcel in exchange for his allotment on the reservation, which the government took over for use at Fort Lewis, an army post.

25. White interview.

26. White manuscript, n.p., copy in author's files.

27. White manuscript, n.p.

28. White manuscript, n.p.

29. White interview.

30. For Stern's statement, see *The Helix*, September 4, 1968; White interview; and Robby Stern, interview by author, July 7, 2005. For Adams's quote, see "Memorandum to Selected Indian Person," "General Correspondence, 1971" folder, box 80, FHUW. Stern claimed that in 1965–1966 there were 6,373 deaths among 472,000 American soldiers in Vietnam but 10,178 deaths among 400,000 Indians in the United States.

31. *The Helix*, September 4, 1968.

32. White manuscript, n.p.

33. *DO*, September 9, 1968. That these kinds of supporters did not win universal Indian support is apparent in the same article: "Some disgusted Indian leaders were asking Fisheries officials how they could become disassociated with their unwashed, bearded, bare-chested supporters from Seattle."

34. *DO*, October 14, 1968; *PI*, October 14, 1968.

35. *ST*, August 13, 1970.

36. *ST*, September 18, 1970. See also Wilkinson, *Messages*, 168–172.

37. AFSC, *Uncommon Controversy*, xviii, xxix. See also Robert Johnson, "Indian Fishing Controversy," *PI*, November 22, 1971.

38. AFSC, *Uncommon Controversy*, xxix.

39. Wilkinson, *Messages*, 170.

9 Talking the Language of the Larger World

Politics in Cold War (Native) America

Daniel M. Cobb

The decade of the 1960s is often seen as a nebulous midway point between the termination era of the 1950s and the self-determination era that came into its own during the 1970s. Scholars acknowledge the role that the War on Poverty played in strengthening tribal institutions and fostering an acceptance of self-governance in Washington DC, even as local communities encountered problems with implementation (see table 4). In the past, however, they have focused on policymakers or individual communities.[1] Meanwhile, studies of activism continue to focus primarily on the militancy of the late 1960s and after.[2] In this chapter, Dan Cobb takes a different approach. He explores a diverse array of Indian and non-Indian reformers, youths, social scientists, and tribal leaders whose ideas and actions were deeply influenced by the struggle for black equality, the youth movement, decolonization, and the Cold War. By locating them as, at once, influenced by and shapers of the larger domestic and international histories of which they were a part, he shows how attending to Native people's experiences can contribute to a fuller understanding of politics in Cold War America. Finally, by de-emphasizing militancy, he provides a more complex and variegated picture of American Indian activism during the 1960s.

Imagine Standing Rock Sioux activist and intellectual Vine Deloria Jr. sitting on a sofa in his den. A cup of coffee and a row of carefully aligned Pall Mall cigarettes rest on a nearby end table. A box of donuts lies open on a coffee table in front of him. On this brisk fall morning, he is bedecked in a white sweatshirt and matching pair of white sweatpants. Over several hours, he methodically works his way through one smoke after another while telling stories about his tenure as executive director of the National Congress of American Indians during the mid-1960s. This is how I remember my first encounter with one of the towering figures of the twentieth century, a man who shaped not only the course of American Indian history but also the way we think about it. It was October 2001, a little more than five years before his passing. I was a doctoral candidate at the University of Oklahoma then, and the two days I spent interviewing him at his home in Golden, Colorado, fundamentally altered the way I conceptualize my work.

This chapter explores four important aspects of the politics of tribal self-determination during the 1960s—the Workshop on American Indian Affairs, the American Indian Chicago Conference, the War on Poverty, and the Poor People's Campaign. The analytical thread holding each of them together derives from one of the many poignant observations Vine Deloria made during our conversations. "At NCAI," he told me, "I was looking for some kind of intellectual format of how you would justify overturning termination and at the same time escape this big push for integration that civil rights was doing." To make this distinction, he situated tribal issues in the context of what he called "an era of resurgent nationalism among dark-skinned people the world over." He remembered telling tribal leaders, "If we're gonna say we're nations and we got sovereignty and our treaties are as valid as other treaties, then we gotta talk the language of the larger world."[3]

In arguing this point, Vine Deloria added his voice to a conversation that had been under way for more than a generation. Indian activists began drawing parallels between themselves and nations emerging from colonialism after World War I, but the advent of the Cold War following the Second World War added a new sense of urgency.[4] In 1954 and again in 1957, Native and non-Native advocacy organizations launched aggressive campaigns for what they called an American Indian Point IV Program, a strategy that invoked President Harry S. Truman's plan to provide technical assistance and scientific training purportedly needed by developing nations to "modernize" their cultures, political systems, and economies. These reformers presented their appeal as more than just an alternative to termination (see table 3). They argued that it represented a Cold War imperative: if the United States expected to prevail in its ideological contest with the Soviet Union in Latin America, Asia, Africa, and the Middle East, they argued, it would have to demonstrate to the rest of the world that it treated the indigenous peoples within its own borders with justice and honor.[5]

Among the earliest and most eloquent advocates of this position was D'Arcy McNickle. Born on the Flathead Reservation to a Cree mother and Scots-Irish father in 1904, McNickle entered the Indian Service during the 1930s, just as Commissioner of Indian Affairs John Collier initiated the Indian New Deal, a wide-ranging reform agenda that intended to bolster tribal self-government. McNickle helped to found the National Congress of American Indians in 1944, before resigning from the Bureau of Indian Affairs (BIA) ten years later, disgusted by the advent of termination (see table 2). Like Deloria, McNickle believed that Indians shared "the world experience of other native peoples subjected to colonial domination." In the 1950s he set about extending "the process of decolonization to the United States" through an organization called American Indian Development (AID).[6]

In 1960 McNickle committed AID to sponsoring the Workshop on American Indian Affairs, a six-week program for Indian college students, initiated by University of Chicago anthropologist Sol Tax in the summer of 1956. At the outset, the workshops endeavored to offer course credit through the University of Colorado, provide an incentive for Indian youths to complete their degrees, and cultivate a new generation of leaders—a particularly important goal, given the threat that termination posed to many Native communities. The workshops metamorphosed into something greater still after Robert K. Thomas, a Cherokee doctoral candidate at the University of Chicago, placed his mark on the curriculum (figure 6).[7] Through a combination of reading about Robert Redfield's anthropological work in Latin America, studying under Edward Spicer and Sol Tax, and reflecting on his own personal experiences, Bob Thomas began thinking about American Indians as a folk people adjusting to contact with and colonization by an urban industrial society.[8]

Thomas contended that Indian students, like their peers in so-called underdeveloped countries, traditionally received vocational training to learn specific skills. When they did go to college, they dropped out in inordinately high numbers because they felt marginal, and they felt marginal because of the messages they received about who they were and where they did or did not fit in. Under his direction, workshop students learned that they were not forsaking their relatives or somehow abandoning Indian culture by going to and succeeding in college. "These kind[s] of bullshit dilemmas are false and come from high school teachers," he seethed. When students recognized that the problems they confronted personally, within their families, and in their communities were not their fault and that they were not alone, they could see these problems for what they were, objectify them, and deal with them "intellectually instead of in a personal, secret, unformalized way." Social science would make this possible by serving as a

Figure 6. Cherokee anthropologist Robert K. Thomas and Standing Rock Sioux activist Vine Deloria Jr. shaped the intellectual development of several generations of Native youths. This dining establishment clearly afforded a photo op neither of them could pass up. Thomas not only went by "Bob" but also welcomed readers of a column he wrote for *Indian Voices* with the greeting "Howdy Folks!" Photo courtesy of Daniel M. Cobb.

vehicle for the liberation of their minds and, with it, the redemption of their communities.[9]

The curriculum Bob Thomas constructed compelled students to confront the idea of internal colonialism and to apply it to analyses of federal policies, their own communities, and even themselves.[10] In 1962 Thomas asked workshop students to "[d]escribe the consequences for the world and social relations of a folk people under a colonial administration" and, even more pointedly, asked, "Is it possible for a government, given a colonial situation, to determine the destiny of the governed people and also to terminate their colonial status with success?" The final exam in 1963 read: "Compare the structure and consequences of colonialism or minority group status in one of the following: India, Kenya, Ghana, Maori in New Zealand, aboriginal people in the Philippines, with the structure and consequences of the relationship between either American Indians or a specific group and the wider American society."[11]

D'Arcy McNickle later remarked that the workshop experience served as "an awakening" for many of the students who attended.[12] The essays they wrote during their summers in Boulder lend credence to his assessment. "I had never before thought of the Indians as compared to colonialism," Frank Dukepoo (Hopi) reflected. "I thought colonialism existed only in the older countries like southern Europe or in places such as Africa."[13] Clyde Warrior (Ponca) detected similar resonances. "Another thing I learned is that all over the world tribal peoples are coming in contact with the outside world," he noted, "and basically they all have the same reactions."[14] What this young person—who was instrumental to the formation of the National Indian Youth Council in August 1961—meant by "same reactions" was, of course, rebellion. Makah tribal member and NIYC member Bruce Wilkie explained why: "[A]s long as there is a colonial agency set up to administer to Indian affairs," one of his papers read, "there will always be an Indian social problem."[15]

In a perceptive essay written in 1962, Sandra Johnson, another Makah from the Neah Bay area, extended a Cold War analogy to this discourse on colonialism and wove it into issues of identity. "It is not that Indians reject white culture, per se. It is that they reject white culture when they are forced to adapt to it by losing what they are and [what] they value. One does not painlessly reject oneself," she asserted. Searching for an appropriate metaphor, she asked how non-Indians might respond to the prospect of being forced to live under Soviet domination: "Many would cry, 'Better dead than Red.' And yet, another battle between the Reds and the Whites is being fought within our own borders. Given this different context it may be easier for white citizens to understand our cry which would sound more like, 'Better Red than dead.'"[16]

The workshop's emphasis on decolonization and ethnic pride clearly informed students' rejection of termination and assimilation. Moreover, many of the "Workshoppers," as they called themselves, carried these ideas with them as they went on to become elected tribal leaders, educators, doctors, lawyers, documentary filmmakers, artists, writers, and founders of activist organizations such as the National Indian Youth Council. From this generation arose persons who, over the course of the succeeding fifty years, would become influential promoters of change in Native America—youth activist Clyde Warrior, tribal leaders Mel Thom and Bruce Wilkie, filmmaker Sandy (Johnson) Osawa, former Institute of American Indian Arts president Della (Hopper) Warrior (Otoe-Missouria), lawyer Browning Pipestem

(Otoe), tribal college administrator Phyllis Howard (Mandan), Stockbridge-Munsee community leader Dorothy Davids, Mary Hillaire (Lummi), Evergreen State College's first Native staff member, and many, many others (Warrior, chapter 16, this volume). All of them have been active in decolonizing a wide range of spheres, from art and education to mass media and federal–Indian relations.[17]

A second example of how international affairs shaped Indian politics during the 1960s can be found in the American Indian Chicago Conference. Seizing upon a United Nations proclamation that the 1960s would be the "Decade of Development," Sol Tax proposed a meeting that would bring delegates from across Indian Country to Chicago in order to finalize a comprehensive "Declaration of Indian Purpose." This statement would, in turn, be presented in person to John F. Kennedy, the newly elected president of the United States. The National Congress of American Indians endorsed the idea in December 1960, and D'Arcy McNickle quickly took the lead in authoring a draft document. Then, during the spring, Sol Tax coordinated a series of regional meetings in which Indian and non-Indian people discussed and critiqued it. Long an advocate of the Point IV philosophy, McNickle infused the initial statement with the spirit of international development. The final declaration even resurrected the Cold War imperative by intoning, "[T]he problem we raise affects the standing which our nation sustains before world opinion."[18]

Looked at from a different perspective, the Chicago conference reveals still another dimension to politics in Cold War Native America. Indeed, one of the untold stories of the event is the extent to which it was plagued by the politics of anticommunism. If the Chicago conference's proponents sought to harness the Cold War as a means of advancing a progressive agenda, its detractors used the fear of communist subversion as a bulwark against change. Earl Boyd Pierce, general counsel of the Cherokee Nation of Oklahoma, proved instrumental in this regard. Born and raised in Ft. Gibson, a small town in Muskogee County, Oklahoma, he saw himself as a champion of the American way of life, venerated Federal Bureau of Investigation director J. Edgar Hoover, and kept an autographed copy of the zealous anticommunist's book, *Masters of Deceit*, in his personal library. Although he actively pursued Cherokee legal claims against the federal government, he was suspicious of strident acts of protest, such as civil rights demonstrations and antiwar rallies.[19]

The Chicago conference came under close scrutiny in January 1961 when the Inter-Tribal Council of the Five Civilized Tribes convened in Muskogee, Oklahoma.[20] Detecting a nefarious scheme, Cherokee principal chief W. W. Keeler, an executive for Phillips Petroleum, recalled a trip to the

Soviet Union he had taken in August 1960: Some Russians "took me aside and explained to me how they would like to work with me in working out plans to set up some *Indian Republics* here in the United States. [T]hey talked about *freeing the Indians*...they had the idea Indians are held as prisoners... they spoke of the Indians in leg-irons...." But that was not all. "They said it came from the reports of the *University of Chicago*." Earl Boyd Pierce added his own premonition that Sol Tax, D'Arcy McNickle, and others intended to lay a "booby trap" in Chicago that would culminate in nothing less than "an overall Governmental State."[21]

With deep suspicions in tow, Pierce traveled to Chicago in February to attend a meeting of Indian leaders who had been chosen to serve as the steering committee for the conference. He proceeded to bait the participants and to underscore that Indians were no longer sovereign nations—that they must remain loyal to the United States government.[22] Repeatedly, the Cherokee general counsel argued that the Interior Department and the Bureau of Indian Affairs should be consulted before Indians took any definite actions. By being too forceful, he feared, they would come off as "an unhappy minority."[23] Pierce had to leave before the steering committee disbanded, and he suspected rightly that he had earned their derision.[24] He also knew that a tape recorder had been running throughout all but the first session. Upon his return to Oklahoma, he requested copies. An incredible game of cat and mouse followed, with Pierce pursuing what had become, in his mind, a "black plot against him" and assistant coordinator Nancy Lurie, an anthropologist and a former student of Sol Tax, doing all in her power to forestall the inevitable surrender.[25]

In the months that followed, opponents of the Chicago conference spread rumors that Tax, a Jew whose socialist parents emigrated from Germany, was a communist in disguise.[26] If Pierce could not destroy the conference by whispering such intimations, he resolved personally to see that no one advanced a radical agenda. When the hundreds of tribal delegates finally descended on Chicago in June 1961, he and his allies worked diligently to secure passage of a stridently anticommunist "American Indian Pledge" that ultimately prefaced the "Declaration of Indian Purpose."[27] In ultrapatriotic prose targeting Tax and his allies, it denounced "the efforts of the promoters of any alien form of government." When representatives from the Chicago conference finally had their personal meeting with John F. Kennedy, it appears that the "American Indian Pledge" was the only part of the declaration the president actually read.[28]

This aspect of the Chicago conference suggests that the intersection between domestic and international politics did not occur merely in the realm of ideas. Rather, it literally shaped behavior and, with it, the course of events. In this instance, the Cold War served as a powerful backdrop. Just as decolonization informed the organizers' embrace of development through democratic self-determination, fear of communist subversion inspired its opponents.

Another unanticipated manifestation of these ideational border crossings—one that extended into the realm of action—can be found in the strategy Vine Deloria carved out for the National Congress of American Indians. Upon assuming the executive directorship in 1964, not only did he adopt rhetoric reminiscent of that found in anticolonial movements across the globe, but he also used similar approaches for affecting change. In a study of Cold War foreign policy, historian John Lewis Gaddis observed that although "Third World" countries could not challenge the Soviet Union or the United States militarily, they could manipulate these world powers "by laying on flattery, pledging solidarity, feigning indifference, threatening defection, or even raising the specter of their own collapse and the disastrous results that might flow from it."[29] Under Deloria's direction, the NCAI engaged in precisely this kind of veiled resistance by adopting a carefully orchestrated play-off system involving several government agencies.

President Lyndon Baines Johnson unwittingly handed him the primary vehicle he would use to push for reform, when Johnson launched and then proceeded to escalate the War on Poverty (see table 4, 1964). Deloria immediately formed a significant relationship with James J. Wilson, an Oglala Lakota brought in to oversee all the War on Poverty's Indian programs in the spring of 1965. Channeled through what Deloria called "inside-outside politics," they seem to have agreed to use each other in order to manipulate the federal bureaucracy from within rather than confront it from without. Both of them well knew that the War on Poverty—and particularly the Community Action Program, given its direct funding of tribes and emphasis on local initiative—offered a potent critique of wardship and paternalism. Having the dubious distinction of being the quintessential symbol of these unsavory concepts, the Bureau of Indian Affairs became the central focus of their attacks.[30]

The political strategy Wilson and Deloria devised evidenced itself during the National Congress of American Indians' annual convention in Scottsdale, Arizona, in November 1965. Through the spring, summer, and fall of that year, the Office of Economic Opportunity, which served as the administrative headquarters to the War on Poverty, was embroiled in tremendous controversy, in large part because of the explosion of the Watts riot in Los Angeles. Members of Congress and city mayors intimated that federal money was being used to incite racial and class conflict. At the same time, the rising cost of the war in Vietnam meant potential budget cuts for the War on Poverty.

R. Sargent Shriver, the director of the Office of Economic Opportunity, found himself fighting two battles. First, he argued with President Lyndon Johnson over how much money it would take to win the antipoverty campaign. Second, he had to struggle with city mayors and congressmen to save the grassroots-centered approach of Community Action.[31]

Vine Deloria and Jim Wilson understood that they could leverage these struggles to advance tribal interests. Networking with other Washington insiders, they suggested to R. Sargent Shriver that he attend the NCAI convention and use it as an opportunity to fight back. Given the depth of bitterness directed toward BIA paternalism and the popularity of Community Action in Indian Country, there could be few better places for Sargent Shriver to reaffirm his commitment to the idea of maximum feasible participation of the poor. This calculated maneuver paid off. "He was almost like a conquering hero returning," one observer remembered of Shriver's arrival at the convention. Deloria had a similar recollection of the event. "I can remember him coming into the hotel, and, by God, it took him ten minutes to get up on the podium.... All these people wanted to show him pictures of their projects or talk to him. Everybody was just shaking hands with him. I hardly had a chance to say two words to him, and I was running the whole thing...."[32]

Shriver used his address to proclaim the Office of Economic Opportunity's commitment to tribal self-determination. Reservation communities, he argued, could be likened to underdeveloped nations, and, therefore, the same kinds of prescriptions for change applied to them. "[W]hite imperialism, white paternalism," he argued in a thinly veiled reference to the BIA, "cannot be replaced by the paternalism of experts, the imperialism of professionals." He also said, "The money is yours—because the whole basis of the poverty program is self-determination—the right of the people—individually and collectively—to decide their own course and to find their own way."[33] Deloria considered Shriver's performance a tremendous success. The War on Poverty received the positive media coverage it needed, while he gained additional leverage to use against the established bureaucracy. With OEO on his side, Deloria recalled, he could go to the BIA and say, "Okay, we'll listen to the commissioner, but this better be good."[34]

Vine Deloria allowed the Office of Economic Opportunity to cultivate a romantic image of Community Action. But did that mean he really believed in it? Consider this remembrance from my interview with him: "I never liked most of the OEO people cause they were so...snobby, and they were all Ivy League people, you know?" They might talk a good game about empowerment and representation, he remembered, but they had no idea what it was like to live in poverty. "[If] you took one of these OEO guys and put him in the towns we grew up in, they'd make a total ass of themselves," he stated flatly. "They'd be run out of town in a half hour."[35]

This observation needs to be balanced with the following exchange Deloria had with a non-Indian social scientist named Murray Wax. Wax took particular umbrage at the War on Poverty's Head Start preschool program, basing his assessment on extended on-site evaluations in centers across Indian Country. "I have looked closely at poverty programs on Indian reservations and I assure you they violate the fundamental principle of Indian self-determination," he wrote to Deloria. "Do Indian parents really need Head Start programs so as to transform their children into Whites?!?" Deloria offered a response rich with irony. "I don't believe you are understanding what is taking place in regard to poverty programs and Indianism —the more educated they get, the more nationalistic they get also," he wrote. "Head Start just provides us with a chance to get them a solid basis for becoming nationalists 2 years sooner."[36]

Vine Deloria not only talked the language of the larger world but also walked the walk. "In any fight with an institution, the institution will always win because it's going to be there longer than you," he later explained to me. "So you gotta screw up the way it operates itself, turn it in on itself, create a crisis for it. And then, they'll give you what you want and alter things." In public addresses, congressional testimony, formal resolutions, and the pages of the NCAI's publications, Deloria proceeded to use innuendo, warnings of impending crises, fulsome praise, and caustic ridicule to play Congress, the Interior Department, the Bureau of Indian Affairs, the Office of Economic Opportunity, and even tribal leaders against one another. "The only way we're going to get anywhere," he later said in justification of this approach, "is to praise one agency while kicking the ass of another and get those two competing with each other."[37]

This logic was certainly operative in Scottsdale in 1965, but another event in April of the following year may provide the single best example. By the spring of 1966, heightened anxieties over the resignation of one Indian Affairs commissioner and the appointment of another, rumblings of support for termination in the Senate, and rumors of the BIA's designs to take over the Office of Economic Opportunity's Indian programs permeated Indian Country. Amidst this tumult, Interior secretary Stewart Udall organized a policy meeting for federal employees and interested congresspersons in Santa Fe, New Mexico. Arguing that Indian people deserved the right to have a voice in making decisions that affect their lives, Deloria requested permission to send NCAI observers to the four-day conference. To his exasperation, Udall declined.

Deloria had had enough. Likening the Interior Department to a giant piñata, he remembered thinking, "Let's take the closest thing we have and hit that thing as hard as we can and see what's going on." To do so, he called an emergency meeting. In short order, two hundred representatives from sixty-two tribes descended on Santa Fe to hold countermeetings a mere three blocks away from Udall's closed session. Taking the civil rights movement as his model, Deloria sought to create a "media phenomenon" that would dramatize the BIA's complete disregard for basic democratic principles. For three days, the NCAI railed against the Indian bureau as a reporter from the *New York Times* recorded every detail.[38]

Throughout the confrontation, members of the NCAI juxtaposed the "spectacular success" of local initiative via Community Action with the BIA's penchant for paternalism. The *New York Times* articles, according to Deloria, delivered the following message: "Here are the Indians who are managing their own affairs, and they've got poverty programs and everything. Here's the Bureau trying to put them back in the nineteenth century." Praising the War on Poverty while criticizing the Indian bureau fostered the kind of competition that Deloria hoped would prove advantageous to tribes. To be sure, the Office of Economic Opportunity could ill afford to lose one of the few friends it had left, and the last thing the much maligned BIA needed was to appear to be perpetuating dependency.[39]

In the wake of Santa Fe, Deloria continued the strategy. "Certainly there has been no single program or theory of government that has caused such excitement on Indian reservations in 100 years as the Poverty Program," he expounded in the pages of the *NCAI Sentinel*. But in keeping with the strategy employed by other developing nations during the Cold War, he added a dire warning: "There is now a good chance for wholesale collapse of enthusiasm on reservations if the basic philosophy of the OEO is changed to conform to what is happening in the large cities." Through the spring and summer of 1966, black-white coalitions fragmented, calls for Black Power and welfare rights peaked, and the inner cities exploded. Through it all, the National Congress of American Indians continued to cultivate an image of Indians as the one minority group that Lyndon Johnson's administration could safely champion without fear of white reprisal. Why? To advance a nationalist agenda to promote tribal sovereignty.[40]

After Vine Deloria resigned from the NCAI in 1967 to pursue a law degree at the University of Colorado, John Belindo (Kiowa/Navajo) carried his efforts forward. In March 1968 the organization scored a victory when President Johnson issued "The Forgotten American," the twentieth century's first presidential statement devoted exclusively to Indian affairs. The address did not renounce termination outright, but it did indicate that the Johnson administration wanted to end the debate by committing the federal government to a policy of "self-help and self-determination."[41] Showing himself to be equally adept at leverage seeking, Belindo assured Johnson's advisers that if the NCAI were given an audience with the president, then it would "include quotes like 'The Johnson Administration has done more for Indians than any other president'" and would also "support the President's Viet Nam stand."[42] Following closely on the heels of the disastrous Tet Offensive in Vietnam, this must have been inviting, indeed.

The Poor People's Campaign, a massive six-week protest in the heart of Washington DC, revealed that even as the NCAI's patient incrementalism seemed to be producing results, the political climate was becoming increasingly radicalized. Less than two months after Johnson issued "The Forgotten American," thousands of poor whites, blacks, Chicanos, and American Indians converged on the capitol, taking up residence in Resurrection City, a makeshift community located just off the National Mall, and in churches and schools throughout the city. Together, they marched, picketed, testified before Congress, conducted sit-ins, and allowed themselves to be arrested— all in an effort to expose what they considered to be the grave injustices visited upon those who lived in America's shadows. Over the course of the Poor People's Campaign, a demonstration was staged outside the Supreme Court to protest the anti-treaty fishing rights *Puyallup* decision, and a spontaneous sit-in occurred at the Bureau of Indian Affairs headquarters.[43]

Indian involvement in what many perceived to be a primarily African American demonstration created deep divisions within tribal communities. The National Congress of American Indians, as well as a number of tribal governments, refused to endorse the Poor People's Campaign. Although Vine Deloria understood the Indian participants' anger and reasons for being there, he questioned their tactics. "The temptation to be militant overcomes the necessity to be nationalistic," he later wrote in *Custer Died for Your Sins*. "Anyone can get into the headlines by making wild threats and militant statements. It takes a lot of hard work to raise an entire group to a new conception of themselves. And that is the difference between the nationalists and the militants."[44]

Mel Thom did not see it this way. On May 1, 1968, Thom—a participant in the American Indian Chicago Conference, a student in the Workshop on American Indian Affairs, a founding member of the National Indian Youth Council, and director of the Walker River Paiute Community Action Program—stood as one with a multiracial delegation of the poor called the Committee of One Hundred as it met face-to-face with members from President Lyndon Johnson's cabinet. In an impassioned speech delivered before representatives from the Bureau of Indian Affairs, Thom spoke of poverty as a product of internal colonialism. "There is no way to improve upon racism, immorality and colonialism; it can only be done away with," he railed. "The system and power structure serving Indian peoples is a sickness which has grown to epidemic proportions. The Indian system is sick. Paternalism is the virus, and the Secretary of the Interior is the carrier...."[45]

By drawing analogies between Indians and others, and particularly by locating the struggle of Native people squarely in the context of decolonization, Mel Thom followed in the tradition of D'Arcy McNickle, Sol Tax, Robert K. Thomas, and even Vine Deloria Jr., though he came to a different conclusion. As he wove together issues regarding race, poverty, identity, and power, he made a demand not only for self-determination but also for national liberation. The time for talking was over. "The day is coming when we're gonna move," he warned during a second encounter with government officials, this time representatives from the Office of Economic Opportunity. "And when we move, like I said, watch out!"[46] As Mel Thom hammered his fist against a table, he offered an accurate premonition of things to come. Later that summer, in Minneapolis, Minnesota, members of an embattled urban community formed an organization they eventually called the American Indian Movement, and in California a small contingent of college students launched an abortive attempt to occupy and lay claim to Alcatraz Island as Indian land (see table 4). The rest, as they say, is history.[47]

This analysis of the Workshop on American Indian Affairs, American Indian Chicago Conference, War on Poverty, and Poor People's Campaign illuminates several new dimensions of American Indian politics and activism during the 1960s. It shows how a generation of Indians and non-Indians situated themselves and the struggle for tribal self-determination in the context of domestic controversies involving race, class, and war, as well as global concerns over the rights of indigenous peoples and the Cold War. But talking the language of the larger world, no matter how conceptually powerful it proved to be, did not necessarily produce results—for it was one thing to speak, another to be heard, and still something different to be understood. Indeed, as Mel Thom stood in solidarity with the Committee of One Hundred, he had reached the point of exasperation for the very reason that Indian people had been listened to but not understood. Despite drawing analogies and assiduously pointing out parallels, the dominant society simply could not or would not make the translation. It is a problem that continues to this day.

Notes

1. Robert Bee, "Tribal Leadership in the War on Poverty: A Case Study," *Social Science Quarterly* 50 (December 1969): 676–686; Francis Paul Prucha, *The Great Father: The United*

States Government and the American Indian, 2 vols. (Lincoln: University of Nebraska Press, 1984), 1087–1109; Kenneth Philp, ed., *Indian Self-Rule: First-Hand Accounts of Indian–White Relations from Roosevelt to Reagan* (Salt Lake City: Howe Brothers, 1988; Logan: Utah State University, 1995), 186–259; Päivi Hoikkala, "Mothers and Community Builders: Salt River Pima and Maricopa Women in Community Action," in *Negotiators of Change: Historical Perspectives on Native American Women*, ed. Nancy Shoemaker (New York: Routledge, 1995), 213–234; George Pierre Castile, *To Show Heart: Native American Self-Determination and Federal Indian Policy, 1960–1975* (Tucson: University of Arizona Press, 1998); Daniel Cobb, "Philosophy of an Indian War: Indian Community Action in the Johnson Administration's War on Indian Poverty, 1964–1968," *American Indian Culture and Research Journal* 22, no. 2 (1998): 71–103; Thomas Clarkin, *Federal Indian Policy in the Kennedy and Johnson Administrations, 1961–1969* (Albuquerque: University of New Mexico Press, 2000); and Daniel Cobb, "'Us Indians understand the basics': Oklahoma Indians and the Politics of Community Action, 1964–1970," *Western Historical Quarterly* XXXIII (Spring 2002): 41–66.

2. Paul Chaat Smith and Robert Allen Warrior, *Like a Hurricane: The Indian Movement from Alcatraz to Wounded Knee* (New York: The New Press, 1996); Troy Johnson, *The Occupation of Alcatraz Island: Indian Self-Determination and the Rise of Indian Activism* (Urbana: University of Illinois Press, 1997); and Troy Johnson, Joane Nagel, and Duane Champagne, eds., *American Indian Activism: Alcatraz to the Longest Walk* (Urbana: University of Illinois Press, 1997).

3. Vine Deloria Jr., interview by author, tape recording, Golden, CO, October 18, 2001. The quote regarding "resurgent nationalism" is from Stan Steiner, *The New Indians* (New York: Dell Publishing Co., 1968), 44.

4. For examples of the earlier generation's rhetoric, see Frederick Hoxie, ed., *Talking Back to Civilization: Indian Voices from the Progressive Era* (Boston: Bedford/St. Martin's, 2001).

5. Daniel Cobb, "Indian Politics in Cold War America: Parallel and Contradiction," *Princeton University Library Chronicle* LXVII (Winter 2006): 392–419; and Paul Rosier, "'They Are Ancestral Homelands': Race, Place, and Politics in Cold War Native America," *Journal of American History* 92 (March 2006): 1300–1326. For an extended discussion of the ethnocentric underpinnings of ideas such as modernization and development, see Michael Latham, *Modernization as Ideology: American Social Science and "Nation Building" in the Kennedy Era* (Chapel Hill: University of North Carolina Press, 2000).

6. D'Arcy McNickle, *They Came Here First: The Epic of the American Indian* (1949; New York: Harper and Row, 1975), 284; and Frederick Hoxie, "'Thinking like an Indian': Exploring American Indian Views of American History," *Reviews in American History* 29, no. 1 (2001): 9. Also see Dorothy Parker, *Singing an Indian Song: A Biography of D'Arcy McNickle* (Lincoln: University of Nebraska Press, 1992).

7. For more on Robert K. Thomas, see Steve Pavlik, ed., *A Good Cherokee, A Good Anthropologist: Papers in Honor of Robert K. Thomas* (Los Angeles: UCLA American Indian Studies Center, 1998).

8. "Carnegie Cross-Cultural Education Project-Miscellaneous" folder, Sol Tax Papers, NAES College Archives, Chicago. Seventh Annual Workshop on Indian Affairs Brochure, folder 195, box 23, and Staff Meeting, June 16, 1962, folder 211, box 24, McNickle Papers; Education for Leadership, p. 3, "Topical Files—American Indian Development, Sept. 1960–May 1962" folder, Robert Reitz Papers, NAES College Archives, Chicago. See also Robert Thomas, "Colonialism: Classic and Internal," *New University Thought* 4, no. 4 (1966–1967): 37–44.

9. Bob Thomas to Clyde Warrior, n.d., folder 31, box 3, National Indian Youth Council Papers, Center for Southwest Research, University of New Mexico, Albuquerque. See also Rolland Harry Wright, "The American Indian College Student: A Study in Marginality" (Ph.D. diss., Brandeis University, 1972), 20–21.

10. Students read works by Ruth Benedict, Karl Manheim, Dorothy Lee, Everett and Helen Hughes, George Simmel, David Riesman, Robert Redfield, Bob Thomas, D'Arcy McNickle, Felix Cohen, and others. Workshop on American Indian Affairs 1963 Report, pp. 6–9, "AID Subject File Reports" folder, box 25, Helen L. Peterson Papers, National Anthropological Archives, Smithsonian Institution, Suitland, MD.

11. Workshop on American Indian Affairs 1962 Report, pp. 6–7, 16, "Topical-Education-Summer Workshops-1962" folder, Reitz Papers; Workshop on American Indian Affairs, July 26, 1962, Final Examination, folder 211, box 24, D'Arcy McNickle Papers, The Newberry Library, Chicago; Gloria Keliiaa, untitled essay, "Workshops 1962 Student Papers 2" folder, and Georgianna Webster, untitled essay, and Ona White Wing, untitled essay, "Workshops 1962 Student Papers 4" folder, box 29; Workshop on American Indian Affairs 1963 Report, "AID Subject File Reports" folder, box 25, Peterson Papers; and Lenore LaMere, untitled essay, July 24, 1962, "Topical-Education-Summer Workshops-1962 Student Papers" folder, Reitz Papers.

12. Quoted in Parker, *Singing an Indian Song*, 196.

13. Frank Dukepoo essay, July 16, 1962, "Workshops 1962 Student Papers 1" folder, box 29, series 19, Peterson Papers.

14. Clyde Warrior essay on *Where Peoples Meet*, "Workshops 1962 Student Papers 4" folder, box 29, series 19, Peterson Papers.

15. Bruce Wilkie essay, "Workshops 1962 Student Papers 4" folder, box 29, series 18, Peterson Papers.

16. Sandy Johnson, "Final Conclusions," "Workshops, 1964 Miscellaneous Student Papers and Exams 2" folder, box 30, Peterson Papers.

17. I thank Denise Howard, a student in my 2005 senior seminar on American Indian politics and activism at Miami University, for compiling a complete list of workshop students, making this follow-up research possible.

18. American Indian Chicago Conference, "Declaration of Indian Purpose: The Voice of the American Indian" (Chicago: University of Chicago, 1961), 4–5, 7, 16–18, 19, 20.

19. Earl Boyd Pierce (Cherokee), May 6, 1967, vol. 17, Doris Duke Oral History Collection, Western History Collections, University of Oklahoma, Norman. The copy of *Masters of Deception* is held by the Cherokee National Archives in Tahlequah, OK. For more on how anticommunism shaped Indian politics at the local level, see Daniel Cobb, "Devils in Disguise: The Carnegie Project, the Cherokee Nation, & the 1960s," *American Indian Quarterly*, 31, no. 3 (2007): 201–237.

20. *Five Civilized Tribes* refers to the Cherokee, Choctaw, Chickasaw, Creek, and Seminole nations.

21. Report of the Meeting of the Inter-tribal Council of the Five Civilized Tribes, Muskogee, OK, January 11, 1961, 10:00 a.m., pp. 20–21, folder 36, box 82, Alice Marriott Collection, Western History Collections, University of Oklahoma, Norman.

22. Nancy Lurie to Alice Marriott, 3 March 1961, "Ma…(cont'd)" folder, box 8, series III, American Indian Charter Convention Records, National Anthropological Archives, Smithsonian Institution, Suitland, MD.

23. Roy Stewart, "Indian Charter Groups Merit Long Look," *Daily Oklahoman*, April 2, 1961, A3.

24. Nancy Lurie to Sol Tax, 16 February 1961, "N. O. Lurie, Jan–Feb 1961" folder, box 8, and Nancy Lurie to D'Arcy McNickle, 22 February 1961, "D'Arcy McNickle" folder, box 9, series III, Records of the American Indian Charter Convention, National Anthropological Archives, Smithsonian Institution, Suitland, MD.

25. Nancy Lurie to Alice Marriott, 3 March 1961, "Ma...(cont'd)" folder, box 8, and Nancy Lurie to D'Arcy McNickle, 22 February 1961, "D'Arcy McNickle" folder, box 9, series III, AICC Records. For Pierce's correspondence, see Earl Boyd Pierce to Nancy Lurie, 18 February 1961, Earl Boyd Pierce to Nancy Lurie, 20 February 1961, Earl Boyd Pierce to Nancy Lurie, 21 February 1961, and Earl Boyd Pierce to Nancy O. Lurie, 6 March 1961, "P general" folder, box 9, series III, AICC Records.

26. Alice Marriott and Carol Rachlin to Sol Tax, 9 April 1961, and Agenda for Meeting of the Inter-tribal Council of the Five Civilized Tribes of Oklahoma to Be Held at Muskogee, Oklahoma, District Court Room, Federal Building, April 12, 1961, 9:45 a.m., folder 36, box 82, Marriott Collection; D'Arcy McNickle to Sol Tax, 31 March 1961, "D'Arcy McNickle" folder, box 9, and Nancy Lurie to Alice Marriott, 3 March 1961, "Ma–(cont'd)" folder, box 8, series III, AICC Records.

27. Nancy Lurie, "The Voice of the American Indian: Report on the American Indian Chicago Conference," *Current Anthropology* 2 (December 1961): 495; and Nancy Lurie, "Sol Tax and Tribal Sovereignty," *Human Organization* 58, no. 1 (1999): 112, 114.

28. AICC, "Declaration of Indian Purpose," inside front cover; Clarkin, *Federal Indian Policy*, 80.

29. John Lewis Gaddis, *We Now Know: Rethinking Cold War History* (New York: Oxford University Press, 1997), 154.

30. James J. Wilson, interview by author, tape recording, Rapid City, SD, 7 October 2001; and Deloria interview, 18 October 2001.

31. Susan Abrams Beck, "The Limits of Presidential Activism: Lyndon Johnson and the Implementation of the Community Action Program," *Presidential Studies Quarterly* 27 (Summer 1987): 547–548, 553–555; Michael Gillette, ed., *Launching the War on Poverty: An Oral History* (New York: Twayne Publishers, 1996), 143; and Robert Alan Bauman, "Race, Class, and Political Power: The Implementation of the War on Poverty in Los Angeles" (Ph.D. diss., University of California, Santa Barbara, 1998), 76–79, 139–167.

32. James J. Wilson, interview by author, tape recording, Rapid City, SD, 5 October 2001; Forrest Gerard, interview by author, tape recording, Albuquerque, NM, 30 May 2002; and Vine Deloria Jr., interview by author, tape recording, Golden, CO, 19 October 2001.

33. Sargent Shriver, "Tribal Choice in War on Poverty: Rubber Stamp or Communal Decision?" *Journal of American Indian Education* 5 (January 1966): 8–13, quotes at pp. 12 and 8.

34. Deloria interview, 19 October 2001.

35. Deloria interview, 19 October 2001.

36. Murray L. Wax to Vine Deloria Jr., 29 April 1966, and Vine Deloria Jr. to Murray L. Wax, 2 May 1966, in author's possession. I would like to thank Murray Wax for giving me these and many other letters.

37. Deloria interview, 19 October 2001; and Deloria interview, 18 October 2001.

38. Deloria interview, 18 October 2001. See also Joe Herrerra to delegates of NCAI, n.d.; Vine Deloria to All Indian Tribes, n.d.; and Remarks of Secretary of the Interior Stewart L. Udall at his Bureau of Indian Affairs Conference, Santa Fe, New Mexico, April 14, 1966, p. 2, "1966 NCAI Santa Fe Conference" folder, box 20, Earl Boyd Pierce Collection, Cherokee National Archives, Cherokee Heritage Center, Tahlequah, OK. I have also drawn from Donald Janson, "Indian Bureau Parley Rebuffs Tribes," *New York Times*, April 14, 1966, reprinted in *NCAI Sentinel* 11 (Spring 1966).

39. For first quotation, see Janson, "Indian Bureau Parley Rebuffs Tribes." The second quotation is from Deloria interview, 18 October 2001.

40. Editorial, *NCAI Sentinel* 11 (Summer 1966).

41. *The Public Papers of the Presidents of the United States. Lyndon B. Johnson, Containing the Public Messages, Speeches, and Statements of the President, 1968–1969*, book 1 (Washington DC: GPO, 1970), 336.

42. Joseph H. Carter to James R. Jones, 28 February 1968, "EX IN Indian 3/1/68-9/30/68" folder, box 1, EX IN Indian Affairs, Lyndon Baines Johnson Presidential Library, Austin, TX.

43. "Poor Marchers Besiege Supreme Court," *Washington Post*, May 30, 1968, A1, A12; and "Five Supreme Court Windows Smashed," *The Evening Star* (Washington DC), May 29, 1968, A1, A3.

44. Vine Deloria Jr., *Custer Died for Your Sins: An Indian Manifesto* (1969; New York: Avon Books, 1970), 270.

45. "Statements of Demands for Rights of the Poor Presented to Agencies of the US Government by the Southern Christian Leadership Conference and Its Committee of 100, 29–30 April and 1 May 1968" attached to Ralph Abernathy to Congressman Harris, n.d., folder 30 [1 of 3], box 48, Carl Albert General Collection, Carl Albert Center for Congressional Research and Studies, University of Oklahoma, Norman. On the Poor People's Campaign generally, see Robert Chase, "Class Resurrection: The Poor People's Campaign of 1968 and Resurrection City," *Essays in History* 40 (1998): 8, 10, 14–16, 20.

46. Poor People's Campaign, tape 381.238, Motion Picture, Sound, and Video Research Room, National Archives and Records Administration II, College Park, MD. Robert K. Thomas also predicted that the nationalistic youth movement would lead to violence.

47. Smith and Warrior, *Like a Hurricane*, 1–17, 127–136.

10 In the Arena
An Expert Witness View of the Indian Claims Commission

Helen Hornbeck Tanner

Assessments of the Indian Claims Commission (ICC; see table 3) stress the problems that stemmed from the adversarial approach of the court, as well as its reliance on monetary awards rather than on return of land. Other scholars point to distortions of Indian history resulting from the expert witnesses' adoption of models of evolutionary cultural development and definition of boundaries that little resembled the way Native people related to the landscape. The court favored simplistic portraits of Native people instead of more realistic, albeit complicated, perspectives.[1] Tribes had to contend with these limitations just as they had had to cope with earlier challenges of not being allowed to sue the government for the treaty violations and, later, having to convince Congress to pass special legislation to allow them to sue in court. Tribal leaders began pressing the government to provide redress for treaty violation in the early nineteenth century, and they relied on help from Indian communities to raise money for delegations to petition for the right to hire attorneys and meet with Congress. Even after the ICC settled claims, tribes continued to protest the injustice of those settlements. Helen Tanner, an expert witness in sixteen cases before the ICC, provides a firsthand account of the practices that denied Indians an opportunity to make their case for just settlement. She highlights how the court ignored Indian testimony or viewed Indian witnesses in stereotypical ways that weakened or negated their testimony. Also, she notes how Native people worked behind the scenes through non-Indian friends and allies to influence the legal process (Smith, chapter 8, this volume).

The slippery path into the arena of hotly contested Indian Claims Commission litigation began, of course, with an innocuous introduction. In the late fall of 1961, at a meeting of the Women's Research Club at the University of Michigan, well-known anthropologist Nancy O. Lurie turned to me and casually said that I ought to help her lawyer friends with some research she could not undertake because she was about to leave Ann Arbor to start a new and demanding job in Milwaukee. As a new Ph.D., effectively tied to my home base as a faculty wife with four children, I was teaching only a couple off-campus graduate courses in Latin American history. The opportunity to work a flexible schedule was appealing. She said that the lawyers wanted to find out which Indians lived around Ann Arbor at the time of the American Revolution.

This seemed like a reasonable request, for we lived only a few blocks from the campus and I had already done considerable research at the William L. Clements Library, which specializes in the Revolutionary War era. Very soon, I had an interview with a lawyer from the Upper Peninsula, a member of the state judiciary who described the same subject for historical investigation. When I agreed to his proposal to conduct research at an hourly rate, he immediately gave me a $500 check as an advance. What a shock! I had never known of such a lucrative academic assignment. It seemed that research for lawyers might be more profitable than writing journal articles.

With Nancy Lurie's suggestions about where to begin reading, I started out in the frame of mind that I was working on a seminar paper on a totally unfamiliar subject. I knew little American history, though I had intensively studied the colonial era in the Gulf Coast area and the Florida-Georgia border, and I had never taken a course in anthropology. But I felt confident that I could deal with local history. For the Indian information, I camped out at the Museum of Anthropology and received a running "tutorial" from the very helpful faculty who turned up at the museum library.

Of course, my initial assumption about the simplicity of this task was incredibly naive. After agreeing to do the research and write a summary report, I gradually became aware of the complications and ramifications of the legal cases that necessitated the research. Actually, Ann Arbor was just the edge of the total area of interest to these lawyers. They wanted to find out which tribes were "occupying" which areas of southeastern Michigan and Ohio at the time of American independence, as well as at the time the tribes signed treaties ceding the land to the United States. This information would be presented to the Indian Claims Commission in Washington DC, with the prospect of getting an award if the original selling price, usually a few cents an acre, was judged insufficient and unfair at the time of government acquisition. (Base price for government land on sale to prospective settlers was $1.25 an acre.) There were also other matters for consideration, such as evidence of fraud.

Learning more about this special tribunal, I discovered that such a court to hear cases of Indian treaty violations had been recommended as early as the famous Meriam Report of 1928 but none was established until 1946 after World War II. Apparently, United Nations delegates resented American criticism of the treatment of minorities in other countries. The reaction abroad was, "Go settle your Indian problems before you talk to us!" Within a few years after the Indian Claims Commission Act was passed, more than six hundred cases had been filed, but only two-thirds were accepted. According to the provisions of the act, these were to be settled in five years—which proved to be a ludicrous deadline. The Indian Claims Commission officially came to an end in 1978, but cases still unsettled continued to be heard by the Court of Appeals in Washington DC for more than a decade.

This new effort to settle claims of Indian people against the federal government was a remarkably cumbersome process. The Indian Claims Commission Act was intended to overcome the disadvantage of the nineteenth-century procedure, which compelled a tribe to secure legislation granting permission to sue the "sovereign nation," the United States of America. This procedural barrier, and resulting delay, was removed. The litigation could have been more streamlined. Under provisions of the act, the commission had the opportunity to operate as an administrative court, employing its own staff of research specialists for all the cases. The Department of Justice, for its part, rapidly rushed into battle position, insisting that if the federal government was going to be sued, then it had to be defended. Immediately, a whole new division was set up in the Department of Justice to defeat the claims that Congress had invited the Indian tribes to initiate.

Furthermore, a procedure was established whereby each case had to be litigated three times. In the first phase, a decision was handed down establishing the territory for which a tribe had proved "ownership." In the second phase, yet another decision fixed the value per acre of the ceded land. This figure, multiplied by the number of acres, determined the monetary value of the initial ICC financial award. (Though most tribes would have preferred land, the Indian Claims Commission Act specifically stated that no land would be returned.) Finally, a third hearing determined any "offsets" that the federal government might claim because of its subsequent solicitous care for that particular Indian tribe. Sometimes the sum awarded in phase two was severely reduced by this final computation, and on rare occasions, entirely wiped out.

As I began my own adventurous research, I thought that I would find a simple initial guide by consulting the appropriate maps that would portray the location and general distribution of tribal people in the United States. Always interested in the geographic setting of historical events, I had great faith in the visual power of maps, so I turned to large maps published by the Smithsonian Institution and the National Geographic Society. To my dismay, I discovered that the Ohio country and part of the Great Lakes area was just a gray expanse in the center of the map of the United States, surrounded by colorful areas with tribal names. Across the gray area was the legend "little known" or "insufficient data." It did not seem reasonable that the lands in all the rest of the United States were apparently mapped with confidence but that this blank existed in an area of relatively early settlement.

I soon realized that both anthropologists and colonial historians had avoided the early history of the Ohio country and much of the Great Lakes. Anthropologists prefer to "study" pristine "cultures" uncontaminated by the influences of western Europeans, so they pursued research in the Southwest or the exotic Northwest coast. By contrast, the Ohio valley scene was fast changing with the early-eighteenth-century presence of competing French and British traders. American colonial historians, in general, were very British oriented and avoided the area because it was initially penetrated by the French and involved too many Indians of different tribes. This "no man's land" of historical and ethnological research was a challenge to all the plaintiff law firms and to the Department of Justice in planning for the adjudication of ICC cases dealing with land in this region.

To collect adequate evidence for litigation in this particular geographical area, the Department of Justice assigned a half-million-dollar research grant to Indiana University to establish the "Great Lakes–Ohio Valley Research Project," headed by anthropologist Erminie Wheeler-Voegelin. With the assistance of a group of graduate students, she organized vast files of maps and documents, arranged by tribe. Reports were written about the Indian use and occupancy of the area ceded to the federal government by each treaty. Usually, the reports began with the statement that the American government had assumed sovereignty over the land by terms of the Treaty of Paris in 1783.

I did not find out that my own solitary research efforts would very likely be contested by the big research operation at Indiana University until a few weeks before I was scheduled to go to Washington in November 1962. An Indian book dealer phoned me to try to sell me some rare volumes that he assured me were indispensable to my writing—but I had obtained library copies. At the time, I was too busy completing a report on my own multi-tribal investigations to worry about what would happen in Washington. Besides, I was still assuming that I would turn over my research results to Nancy Lurie, who had experience with Indian claims litigation and would present the facts to the commission. Her lawyer friends, with whom I was now associated, represented several tribes that were making claims to land in Michigan and Ohio: the Wyandot, Shawnee, and Saginaw Chippewa. Subsequently, the lawyers asked me to undertake some supplementary, short-term research for lawyers representing contingents of the Potawatomi and Miami.

The principal treaties that were the basis for the upcoming hearings had been signed between 1805 and 1818. In the regional history, the first and most important treaty was the Treaty of Greenville in 1795, breaking the Ohio River boundary that had been the accepted dividing line between areas of white and Indian occupation since the British Treaty of Fort Stanwix in 1768. By the Greenville treaty, the federal government acquired the long coveted area of southern and eastern Ohio and the main portage points.

Because the regional treaty history obviously began with the Greenville, why was it not tried first? Legal strategy was the answer. Apparently, an early decision of the Indian Claims Commission had held that the federal government, in the Greenville treaty, recognized the Indian ownership of all the land northwest of the Greenville cession. "Recognized title" was an important legal asset in establishing a land claim. Generally, a tribe had to present evidence establishing "aboriginal occupancy," involving laborious research. Because the Treaty of Greenville in 1795 provided an important legal underpinning for many legal cases, the decision was made to postpone a hearing on this basic treaty until the very end. The Michigan-Ohio cases were heard in late 1962 and 1963, but the Greenville treaty land was not officially brought before the Indian Claims Commission until the summer of 1969, after the whole subject had been so frequently discussed that it had become almost tiresome.

Because each treaty in the Michigan-Ohio area was signed by representatives of several tribes, the litigation for each one included multiple competing claimants. For this reason, the dockets were consolidated for a joint hearing involving additional expert witnesses for the Ottawa, Delaware, Seneca, and Miami. The plaintiffs' side of this particular litigation was further complicated by the participation of three rival Potawatomi lawyers representing different bands—two or three contesting Shawnee groups, the eastern Miami who had remained in Indiana, and the Miami who had been removed to an Oklahoma reservation.

All assembled, quite a roomful of lawyers, expert witnesses, and ICC staff gathered for the opening of the session of "direct testimony" about the "use and occupancy" of the area covering northern Ohio and extending west of Lake Erie and north into Michigan. According to instructions, I had prepared a brief summary report of the regional history and xeroxed all the information I cited as "evidence." Yet I was, frankly, intimidated by the scene. The six commissioners sat in a row at the front of the room in big, high-backed, swiveling chairs, and the witness box was off to the right side. The initial questioning by one of my lawyers aimed to establish my status as an expert witness for the several tribes these lawyers represented. I had been told that, in all the early cases brought before the Indian Claims Commission, the expert witnesses were eminent anthropologists with established reputations and connections with prominent educational institutions. Apparently, I was the first historian to turn up in court, and somehow a doctoral degree from Michigan proved to be a sufficient qualification to be accepted as an "expert" on four Indian tribes. I wondered whether there were any specific "credentials" for an expert witness.

When the federal government defense attorney began the cross-examination, I concentrated on giving a clear and accurate account of where tribal people lived and hunted and also where they fought the Americans, mostly in Ohio. After several minutes, when I thought that the grilling was over, the lawyer suddenly exclaimed, "I move that all this testimony be stricken from the record as incompetent, irrelevant, and immaterial." Though usually tolerant, I have a short fuse when it comes to personal honor and integrity. I did not hear past "incompetent" and was instantly on my feet, pounding the table and shouting, "I have never been called incompetent in all my life, and I am not about to take it here!"

This outburst necessitated an intermission in the hearing. Four lawyers escorted me to an outside room to explain the rules of the legal game. In the first place, they said, I should have heard the suppressed laughter from other lawyers, who were astounded that this "Perry Mason" tactic had been used in the hearing room. Then they explained that I should be pleased and honored at the request to have my testimony stricken (which, of course, did not happen). If what I said *was* inconsequential, then my statements would not be contested. Of course, if my testimony might influence the decision in favor of the tribes, then the government lawyer would try to have it deleted. I recovered my composure, apologized, and gratefully accepted the peppermints offered by the nearest commissioner to help me "keep cool."

This initial experience turned me into an "activist historian." I felt as though I had been "flung into the arena," in danger of being intellectually chewed up by opposition forces inimical to the historical profession. I could not believe that the strategy of winning an ICC case could include suppressing historical information. In fact, as I discovered, the whole Anglo Saxon legal system seems inimical to history. I had taken great pains to locate the most recent, historical scholarship in books and periodicals, only to find out that the lawyers are suspicious of modern research and have a sacrosanct feeling about "original documents." I tried to explain that, without much information about the context for any written "document," such writing can often be very misleading or convey outright falsehoods. But the rule was that no one could cite a living author without bringing in the author for cross-examination. If the author fortuitously dropped dead, then his or her publications would be acceptable legal evidence. One rival lawyer later told me with triumphant glee that he had removed from my submitted evidence the fine modern work of Howard H. Peckham concerning the Pontiac War in 1763, leaving only the mellifluous nineteenth-century prose of Francis Parkman in the official record.

As an enthusiast for written history, I was surprised at the emphasis on oral testimony. The historical narrative is hard to follow in the staccato question-and-answer routine of a courtroom. The continuity is broken, and as much confusion as clarity can be introduced by impromptu questions from the commissioners. Recounting historical events is a different mental process from recalling personal experiences and observations that are apt to be the subject of other kinds of courtroom inquiry. Even more puzzling was the intrusion of concepts of English property law into the discussion of tribal territories. When I first testified before the Indian Claims Commission, the general guideline was that in order to establish a land claim, a tribe had to prove "exclusive use and occupancy" of the claimed territory "from time immemorial" up to the time of the treaty.

For southern Michigan and the Ohio country, this was a ludicrous requirement. The area was a corridor for invading Iroquois war parties at intervals in the last half of the seventeenth century and became an active war zone even before the American Revolution and continuing through the War of 1812. The very term *exclusive* is inappropriate for discussing Indian behavior, which constantly emphasizes the value of "sharing." When I described the presence in Ohio of allies from other tribes, a couple commissioners tried to class this situation as "adverse occupancy," inferring that the host tribe gave up some of its land to the temporary residents. I finally had some success in laying out a different vocabulary, stressing the reality that some areas were shared territory of "joint occupancy" and that the presence of other Indian contingents was usually evidence of the "hospitality" regularly accorded to visitors.

More confusing was my attempt to explain the significant economic loss represented by inclusion of an important river portage in the area of a land cession treaty. The tribe controlling a portage usually collected a fee for helping to move canoes, people, and cargo across the land route between two watercourses—a kind of an Indian toll road. When the American government acquired the land at the portage site by treaty, this source of revenue was no longer available to the tribe. To my astonishment, one of the commissioners immediately launched a disquisition on the subject of "riparian rights" according to English common law, and the lawyers had a round of commentary.

I discovered, to my great relief, that I did not have to worry about the general direction and conclusions of my research. In my brief report, I stressed the value of the same captivity narratives that were given special consideration by Erminie Wheeler-Voegelin in her far longer presentation of evidence. I still think that much time could have been saved by letting us collaborate freely. I am sure that we were in agreement about the basic "facts"; then the lawyers could wrestle over the legal import.

My introductory experience at the Indian Claims Commission was brief, cut short by the emergency announcement in the early afternoon of November 22 that President John Kennedy had been shot and killed in Dallas, Texas. Washington came to a halt. The hearings were recessed. It was also my wedding anniversary, and I could head for home. On the way to the airport, I watched the flags along Pennsylvania Avenue being lowered to half-mast. Hearings for the consolidated Michigan-Ohio cases resumed the following summer, with an endless amount of time spent on descriptions of canoe travel. The expert witness for the Ottawas had not written a report, but the lawyer was determined to get as much "evidence" as possible into the record of direct testimony. Because the witness was an avid paddler, he provided daily installments vividly describing a whole series of canoe journeys. Some of the other lawyers became visibly restive, but several commissioners seemed to enjoy the accounts of wilderness adventures.

One day, when I was briefly back on the witness stand, I suddenly caught a glimpse of a large man quietly entering the back of the room. He sat down, with chin resting on his left hand, and fixed a steady gaze on the row of commissioners. The chief commissioner called for an intermission to find out the identity of the surprise visitor. I later heard that there was some apprehension that a member of Congress might be checking up on the commission to find out why cases seemed to progress so slowly. Actually, the "stranger" was my husband. He had flown to Washington to find out why these hearings were continuing for such an infernally long time and when I would be home in Ann Arbor.

During the couple days my husband spent in Washington, he infused a bit of effervescent spirit in the generally staid and formal courtroom scene. He later confessed that he had cornered the long-winded canoe hobbyist witness in the men's room and sternly admonished him to answer questions with brevity, just to admit it when he had no ready answer. To ease the minds of the commissioners, he was formally introduced as a harmless psychology professor. It was his idea to host alone a convivial lunch for the principal government lawyer and expert witness Erminie Wheeler-Voegelin, a social experience forbidden to me as an "expert witness" for a plaintiff party. Then he joined a "happy hour" conversation with the plaintiff lawyers. (I would have liked to include Erminie Wheeler-Voegelin.) One of the peculiar restrictions of the adversarial legal system is the barrier to any kind of fraternization between the plaintiff and defendant personnel, which seemed to me to be artificial and unnecessary.

After my husband's brief appearance on the ICC scene, a more relaxed mood prevailed in the commission quarters. The hearing proceeded with more alacrity, and we all wanted it to end. After weeks together, we felt more like "comrades in arms" and decided to have a joint celebration when these extended hearings were over. In this legal arena, all were opponents to some degree. Among the lawyers, very real conflicts existed concerning rival claims to adjacent areas of tribal territory, as well as the government's official stance of trying to deny all claims. Among the lawyers, I became aware of two groups. I learned that "my" lawyers, who principally came from Minnesota and northern Michigan, were identified as "the independents." Then there was a collegial group, called "the syndicate," representing cooperating firms based in Chicago and other big cities. Of course, rumors circulated about the possibility that some judge was influenced by the claims brought by an individual lawyer or by the syndicate. The matter never became the subject of serious conversations.

The urbane lawyer for the Seneca decided that the celebratory function should take place at the fashionable Hunt Club. The invitation list included all the plaintiff lawyers and expert witnesses, government lawyers and staff, and the commissioners, some of whom actually attended. We toasted "justice" and one another, consumed fine food, and disbanded. This had been the lengthiest hearing in the history of the Indian Claims Commission, consuming seven weeks in the final summer. I heard that stacked pages of the transcript stood more than three feet high. I wondered who read it and how reliable was the text. All these words had to be hand-entered in a stenographic machine used by court reporters in the sixties. When I occasionally had a chance to review and correct my own spoken testimony, I found the transcript full of errors.

The unreasonable amount of verbiage in the direct testimony for the consolidated Michigan-Ohio cases brought about a change in the rules at the Indian Claims Commission. Thereafter, all direct testimony of expert witnesses had to be presented in written form, with copies of the references and footnoted information supplied as separate items of evidence.[2] The hearings before the commission henceforth entailed only cross-examination and occasionally re-direct testimony, as well as re-cross-examination.

From the beginning, the absence of any visible Indian participation in the ICC process struck me. Tribal representatives rarely turned up in court. Of course, the Indian elders know the history of their people but have a very different perspective in viewing the relative importance of past events. According to Indian custom, a leader would not make any extended statement without first explaining his personal history and genealogy, recounting his services to his people and, in general, establishing his qualifications for speaking on behalf of his tribe. He might also have a specific message in mind to convey to the court as a kind of opening statement. The commissioners were apt to consider this preamble a waste of time. Then there was the problem of asking questions. In Indian society, white people who ask questions are considered rude. If a reasonable question is posed, then the Indians feel that all sides of the query should be thoroughly explored, using as much time as it takes for everyone to state an opinion. To ask a series of questions and expect immediate brief replies is unspeakably rude. Questioning revered elders is unthinkable.

Lawyers representing tribal people at ICC hearings were sensitive enough to appreciate the problems for Indians appearing in court, where questioning was a normal part of the procedure. There was a further problem because the rules of evidence actually restrained an Indian from appearing as an "expert witness" on his or her own tribal history. "History" was a professional field, controlled by academics trained in the accepted methods for presenting impartial research and given the stamp of approval—a doctoral degree. Indian people were allowed to talk about "oral tradition," a body of information with less legal standing because there were no "documents." Among the Saginaw Chippewa in eastern Michigan, one tribal member had been assiduously collecting information about the current location of all the members of his tribe. He was working on a list of prospective claimants for a monetary award anticipated at the conclusion of the claims litigation. He also picked up a lot of genealogical information.

The lawyer wanted to have the Chippewa claims worker present his ongoing survey results to the commission as evidence of the geographic expanse of "use and occupancy" of ceded land around Saginaw Bay. This Saginaw Chippewa was an ardent supporter of tribal re-energizing. Although he was of mixed ancestry, his Indian heritage had been stamped firmly as a youth when his grandmother ceremoniously gave him an Indian name. She also taught him about Chippewa history and pointed out that her own knowledge was verified in the published county history. This factor was a problem for the claims worker's appearance in court. If he admitted that he had read in a book any information he recounted, then his oral testimony would be rejected. Apparently, the most acceptable Indian witness should be absolutely illiterate, informed exclusively by stories recounted by elders. The claims worker was coached carefully to make no mention of anything he had ever read, concentrating on what he had learned from his grandmother and what he had found out from his personal surveys. To everyone's relief, he performed well, answering all the questions from the commissioners and the Department of Justice lawyer with clarity and composure. Later, Erminie Wheeler-Voegelin said that she was impressed by his sincerity and the information he had collected.

I came in contact with more Indian people involved in pursuing awards from the Indian Claims Commission after I was appointed to the State Commission on Indian Affairs, established in Michigan in 1967 (figure 7). At meetings in Indian communities to hear requests for local assistance, I was often asked about the current status of the Michigan land claims cases that were progressing so slowly through the court system. Elderly people, many in severe financial distress, had been waiting for more than a decade, anticipating a financial award that would alleviate the strain, as well as the sense of past injustice. They knew that, in addition to the question of land value, money sums were due them from specific terms of the treaties. It was heartbreaking to realize that most of them would be dead before the long anticipated financial reward became reality.

Lawyers for the Indian tribes did not seem to maintain close contact with their Indian clients. The changes in tribal leadership complicated the situation, and, of course, the Bureau of Indian Affairs was monitoring activities. I believe that the lawyers thought that it was desirable to produce minimal paperwork, with cryptic correspondence. I did attend one big meeting in Indiana, when the local Miami gathered in a school gymnasium to hear reports on ICC cases from their leaders and legal representatives. My assignment seemed to be to field all kinds of miscellaneous inquiries as I mingled with the crowd.

In Washington, as I have pointed out, an Indian was seldom seen in the hearing room. Occasionally, a government staff member, who might be

Figure 7. After more than four decades of work as an expert witness on behalf of tribes, Helen Tanner has deep ties and close friendships in many Native communities. She is seen here (middle row, in white blouse) with a Caddo dance group in May 2005. Photo courtesy of Helen Hornbeck Tanner.

Indian or Chicano, appeared briefly on an unexplained mission. It was a real surprise one morning to find seated in the courtroom an Indian resplendent in white buckskin regalia, complete with a full-feathered headdress. All alone, he seemed to be ignored completely by everyone present. Finally, I decided that he should be accorded a little hospitality and went over to talk to him during a morning break. He explained that he was from the West Coast and had attended a special hearing that the commission had held in California. I was really interested in this western excursion of the ICC commissioners, so we continued talking throughout the intermission. He clearly thought that the chairman of the commission, Arthur V. Watkins, should be disqualified and removed from office. (As a senator, Watkins was a strong proponent of termination and relocation programs for Indian people and expressed doubts about the validity of treaties.)[3] When the hearing was about to resume, he abruptly handed me a notarized sheet of paper and asked me to give it to the lawyers I knew. Then he left the room.

The sheet of paper was a copy of a notarized affidavit signed by an Episcopal priest who had been in the company of the commissioners at some time during their California tour. In the statement was the charge that he had heard Watkins say that all American Indians should be sent back to Asia (or China) where they came from. It was an embarrassing revelation of the personal attitude of the man who was supposed to lead efforts to bring justice to the country's original inhabitants. I turned over the paper to my Minnesota lawyer, who relayed it to a Washington lawyer he knew had influential political connections. Later, I heard that this affidavit played a part in ending Watkins's career on the Indian Claims Commission. His original appointment was made by President Dwight Eisenhower after Watkins lost his bid for re-election to the Senate.

In the course of prosecuting the ICC cases, the legal personnel seldom discussed "justice" in their presentations or referred to the commission's supposed responsibility for according long overdue justice to America's diverse Indian population. The legal arena was obviously dominated by the adversarial system of Anglo law. The emphasis was not as much on the achievement of abstract "justice" as on "winning." The ICC cases became a specialized professional operation aimed at lucrative results when the three stages of litigation were finally completed. This litigation was a speculative enterprise for lawyers. When a tribal client hired them, the contract had to be government approved, and the fee for legal service was limited to 10 percent of whatever sum was finally awarded to the tribe. The litigation could go on for years, requiring the expenditure of significant financial resources before any payment was received. On one hand, many well-intentioned lawyers undertook claims for tribes but were ultimately forced to abandon the cause for financial reasons. On the other hand, in the course of ICC litigation, several firms gained prominence in this specialized legal field.

Expert witnesses did not face the financial hazards that the lawyers did. The "experts" had to be paid regularly. At the beginning of each hearing, a witness had to state under oath that full payment had been received for research and writing services in preparing the case and that remuneration was in no way dependent on the trial's outcome. I do not know the extent of the other expert witnesses' contributions to ICC cases, but I usually continued as a consultant during court session. Occasionally, I suggested lines of questioning for other witnesses and later drafted "Findings of Fact" to assist the lawyers preparing legal briefs. It was important to have the historical "facts" well stated.

Over the course of ICC litigation, the field of historical research developed into a specialized consulting profession. Although the suggestion was made, I did not feel like establishing a business enterprise of this kind, but others with scholarly credentials formed consulting firms to undertake historical research for the numerous Indian cases. In academic circles, ICC work was not professionally advantageous, though *action anthropology* became a new term. In general, the ivory tower attitude prevailed, and association with lawsuits tended to downgrade status in a university department. I know that Erminie Wheeler-Voegelin felt that her own energetic research work for the Department of Justice estranged her from her strictly academic colleagues. I was immune to these departmental tensions because I was a freelance historian and found an element of excitement in the legal game.

Not all cases within the purview of the commission's legal arena were claims against the federal government. The most intense dispute I experienced was a case involving two well-known Washington law firms representing two adjacent Sioux reservations on opposite sides of the Missouri River. Lawyers for the east bank reservation claimed for their clients a considerable proportionate interest in the west bank reservation. Although the title of the case named two tribes as plaintiff and defendant, this was really a battle between the lawyers. When I was asked to figure out the merits of this invasive claim, my first reaction was that it was an affront to history. The two tribes were friendly neighbors with a broad river between them as an obvious, recognized boundary line. There was no evidence of enmity and, in my opinion, no reasonable excuse for hostile legal action. But a reasonable amount of money was at stake, and it appeared to me that this was the sole basis for bringing suit. If successful, the east bank lawyers could get a significant part of the final award for the west bank reservation.

When I could not persuade a real Sioux expert to take over this unappealing case, I buckled down to study the "evidence." Obviously, people went back and forth across the Missouri River and engaged in many joint, sociable events. The east bank Sioux occasionally went farther west into the interior on hunting expeditions or traveled across the entire west bank reservation on their way to other destinations. This type of activity was part of normal Indian hospitality and reciprocal relationships. In the legal arena, however, these casual incidents could be collectively emphasized and distorted to present a case for "adverse occupancy," evidence that the west bank Sioux had been dispossessed of part of their own reservation.

This strange case was scheduled for hearing by only a single judge. After the Indian Claims Commission was officially disbanded, remaining cases were divided up between commissioners to try to complete the list of dockets as rapidly as possible, using several courtrooms. From the outset, the atmosphere was more formal and tense. In the witness stand, I was firmly questioned about my sources of information. I remember a critical reference to the fact that I had placed in evidence the translation of a French fur trader's journal without checking the original manuscript. In response, I explained that I found nothing in the printed journal that I thought needed checking and that a well-footnoted edition in English seemed to me more useful to the court than pages of French handwriting.

The expert witness for the opposing east bank lawyers was a member of a recently formed historical consulting firm in the Washington area. To establish his superior status as an expert witness, he called attention to the original French documents he was presenting in evidence. These included the trader's journal and other correspondence from the Missouri Historical Society. He also presented a map that displayed hunting activities of the west bank Sioux in a broad area almost entirely outside their reservation lands. The map created the false impression that the west bank Sioux did not "use and occupy" their own reservation land but that this area, to a large extent, was "used and occupied" by their east bank neighbors. I could see that, in addition to the obvious omission of pertinent data, the map had some geographical errors. Checking sources for the information on the map, I soon concluded that important watercourses had not been identified accurately, and I suspected that the problems came from misreading the French source material. I suggested that the cross-examination for this expert include a check of his knowledge of French. The lawyer was a fluent speaker and conducted a painful line of inquiry, finally forcing the expert witness to admit that he could not read any of the French documents he had introduced, with so much flourish, as evidence.

Beyond the ICC hearing room, this unhappy incident had repercussions potentially disastrous for my career. While I was in Washington, I took the opportunity to visit the office of the National Endowment for the Humanities, where the staff was considering a project, under my direction, to create an atlas of Great Lakes Indian history. The conference was reassuring, and I returned home feeling encouraged. Very soon, though, I had a disturbing phone call from a good friend in Washington, a woman whom I first knew as a judge on the Indian Claims Commission. A friend of my lawyers as well, she was also a strong supporter of local ballet performances; her daughter was a student ballerina. The core of her message was that my grant application at NEH was in serious trouble. She thought that I should have some distinguished scholars send in letters immediately assuring the endowment that I could conduct respectable research.

The story that unfolded in subsequent telephone conversations seemed preposterous. Apparently, the NEH staff member wanted to find out more about what I was doing currently and decided to call in the opposing expert witness for an interview. The witness took the opportunity to make some critical comments—enough to stall the grant application. Learning of this situation, my law firm threatened to sue the opposing law firm if NEH did not award the grant, and the opposing law firm fired the expert witness. The situation was actually saved by a fortunate coincidence. A secretary in the NEH office, also a ballet student, knew that the mother of a fellow ballerina was a judge on the Indian Claims Commission. She suggested calling my friend, just to check on the information. The phone call from NEH brought rapid results. My friend wrote a letter explaining, among other points, that my research was very helpful to the commission. She secured another letter of support from the judge who presided at the hearing, and then she carried both letters to the NEH offices for a personal conversation. Although delayed, the grant application was approved. This experience was a warning that expert witness work could be professionally hazardous.

The intense dispute over allocation of the financial award was tangential to the general course of Sioux litigation in the ICC proceedings. The Sioux received much newspaper coverage as a consequence of the confrontations at Wounded Knee on the Pine Ridge, involving Bureau of Indian Affairs–supported leaders, the American Indian Movement, and the FBI. In the ICC litigation, the controversy over the Black Hills became a central focus. Legal opinion clearly stated that the American government's action in taking over the Black Hills (after gold was discovered) was blatantly illegal, but the land could not be returned under terms of the Indian Claims Commission Act. To get on with the litigation over the balance of the western Sioux country, the Sioux case (Docket No. 74) was divided, with "74 A" covering the majority of Sioux land and "74 B" limited to the Black Hills claim. The tortuous progress of Sioux Docket No. 74 did not come to my attention until after 1980, when I thought that ICC cases were finished. It was a complete surprise to receive a phone call requesting another research report for the Sioux. To overcome my reluctance, the lawyers pointed out that this case provided the opportunity to put an end, finally, to the Sioux case. Although I was doubtful, the idea of helping to end an ICC case was appealing.

As the lawyers explained, Sioux Docket 74 A had reached the third and final stage of the ICC process. I had always viewed the final step as an accounting process in which the federal government calculated the "offsets" to be deducted from a prospective financial award. But the lawyers for the Sioux had presented an additional claim, for unfair treatment through the long course of interaction with American agencies and officials. Now, as a grand finale, they needed a summary account of "the entire course of dealings" between the federal government and the Sioux Nation. Because the Indian Claims Commission had come to an end, the final judgment would be handed down in the Court of Appeals in Washington DC by a judge who had never heard an Indian case.

Seeking the advice—and, hopefully, the assistance—of a real expert on

Sioux affairs, I was told that he could not possibly undertake the research, which would require ten years. But he offered to locate a graduate student to assist in the collection of documents, which would probably be voluminous. With only a year to complete the research, I decided that a mass of data and historical generalizations covering the entire area for much more than a century would be mind-boggling. After surveying the measures that the government had taken to force the Sioux to stop behaving like Indians, I decided to concentrate on selected examples of the results of these measures. To demonstrate the consequences of each policy change, I described a specific incident, distributing the examples so that all reservations were covered. The report had to have impact. Instead of stating blandly that Indian children received boarding school education, I noted that five-year-olds on the reservation were grabbed and thrown into high-sided wagons, effectively kidnapped, and taken from their homes in order to train them to be "civilized." Instead of calling attention to the substandard blankets and clothing distributed among the Sioux, I cited an account of a Sioux mother's travel to agency headquarters in winter, arriving badly frostbitten. The baby carried on her back, wrapped in a flimsy government-issue blanket, had frozen to death.

The cumulative account of unfortunate results and mismanagement of each successive federal project became impressive. I wondered why there had not been more open rebellion in Sioux country. The graduate student assembling the "evidence" did an absolutely heroic job, beginning with "mining the archives," as the process of government documentary research has been described. Additional material came from missionary journals, newspaper reports, travel accounts, and already published research. In ICC research, historical data—conveniently stored in libraries and archives—was much easier to acquire than information about more recent occurrences.

A little-known event of the World War II era was the abrupt seizure of the northwest section of the Pine Ridge Reservation to use for an aerial gunnery range, giving more than a hundred frightened Sioux families only forty-eight hours' notice to evacuate their homes. They believed that "the Japanese were just over the hill." Finding out what happened to the refugees required the assistance of the Washington lawyers, who located transcripts of congressional hearings on the subsequent hardships. One poignant detail of the flight noted the death of a ninety-year-old man who had survived the Wounded Knee Massacre of 1890, shielded by his mother's body from the gunfire directed at a group of religious dancers.

Recent reports and correspondence from field offices of the Bureau of Indian Affairs were not readily available. In 1981, the 1950s records were just being "declassified," and the archivists were only through the letter C. Although I wanted to investigate Pine Ridge and Rosebud, the choice became the Cheyenne River Reservation. It proved to be an interesting case because the documents revealed that as one branch of the government was planning a new high school for Cheyenne River, the Army Corps of Engineers was planning to flood the area where the school was supposed to be built. To find out more about flooding reservation lands, the resourceful graduate student drove to the Army Corps project headquarters at Ft. Abercrombie. He arrived on the day that a whole series of research reports and "impact statements" were being shredded, but he managed to salvage copies relating to each Sioux reservation along the Missouri River.

These are examples of the diverse sources of information that could be assembled for an ICC case. To manage the mass of material, the 424 individual items (some, entire books) were classified according to the eight reservations involved, with an additional "general" category. The guide to this body of evidence was a sixty-five-page list and digest, with an entry for each item. There may be some truth in the jesting remark about legal cases being settled by the "weight of the evidence"—in pounds. The short, written report of about eighty pages, just a sampling of the collected material, seemed rather disconnected to me when I finished. To summarize, I crafted a final paragraph using emotional language and ending with the statement that the Sioux had been "the human victims" of the entire series of government policies. I hoped that the lack of restraint would not bring criticism.

All the printed sources and handwritten correspondence (with typewritten copies) made up only one element in the preparation for an important claims case. The legal arena also has a theatrical element, even when the case presented is far less exciting than the crimes and melodramatic topics that usually dominate the press, radio, and television. Costuming is important, and expert witnesses for tribal people need to present a nonpartisan appearance, with no evidence of Indian jewelry, pins, or emblems. I learned to "suit up" for court, always carry a leather brief case, and maintain a pleasant but bland expression. At early ICC hearings, people sitting in the courtroom told me that they watched my changing facial expressions when other witnesses were in the stand, to get my visual commentary on the testimony. Those transparent reactions had to be avoided.

The legal arena is also a type of combat zone where competing lawyers devise strategies to win through declamation and questioning. With good reason, one of the Indian terms for lawyer is *word warrior*. I was very apprehensive about the kind of cross-examination I might face at the Court of Appeals. I wondered how much of all the collected "evidence" I might be expected to have in my head. I decided that the opposing expert witness in this case would probably be an anthropologist and the questioning would be in that field. To help fill this void in my knowledge, I arranged an intensive tutorial course, spending two weeks driving across six of the eight Sioux reservations with a friend who had a thorough understanding of the society and its history. We saw schools, mission churches, already decaying housing projects. We viewed the gaunt, dead trees in the flooded land along the Missouri River, and we attended a powwow. All the time, I heard concise lectures on kinship, ritual, origin stories, and current politics. We even stopped at the cemetery at Wounded Knee, at my request, staying in the car for fear of being shot if we stepped outside. Hostilities against outsiders were still prevalent in the aftermath of the armed conflict of Wounded Knee II. It was a strange experience to cross miles of almost vacant grasslands, with the car radio reporting from England on Charles and Diana's royal wedding.

The traveling tutorial provided most of the information I expected to need for cross-examination. Because I had also attended a conference in Bismarck on Sioux religion, I felt armed for the predicted line of questioning. The hearing was brief, and to my surprise, the judge jumped right into the questioning. He did not appear much interested in Indians, but he did want to hear more about the buffalo. The final minutes of the time allotted for the hearing were spent describing the US Army's role in the deliberate destruction of the herds that were the indispensable resource for the Sioux and other Plains nations.

Although the judge had appeared rather inattentive in court, his decision awarded about $40 million to the Sioux Nation after a review of the "unconscionable dealings." My personal opinion, expressed in as melodramatic prose as I could create at the conclusion of my report, was quoted in full in the "Findings of Fact." But Sioux Docket No. 74 did not come to an end, as I had been led to hope. The Sioux refused to accept the money, just as they had previously refused the $106 million settlement for the Black Hills. Currently, the sum is part of a steadily increasing fund that has surpassed $800 million. Real justice has no price.

One further case in the Indian Claims Commission category turned up a decade later. This case, concerning Canadian Potawatomi, is worthy of mention because it is one controversy that finally was settled in a somewhat reasonable manner, using "alternative dispute resolution" instead of the adversarial system. The late appearing Canadian Potawatomi case was really a castoff from earlier ICC litigation and had a remarkably long history. The claimants were descendants of Potawatomi who had fled to Canada, primarily between the 1830s and 1850s, during the period of forced removal west of the Mississippi. When they left, the United States government still owed them payments according to terms of past treaties. Although the claims of the refugee Potawatomi were ignored for some time, Congress in 1906 finally sent a representative to Canada to report on the situation. The report, completed in 1980, included a census of more than two thousand Potawatomi living in Canada who were descendants of the tribal members owed money at the time they left the United States. The report calculated that these Indian people were due $1.5 million, but congressmen would not appropriate any money for "foreign" Indians.

The Potawatomi descendants living in Canada continued to press their claims, bringing their case to the attention of tribunals in Canada, England, Geneva, and The Hague. Descendants of some Potawatomi refugees who later returned to the United States eventually received compensation as part of the settlement of an ICC case. The Indian Claims Commission, however, refused any award for Potawatomi living outside the United States. I had a vague idea about this situation from a brief remark, probably back in the 1970s, by a lawyer working on behalf of the Hannahville Indian community, a group including refugee and displaced Potawatomi families. While waiting to catch a taxi, he pointed out his well-worn briefcase and commented, "That's the Canadian Potawatomi. Sometime they will have their day in court." At that moment, I did not know what he was talking about.

Twenty years later, I learned about the cause of the Canadian Potawatomi after they received support from the Native American Rights Fund and its representatives in Washington DC. Senator Daniel Inouye of Hawaii was instrumental in securing congressional approval of a bill allowing the Canadian Potawatomi to present their case in the Court of Appeals at Washington. The bill specified that they were to be treated as if they were living in the United States. At this advanced stage of attempted settlement, the case involved the State, Justice, and Interior departments, as well as the Canadian legation.

Serving as expert witness for this unusual Indian claim was a different experience. Working with Indian lawyers of the Native American Rights Fund was more like being a member of a team. In a discussion of strategy, I could recommend that these clients always be called "refugee Potawatomi," with a focus on their reasons for escaping to Ojibwe reserves on the Canadian shores of Lake Huron. Use of the term *Canadian* should be avoided. Preparation for this case required careful thought about possible ramifications. The status of the "refugee Potawatomi" in Canada was being reviewed with the possibility of some kind of legal or legislative action. In Washington, I went along to the conference at the Canadian legation, where it was clear that the staff, though sympathetic to the Potawatomi cause, did not want to be viewed as interfering in American Indian affairs. An element of diplomatic sensitivity was evident.

The preliminaries for going to court seemed a tedious process. First, both sides prepared the long lists of interlocutory questions. I had never thought that any historical narrative could be well understood by the question-and-answer process, which produces only a succession of bits of information. Then there were "Proposed Findings of Fact." Of course, the statements of "fact" were apt to be loaded, so they really constituted an argument. In this form of writing, the historical critique was most important, for the selective use of information can imply an inaccurate conclusion. These reactions took form in the "Objections" to the proposed "facts." To me, the whole obligatory process was tedious, but challenging. Repeatedly, the Department of Justice representatives contended that the Indians bringing suit were not part of the Potawatomi tribe because the real Potawatomi were the communities removed finally to Oklahoma and Kansas. The response on behalf of the "refugees" insisted that membership in a group of tribal people depended on kinship relations without regard for geographic boundaries.

The main points of contention were clearly established before everyone interested appeared at the Court of Appeals for the beginning of the formal trial. The presiding judge, a very sharp woman with a practical outlook, made a surprising opening speech. She explained that although she did not yet fully understand the historical circumstances leading to the original award calculation in 1906, she had read enough to determine that there were some weaknesses in the arguments brought by both sides. She estimated that it would take seven years for this new case to reach a decision in the court system and the final outcome was problematic. As a substitute, she recommended that the case be decided speedily by following the procedure for "Alternative Dispute Resolution." After some initial hesitation, both sides agreed to look forward to her decision.

Some months later, everyone immediately involved assembled in a conference room, a setting more relaxed and informal than a courtroom. The group seated at the big table now included leaders of the Potawatomi organization in Canada. With clarity and a note of apology, the judge announced her decision, explaining her rationale for awarding as a final settlement the sum of only $1.5 million, the exact sum recommended in the original congressional report in 1908. She admitted that the settlement was undoubtedly far less than the Potawatomi and their lawyers had hoped for, but she had taken into account another factor. She felt that present members of Congress might be very reluctant to approve any money at all for this purpose, regardless of the sense of obligation evidenced by the Congress in 1906. The $1.5 million had the least chance of strong opposition. Both sides accepted her decision, but the underlying problem remained unsolved. After a century of deliberation in a variety of settings, the legal saga of the

Potawatomi refugees in Canada has not yet come to an end, because the requisite legislation for payment of the award has not made its way through Congress.

In retrospect, frustration was a major element in the expert witness experience dealing with the Indian Claims Commission. In the majority of cases, it was difficult to have a feeling of accomplishment, because the elapsed time was so long between the completion of a research report and news of a decision. But historical research for ICC cases also provided an exciting series of educational opportunities. In moments of cynicism, I wonder how many trees were sacrificed to make the reams of paper for reproducing the reports and "evidence" for the hundreds of cases, filling boxes, closets, garages, file drawers, and archives. I also know that an important legacy of ICC research has been new sources and new data, as well as monographs being used by graduate students working for advanced degrees. Many of these students are now attending tribal colleges or taking advantage of the new American Indian Studies programs at major universities. A number of research reports became available in the American Indian Ethnographic Series, published in 1974 by the Garland Press. These are all very positive results. Nevertheless, it is sobering to realize that the hard-fought cases brought to the Indian Claims Commission do not seem to have ended this type of litigation. Entrepreneurial investigators, backed by prospective developers, are poring over the final decisions in the land claims cases and the nineteenth-century treaties these involved, searching for loopholes or omissions to justify additional lawsuits. In Indian affairs, lawsuits do not end—they multiply.

Meanwhile, many Indian communities have ultimately achieved rewards and have benefited from ICC decisions. In the United States, at least, the opportunity has existed for them to bring many of their problems to court. Across the border in Canada, where a number of Indian treaties have also been negotiated, the original inhabitants are similarly engaged in lawsuits concerning land and resources. However, those living in British Columbia are handicapped because they have no treaties to use as a basis for dealing with their government. In New Zealand, the Maori signed only one treaty with the British colonizers, but it has been the basis for a thousand legal cases. All of these are examples of original inhabitants' universal spirit of resistance against foreign domination.

Notes

1. Nancy Lurie, "The Indian Claims Commission," *Annals of the American Academy of Political and Social Science* 436 (March 1978): 97–110; Imre Sutton, ed., *Ireedeemable America: The Indians' Estate and Land Claims* (Albuquerque: University of New Mexico Press, 1985); Harvey

Rosenthal, *Their Day in Court: A History of the Indian Claims Commission* (New York: Garland, 1990); R. Warren Metcalf, "Lambs of Sacrifice: Termination, the Mixed-Blood Utes, and the Problem of Indian Identity," *Utah Historical Quarterly* 64 (Fall 1996): 322–343; and Roundtable on Politics and Theory from the 1950s, Annual Conference of the American Society for Ethnohistory, November 17, 2005, Santa Fe, New Mexico.

2. The idiosyncrasies of the American court system are amazing. Carefully following the rules of the Indian Claims Commission, I later wrote a report for another division of the Department of Justice, a district court in Michigan. Though every sentence was documented, mostly from photographed National Archives correspondence, the judge in Michigan initially declared the report "a clear case of hearsay evidence."

3. Charles Wilkinson, *Blood Struggle: The Rise of Modern Indian Nations* (New York and London: W. W. Norton & Co., 2005), 66–71, 178S.

4. Helen Hornbeck Tanner, "History v. The Law: Processing Indians in the American Legal System," *University of Detroit Mercy Law Review* 76, no. 3 (1999): 693–708.

Part III

Sovereignty in Action: Contemporary Perspectives

Loretta Fowler

During what is known as the sovereignty era, Congress and federal courts have affirmed, at least in part, the inherent sovereignty of tribal nations; ostensibly, they have also provided tribal nations with the necessary tools to implement sovereign rights. In reality, the sovereignty process has created both opportunities and obstacles: recent federal legislation and Supreme Court decisions simultaneously affirm and limit the exercise of tribal sovereignty. As in earlier eras, Indian political activists focus on advocating for sovereignty and compensating for the shortcomings of legislative and judicial actions, in a variety of ways.

Since the mid-1970s, the federal policy of self-determination has led to legislation promoting tribal control over minerals, education, law and order, and economic development (see tables 4–7). Tribes have received encouragement, for example, to contract for the operation of programs formerly operated by the government. Nonetheless, Thomas Biolsi maintains, contracting is a way to offload federal responsibility; it is a new form of "termination." Randel Hanson considers new economic development opportunities to be market-based ventures that actually can undermine the quality of life on reservations at the same time they create jobs. Bruce Miller argues that the recent willingness of the federal government to grant recognition to tribes has resulted in some Indian communities accepting hegemonic concepts about identity. For example, in the Puget Sound area, recognized tribes have denied fishing rights to unrecognized tribes. After the passage of the Indian Self-Determination and Education Assistance Act in 1975 (also known as Public Law 638), the Cheyenne and Arapaho nations began to contract programs. But reduced funding and complicated federal regulations surrounding contracting have made it difficult for the tribal government to meet the raised expectations of their constituents. As one official remarked, "638 became a reason to fail."[1]

That said, Indian communities do have more control over their resources and community life, in general, and try to take advantage of new opportunities as much as possible. Recent studies explore tribal nations' strategies, given particular community circumstances. Joseph Jorgensen looked at the effects of the controversial Alaska Native Claims Settlement Act (ANCSA) on three Inuit villages (see table 4). With the ANCSA, land, the claim to which was based on aboriginal title, was transferred to Native corporations without trust status. Tribes had sovereignty over members but not over territory they occupied and used. This led to fears that subsistence priorities would be undermined by desire for corporate profits. The three villages in Jorgensen's study made their ANCSA corporations instruments of elected tribal officials and pursued sovereignty goals that challenged the ANCSA, particularly in the areas of subsistence hunting and fishing. The Native language program in a Navajo contract school that encouraged literacy in Navajo was "empowering," Daniel McLaughlin reported. Navajo literacy became important in transforming inequities and altering perceptions; English literacy became separate and complementary. Patricia Erikson found that a tribal museum, largely established as a result of the War on Poverty and strengthened by self-determination legislation, helped the Makah take control of the representation of their community, despite the incorporation of aspects of Western museology. Jessica Cattelino examined changes in the housing program after Seminoles took charge. Under Seminole control, the housing program reaffirmed Seminole culturally distinctive concepts of gender, family, and space. The Seminole Nation incorporated Seminole dwelling norms and practices into housing policy, such as the funding of *chickee* building and scattered settlement patterns. Federal constraints could be bypassed because the Seminole Tribe used proceeds from gaming to fund many of the program's initiatives. Loretta Fowler found that when the Cheyenne and Arapaho nations contracted programs, they indigenized them. For example, the child welfare program used different guidelines for the selection of foster parents than did the State of Oklahoma. The tribes paid less attention to economic status, space, and privacy for children when selecting foster families. Moreover, the Cheyenne-Arapaho health department operated a substance abuse program with therapies that included pow-wows, sweat lodges, and peyote meetings sponsored for patients. Robert

Yazzie and James Zion argued that the Navajo Nation's Peacemaker courts use Navajo ideas and institutions for social control and dispute resolution.[2]

To avoid federal constraints by pursuing other kinds of partnerships, tribes have sought to work through international agencies (Helton and Robertson, chapter 3, this volume). They cooperate with national organizations, such as the Native American Rights Fund (see table 4) and environmental groups. Kathleen Pickering has explored how the Lakota Fund, a private nonprofit organization modeled on Grameen Bank in Bangladesh, loans money to support microenterprises or small businesses, such as sewing, beadwork, food sales, car repair, and babysitting, that operate out of homes on the Pine Ridge and Rosebud reservations. These businesses can be run in ways compatible with Lakota values. Daryl Baldwin and Julie Olds (chapter 15, this volume) discuss how the Miami Tribe of Oklahoma established a relationship with Miami University to develop their language and culture revitalization program. In the sovereignty era, given the tension between opportunities and limitations, tribal nations sometimes also try to establish a beneficial relationship with states.[3]

Circe Sturm (chapter 12, this volume) discusses how some tribes have sought recognition from state, rather than the federal, government. Federally recognized tribes also have important relations with states, whether or not they want to. Even though tribal nations have sovereign rights in matters of hunting and fishing on trust land and taxation of oil company profits, for example, they often have to negotiate with states in order to exercise their sovereignty. Sometimes negotiation is an economic necessity because long-term litigation with states is prohibitively expensive for tribes but not necessarily for states. Federal mandates for negotiation, as with Class III gaming, also result in negotiations between tribes and states. The states may refuse to negotiate over gaming unless tribes compromise on other issues, such as taxation.

On one hand, Jessica Cattelino (chapter 14, this volume) presents a case in which gaming revenue was used by the Seminole to influence public attitudes and state policy so that the Seminole became more influential in the region. On the other hand, Larry Nesper (chapter 13, this volume) points to the Ojibwe's accommodation with Wisconsin in the course of adopting hunting and fishing codes in the wake of their court victory; he raises questions about the implications of compromising community values in order to establish these tribal codes. Similar kinds of negotiation, as well as joint management, occurred in the Pacific Northwest as a result of the Boldt decision (see table 5). In Plains communities, Loretta Fowler (chapter 11, this volume) found significant resistance to negotiation with the state on matters such as water rights, hunting and fishing regulation, and taxation. The efforts of tribal governments to negotiate cross-deputization agreements generated suspicion from constituents, who had experienced brutality and discrimination from non-Native authorities. Fowler argued that the implementation of state policies, perceived as hostile, generated grassroots support for aggressive sovereignty agendas and sometimes led to criticism from constituents when tribal leaders tried to negotiate with states in order to avoid litigation.

In addition to dealing in various ways with states, tribes have worked to exercise their sovereignty through cooperation with other tribes or, in some cases, through conflict with them. New opportunities, such as the passage of the Indian Child Welfare Act (see table 5), have led to new challenges. This act gave tribes jurisdiction over custody of children of members, but intermarriage between people from different tribes complicated these arrangements. In South Dakota, Sioux tribal court justices have been negotiating to find a way to resolve these cases. Black Hills treaty groups on Sioux reservations in South Dakota grew stronger after the court victory (see table 5). Their memberships have lobbied Congress, as well as crosscut tribal entities and developed local power bases that figure in politics on these reservations. Spearfishing activists used prophesies, ritual, and alliances in northern Wisconsin to build pantribal consensus about fishing rights; in the process, they constructed new social identities. Similar intertribal movements exist elsewhere, for example, among Iroquois in Canada and the United States. Regionally based organizations work to gain more leverage than individual tribal nations can manage on their own, for example, the Council of Energy Resources Tribes among the "energy tribes" in the western United States (see table 5).

New opportunities also have set in motion conflicts among tribal nations, for example, over recognition (Sturm, chapter 12, this volume). In Oklahoma, the small tribes in the western and northern part of the state have to contend with the different political strategies of the larger Indian nations in the eastern part of the state. The larger tribes negotiated with the state over cigarette and fuel taxes, which made it virtually impossible for the smaller groups to hold out for better terms. In Oklahoma, large nations with membership criteria not tied to "blood" have qualified for a greater relative share of federal services than have the smaller groups in the western part of the state that have blood degree requirements. In the Southwest, the Hopi and Navajo nations struggle over rights to land and its use. In Montana, when Native people recently gained control over the public program at the Little Big Horn Battlefield National Monument (formerly, Custer Battlefield) historical site, conflict between different Indian nations occurred over representations of history. Similarly, Native communities potentially find themselves in competition over the repatriation of objects in museum collections. Part of the process of exercising sovereignty, then, involves working out new relationships and understandings among Indian nations.[4]

Tribal nations' attempts to exercise sovereignty in the wake of favorable legislation and court decisions have created new problems and opportunities in intracommunity relations. New and expanded bureaucracies emerged as tribal nations exercised sovereignty, and jobs for women, elders, and college-educated individuals increased, drawing people back to their home communities or establishing new roles and statuses for some members. Local hierarchies and challenges to these hierarchies developed. In these communities, Native people developed new social institutions and began constructing new identities. In what ways have these developments shaped local politics in the sovereignty era?

In the case of the Upper Skagit, federal recognition and the subsequently successful effort to obtain a reservation land base created conditions for the construction of a tribal identity. Small family groups formerly had lived along the Skagit River in relative isolation from other family groups. Their relocation to the reservation precipitated economic and political reorganization that allowed for a balance between the tribal and family models of community. The Pequots' casino simultaneously became an opportunity to revive the local economy and an opportunity to work at constructing an identity that affirms indigenous heritage both for members and for the surrounding community.[5]

Elsewhere, tribes had to contend with how to redefine their memberships as their circumstances changed. New local opportunities that resulted in return-migration or a reduction in out-migration of members forced tribal governments to provide more jobs and services. Under what circumstances would membership criteria be expanded or, conversely, restricted? To what extent would blood criteria be used? Would historical and cultural influences, such as the restriction of membership to children of a male member or a female member, remain important? In an effort to expand services to their community, the Comanche Nation changed the blood degree requirement from one-fourth to one-eighth. Other tribal nations have dropped members from their rolls. At Fort Peck reservation, the Assiniboine and Sioux tribes developed a series of membership categories that clearly define the rights of people in the reservation community: individuals who were recognized as members of tribes with treaty rights at Fort Peck and the lineal descendents of these individuals who are US citizens and one-fourth Assiniboine and/or Sioux blood; adoptees; children of members who also have one-fourth Assiniboine and/or Sioux blood and were born after 1960; and associate members, who are children of members, have at least one-eighth Assiniboine and/or Sioux blood, and are US citizens. By restricting membership to US citizens, they deny membership to Assiniboine and Sioux who settled in Canada rather than sign a peace treaty with the United States. Associate members are ineligible to vote or share in tribal funds or property but are eligible for benefits as Indians. Membership categories also are taken into account in relation to hunting and fishing rights, jobs, and other matters. Until recently, the Northern Arapaho restricted membership to children of male members and had an associate membership category for others, but pressure from Arapaho women not married to Arapaho men resulted in the adoption of more inclusive criteria. The Blackfeet and Crow are threatened with the loss of much of their land base because recently the Supreme Court allowed the taxation of fee land on these reservations. The Blackfeet have so far refused to enroll descendents of members who cannot meet the blood requirement and therefore cannot obtain a trust patent on their land. Changing membership criteria would help keep reservation land in trust status. Rather than make enrollment less restrictive, the Crow have used tribal funds to pay taxes on fee land. Deciding who has what rights in tribal communities has become a more pressing problem subsequent to developments in the self-determination era. Conflict over membership and other issues has increased.

Perceived power differentials give rise to intracommunity struggles, including the potential for class conflict. Tribal nations have new powers, to the extent that (Nesper suggests) they can be viewed as states. The norms that support the state may conflict with community norms (Nesper, chapter 13, this volume). Tribal nations also are a special kind of corporation charged with operating businesses staffed with Native and non-Native employees, at the same time protecting sovereign rights in such matters as taxation, environmental conditions and sacred sites, and labor policy. Tribal nations can be advocates for equal employment opportunity, as Colleen O'Neill suggests, or workers' rights may clash with the tribal government's aims. David Kamper points to efforts on the part of Navajo workers to unionize in order to gain more influence over the self-determination process, that is, to organize a "grassroots model of self-determination based on the belief that workers and [other] community members should have a say in the administration of tribal healthcare at the hospital." Loretta Fowler (chapter 11, this volume) argues that, as "shareholders" of tribal corporations, members also may demand the distribution of the corporation's income in per capita payments—a challenge to perceived economic inequalities—or organize constitutional revision movements to diffuse authority positions.

These kinds of grassroots challenges have been widespread and have taken different forms in different local circumstances. Although the Alaska Native Claims Settlement Act ostensibly was a way for Native peoples to gain control over their lives and resources, Tlingit and Haida corporation councils became an elite in control of jobs and resource management. Kirk Dombrowski found that a marginalized sector of the population was the result and that this sector opposed Native cultural programs and other ventures sponsored by the ANCSA councils. Circe Sturm examined how, in Cherokee national politics, Cherokee elites manipulated a "race-as-nation" ideology to maintain power and to obtain expanded federal services. "Fuller" blood Cherokees used a "race-as-blood quantum" ideology to contest power relations in the nation. Bruce Miller described how women, hired by the tribal corporations in large numbers, could use their employment as a political base and compete for and attain political office, challenging gender hierarchies in the process. Political interest groups have formed around repatriation issues so that these groups challenge elected officials for control of repatriation efforts.[6]

In the self-determination era, tribal nations have taken advantage of legislation and court decisions when they could. They have developed innovative strategies to press for greater control over their resources and their communities when faced with obstacles. Groups and individuals also have struggled to exert influence over the self-determination process (see the "Political Activism" column in tables 4–7). The chapters in Part III examine the exercise of sovereignty, given the contradictions and complexities that emanate from new kinds of relations with federal agencies and states, from intertribal politics, and from intratribal relationships.

Notes

1. Loretta Fowler, *Tribal Sovereignty and the Historical Imagination: Cheyenne-Arapaho Politics* (Lincoln and London: University of Nebraska Press, 2002); Bruce Miller, *Invisible Indigenes: The Politics of Nonrecognition* (Lincoln: University of Nebraska Press, 2003); Thomas Biolsi, "Political and Legal Status ('Lower 48' States)," in *A Companion to the Anthropology of American Indians*, ed. Thomas Biolsi, Blackwell Companions to Anthropology (Malden, MA: Blackwell Publishing, Ltd., 2004), 231–247; and Randel Hanson, "Contemporary Globalization and Tribal Sovereignty," in ibid., 284–303.

2. Joseph Jorgensen, *Oil Age Eskimos* (Berkeley: University of California Press, 1990); Daniel McLaughlin, *When Literacy Empowers: Navajo Language in Print* (Albuquerque: University of New Mexico Press, 1992); Robert Yazzie and James Zion, "'Slay the Monsters': Peacemaker Court and Violence Control Plans from Navajo Nation," in *Popular Justice and Community Regeneration: Pathways of Indigenous Reform*, ed. Kayleen M. Hazelhurst (Westport, CT: Praeger, 1995), 57–88; and Robert Yazzie and James Zion, "Navajo Restorative Justice: The Law of Equality and Justice," in *Restorative Justice: International Perspectives*, ed. Burt Galaway and Joe Hudson (Monsey, NY: Criminal Justice Press, 1996), 157–174; Patricia Pierce Erikson with Helma Ward and Kirk Wachendorf, *Voices of a Thousand People: The Makah Cultural and Research Center* (Lincoln: University of Nebraska Press, 2002); Jessica Cattelino, "Florida Seminole Housing and the Social

Meanings of Sovereignty," *Comparative Studies in Society and History* 48, no. 3 (2006): 699–726; and Fowler, *Tribal Sovereignty.*

3. Kathleen Ann Pickering, *Lakota Culture, World Economy* (Lincoln: University of Nebraska Press, 2000).

4. Richard Clemmer, *Roads in the Sky: The Hopi Indians in a Century of Change* (Boulder, CO: Westview, 1995); Brad Bays, "Tribal–State Tobacco Compacts and Motor Fuel Contracts in Oklahoma," in *The Tribes and the States: Geographies of Intergovernmental Interaction*, ed. Brad Bays and Erin Hogan Fouberg (Lanham, MD: Rowman and Littlefield Publishers, 2002), 181–209; and Larry Nesper, *The Walleye War: The Struggle for Ojibwe Spearfishing and Treaty Rights* (Lincoln: University of Nebraska Press, 2002).

5. Bruce Miller, *The Problem of Justice: Tradition and Law in the Coast Salish World* (Lincoln: University of Nebraska Press, 2001); and John Bodinger de Uriarte, "Imaging the Nation with House Odds: Representing American Indian Identity at Mashantuckett," *Ethnohistory* 50, no. 3 (2003): 549–565.

6. Bruce Miller, "Women and Politics: Comparative Evidence from the Northwest Coast," *Ethnology* 31, no. 4 (1992): 367–383; Kirk Dombrowski, *Against Culture: Development, Politics, and Religion in Indian Alaska* (Lincoln: University of Nebraska Press, 2001); Circe Sturm, *Blood Politics: Race, Culture, and Identity in the Cherokee Nation of Oklahoma* (Berkeley: University of California Press, 2002); and Colleen O'Neill, "Labor Rights vs. Sovereignty?: Regulating Working Conditions in Postwar Reservation Communities," and David Kamper, "The Work of Tribal Sovereignty: Navajo Healthcare Worker Activism," papers presented at "Indians, Labor, and Capitalist Culture: A Colloquium of Historians, Ethnohistorians, and Anthropologists" at the Newberry Library, Chicago, September 22–23, 2006.

11

Tribal Sovereignty Movements Compared
The Plains Region

Loretta Fowler

Plains tribes are among the "energy tribes" of the Western states. In 1938 they gained more control over energy development, but in the 1980s, even with a favorable Supreme Court decision in 1982, control over income from minerals remained problematic (table 2, 1938; table 5, 1982; table 6, 1985, 1989). Today, isolated from markets, they are impoverished despite their mineral wealth. In Western states, oil and gas, coal, and uranium are important to both state and tribal economies. Tribal leaders struggle to protect and develop resources and ward off state efforts to siphon off income from mineral development. There are pressures for tribes to negotiate with states over shared taxation.[1] Fowler's chapter discusses how tribal control over management, distribution of income, and environmental impact affects relations between grassroots community groups and elected officials, and she addresses the social repercussions of negotiation for tribes attempting to exercise sovereignty.

The tribal sovereignty movement has taken hold in all High Plains communities. Yet sovereignty is implemented in different ways, aspects of sovereignty are given different degrees of emphasis, and sovereignty agendas may be based on community consensus or subject to contention between officials

Figure 8. An American Indian Movement rally in South Dakota to oppose the reinstatement of a local sheriff accused by the community of discriminatory behavior toward Native Americans. David Bartecchi and Kathleen Pickering © 2004. Used with permission.

and grassroots groups. Through a comparison of twelve communities in South Dakota, Montana, Wyoming, and Oklahoma during the 1990s, I situate sovereignty movements within regional and local contexts to examine how different political views and choices about economic and cultural rights emerge.[2] A focus on the local exercise of sovereignty complements a large literature that deals almost exclusively with federal policy and legal cases in the sovereignty movement in the United States.[3]

State by state, I discuss how state–tribe relations influence commitment to the exercise of tribal sovereignty. I also describe the political organization of each tribe in the state and examine how that organization affects the local expression of sovereignty. What the comparisons show is that, first, for a tribe to attempt to exercise sovereignty fully, grassroots commitment is necessary and grassroots commitment to sovereignty issues is influenced by state actions, especially by the perception of state violence against Indians (figure 8). The greater the fear of violence, the greater the support for a sovereignty agenda. Second, where defense of a homeland (maintaining control over a sizable land base or recovering land through a treaty-based claim) is possible, grassroots groups can be more easily mobilized to support the exercise of tribal sovereignty. Third and finally, the more that political authority is diffused in a community, the more likely that broad-based consensus exists between grassroots groups and officials. In fact, grassroots groups have been working toward greater participation in self-determination by supporting constitutional revisions that decentralize tribal government.

South Dakota.

Earl Bordeaux, one of the Rosebud councilmen, remarked: "Look what the State of South Dakota is doing to her Indians, you know. They show in a glowing picture. Those of us who live within the State of South Dakota really know the spirit of the South Dakota non-Indian world. It's not a true reconciliation. They won't recognize our Treaty Rights. They won't recognize our jurisdiction." Suspicion and hostility appear to be mutual. The four Sioux reservations in the western part of the state are large: Pine Ridge is 3.1 million acres; Rosebud, 3.2 million acres; Cheyenne River, 2.8 million acres; and Standing Rock, 2.7 million acres. In the 1990s all these reservations were in conflict with the state over several issues, one of which was juvenile justice. Sioux people argued that the state judicial system was biased against the Sioux. In fact, South Dakota's incarceration rate was the highest for a state with an Indian population. Sixty percent of youths in South Dakota's prison system were Indian; yet Indians made up only 10 percent of the population in the state. In contrast, in Montana, youths composed 25 percent of the prison population, and the state's Indian population was 6.5 percent; in Oklahoma, youths were 18 percent of the prison population, and Indians, 8.1 percent of the state population. Sioux advocates referred to Indians as a "cash crop" in the state, where Indians were discriminated against in terms of fines. Child custody was another point of contention. South Dakota had the highest rate of termination of Indian parents' rights in the nation; 60 percent of cases were Indian. The state and the tribes battled over highway jurisdiction, game and fish regulations, and taxation in Indian Country. Also, the tribes took special umbrage at the state's opposition to the return of tribal land not used by the Oahe Dam project.[4]

The Oglala Sioux Nation of the Pine Ridge Reservation has a history of conflict between "hostiles" and "friendlies" that pre- and postdates reservation settlement. The American Indian Movement precipitated an "Indian Renaissance," to use Herbert Hoover's terminology, and, from the 1970s on, the sovereignty movement grew. The number of participants increased significantly as the years passed, and, in the aftermath of the civil war during the Wounded Knee takeover, there was a reconciliation of sorts between the hostiles and the friendlies (who were both Full and Mixed Bloods, sociologically and culturally defined). By the 1990s the sovereignty agenda had extensive and passionate grassroots support, nourished by the State of South Dakota's intransigence over sovereignty questions and its general pattern of state violence toward Indians.[5]

On Pine Ridge (settled by Lakota Sioux of the Oglala division) during the 1990s, Oglala political organization was based on the principles of diffusion and circumscription of leadership. The elected tribal council consisted of eighteen representatives from districts in which they resided. The districts had councils of representatives from smaller "communities" within each district. The districts effectively exerted pressure on their representatives. Much of the tribal council's work was done by committees and boards made up of people from all the districts, as well as tribal council members. Districts also administered tribal and private funds, as did political advocacy groups that crosscut districts. During the 1990s the tribal council was committed to mitigating tensions between the council and the people in districts and advocacy groups (such as treaty committees, women's rights organizations, and the tribal college movement).[6]

These advocacy groups pursued an aggressive sovereignty agenda. Petitions from grassroots groups dissuaded the tribal council from waiving sovereignty to get a bank loan, and petitions helped persuade the tribal council to file a court case against South Dakota for trespass by law enforcement agencies. The constitution (accepted along with the Indian Reorganization Act) was revised in 1985, and voters eliminated provisions that the secretary of the interior had to review tribal council decisions. After the successful claim filed against the federal government for the violation of the Treaty of 1868 (described by one leader, Harold Salway, as "divine intervention from the spirit world"), the grassroots community in the 1990s consistently rejected a monetary settlement (see table 5). "The Black Hills is not for sale" has been central to the ideology of the sovereignty movement and used by communities to reject the establishment of dumps or the building of pipelines on community land. The tribal law and order code was revised in response to grassroots pressure. In 1996 the tribal court adopted a position of leniency in sentencing, stressing rehabilitation instead. Counseling and supervision by groups of elders became mandatory in domestic abuse cases. Court decisions could be reviewed by a board of elders, and officers of the court did not have to have law degrees. Even though the reservation community was very poor and the tribal government had to rely on taxes (of business activity on tribal land, usually non-Indian businesses) and federal programs, public sentiment favored precedence of treaty and cultural rights over economic development projects or per capita payments. As one leader at Oglala Lakota College explained, they were "beginning an intellectual revolution" in order to reverse the damage done to them by "alien concepts."[7]

The other three Sioux reservations also participated in the Indian Renaissance. Passionate support for a sovereignty agenda existed at Rosebud, and considerable grassroots commitment to it, at Cheyenne River and Standing Rock in the 1990s. All three reservation communities rejected a monetary settlement for the Black Hills. Charles Murphy, a Standing Rock leader, remarked, "We cannot forget the sufferings our people endured by signing these treaties—that is our driving force [that their suffering will not be in vain]." At Rosebud (settled largely by Lakota Sioux of the Brule division), the tribal council officers were elected at-large, and eight districts elected community residents as representatives to the tribal council. Each district also elected a council that chose officers, held meetings, met with the tribal council, and owned enterprises. A recent amendment to the IRA constitution eliminated provisions that required review of tribal council actions by the secretary of the interior. Only 27.2 percent of the reservation land is Indian owned (compared with 55 percent at Pine Ridge), which feeds the conflict between Indian and white residents. Descendents of four Lakota Sioux tribes settled on the Cheyenne River Reservation, 49.5 percent of which is Indian owned. An IRA constitution provided for a tribal council with officers elected at-large and councilmen elected from thirteen districts. Districts also had councils with elected officers. Standing Rock (which straddles North and South Dakota) was settled by people from two divisions of the Lakota Sioux and from Yanktonais bands, whom the United States regarded as hostile factions resisting the surrender of the Black Hills. Sitting Bull was a symbol of resistance and, after he was murdered on the reservation, a martyr to the cause. Like the residents of Cheyenne River, these Sioux were particularly damaged by the Oahe Dam. Only 32.1 percent of reservation land is Indian owned. Land recovery has been a major issue here, and the constitution requires that sale, exchange, or leasing of tribal lands be approved by a vote of the membership. Standing Rock rejected the IRA but adopted a constitutional government: the tribal council officers are elected at-large, six members of the council are elected at-large, and eight are elected from eight districts. Tribal council members are required to attend district council meetings. In the 1990s multiple committees took responsibility for programs and other activities on the reservation, including defending treaty rights.[8]

Montana.

Montana is less overtly hostile than South Dakota, although not really supportive of Indian communities. Backlash usually follows state legislature efforts to support Indian issues, but Indians have some leverage with the Democratic Party and moderate Republicans because the Indian vote can determine the outcome of close elections in some parts of the state. Whereas the Sioux in western South Dakota were regarded as "hostile," only two tribes in Montana had this kind of reputation. Despite the seemingly greater tolerance in Montana than in South Dakota, state officials have opposed even changing place names that are offensive to Indians (for example, Custer Battlefield and geographical features named Squaw). Indian leaders have complained of state violence and discrimination against Indians in judicial, child custody, and welfare matters. Compared with the Sioux tribes in South Dakota, the Blackfeet, Crow, Fort Peck Assiniboine and Sioux, Northern Cheyenne, and Fort Belknap Assiniboine and Gros Ventre have less grassroots involvement in the sovereignty movement generally, although people from all these communities once participated in a mass demonstration to protest "anti-Indian" legislation. In Montana, grassroots passion usually focused on local, land-related issues in the 1990s. Most of these tribes were better off economically than the tribes in South Dakota. In fact, almost 48 percent of Indian families in South Dakota had incomes below the poverty level; at Pine Ridge and Rosebud, a higher percentage. In Montana, the percentage for impoverished Indians in the state was 39 percent. At Fort Peck, it was 46 percent; Northern Cheyenne, 43 percent; Fort Belknap, 37 percent; Crow, 32 percent; and Blackfeet, 31 percent. Subsistence hunting and fishing were important, to some degree, on all these large reservations.[9]

The Blackfeet have a 1.5 million-acre reservation and were relatively wealthy in oil and gas in the 1990s. Together, the tribe and individual Blackfeet owned 63 percent of the reservation. Some of that land was in fee status, owned by nonmembers who were descendants of Blackfeet; this land was in jeopardy of passing out of Indian ownership. Despite the mineral resources, 64 percent were unemployed. The tribe used most of its income from oil and gas for social programs, attorneys, and land purchase, but, at public insistence, a portion went to make one or two small per capita payments a year.[10]

Most authority was concentrated in the business council, which had nine members elected at-large from four districts. To run as a district representative, an individual had to reside in the district but did not have to win a majority of votes in that district. The business council appointed committees that included people from the districts (but did not always respond to their concerns). An honorary council of elderly men, all Blackfeet speakers, who had lifetime appointments and were selected by the business council, was the most important mitigating influence on the business council, although the former was not mentioned in the constitution.[11]

The constituency had less input than was the case on the Sioux reservations, and the grassroots support for a sovereignty agenda was less pervasive or wide ranging. Leadership for sovereignty implementation primarily came from the business council, except for protection of wilderness areas, in which several grassroots groups took passionate interest. Speaking in opposition to proposals to drill for oil in a wilderness area, Leland Ground linked religious duty to prevention of drilling: "In the name of Creator, don't do this." The business committee focused on negotiating with Montana on legal jurisdiction, water, and taxation issues. On one hand, their constituents expressed concern that these efforts would undermine Blackfeet sovereignty, frequently charging that the council would not properly manage tribal assets. On the other hand, constitutents supported land purchase and lobbied the business council to file suit against the United States for fraudulent land sales. The Blackfeet constitution (accepted under the auspices of the Indian Reorganization Act) was revised to allow the business council to buy fee land. In fact, part of the tribe's income was used annually to buy land.

In an 1895 agreement between the Blackfeet and the United States, the land that is now Glacier Park was transferred to the United States. The Blackfeet people believe that they did not cede the rights to hunt, fish, gather wood and other plants there, and visit and protect sacred sites in the park. Michael Desrosier put it this way: "Ever since we live in the country, we camp, hunt, gather from the mountains, and, since horses, graze them there. We have lived and died, we have played and dreamed and roamed those mountains and hills for more than a thousand years.... It belongs to us and we belong to it." During the 1990s grassroots organizations demonstrated and sought international support for Blackfeet rights there, and the honorary council pressured the business council to sue to establish Blackfeet rights in the park. The business council cooperated with grassroots organizations, such as traditionalist groups, and with individuals whose rights to operate businesses in the park were challenged by park officials. Many Blackfeet supported a traditionalized tribal fish-and-game program—for example, with no hunting seasons for people in need and designated hunters for the elderly.[12]

The Crow, who have a history of alliance with Americans in the nineteenth century, have a 2.2 million-acre reservation, with large deposits of coal and oil in their home territory. In the 1990s the Crow was the wealthiest tribe in Montana. The tribe and Crow individuals owned 65 percent of the land, but some of it was in fee status. The Crow used tribal income for some land purchase, small per capita payments, and job creation to supplement federal programs. Unemployment was high—57 percent.[13]

The Crow's 1948 (non-IRA) constitution provided that every two years the Crow elect four officers. These officers managed the tribe's programs and represented the tribe to the state and federal governments. The constitution also provided that major decisions and budget ratification were the responsibility of the "tribal council," a meeting open to all adult Crows. By tradition, decisions have been made by voice vote or "walking through the line" (standing with representatives of a position). Both practices subjected participants to peer pressure. Thus, clan leaders and/or tribal officials often have had the opportunity to influence tribal members to support a particular position. Also, a committee of district representatives—two elected officials from each of the six districts and two from off the reservation (Billings)—were supposed to offer advice to the four tribal officials. Frequently, the district elections were by acclamation; in practice, these representatives have had little influence. In 2001 the Crow amended the constitution, most significantly, to provide for separation of executive, legislative, and judicial powers—a checks and balances system. Representatives from six districts thereafter constituted a "legislative branch," which could adopt ordinances and codes and approve executive (the four officers') decisions. The executive branch could veto legislation, and tribal members elected judges.[14]

In the 1990s grassroots people and tribal officials alike viewed the United States' disregard of the Crow Act of 1920 as a serious betrayal in light of the support the Crow gave the United States during the Indian wars. This act, which provided for allotment, precluded non-Indians from owning more than 3,200 acres of reservation land. In fact, non-Indians acquired much more, and many Crows were unilaterally given fee patents on their land; therefore, less than half the reservation is in trust status. The land issue and associated water rights were the driving force of a grassroots-supported sovereignty agenda, largely because ranching is important to Crow identity. The Crow Tribe pursued legal action in the Crow Act case, despite the expense. Tribal officers also have obtained tribal council consent to buy land and to pay taxes on fee land owned by Crows so that the land would not be sold to non-Indians. Crow officials retained consistent public support through the 1990s by using a large portion of tribal income for job creation. Unemployment dropped by half, and the tribal employees increased from 450 in 1989 to 1,300 in 2000. In 2000 most of the tribe's $12 million budget was spent on wages. Some income from leasing tribally owned land and minerals was used for moderately-sized per capita payments. Income from court settlements against corporations was programmed, for example, to help the Little Big Horn College and the tribal court (whose judges are fluent in Crow). But the tribal college, established in 1980, was not as central to the sovereignty agenda as on Sioux reservations. In 1990 the college president, commenting on the college's recent accreditation noted, "People will start to believe that we are a real school now."[15]

At Fort Peck are Assiniboines, historically allies of the United States, and Sioux, who agreed to peace when they settled there. The Fort Peck Reservation is 2 million acres, only 43 percent of which is Indian owned. More than 56 percent is in fee status, creating a reduced land base for development and conflict over jurisdiction with the state (for example, over hunting and fishing on fee land within the reservation). Half the residents are non-Indians, and they have controlled the school system on the reservation. Unemployment was about 53 percent in the 1990s, even though the tribes had the largest income from oil in the state. Tribal income was used to purchase land, purchase and support tribally owned businesses, and supplement federal programs. The tribes made a small, annual per capita payment from the mineral leases and tax income.[16]

The Tribal Executive Board (TEB)—twelve representatives, a chair, vice chair, and sergeant-at-arms, all elected at-large every two years—managed the tribal businesses, programs, and income. This body was very stable throughout the 1990s, with most incumbents achieving re-election. The 1960 non-IRA constitution (amended in 1971) provided for the possibility of a "general council" to initiate a decision or reject enactments by the TEB, but meetings of the general council of adult enrolled members have been rare (only one in the 1990s). Authority and resources were broadly diffused (as was the case on Sioux reservations in South Dakota). In addition to the TEB, there were several "community organizations," the largest and most important of which were Poplar (a Sioux community) and Wolf Point (an Assiniboine community). These organizations elected officers, had sizable budgets (from treaty claim settlements), owned their own businesses in the community, gave assistance to individuals, and had control over some programs. They obtained loans and funds from the TEB. There also were two tribal organizations with elected officers that managed funds from treaty claim settlements. They made per capita payments, operated businesses, and bought land. In addition, the TEB appointed community members to all the boards that directed tribal businesses, the tribal college, and certain programs and to the oversight committees and commissions (for example, the fish and wildlife commission).[17]

Some grassroots groups pursued particular sovereignty issues and, toward that end, effectively put pressure on the TEB. People in the communities were outraged at the state's attempt to interfere with the traditional ways they had handled hunting and fishing on the reservation. The reservation has had a tradition of restricting hunting and fishing to Indians even though half the residents are non-Indians. Tribal fish and wildlife officers enforced tribal code. Through public pressure, grassroots communities prevented the TEB from negotiating an agreement to share authority with the state. The communities also spearheaded an effort to tribalize the educational system on the reservation, by working to elect Fort Peck Assiniboine and Sioux individuals to school boards and by supporting Native language and culture curriculum. However, the constitution still required that the secretary of the interior review TEB actions with regard to non-Indians on the reservation, the tribal court system, and loans and contracts to which the tribal government was party. And the Sioux at Fort Peck expressed willingness to accept money for the Black Hills treaty claim.[18]

After the Northern Cheyenne ended their war with the United States and settled on their reservation in 1884, they embarked on a strategy of isolation, determined to maintain their traditions. In fact, the tribe waives a one-half blood requirement for membership for individuals who reside in the reservation community. At 445,000 acres, their reservation is one of the smallest, but the tribe and Cheyenne individuals own 99 percent of the land. In the 1990s they did not exploit potential mineral wealth but rather concentrated on negotiating for jobs in local, energy-related industries and the Tongue River Dam project. Unemployment was about 50 percent. Leases on grazing land and timber and taxes were the main sources of tribal income; much of it has been used for small per capita payments. Tribal income in the 1990s was very low compared with that of the Blackfeet, Crow, and Fort Peck, but tribal leaders in prior decades had made a policy of buying back all the land alienated after allotment and had obtained federal assistance to do that.[19]

In 1935 the Cheyenne accepted the Indian Reorganization Act and a constitutional government, largely to enable the older, traditionally oriented men to gain more political influence during a time when the tribal government was dominated by younger, "progressive" men. The constitution was revised in 1960. It provided for a president elected at-large and a tribal council elected by the districts in which they lived (ten individuals from five districts). The districts have had frequent meetings. The 1960 constitution required that the secretary of the interior review most of the tribal council's actions. In 1996 the constitution was amended again: Cheyennes approved a "separation of powers" provision so that some tribal judges attained office by election and some (appellate judges) by appointment by the tribal president. In the 1990s there was great turnover in the positions of president and council member, producing instability in leadership and policy. This pattern developed, in large part, because of disagreement over coal leases.[20]

The issue that generated the most grassroots passion in the 1990s was the plan for the creation of a reservationwide school district so that Cheyennes could control the education of their children, who were bused off the reservation. Cheyenne communities worked on this project for thirty years and finally succeeded in 1994, overcoming strenuous opposition from the local, non-Indian-controlled school districts. They obtained money from Congress to build the school. "Traditionalists" have been very influential in grassroots politics. They have resisted coal mining on the reservation, because it would bring outsiders to their community and would damage the environment: these objections were presented as tradition or religion based. Conflict erupted over this decision because many Cheyennes wanted the per capita payments that coal mining would bring. Cheyenne leaders, working with environmental groups, focused on negotiating air quality agreements with companies near the reservation. Traditionalist interest groups also put pressure on the tribal council to create a leadership sphere for themselves in response to repatriation issues following NAGPRA and issues associated with the Sand Creek Massacre (see table 6). The tribal court has used a traditional model of social control relatively more than the other Montana reservations.[21]

The Gros Ventre and Assiniboine, historical allies of the United States, share Fort Belknap Reservation. The cession of the southern portion of the reservation in 1895 removed from their control the major mineral resources on the 650,000-acre reservation. The reservation land is 95 percent Indian owned, but the tribes (which own about 28 percent of the land) received little income from leasing tribal land. With no mineral resources on the reservation, the Fort Belknap community government was largely dependent on federal programs and contracts, and the reservation had an unemployment rate of 52 percent. Fort Belknap leaders attempted to sue in order to force the state to negotiate a gaming compact, but their suit was unsuccessful, as was an attempt to stop mining companies from polluting the water on the reservation. Elected leaders negotiated agreements with the state concerning taxes and water; Fort Belknap tried unsuccessfully to secure the right to market water.[22]

In 1935 Fort Belknap accepted a constitution under the auspices of the Indian Reorganization Act and instituted a twelve-member community council consisting of six Gros Ventres and six Assiniboines elected at-large. The constitution required that the secretary of the interior review most of the council's actions. In 1993 the constitution was amended; thereafter, the community council consisted of two Gros Ventres and two Assiniboines elected by their respective districts and a president and vice president elected at-large. The president–vice president team consisted of one Assiniboine and one Gros Ventre tribal member. The 1993 constitution also provided for the recall of these officials. There is a Gros Ventre treaty committee and an Assiniboine treaty committee, each with its own funds.[23]

In the 1990s grassroots efforts at Fort Belknap centered on amending the constitution to allow for more community participation and for acknowledgment of tribal identity, as well as on revising the law code. In the new 1999 code, the judges of the tribal court are appointed by the community council; judges must have a high school diploma. Laws regarding fish and wildlife conservation and child welfare received the most attention. Regarding fish and wildlife conservation, the Fort Belknap community assumed exclusive jurisdiction over non-Indians on trust land and established a committee of community members to oversee the tribes' Fish and Wildlife Department. The code authorized cooperative agreements with the state, county, and federal governments. It was to be enforced by tribal officers or federal officers; state conservation officers would need an agreement in place before they could enforce the code, and they would have to institute proceedings in tribal court.[24]

Wyoming.

In Wyoming, there is only one reservation, shared by the Eastern Shoshone and the Northern Arapaho. The Indian population in Wyoming is only 3 percent of the total and has less clout than the Indians in Montana, even though the oil and gas resources on the Wind River Reservation make it the wealthiest of all the reservations considered here. The state has shown great intransigence toward Wind River sovereignty, forcing the tribes there to go through expensive court proceedings over water rights and other matters of jurisdiction. Even when the water rights case was decided in Wind River's favor in 1989, the state refused to cooperate in the administration of those rights.[25]

Eighty-five percent of the oil and gas income is distributed in monthly per capita payments (from 40 to 325 dollars a month). The tribal governments rely on the remaining 15 percent, plus money from taxation, to hire legal assistance and create jobs by establishing tribally owned businesses. During the 1990s unemployment was about 51 percent, and 39 percent of the families lived below the poverty line. The establishment of fisheries and businesses that take advantage of the huge 118,000-acre wilderness area on the reservation has been thwarted by the state's opposition to the tribes' exercising their water rights.[26]

Each tribe has its own six-member business council, elected at-large every two years, and each has a general council (a meeting of voters) that can overrule the business council, initiate policy, and even disband the business council and hold a new election. A combined Shoshone-Arapaho business council has responsibility for managing the tribally owned trust lands. Neither tribe adopted a constitution, and both rejected the Indian Reorganization Act. The lack of a constitution is regarded as the perpetuation of "tradition." This means that the business councils must have the general councils' support for the sovereignty agenda.

The large 2.3 million-acre reservation is 90 percent Indian owned, but water rights are an issue. Arapahos boycotted merchants in neighboring towns for several weeks to protest lack of support for the tribes' "treaty-based water rights," a matter of "dignity" and "respect," and fairness, one council member insisted. Shoshone councilman Wes Martel explained that, in the matter of water rights, the "Creator and Creation" guided them. Both general councils have supported the pursuit of water rights. In the 1990s the Arapaho general council approved the separation of joint Shoshone and Arapaho federal programs into tribally controlled ones. With general council approval, Arapaho elders initiated a Native language program with tribal funding, and Shoshones, a cultural center. In the late 1960s the Arapaho led the successful effort to tribalize the school system on the reservation. During the 1990s, even with considerable turnover on the business councils, there was consistency in sovereignty goals. Also, in an effort to diffuse authority, the general councils created boards of tribal members to oversee tribal businesses, economic development, and water resources.[27]

Oklahoma.

In western Oklahoma, the non-Indian and the Cheyenne, Arapaho, Kiowa, Comanche, and Plains Apache populations live in small towns, where their children attend the public schools. In the 1990s Indians made up about 8 percent of the state population, but less in western Oklahoma. Nineteen percent of Indian families in the state had incomes below the poverty level; among the Cheyenne and Arapaho, 23 percent, and among Comanche, 27 percent on average—significantly lower than on Northern Plains reservations. Western Oklahoma Indians have access to urban centers, where they obtain employment, and these areas are close enough to allow them to return to western Oklahoma for tribal meetings and celebrations. State violence against Indians is less an issue here than on the Northern Plains. The majority population in Oklahoma employs romantic Indian imagery mostly to promote tourism. In eastern Oklahoma, where there has been extensive intermarriage with non-Indians, state officials often promote projects that recognize Indian heritage. Yet in western Oklahoma the treatment of Indians has come under fire by the civil liberties organizations. As I have argued elsewhere, the majority population has promoted an Indian imagery that works to marginalize and trivialize the Indian way of life, as well as undermine Indian confidence in their own political institutions.

The Cheyenne and Arapaho settled on a reservation in western Oklahoma in 1869. After the reservation was allotted in 1892, the federal government permitted the ownership of the remaining "surplus lands" to pass into the hands of non-Natives. About 10,000 acres were assigned to the federal government and have since been recovered and put in trust status, owned by the tribes. The tribes' oil and gas income is derived from these lands. Most of the allotments eventually were sold.

During the 1990s the elected Cheyenne-Arapaho business committee initiated efforts to implement sovereign rights over trust land, primarily so that they could generate income on these lands. The business committee has eight members, four from two Arapaho districts and four from four Cheyenne districts. There is no residency requirement for candidates or voters. The Arapaho and Cheyenne pre–World War II rural communities have largely been replaced by housing projects in small, multiethnic towns. The constitution written under the auspices of the Oklahoma Indian Welfare Act (and amended in 1975 and 1993) provided for an annual meeting of the general council, as well as a business committee (see table 2). Although the meeting is open to all enrolled tribal members, about 75–130 people attend, and here they vote on a budget presented by the business committee. All the tribes' income from oil and gas is budgeted for a small, annual per capita payment. In the 1990s the business committee operated as independently of the general council as possible.

The Cheyenne-Arapaho business committee drove the sovereignty agenda. Its constituents supported the committee in the unsuccessful struggle to prevent the state from taking income from cigarette and fuel businesses on trust land, but the general council voted down land-buying proposals and there was no grassroots sentiment for such an effort. Cheyennes and Arapahos celebrated Native traditions in powwows, but no grassroots pressure for a tribal college emerged. Most Cheyenne and Arapaho people favored the per capita distribution of all tribal income (although not all tribal income can be distributed per capita, because of federal constraints). The business committee implemented a program to tax non-Indian and tribal businesses, despite objections from constituents, and this income largely supplemented federal programs. There was no grassroots pressure to traditionalize the tribal court, although, in sentencing, the code provided for banishment, which reflects Cheyenne legal tradition. Cheyennes and Arapahos generally did not view their tribes or the combined tribes as a corporate entity within which individuals are subsumed. Rather, the "tribe" was viewed as a collection of individual members, each with an equal share in whatever resources the tribe has. The sovereignty movement was kept alive and pursued by a small group of elected officials either descended from the chiefs who fought and eventually won payment for the United States' violation of the 1851 treaty or from individuals who were exposed to American Indian Movement ideology in the 1970s while living in cities away from western Oklahoma.[28]

The Comanche Nation lost most of its reservation land at the time of allotment but in the 1990s had some income from oil on the remaining trust land. The Comanche refused to organize their government under the Oklahoma Indian Welfare Act but eventually adopted a constitution. The Comanche constitution provides for a tribal council, which meets at least once a year and has authority to approve budgets and leases and contracts on tribal property. Comanche voters also elect a seven-member (including three officers) business committee at-large. As among the Cheyenne and Arapaho in the 1990s, grassroots political activity focused on revising the constitution to restrict the business committee's powers. In the revised constitution, voters did not strike a provision that required the secretary of the interior to review tribal council actions. They did change enrollment requirements so that descendants of allottees need one-eighth Comanche ancestry (instead of one-fourth) to be members of the Comanche Nation. Opposition to business committee actions interfered with the development of several projects, but the business committee contracted programs, issued licenses, and operated small businesses.[29]

Comparisons and Conclusions

Tribal officials in all the Plains communities saw the exercise of sovereignty as entwined with control over tribal land and resources. Where they could generate income from energy resources and businesses established on tribal land, they tried to commit at least some of that income to strengthening the tribe as a corporate entity, for example, by buying land and putting it in tribal ownership. Grassroots commitment to a sovereignty agenda, however, was an equally important component of sovereignty movements. Tribal officials' success largely depended on the extent to which grassroots groups supported their goals. With strong grassroots support, there also were aggressive efforts to protect and extend cultural rights, for example, to indigenize the educational system. The extent to which the exercise of sovereignty had grassroots support depended on several factors: tribal–state relations, a "sustainable homeland," and a tribal government that allowed for diffusion of authority.

The degree to which grassroots people believed that they had a problem with state-supported violence against Indians varied among the four states considered here. Indians were visible minorities in Plains states and owned significant amounts of land in trust status—more so in some states than in others. Presumably, states with larger Native populations acted in response to a perceived threat. In any case, during the 1990s grassroots commitment to tribal sovereignty was greatest where Native people most feared state violence.

Plains communities were established as the result of treaties, but some land bases offer more potentially sustainable homelands than others do. A sustainable homeland has adequate economic resources to enable its residents to have real control over economic development, education, health care, and other aspects of life. Where the grassroots community was committed to the defense of a sustainable homeland, tribal members viewed the "tribe" as a corporate entity and supported investing tribal income to augment and protect the land base rather than distribute all tribal income per capita. Defense of homeland was rooted in collective memories about the treaty era in which these homelands were established in South Dakota, Montana, Wyoming, and Oklahoma. Treaty symbolism propelled modern sovereignty agendas and was linked to ideas about the connection between contemporary and ancestral peoples and among the natural, social, and sacred realms of life. During the 1990s tribes with sustainable homelands (Blackfeet, Crow, Northern Cheyenne, Northern Arapaho, Sioux, and Assiniboine) or potentially sustainable homelands (Sioux of South Dakota), which included wilderness areas and mineral resources, had some grassroots commitment to a broad sovereignty agenda and to resistance to compromises with states. The Gros Ventre and Assiniboines and the tribes of western Oklahoma have homelands that currently lack substantial economic resources.[30]

The exercise of sovereignty by tribal governments created conditions for alienation of constituents from elected leaders. A constitutional revision movement emerged on many Plains reservations. These movements worked for greater diffusion of authority. Where authority was widely diffused, grassroots support for sovereignty goals developed, and the idea of tribal corporateness was strengthened. Where there was little effort to diffuse authority, an individualized notion of "tribe" prevailed, and public pressure developed to distribute all tribal resources per capita.

In the 1990s grassroots commitment was greatest among the Sioux of South Dakota, who exhibited the most fear of state violence. Among these Sioux was passionate support for multiple spheres of a sovereignty movement: recovery of the Black Hills, protection of the homeland environment, protection of legal jurisdiction on reservation land, and cultural rights (especially an indigenized tribal court and educational system). The Sioux had a strong sense of "tribe" as a corporate entity, and they had the most developed system for the diffusion of authority positions.

At the other extreme, in western Oklahoma, Native people lived in counties where non-Indians outnumbered them ten to one. The tribes' land base is very small. The fear of state violence was less than on the Northern Plains. There was little grassroots commitment for and considerable controversy over a sovereignty agenda, and that agenda, which was pursued by elected officials, was narrowly defined (collection of taxes and establishment of businesses to generate income for distribution). In western Oklahoma, an individualized notion of "tribe" prevailed, and sporadic efforts to diffuse authority positions throughout the Native community have not succeeded.

Federal policy changes in the 1970s and 1980s opened the door for aggressive pursuit of sovereignty agendas. But the growth and direction of sovereignty movements on the Plains also was influenced by local circumstances and local views—and by Indian people taking the initiative and developing localized versions of sovereignty and sovereignty goals.

Notes

1. Marjane Ambler, *Breaking the Iron Bonds: Indian Control of Energy Development* (Lawrence: University Press of Kansas, 1990); Richard White, *It's Your Misfortune and None of My Own: A New History of the American West* (Norman: University of Oklahoma Press, 1991); and Brad Bays and Erin Hogan Fouberg, eds., *The Tribes and the States: Geographies of Intergovernmental Interaction* (Lanham, MD: Rowman and Littlefield, 2002).

2. The term *community* refers to ten reservations on the Northern Plains, the Cheyenne-Arapaho people in west-central Oklahoma, and the Comanche people living in west-central Oklahoma. The research for this chapter was supported by Wenner-Gren Foundation for Anthropological Research and is based on records from the 1990s.

3. For example, see Russell Lawrence Barsh and James Youngblood Henderson, *The Road: Indian Tribes and Political Liberty* (Berkeley: University of California, 1980); Vine Deloria Jr. and Clifford Lytle, *The Nations Within: The Past and Future of American Indian Sovereignty* (New York: Pantheon, 1984); Lyman Legters and Fremont Lyden, eds., *American Indian Policy: Self-Governance and Economic Development* (Westport, CT: Greenwood, 1994); David Wilkins, *American Indian Sovereignty and the United States Supreme Court: The Masking of Justice* (Austin: University of Texas Press, 1997); Troy Johnson, ed., *Contemporary Native American Political Issues* (Walnut Creek, CA: Alta Mira, 1999); Dean Howard Smith, *Modern Tribal Development: Paths to Self-Sufficiency and Cultural Integrity in Indian Country* (Walnut Creek, CA: Alta Mira, 2000); David Wilkins and K. Tsianina Lomawaima, *Uneven Ground: American Indian Sovereignty and Federal Law* (Norman: University of Oklahoma Press, 2001); and David Wilkins, *American Indian Politics and the American Political System* (Lanham, MD: Rowman and Littlefield, 2002).

4. *Lakota Times*, see March 20 and July 31, 1990; October 23, 1991 (quoted in); vol. 2, nos. 5, 9, 15, 37, 47, 48 (2001); Herbert Hoover and Carol Goss Hoover, *Sioux Country: A History of Indian–White Relations* (Sioux Falls, SD: Center for Western Studies, Augustana College, 2000),

171. Also see Thomas Biolsi, *"Deadliest Enemies": Law and the Making of Race Relations on and off Rosebud Reservation* (Berkeley: University of California Press, 2001).

5. Hoover and Hoover, *Sioux Country*, 164–171; Herbert Hoover, personal communication, February 2004; and Frank Pommersheim, personal communication, February 2004.

6. Constitution and By-Laws of the Oglala Sioux Tribe of the Pine Ridge Reservation, South Dakota, 1935, amended 1985; on the districts' political role, see, for example, *Lakota Times*, May 20, 1990.

7. Constitution and By-Laws of the Oglala Sioux Tribe; Oglala Sioux Tribe's Law and Order Code Book, 1996; on grassroots sovereignty activity, see *Lakota Times*, October 10, 1989, February 6, 1990, February 5, 1991, and May 7, 2001. Quotations are from February 6, 1990, and May 24, 1991. My study and comparison of tribal law codes was inspired by Bruce Miller's "Contemporary Tribal Codes and Gender Issues," *American Indian Culture and Research Journal* 18, no. 2 (1994): 43–74.

8. Hoover and Hoover, *Sioux Country*; Constitution, Bylaws and Corporate Charter of the Rosebud Sioux Tribe, 1935, amended 1962, 1966; and *Lakota Times*, vol. 9 (17, 18:1889), and November 16, 1990. On grassroots activity, see *Lakota Times*, January 9, 1990, vol. 1 (47:2000) and vol. 2 (22, 24:2001). The quotation is from *Lakota Journal*, November 13–19, 2000. Constitution and By-Laws of the Cheyenne River Sioux Tribe, South Dakota, 1935, amended 1960, 1980; Constitution of the Standing Rock Sioux Tribe, 1959, amended 1961, 1963, 1974, 1984. On committees at Standing Rock, see *Lakota Times*, vol. 2 (44:2001).

9. *Big Horn County News*, October 9 and November 4, 1992; James Lopach, Margery Hunter Brown, and Richmond Clow, *Tribal Government Today: Politics in Montana* (Boulder: University Press of Colorado 1998), 17, 36. Data on poverty levels are from 2000 Census, Summary Social, Economic, and Housing Characteristics, for South Dakota, Montana, Wyoming, and Oklahoma.

10. Lopach, Brown, and Clow, *Tribal Government Today*, 204–205; see also Native American Development Corporation (NADC), *Tribal Economic Contributions to Montana* (n.p., 2004), 11–12. There has long been tension between the so-called Full Blood group and a group of Blackfeet who are descendants of American Fur Company employees. The American Indian Movement influenced the younger generation of both groups, and this has resulted in support for sovereignty from both groups. Stanley Clay Wilmouth, "The Development of Blackfeet Politics and Multiethnic Categories" (Ph.D. diss., University of California at Riverside, 1987).

11. Constitution and By Laws of the Blackfeet Tribe of the Blackfeet Indian Reservation, 1935, amended 1978. On the honorary council, see *Glacier Reporter*, January 26, 1995, February 13, 1997, and January 22, 1998.

12. On land issues, see *Glacier Reporter*, February 5, 1998, and April 15, 1999. On Glacier Park, see *Glacier Reporter*, March 7 and 17 and October 17, 1991, May 14, 1992, March 18 and June 17, 1993, March 10, 1994, April 14, 1994, February 13, 1997, July 16, 1998, and January 13, 2000. Ground is quoted in March 7, 1991, and DesRosier in October 10, 1991.

13. Lopach, Brown, and Clow, *Tribal Government Today*, 204–205; and NADC, *Tribal Economic Contributions*, 12–14.

14. Constitution and Bylaws of the Crow Tribe of the Crow Reservation, 1948, amended by resolution in 1959, 1986, and 2001; and *Big Horn County News*, October 8, 1997.

15. *Big Horn County News*, July 4, 1990 (quoted in), January 27, 1993, November 22, 1995, January 10, June 5, and October 9, 1996, February 18, 1998, May 26, 1999, March 29, May 10, August 16, and November 29, 2000.

16. Lopach, Brown, and Clow, *Tribal Government Today*, 204–205; and NADC, *Tribal Economic Contributions*, 15–16.

17. Constitution and Bylaws of the Assiniboine and Sioux Tribes of the Fort Peck Indian Reservation, 1960. *Wotanin Wowapi*, August 26, 1993, August 18, 1994, January 30, 1997, and July 22, 1999; on taxes, July 11, 1991, April 2, 1992, July 3, 1996, and July 16, 1998; on gaming, December 16, 1993, and January 26, 1995; and on water rights, December 6, 1991, and September 22, 1994.

18. *Wotanin Wowapi*, on hunting and fishing, February 3, June 2 and 30, August 25, and September 1, 1994; on the Black Hills Claim, July 2, 1998; and Constitution of the Assiniboine and Sioux Tribes, VII, 3, 5 and X, 6–8.

19. Lopach, Brown, and Clow, *Tribal Government Today*, 204–205; and NADC, *Tribal Economic Contributions*, 17–18. The Cheyenne also face considerable hostility from the Crow, whose reservation borders theirs. The Crow often challenge Cheyenne rights to land and resources in what was once Crow land.

20. Constitution and By-Laws of the Northern Cheyenne Tribe of the Northern Cheyenne Indian Reservation, 1935, amended 1960, 1996; Graham Taylor, *The New Deal and American Indian Tribalism: The Administration of the Indian Reorganization Act, 1934–1945* (Lincoln: University of Nebraska Press, 1980), 104; and Separation of Powers Code, 1997.

21. On the new school district, see *Big Horn County News*, January 16 and July 3, 1991, September 30, 1992, June 30 and November 10, 1993, and August 17, 1994; on coal mining and tribal income, February 3 and October 6, 1993, and September 4, 1996, and *Wotanin Wowapi*, April 25, 1991. On traditionalist issues, see Tribal Code of the Northern Cheyenne Reservation, 1987; and *Wotanin Wowapi*, March 14, 1991, March 3, 1994.

22. *Wotanin Wowapi*, January 27, 1994; Lopach, Brown, and Clow, *Tribal Government Today*, 204–205; and NADC, *Tribal Economic Contributions*, 14–15.

23. Constitution and By-Laws of the Fort Belknap Community of the Fort Belknap Reservation, Montana, 1935, amended 1993.

24. The Laws of the Gros Ventre and Assiniboine Tribes of Fort Belknap, 1999.

25. *Wind River News*, February 6 and August 20, 1990, April 9, 1991, April 21 and 28, 1992, and December 13, 2001.

26. *Wind River News*, January 2 and 23, February 27, and June 19, 1990, September 7, 1993, May 11, June 29, July 27, and November 9, 2000. Also see Geoffrey O'Gara, *What You See in Clear Water: Indians, Whites, and a Battle over Water in the American West* (New York: Vintage, 2000).

27. *Wind River News*, January 2, March 20, April 10, May 20 (quoted in), September 25 and October 2 and 9, 1990, August 13, 1991, January 14 and July 7, 1992, May 9, 1995, September 25, 1997, and November 10, 1998.

28. On the Cheyenne-Arapaho, see Cheyenne-Arapaho Tribes of Oklahoma Law and Order Code, 1988; and Loretta Fowler, *Tribal Sovereignty and the Historical Imagination: Cheyenne-Arapaho Politics* (Lincoln and London: University of Nebraska Press, 2002).

29. Constitution of the Comanche Nation, 1966, amended 1976, 1978, 1979, 1981, 1984, 1985, 1994, 2002.

30. The term *sustainable homeland* is Earl Old Person's, *Glacier Reporter*, May 9, 1991. The Rocky Boy Reservation was settled by Native people who did not sign a treaty with the United States.

12 States of Sovereignty

Race Shifting, Recognition, and Rights in Cherokee Country

Circe Sturm

In 1978 the Branch of Acknowledgment and Research (BAR) established criteria for tribes to obtain federal recognition (see table 5). Despite revisions in 1994, the legitimacy of these criteria remains a subject of debate. For instance, tribes must document evidence of social and political continuity, even though their survival often depended on lack of visibility and they frequently had little control over what happened in their communities. In addition, the dominant mode of race thinking in some regions caused Indians to be defined as either "white" or "colored" and treated accordingly. As if this was not enough, the recognition process is also long and expensive; even with legal assistance from organizations such as the Native American Rights Fund (see table 4), many tribal groups with strong claims have been unable to navigate successfully through it.[1] Nonetheless, as historian Mark Miller observes, tribal recognition represents a "pivotal development in post-war Native American policy" because it confirmed the right of tribes to exist in modern America.[2] Typically, scholars focus on the federal level, but Circe Sturm discusses the issues surrounding state recognition, including the opposition of recognized tribes to the acknowledgment of new tribes and the advantages and disadvantages of recognition for both states and Indian communities.

Almost anyone working or living in Native North America is aware of the tensions between legal definitions of "Indianness" and local understandings of community belonging. Achieving the legal status of "Indian tribe" has never been the clear-cut proposition that outsiders might expect. In recent decades, the process has become even more fraught with confusion. Traditionally, Native American tribes have been legally acknowledged as such by the federal government and its agent, the Bureau of Indian Affairs (BIA), though federal standards for official recognition are immensely variable. In federal legis-lation alone, thirty-three definitions of "American Indian" are in use, including those based on blood quantum, tribal citizenship, residency, self-identification, or any combination of the above—any of these may or may not correspond to the standards and definitions used by tribal governments.[3] Negotiating the meanings these different sets of rules and legislation hold for Indian lives is challenging enough, but in the past three decades, being indigenous in this country—at least in a legal sense—has become infinitely more complex. State governments have taken an increasingly active role in defining communities as "Indian tribes," something that was not in their purview for most of the twentieth century.[4]

What states are doing is, in many ways, reviving their colonial practices and reflecting ongoing tensions over states' rights that have long character-ized US federalism. Though some state governments and their colonial predecessors recognized the political rights of Native American nations in government-to-government treaties, proclamations, and laws as early as the mid-seventeenth century, most have deferred to the federal government on such matters for much of US history.[5] Only in the past three decades have states become more involved in the process again, recognizing more tribes on an ever more frequent basis. In doing so, states have added a competing element, a sort of wild card, to the already chaotic process of tribal recogni-tion, sparking bitter debates among federally recognized, state-recognized, and self-identified Indian communities. Some of the most intense fighting has been over access to state economic resources; state governments now have to decide whether to privilege federally recognized tribes or their own, state-acknowledged tribes for funding. Other conflicts have emerged over rights of representation. People argue about who should talk to the local Lion's Club, who should have access to local sacred sites, who should repa-triate and conduct ceremonies for dead ancestors, and who should sit on the State Commission for Indian Affairs. At the heart of these debates are two deceptively simple questions: which group is authentically "Indian," and who should decide? Whatever the response, all parties agree that a great deal is at stake.

In all the acrimonious debate about who is really Indian—and on what basis—one term keeps popping up again and again, and that is *sovereignty*. Its ubiquity stems not from the fact that sovereignty is a complex idiom that can be read in many ways. Even if *sovereignty* is used in a variety of contexts to mean different things, it has a common semantic core that refers to political autonomy—the ability to exercise a certain amount of control over one's social, political, and economic life and one's geographic territory. Yet many Native Americans articulate a contradictory stance. They claim, on one hand, an inherent sovereignty as an autonomous, self-governing people (as a nation) and, on the other, a type of sovereignty that stems specifically from their government-to-government relationship with the United States, or at times, even with states.[6] The first type of sovereignty derives from the people and is therefore closely linked to understandings of both "peoplehood" and nationalism, but the second type is less autonomous. In fact, it relies upon negotiation, reciprocity, and relations of interdependence with outside powers.

One of the most critical examples of this interdependence is that tribal sovereignty—not as an ideal, but as a legal right and an actual practice—is often tied to various forms of external recognition, so much so that the nature and exercise of sovereignty depend on who is recognizing whom in which context (Cattelino, chapter 14, this volume).[7] Tribal sovereignty, then, is a form of power that is both independent of and dependent on broader social and political forces. Because of this social and political interdependence, sovereignty is being invoked in the great debates over tribal recognition at the very moment people feel that they are losing control. What we are hearing are the tracings of power being etched into this debate, as contested Native American identities are tied to contested understandings and practices of tribal acknowledgment and sovereignty that have emerged in the wake of colonialism, nation-building, and US federalism. In this chapter, I use examples from "Cherokee country," the case I know best, to illustrate how state recognition of Indian tribes has complicated the nature and meanings of tribal sovereignty and to explore such conflicts and their broader implications.

At the root of this controversy is a demographic explosion in newly identified Indian people and tribes. Nowhere is this more apparent than in Cherokee country, where literally hundreds of unacknowledged communities assert a Cherokee identity and vie for various forms of political recognition that would affirm their status as a sovereign people.[8] In the 1980s the Cherokee Nation and the Eastern Band of Cherokee Indians in North Carolina, seeing the overall demographic trend as a growing problem, started to collect information and documents on what they ominously referred to as "entities using the Cherokee name." As might be expected, the two tribes were concerned not so much with individual claims of Cherokee identity but with those groups asserting a collective, tribal status that might somehow undermine their own rights to sovereignty. In an interview in the summer of 2003, Troy Wayne Poteete, a lawyer and former Cherokee Nation tribal council member, said to me, "Even if they have an ancestor on some roll, join the historical society, chart it all out, study about it, but don't start a damn tribe!" Richard Allen, who works for the executive branch of the Cherokee Nation, was even more forceful. When self-identified and state-recognized Cherokee tribes emerge to claim treaties and rights, he stated, "not only is that, to me, an insult, but it's also an attack on our sovereignty as Cherokee people, as the Cherokee Nation."

What is not understood is the magnitude of this so-called attack. Because of concerns about these new and reemerging tribal groups, the Cherokee Nation's tribal registrar collected a small closet-full of materials on the subject between the mid-1980s and mid-1990s. I used these and other materials to try to figure out the sheer number of competing claims to Cherokee tribal identity. From what I have been able to ascertain so far, at least 247 groups scattered throughout the United States identify themselves as Cherokee tribes, band, clans, or nations.[9] None of these are federally recognized, though at least fourteen are recognized as Cherokee tribes by the states in which they live. Thirty-one have made contact with the Bureau of Indian Affairs, Office of Federal Acknowledgment, and are seeking federal recognition.

"Entities using the Cherokee name" are a coast-to-coast phenomenon, and geography plays a role in the new calculus of tribal sovereignty. Self-identified and state-recognized tribes have made the greatest inroads in asserting their presence in the absence of federally recognized tribes. Now, for the first time, we can get a better sense of the geographic distribution of these organizations. Self-identified Cherokee tribes tend to cluster in the southeast where, historically, Native American populations have been decimated or pushed out by state policies, leaving a presumptive void of Indianness into which these new groups can assert themselves. For example, Georgia has forty-three such groups, three of which are state recognized. This is bitterly ironic, given that Georgia is the state largely responsible for one of the most genocidal episodes in Cherokee history, the infamous "Trail of Tears." A quarter of the Cherokee people died as they were forcibly and illegally removed from their southeastern homelands in the late 1830s. Florida is the runner-up, with twenty-three, and Alabama, Arkansas, and Tennessee each have somewhere between sixteen and twenty. Conversely, many of the states with few, if any, self-identified and state-recognized tribes are historically "Indian" states, such as South Dakota, New Mexico, and Montana. Yet this phenomenon is not confined to the southeast, as some historians and anthropologists have suggested.[10] Thirty-six states have at least one "Cherokee entity" within their boundaries, and states outside the southeast, such as California, Texas, and Ohio, have as many as seven. These new and reemerging Cherokee tribes are everywhere, from Alaska to Vermont.

What is happening in Cherokee country is a microcosm of what is happening throughout the United States, as states respond in fifty ways to these newcomers. Traditionally, two main parties have been involved in negotiations over tribal sovereignty—the federal government and federally recognized tribes. Historical interactions between these parties set legal precedent, established lines of communication, and put in place the fundamentals of the political process. Now, states are blurring these lines. From New England to Montana, state-recognized tribes have become significant players, growing in number and becoming more outspoken about securing their own rights, whatever these may be. Given the increasingly visible role that state-recognized tribes are playing on the national scene, it is surprising how little is known about them—frankly, there are few reliable sources of information on state recognition. Though I had come to expect neat lists of federally recognized tribes available in numerous government documents, scholarly publications, and websites, it took me considerable research to compile my own list of state-recognized tribes. What I have been able to gather (see table 8) is that at least sixty-three tribes are now recognized by eighteen states, including fourteen state-recognized Cherokee tribes—roughly 20 percent of the total. None of the sixty-three is federally recognized, though several have petitions pending (for example, the Shinnecock Indian Nation of New York, with land holdings in South Hampton).[11]

Though state recognition has deep roots in US history, particularly along the eastern seaboard, the majority of state-recognized tribes achieved this status only in the past thirty years. In the wake of the Red Power movement, non-recognized Indians began making stronger demands for official political recognition at both federal and state levels. These demands gathered steam over the past three decades, fueled at times by the lucrative potential of Indian gaming. The upshot has been a rash of newly state-recognized tribes that now outnumber those with longer standing. In Virginia, for example, two of the state's tribes were recognized in colonial era treaties, and the other seven were recognized after 1980 in various resolutions before the Virginia General Assembly.[12] State recognition has much looser standards than does the federal process.[13] In Virginia, the seven new tribes needed only to be organized as corporate entities, to have a tribal roll, and, more important, to be able to lobby for their recognition effectively. Virginia is not idiosyncratic in the apparent casualness of its recognition process—

the same minimal standards and dependence on legislative maneuvering also exist in other states. Louisiana, for instance, requires no documentation whatsoever, only that a petitioning tribe submit concurrent resolutions to the state senate and house of representatives. If the tribe seeking recognition is politically astute and can convince politicians of its legitimacy, then the resolution is likely to pass. In many cases, states say yes because they have little to lose in recognizing a group of Native people and with a resolution that often rests more on symbolism than on anything else, whereas saying no risks bad publicity and expensive legal battles.

State recognition, then, is often an exercise in pure politics, relying on external measures of authenticity less than the federal recognition process does.[14] Because state recognition flows more out of the pragmatism of contemporary politics than the ostensibly detached empiricism of the social sciences (that is, the historical, anthropological, and genealogical impetus behind the federal acknowledgment procedure), the practice varies widely from state to state.[15] A few states imitate the rigorous posture of the federal government, to greater or lesser degree. For example, the Tennessee Commission for Indian Affairs (TCIA) in its 1990 "Recognition Criteria for Native American Indian Nations, Tribes or Bands" reproduced federal standards almost verbatim.[16] In 1976 the North Carolina Commission on Indian Affairs established procedures for state recognition that were slightly less rigid. Both sets of criteria, much like the federal standards, rely heavily on evidence of external recognition by non-Indians—an obvious bias. Then there are the states that have no guidelines or procedures whatsoever. The State of Georgia, for instance, recognized three groups as Indian tribes in 1993 but set up no standards for the process. Other groups seeking recognition from the Georgia state legislature have been defeated, largely because of the efforts of federally recognized tribes, such as the Cherokee Nation of Oklahoma and the Eastern Band of Cherokee Indians in North Carolina. The latter have a historic—albeit unpleasant—connection to the state of Georgia and have lobbied hard that only the federal government should have the right to recognize Indian tribes.

Although federally recognized tribes have urged states to get out of the tribal recognition business, states continue this for many reasons. Sometimes, as in Georgia, the state is seeking to clean up its reputation in regards to indigenous people. From a cynical point of view, a state that forcibly removed its indigenous population in the past tries to make amends by finding and recognizing some remnant Native American communities in the present. Indeed, two of the three tribes currently recognized by the State of Georgia identify themselves as Cherokee. To promote state recognition, local politicians and tribal activists argue that Native American tribes within state borders help to generate tourism. Also, state legislators who have had leadership roles in their state government and in the very same tribal communities seeking state recognition have used their political influence to sway the legislative process. Examples include Georgia state representatives Bill Dover (Georgia Tribe of Eastern Cherokees, Dahlonega) and June Hegstrom (Cherokee of Georgia Tribal Council, St. George), who sponsored bills for state recognition and other Indian-related legislation in the mid-1990s while in office.[17]

Besides the potential for corruption, other difficulties stem from the inconsistencies and variations in the state recognition process. No one is certain what state recognition means. Is it inexpensive symbolism for state legislators or something more legally substantial? With so much procedural variation, does state recognition mean one thing in Louisiana and something else in North Carolina? Bestowing state recognition without any standards and procedures or any efforts to verify the claims of petitioners seems as politically meaningful as naming a street "Elvis Presley Boulevard" in Memphis, Tennessee—a token affirmation of presence that has no teeth. Historical context is equally important. Surely, when the Commonwealth of Virginia signed a government-to-government treaty with the Pamunkey in 1658, it had different intentions than did the State of Arkansas in 1997 when it recognized the contributions of descendents of the Northern Cherokee Nation of Old Louisiana Territory to the state, proclaiming April 8 as Northern Cherokee Day.[18] Both groups claim state-recognized status, yet only one has received any direct benefits. This is not to suggest that contemporary state recognition is little more than symbolism: material resources are also at stake. At times, state recognition may provide nothing more than a mention in a legislative memorial, but at other times, it can mean funding, benefits, and even a reservation. It may even prove to be a stepping stone toward federal recognition.[19]

Among federally recognized, state-recognized, and self-identified Cherokee communities, the political and legal contests between state- and federally recognized tribes produce the most overt tensions. In direct competition with one another, they fight for local political influence and for federal and state funding. Though most federal funding is earmarked for federally recognized tribes, state-recognized tribes are sometimes able to access federal monies. In 2002 the Administration for Native Americans (ANA), an agency under the US Department of Health and Human Services, granted $282,020 to four state-recognized Cherokee tribes in Georgia, Missouri, and Virginia.[20] Not surprisingly, certain federally recognized Cherokees viewed this as a siphoning off of funding intended for them and for other tribes that share federally recognized status. Wilma Mankiller, principal chief of the Cherokee Nation at the time, wrote a letter to members of the Georgia state assembly: "The Cherokee Nation and Eastern band will not tolerate any groups purporting to be a Cherokee Nation.... Steps must and will be taken to investigate how these groups were able to secure state recognition, how these suspect groups are securing federal funds, and how to correct these injustices."[21] State-recognized Cherokees view this in an altogether different light. As Georgia state representative Bill Dover said, "The issue is not federal programs or a land grab. It's the opportunity to preserve our heritage proudly."[22] To Dover and others, gaining federal funding is not a matter of being lucky or of being able to work the system. The awarding of federal funding demonstrates that state-recognized status signifies legitimacy as a sovereign Indian tribe.

In debates about tribal recognition, resources, and rights, all roads lead back to sovereignty. In considering the gradations of sovereignty that are at stake, how do the claims of state-recognized tribes stack up against those of federally recognized tribes and of states themselves? These are questions that have not been addressed on a consistent basis, either within the academy or in the law.[23] In the case of state-recognized tribes, the ambiguities of federalism and its relationship to different practices of sovereignty are readily apparent. For example, a recent case before the Connecticut supreme court involved a member of the state-recognized Paucatuck Eastern Pequot Tribe. The court ruled that state criminal law applies to Native Americans who are members of state-recognized tribes, even if the crime occurs on a reservation. The defendant argued that Connecticut could not assume criminal jurisdiction over his case because it had not followed the procedures set forth by the Federal Indian Civil Rights Act of 1968. The court ruled, however, that the act did not apply because the defendant was not a member of a federally recognized tribe and therefore did not qualify as an "Indian" under federal Indian law (*State v. Sebastian*).[24] To reach this conclusion, the court considered whether the constitutional power of Congress to regulate Indian affairs preempted state law and whether the tribe had any "residual and demonstrable tribal sovereignty under federal case law."[25] The court reasoned that federal recognition was "the very essence of the government to government relationship underlying federal criminal jurisdiction" and that, because the tribe's state recognition had no bearing on federal recognition, it was irrelevant to the case at hand.[26] If the individual had been a member of a federally recognized Indian tribe, then federal law would have applied, and the outcome might have been very different. Even though the individual was an "Indian" in the eyes of the state, he was not an "Indian" for the purposes of determining state criminal jurisdiction. Federal recognition trumped state recognition in this regard. Tribal sovereignty was a concern of the court. It wanted to be certain that its decisions did not infringe upon the tribe's ability to exercise its own sovereignty, at least in a way that was (again) inconsistent with federal law. In the end, the court decided that sovereignty could not be invoked, because it is a collective instead of individual right and the state-recognized tribe itself was not a party to the suit.[27]

State-recognized tribes have an ambiguous status, one that is constantly evolving. The *Sebastian* case seems to imply that, without federal recognition, state-recognized tribes in Connecticut may not exercise tribal sovereignty in the judicial arena. In several court cases, the state courts have determined that, for most purposes, the state has criminal and civil jurisdiction over state-recognized tribes and individuals.[28] Yet in all these cases, the question of whether a state-recognized tribe enjoys sovereignty, and if so, to what extent, has never been directly decided. The closest approximation took place in 2001 when, in seeming contradiction of earlier decisions, the superior court of Connecticut ruled that a corporation could not sue a state-recognized tribe, because it had been recognized as a "domestic dependent nation" and self-governing entity in state statute.[29] In all preceding cases, the state courts linked sovereignty with federal recognition, for they allowed federal recognition to supercede state recognition when determining who had criminal or civil jurisdiction. In this most recent ruling, no such association was made. By virtue of their state recognition, these tribes, at least in Connecticut, enjoy an aspect of sovereignty—sovereign immunity—and are as free from suit as are federally recognized tribes. State courts struggle to interpret the meanings of tribal sovereignty invoked in these varying contexts across the United States; state-recognized tribes add another element to the already baroque complexity of Indian law.

The law is not the only place where debates about sovereignty are heard. Time and again, the public representation of culture—meaning who has rights to represent what and in which context—is a matter of serious debate among Native American people. Though federally and state-recognized tribes tend to lead the discussions, self-identified tribes also voice their opinions and claim rights to represent, display, and perform "their" culture. Nowhere are these debates about cultural representation, tribal status, and sovereignty more hotly contested than among Cherokees. For instance, during Halloween 2000 the Echota Cherokee Nation, a state-recognized tribe in Alabama, staged a huge protest of a local haunted house known as the "Trail of Fears." They believed that it was morally inappropriate to evoke such images of Cherokee suffering in a commercial context. In making these public assertions, the Echota Cherokee laid claim to the "Trail of Tears" as a part of their own history, suggesting that the event belonged to them as a people and not to some commercial property.[30] Of course, this claim is ironic: the

Echota Cherokee would not exist in Alabama if they had not somehow managed to escape the forced removal to the west, a fact not lost on many Oklahoma Cherokees, whose ancestors suffered and died along the trail. Then again, citizens of the federally recognized Eastern Band of Cherokee Indians in North Carolina also claim the Trail of Tears as a part of their collective history, even though most of their ancestors were spared the trauma of removal.

Public representations of Cherokee culture have a powerful effect on discourses and practices of tribal sovereignty. Such representations shape what the public knows, or thinks it knows, about Indians as a whole and about specific tribal groups—and whether a group of people deserves recognition as a Native American tribe. For example, Chief Wilma Mankiller made these connections explicit in 1995 when she provided written testimony regarding the federal acknowledgment process before the US Senate Committee on Indian Affairs. "The Cherokee Nation and other tribes have been embarrassed by groups such as 'The Echota Cherokee Nation' showing up at the National Congress of the American Indian dressed in stereotypical Hollywood garb," she complained. "A tribe's sovereignty, reputation and identity are at stake."[31] For the Cherokee Nation, such public invocations of their name, national seal, and culture are not matters of libel, intellectual property, or copyright, though they have used this language on occasion. Rather, the sentiment is more akin to what US citizens and leaders might feel if a growing number of small countries started to proclaim that they, in fact, were the United States of America and had claims to the United States' cultural identity, its political rights, and even parts of its geographic territory. These claims would seem ludicrous at first but probably more disturbing if other governments in the international community began to recognize them as legitimate. From the Cherokee Nation's point of view, if almost anyone can claim a tribal identity, can achieve new, alternative forms of recognition and the sense of sovereignty that goes with it, then what happens to the hard-fought gains of the Cherokee Nation? Does it risk becoming just another "entity using the Cherokee name?" Federally recognized Cherokee tribes suggest that the answer, at least in some arenas, may be yes. They argue that state recognition of new Cherokee tribes creates public and legal confusion, undermines perceptions of Cherokee historical and cultural authenticity, and defies the principle that tribal sovereignty is fundamentally based on nation-to-nation relationships.

Given these concerns, both the Cherokee Nation of Oklahoma and the Eastern Band of Cherokee Indians have urged state governments, time and again, to leave matters of recognition to the federal government. The tribal council of the Cherokee Nation has even gone so far as to pass a resolution stating that, as a policy, the Cherokee Nation "shall not endorse, acquiesce, or support for federal or state recognition any other group, association or club which identify themselves as a separate tribal entity for purposes of having a government to government relationship because of Cherokee Ancestry."[32] On May 11, 2005, the principal chief of the Cherokee Nation, Chadwick Smith, also asked the federal government to consider passing a moratorium on the recognition of any additional Cherokee groups, stating flatly that the Cherokee Nation opposed such recognition.[33] The United Keetoowah Band of Cherokee Indians, another federally recognized Cherokee tribe, has been more inconsistent in its stance toward state-recognized and self-identified Cherokee tribes, but lately it has taken a more hard-line approach, in keeping with the other two federally recognized Cherokee nations. For all three, a clear political hierarchy seems to be at work: Cherokee newcomers should be recognized by other "legitimate" Cherokee governments first, by the federal government next, and by their respective state governments last, if at all. Of course, as self-identified Cherokees might point out in frustration, the only "legitimate" Cherokee governments are those that are federally recognized in the first place.

In debates such as these, what matters is not whether we think of Native American identity as a social and political construct, an essential property, or something in between, but how these different understandings determine social classification and are used to measure and assign political legitimacy and legal rights. These issues affect Native North America much more broadly, as can be seen in the numerous newspaper articles, tribal publications, and scholarly articles written by Indian people expressing concerns over federal recognition, state recognition, "wannabes," "outtalucks," and other variations on the theme. Most Indian people care deeply about how tribal identity is measured and understood and how these understandings shape practices of social and political recognition. Many also care about how this impacts tribal sovereignty, even though some regard it as an alien and even irrelevant concept.[34] The Cherokee case provides an opportunity to see how the debates have crystallized within a specific context. As more people reclaim a tribal identity, adding fuel to the state recognition process, issues that now seem Cherokee-specific will soon affect other tribal communities as well.

The complexities of the political situation in Cherokee country beg us to reconsider the various processes of recognition and their implications for Native American sovereignty. The discourses and practices of indigenous recognition are quite complex within the US context, but we need to keep in mind that the United States is not alone in this regard. Nation-states often bear the legacies of empire and colonialism, in that the creation of a national body gives rise to multiple populations that access sovereignty in different ways. In the United States, these inequalities surface in the varying abilities of Native Americans to forge relations of autonomy and interdependence, including inequalities in being recognized or acknowledged by other tribal, state, and federal governments. As sovereign powers engage in competing practices of official recognition, we hear increasingly bitter debates about political, racial, and cultural authenticity among Indian people. The great irony at the center of these debates is that as Native American communities assert their indigeneity, they complicate, vie for, and even challenge the political relationships of mutual recognition and interdependence upon which sovereignty rests.

Acknowledgments

This research has been made possible by generous funding from the National Science Foundation, The American Council of Learned Sciences, the National Endowment of the Humanities, a residential fellowship at the School for Advanced Research, and funding from the College of Arts and Sciences, the Office of Vice President of Research, and the Research Council at the University of Oklahoma, Norman.

Notes

1. Jack Campisi, *The Mashpee Indians: Tribe on Trial* (Syracuse, NY: Syracuse University Press, 1991); Bruce Miller, *Invisible Indigenes: The Politics of Nonrecognition* (Lincoln: University of Nebraska Press, 2003); and Renée Ann Cramer, *Cash, Color, and Colonialism: The Politics of Tribal Acknowledgment* (Norman: University of Oklahoma Press, 2005), 41.

2. Mark Edwin Miller, *Forgotten Tribes: Unrecognized Indians and the Federal Acknowledgment Process* (Lincoln: University of Nebraska Press, 2004), 256–257.

3. Eva Marie Garroutte, *Real Indians: Identity and the Survival of Native America* (Berkeley: University of California Press, 2003), 16. The standards of citizenship for tribal governments are equally variable and complex. For a useful comparative overview, see C. Matthew Snipp, *American Indians: First of This Land* (New York: Russell Sage Foundation, 1989).

4. Research for this chapter is part of a larger ethnographic study on the racial and cultural politics of reclaiming Cherokee identity, at both the individual and group levels. Much of this research has been conducted among federally recognized, state-recognized, and self-identified Cherokee tribes in Oklahoma, North Carolina, Alabama, Arkansas, Missouri, and Texas in 1995–1996, 1998, 2000, 2003–2004, and 2005.

5. One of the earliest examples of state recognition is that of the Mattaponi and Pamunkey; the Commonwealth of Virginia recognized both tribes in a 1658 treaty. Kirke Kickingbird and Karen Ducheneaux, *One Hundred Million Acres* (New York: Macmillan Books, 1973), 209; and Gail Sheffield, *The Arbitrary Indian: The Indian Arts and Crafts Act of 1990* (Norman: University of Oklahoma Press, 1997), 72. Other examples include the Shinnecock Indian Nation, originally recognized by the State of New York in 1792, and the Lumbee, whose recognition in North Carolina dates to 1885.

6. David Wilkins and K. Tsianina Lomawaima, *Uneven Ground: American Indian Sovereignty and Federal Law* (Norman: University of Oklahoma Press, 2001); and Thomas Biolsi, "Imagined Geographies: Sovereignty, Indigenous Space, and American Indian Struggle," *American Ethnologist* 32, no. 2 (2005): 239–259.

7. My heartfelt thanks go to Jessica for her comments on an earlier draft of this chapter. She helped me to clarify my arguments and to pinpoint the ways in which our ideas about sovereignty, recognition, and interdependence dovetail with one another.

8. According to the US Census, the Cherokee population has grown at an unprecedented rate over the past thirty years, from 66,150 to almost three-quarters of a million, representing a startling population growth of 1,003 percent. The Cherokee are, by far, the largest tribal grouping on the most recent census, with the Navajo a distant second. Yet only 35 percent are enrolled citizens of one of three federally recognized Cherokee tribes, which means that close to *half a million* individuals claim to be Cherokee outside conventional standards. Though many of these individuals never seek external recognition, many citizens of the Cherokee Nation and Eastern Band of Cherokee Indians believe that new Cherokee tribes emerge from this population of self-identified Cherokees. However, these shifts in census data do not have a one-to-one correspondence with shifts in racial self-identification. Some of this growth results from other social, political, and demographic factors, such as changes in data collection methods. Russell Thornton, *The Cherokees: A Population History* (Lincoln: University of Nebraska Press, 1990); Jeffrey Passel, "The Growing American Indian Population, 1960–1990: Beyond Demography," *Population Research and Policy Review* 16, no. 1/2 (1997): 11; and Angela Gonzales, "The (Re)articulation of American Indian Identity: Maintaining Boundaries and Regulating Access to Ethnically Tied Resources," *American Indian Culture and Research Journal* 22, no. 4 (1998): 199–225.

9. Much of this information comes from three master lists of self-identified Cherokee groups. The Eastern Band of Cherokee Indians in North Carolina provided one of these lists in March 1995. Another was complied by the Cherokee Nation and presented a few months later to the US Senate Committee on Indian Affairs in a hearing concerning proposed changes in the federal recognition process. The third is an overview of Cherokee groups and the federal recognition process, created in 2001 by Virginia DeMarce, a historian working for the Bureau of Acknowledgment and Research (BAR) at the BIA in Washington DC. I also added to these lists with extensive Internet searches and a mail survey conducted in 1996.

10. Barry Brewton, *Almost White: A Study of Certain Racial Hybrids in the Eastern United States* (New York: Macmillan, 1963); William Quinn, "The Southeast Syndrome: Notes on Indian Descent Recruitment Organizations and Their Perceptions of Native American Culture," *American Indian Quarterly* 14 (Spring 1990): 147–154.

11. Data compiled from several published and unpublished sources: Archives of the Tribal Registrar, Cherokee Nation of Oklahoma, Tahlequah; letter from Chief Wilma Mankiller to the governors of twenty-one states regarding federal and state recognition of "other purported 'Cherokee' tribes," 4 January 1993; "Entities Using the Cherokee Name," Isabel Catolster (Eastern Band of Cherokee Indians), March 3, 1995; "Federal Recognition Administrative Procedures Act, Hearing before the US Senate Committee on Indian Affairs, 104th Congress on S. 479," July 13, 1995: 219–241; Sheffield, *Arbitrary Indian*, 63–73; "Overview Cherokee Groups and Federal Acknowledgement Process," DeMarce (OFA) 2001: 5–63; L. Jeane Kauffman, *State Recognition of American Indian Tribes* (Denver: National Conference of State

Legislatures, 2001); "State Recognized Tribes," http://www.acessgenealogy.com/native/staterec-tribes.htm (accessed June 26, 2003); "State Recognized Tribes," http://www.nativedata.com/statetribes.htm (accessed June 26, 2003); "US Federally Non-Recognized Indian Tribes—Index by State," http:://www.kstrom.net/isk/maps/tribesnonrec/html (accessed June 26, 2003); "Alphabetical Index of State Recognized Tribes," *The Spike: The Original Newspaper on East Coast American Indian Events*, http://www.thespike.com/tablest.htm (accessed June 9, 2005); and "State-Tribal Relations, Indian Tribes in the States," National Conference of State Legislatures, http://www.ncsl.org/programs/esnr/tribes.html (accessed June 9, 2005).

12. Sheffield, *Arbitrary Indian*, 72.

13. According to the *Code of Federal Regulations*, a tribe seeking federal acknowledgment must meet the following criteria: outsiders have identified it on an ongoing basis as an American Indian tribe; members live in an area or community that is viewed as distinctly Indian and are descendents of a known Indian tribe; and the group has maintained some form of tribal political organization or influence over its members on a continuous basis (25 CFR § 83 [1993]). The burden of proof rests on petitioners, who have to rely on the work of anthropologists, historians, colonial officers, and various government agents to substantiate their claims. It is not sufficient that a tribe has been organized as such for a century or longer; rather, it must be perceived as an "Indian" entity, by non-Indians, according to non-Indian standards. Susan Greenbaum, "What Is a Label?: Identity Problems of Southern Indian Tribes," *Journal of Ethnic Studies* 19 (Summer 1991): 107.

14. I do not mean to suggest that states are the only ones with variations in their recognition processes. Scholars have long argued that the federal recognition process is much too rigorous and is "woefully inconsistent." Smaller, less aggressive groups and those that suffered colonialism at an earlier date—particularly those on the eastern seaboard—often fail to meet the criteria for recognition because of characteristics or conditions that the federal government created in the first place. Garroutte, *Real Indians*, 29.

15. One could easily argue that even though the process is somewhat arbitrary and the overall effects unclear, state recognition is a useful alternative to federal recognition, given the rigors and inconsistencies of the federal recognition process.

16. TCIA § 4-34-103, August 17, 1990.

17. *The Atlanta Journal-Constitution*, April 29, 1993, D1, and February 20, 1995, B2.

18. Arkansas HCR 1003.

19. Garroutte, *Real Indians*, 173, n40. In recent years, a slew of state-recognized tribes have managed to petition successfully for federal acknowledgment: most notably, the Mashpee Wampanaog Tribe of Massachusetts, the Passamaquoddy Tribe and Penobscot Nation (both of Maine), and the Poarch Band of Creek Indians in Alabama. State-recognized tribes are also covered under the Indian Arts and Crafts Act of 1990 and the Native American Free Exercise of Religion Act of 1993.

20. See "Administration for Native Americans, Summary of Expenditures, FY 2002," http://www.acf.dhhs.gov/programs/ana/programs/grants2002.html (accessed June 26, 2003).

21. Wilma Mankiller to Georgia State Assembly, 15 February 1995.

22. *The Atlanta Journal-Constitution*, April 29, 1993, D6.

23. The standard legal interpretation is that states may assert jurisdiction over Native American nations only with congressional approval. However, various laws and acts have

challenged this hierarchy, including Public Law 280 (1953) and the Indian Gaming Regulatory Act (1988). See Judith Resnick, "Multiple Sovereignties: Indian Tribes, States, and the Federal Government," *Judicature* 79, no. 3 (1995): 118–125.

24. *State v. Sebastian*, 243 Conn. 115, 1997. For more on the Sebastian case and other court decisions regarding state-recognized tribes in Connecticut, see Christopher Reinhart, "Effect of State Recognition of an Indian Tribe," Office of Legislative Research Report, no. 2002-R-0118, Connecticut General Assembly (2002). In 2002 the BIA ruled in favor of acknowledging the Paucatuck Eastern Pequots and the Eastern Pequots as the Eastern Pequot Tribal Nation. The decision was rescinded in 2005.

25. 243 Conn. 115.

26. 243 Conn. 115.

27. 243 Conn. 116.

28. *Schaghticoke Tribe of Kent, Connecticut, Inc. v. Potter*, 217 Conn. 612, 1991; *Golden Hill Paugussett Tribe of Indians v. Southbury*, 231 Conn. 563, 1995; and *State v. Sebastian*, 243 Conn. 115, 1997.

29. *First American Casino v. Eastern Pequot Nation*, no. 541674, July 16, 2001, CGS § 47-59a; Reinhart, "Effect of State Recognition," 5.

30. Joshua Haynes, "Power of the Blood: Identity Construction and the Cherokee Tribe of Eastern North Carolina" (master's thesis, University of Mississippi, 2001), 93–94.

31. Hearing before the US Senate Committee on Indian Affairs on S. 479, Federal Recognition Administrative Procedures Act, 104th Cong., 1st Sess., July 13, 1995.

32. Cherokee Nation Resolution, no. 14-00, March 13, 2000.

33. Hearing before the US Senate Committee on Indian Affairs on Federal Recognition of Indian Tribes, 109th Cong., 1st Sess., May 11, 2005.

34. Taiaiake Alfred, *Peace, Power, Righteousness: An Indigenous Manifesto* (New York: Oxford University Press, 1999).

13 Tribal Courts and Tribal States in the Era of Self-Determination
An Ojibwe Case Study

Larry Nesper

Today nearly 260 Native communities have tribal courts, the authority and resources of which have been strengthened over time (see table 7, 1993). Originally, these were intended to serve as vehicles for assimilation, but many tribes have revised codes to reflect local needs and values. Scholarship has focused on issues related to tribal–state jurisdiction, explored the ways tribal courts reflect indigenous concepts of justice, and examined how these courts create a counternarrative about colonialism.[1] The difficulties that arise when tribal courts attempt to deal with divisions, conflicts, and competing interests in Native communities also have been the subject of studies.[2] In this chapter, Larry Nesper addresses the issue of internal divisions within the Ojibwe legal system. After the Voigt decision (see table 6), Ojibwe communities developed tribal codes and a tribal court to defend their hunting and fishing rights and deal with code violations. Nesper argues that class-based conflict over the codes ensued because the requirements of the new tribal bureaucracy clashed with the value system of Ojibwe subsistence hunters.

For two and half days in late July 2005, nearly three hundred tribal, federal, and state court judges, court commissioners, court administrators, peace-makers, mediators, traditional forum practitioners, attorneys, lay advocates, and other justice system professionals met at the Radisson Hotel and Conference Center operated by the Oneida Nation near Green Bay, Wisconsin. This national conference, titled "Walking on Common Ground: Pathways to Equal Justice," was sponsored by the US Department of Justice's Bureau of Justice Assistance. The 133 tribal, state, and federal judges con-stituted the overwhelming plurality in this assembly and discussed issues such as judicial leadership, choice of forum, judicial review, recognition of one another's judgments and orders, judicial independence, and the Indian Child Welfare Act. All levels of judiciaries, save the US Supreme Court, were represented.

The centerpiece of the conference was the ceremonial signing of a pro-tocol by state and tribal judges from the 9th Wisconsin Judicial District. The second protocol of this nature signed in this state in the preceding four years, it established a procedure for the allocation of jurisdiction in causes of action in this Public Law 280 state, where the tribe and the state have concurrent jurisdiction (see table 3). The Honorable Ernest St. Germaine, former chief judge of the Lac du Flambeau Ojibwe reservation and current Wisconsin tribal appeals court judge, conducted the ceremony, smudging the signatories and the documents with the smoke of burning sage and offering each the pipe he had loaded with tobacco. The conference marked, advanced, and celebrated the commitment of a growing community of tribal, state, and federal judges to ongoing institutional relationships between sov-ereigns. The segment of this community that resides in Wisconsin is the spearhead of this movement among PL 280 states. Indeed, the first protocol between the 10th Judicial District and four Chippewa tribes is believed to be the first of its kind in the nation.

Wisconsin's federal, state, and tribal judges met for the first time in 1999, but relations began earlier, of course, and more informally.[3] It is often said that "success has a thousand fathers" (usually with the punch line that "failure is an orphan"), but cooperation between two "fathers," tribal judge Ernie St. Germaine and Vilas county judge James Mohr, evolved in the 1990s and formed an important strand in this nexus. Judge Mohr had been a proponent of tribal sovereignty since at least the early 1980s, when Lac du Flambeau established a court as a means to implement fully the Indian Child Welfare Act's provisions and to adjudicate disputes over the exercise of tribal off-reservation hunting and fishing rights. He had assisted the tribe in gaining exclusive jurisdiction over regulatory matters such as traffic and domestic restraining orders.

The tribe now has a police force, and tribal prisoners are kept in county jails. Proceeds from the sale of tribal automobile, fishing, and ATV (all-terrain vehicle) licenses usable throughout the state go to the tribe. It has begun to exercise criminal jurisdiction, though it is constrained because criminal justice is so expensive. The prosecutor at Lac du Flambeau now offers non-member Indians the option of accepting the tribe's jurisdiction or swearing in open court that they do not belong on the reservation. In 1978 the Supreme Court's *Oliphant* decision found that tribes do not have criminal jurisdiction over nonmembers, not with much practical standing here.[4] Tribal police do not ask for tribal IDs when they ticket, presuming jurisdiction; they offer nonmembers, at first appearance in tribal court, the option of transferring cases to county court. In sum, the tribe has adopted a self-conscious strategy of duplicating the procedures used by other sovereigns, thus acting in a sovereign state–like manner.

As a result of these decisions and developments, this tribe, as well as many others, is no longer best thought of, or even experienced, as primarily a community of people particularized by relations of blood and marriage. Tribal communities—to greater and lesser degrees, depending on geographic location and proximity to markets for their suite of resources and services—are better thought of and certainly experienced by their members (and, increasingly, "citizens") as "centralized, institutionalized, authoritative system(s) of political rule"—that is, as states.[5]

"It is now becoming clear that there are multiple roads to statehood," writes Ronald Cohen, though he certainly did not have anything like this in mind. Nonetheless, the worldwide revitalization of non-state, so-called tribal or peripheral peoples, which forms the basis of the indigenous movement, appears in the United States as a sovereignty movement by virtue of the tribes' ambiguous status in federal law.[6] Though tribes have come to be subsumed under the plenary power of Congress, they are both pre- and extra-constitutional and were recognized in the famous *Cherokee Nation v. Georgia* Supreme Court case as self-governing, domestic dependent nations.[7] Indeed, the notion that tribes were already states of one sort, and might become states of another, has a long history, extending as far back as the founding of the United States in the eighteenth century.[8]

Decades of Indian activism and federal legislation have brought this change. The Indian Self-Determination and Education Assistance Act of 1975 permitted tribes to contract directly with the federal government for services. The Indian Child Welfare Act (1978) returned to the tribes their jurisdiction over tribal children. Both acts encouraged the development of tribal government. The Indian Gaming Regulatory Act (1988) further accelerated this transformation, not only creating a viable economic base for tribal development but also involving the tribes with their surrounding communities to a greater extent (see tables 5–7). Managing health clinics and housing authorities, zoning and taxing, autonomously removing and placing children, certifying membership and marriages, exercising extensive, exclusive territorial and personal jurisdiction, sponsoring expressive cultural productions, and placing monuments, tribes are becoming "dispersed ensemble(s) of institutional practices and techniques of governance," in other words, statelike (Cobb, Smith, Helton and Robertson, and Cattelino, this volume).[9]

Court, Community, and Tribe

In Wisconsin, these self-determinative and regulatory projects and developments were given impetus by the Voigt decision, as well as by the massive social conflict that followed it. This watershed federal appeals court decision in 1983 preempted the state's jurisdiction over Ojibwe Indian hunting and fishing on the lands ceded to the federal government in the treaties of 1837 and 1842.[10] In both treaties—neither of which established reservations—the bands stipulated for the right to continue living, in the manner to which they had grown accustomed, on the lands they were ceding. "The privilege of hunting, fishing, and gathering the wild rice, upon the lands, the rivers and the lakes included in the territory ceded," Article V of the 1837 treaty reads, "is guarantied to the Indians, during the pleasure of the President of the United States."[11]

The Voigt decision refigured the relationships among the bands of Lake Superior Chippewa Indians and between those bands and the state. It also motivated the development of tribal conservation law and catalyzed the emergence of tribal courts on Ojibwe reservations that did not already have them. Courts are significant institutions because of how they relate to other institutions and change subjectivities. Marc Galanter writes that the most important "radiating effect" of the courts is that they confer endowments not only on member-citizens but also, and more important, on the institutions that constitute the communities within which the courts operate. These endowments take the form of norms and procedures, models for regulatory activity, immunities, and authorizations. Courts have special effects on those they convict and also the general effect of deterrence, enculturation, mobilization, and demobilization on a larger audience.[12] The institutional developments that should cause us to reimagine reservation communities as emergent states, then, are tied in to the development of courts of law.[13]

Tribal courts are local theatrical sites of authoritative ordering, where internal policies and external relations are publicly debated and where different orders of value and law confront each other. The proceedings in tribal courts reveal the processes by which tribal states are being constructed within and against the communities where they are emerging.[14] This opposition appears in ordinary discourse at the Lac du Flambeau Reservation, with member-citizens alternatively using the terms *community* and *tribe* when imagining the reservation and describing moral or political behavior from the perspective of these two orders of value. This new condition suggests the relevance of the concept of legal pluralism.

Sally Merry calls our attention to relations between groups in which multiple normative orders compete because where law is imposed, it is also resisted.[15] This opposition becomes apparent in the process by which the emerging tribal state regulates with law the hunting and fishing practices that form the historic basis for the legal, social, and cultural identity of this Ojibwe community, which had been regulated by custom. It is in the tribal court trials concerning alleged violations of recently codified tribal law that the norms of a community, wherein kinship remains salient, come into greatest conflict with the demands of the rule of law, the means of organizing the operations of a tribal state.

Historically, the hunting mode of production is organized by kinship. There are many indices of its importance to the people of Lac du Flambeau, beginning with the name of the community, which refers to the practice of hunting and fishing by torchlight at night in canoes. In the post-treaty mid- and late nineteenth century, people continued to live by hunting, fishing, gathering, and trapping throughout the region, with few members of the band actually residing on the reservation itself until the 1870s, unlike the bands living closer to Lake Superior. Later, men supplied meat to the increasing number of lumber camps, indirectly facilitating a deforestation process that had the ironic effect of improving conditions for the deer population and success for Ojibwe hunters.[16]

With the rise of the tourist industry in the late nineteenth and early twentieth centuries, resorts hired Indian men as hunting and fishing guides whose patronage encouraged the reproduction of traditional skills, ecological knowledge, and dispositions of the body. In the tribal archives, photos from the first decade of the twentieth century show these guides standing next to their automobiles, holding guns, a deer carcass at their feet (cars were first assimilated as terrestrial "canoes" for hunting the old logging roads in the second-growth forest). When the tribe adopted a constitution under the Indian Reorganization Act, it stipulated a referendum vote on any changes to tribal members' hunting and fishing rights. Finally, when the 7th Circuit Court of Appeals found that the Ojibwe retained their right to hunt and fish in the lands they had ceded in the nineteenth century, the band that exercised those rights the most zealously was a sector of the Lac du Flambeau band.

Figure 9. In the tribal courtroom at Lac du Flambeau, state and community converge. Photo courtesy of Larry Nesper.

The community established a court in 1983, embracing the American adversarial tradition but offering simplified procedures, reduced cost and delay, and the right to appear without a lawyer (figure 9).[17] The compromise represented an ambivalence about movement from social relations ordered by custom toward social relations ordered by law. This distinction was made in the nineteenth century by Henry Maine, as well as by Morton Fried, and finally articulated by Stanley Diamond: "Law is symptomatic of the emergence of the state," and laws "arise in opposition to the customary order of the antecedent kin or kin-equivalent groups; they represent a new set of social goals pursued by a new and unanticipated power in society."[18] Building on the same point and writing about the legal colonization of Hawaii—a process the Hawaiian elite facilitated—Sally Merry concludes that the law "is part of the violence of the incorporative process.... Perhaps its most important role is to enunciate the cultural principles of the new social order."[19]

Vine Deloria and Clifford Lytle addressed the problem of reconciling the law/custom opposition in the very same year that the court at Lac du Flambeau emerged. "The greatest challenge faced by the modern tribal court system is in the harmonizing of past Indian customs and traditions with the dictates of contemporary jurisprudence," they argued. "Tribes are reluctant to abandon their past traditions by placing too much reliance on the whites' legal procedures and practices. While borrowing some Anglo-American notions about the system of justice, tribal courts are struggling to preserve much of the wisdom of their past experiences."[20] Sixteen years later, Russell Lawrence Barsh concluded that tribal courts, to gain respect from the larger society, compromised their credibility in their own communities because of their reluctance to develop a distinctive jurisprudence reflective of community values and conceptions of justice.[21]

The Study

To satisfy, in part, the State of Wisconsin's expectation that the Lac du Flambeau court be a "court of record," the court audiotapes all proceedings and permanently stores the cassettes.[22] In the summer of 2001, I was permitted to make audiotape copies of eighteen years of the hunting and fishing trials in exchange for organizing this archive. While making the copies, I wrote an index of each trial. On the basis of those indices, I transcribed most of the trials. The following analysis and interpretation draws upon these transcripts.

Between 1983 and 1999, an average of thirty-eight defendants per year from Lac du Flambeau—almost all of them men—were cited into court on a total of 1,014 violations of the band's off-reservation hunting and fishing code by either state or tribal wardens.[23] Between 1983 and 1992, the years for which the court kept the most thorough data on this subject matter jurisdiction, 543 citations came to court. This represented 255 individuals bearing a total of eighty-five patronyms, though a full two hundred of these citations were given to the male members of only six families. One hundred twenty-seven trials were conducted between 1983 and 1999. Because there were often multiple citations and defendants per trial—Ojibwes tend to hunt in small groups of related men—these routine violations were contested at a high rate. Defendants pleaded not guilty to 43 percent (233) of the 543 citations brought to court, therefore requiring trials.

On average, there were seven trials per year, rising to a peak of twenty-three in 1988 and declining to one in 1999; the average holds through the mid-1990s. Between 1983 and 1992, 67 percent were found guilty. Accommodating a high unemployment rate of more than 50 percent in the years before gaming (1983–1991), judges typically assessed fines between $20 and $100 for violations that in the state court would call for fines in excess of $1,500.[24] Nonetheless, in the first two years of the court's existence, and concordant with the high rate of not-guilty pleadings, as well as default judgments, hearings to "show cause" for failure to pay the assessed fine were necessary in a third of the cases. Clearly, those referred to as "subsistence hunters" or "treaty hunters" by some tribal court personnel—a veiled reference to class within reservation society—were actively resisting the new regime.

The Pragmatics of Practice in Court

The non-Indian, law school–trained tribal prosecutors employed by the tribal government were effectively socializing both the defendants and the judges—none of whom were lawyers, but all tribal members—into an alien mode of ostensibly discovering truth, via a formal set of discourse rules. The newly minted tribal wardens and the state wardens presented their testimony as evidence supporting the alleged violation in accounts co-constructed with prosecutors and notable for their reliability.[25] Invited to cross-examine the tribe's witnesses, unrepresented tribal members, who were less adept at non-Indian modes of interaction, often began by presenting the main point in their defense in a single sentence. This inclination recalls the preferred way of killing deer, with a single shot to the head.

The traditional conversational pragmatics, even among English-speaking Ojibwes, inhibits conversation partners from interrupting each other. Consequently, defendants usually had presented the main point of their defense testimony before the judge reluctantly interrupted, usually at the prosecutor's behest, to tell them that testifying while not under oath was not permitted. Reminded to ask questions only, defendants typically declined to continue. Here, the informality of the court can work against the interests of the defendants: they are the only people in the courtroom who must question the testimony of others and give narrative testimony of their own. The presence of another set of rules mitigates that disadvantage somewhat, but only somewhat. It effectively establishes a context for the judge to make his decision on the basis of an instrumental rationality, that is, with a certain goal or outcome in mind, rather than according to the demands of rule orientation.[26] This may be what is tribal about tribal court. The particular circumstances of the alleged violation might be taken into account, whereas in a county court setting, for example, the breadth of the inquiry would likely be narrower.

Many of the defendants were speakers of an Ojibwe English that transmits from the parent Ojibwemowin syntactic elements such as the particle *enah* to mark interrogatives and, as indicated above, pragmatic dispositions. Most relevant for this context, speakers of American-Indian English avoid asking direct questions. Ojibwe speakers are inclined to use either imperatives or indirection when asking for things, neither of which facilitates cross-examination, a technical skill requiring considerable practice.[27] Furthermore, defendants' efforts to ask direct questions in standard English were often complicated by uncommon ordering of clauses. Presumably another carryover from the parent language, it obscured the "turn transition-relevant places" in dialogue, resulting in overlapping speech between themselves and their witnesses.[28] This undermined the effectiveness of their cross-examinations and further risked their dignity as competent participants in the court process.

Nonetheless, defendants and their lay advocates—who learned aspects of the new discourse style, as well as mitigated its force by insisting on using vernacular forms—repeatedly referenced normative communitarian understandings of reservation society in their defenses, thus contesting the emergence of the new order. At the top of the list, implicit and explicit allegations of racism on the part of state wardens reminded the court of a long history of state domination, forcing the judges to make extraordinary demands on law enforcement and ease up on fines. Multiple references to "our treaties" and "our fishing people" and reminders about the traditional value of generosity and sharing as a motivation for hunting and fishing had the effect of softening the hard edges built in to standard civil procedure, shifting the court away from its inherently authoritarian forensics toward a more equalitarian, educative deliberation. These strategies also opened the court to considering explicitly the relationship between what were considered the long-standing customs of the community and the recently codified tribal law, along with the effects of embracing the latter over the former.

The Exemplary Case

Instead of continuing to list elements that turn up in many trials, I will discuss a single exemplary, if not representative, case in some detail for purposes of illustrating the ways in which different conceptions of community, law, and custom arise.

In 1995, eleven years into the tribally administered, off-reservation deer-hunting regulatory regime, six defendants consolidated their cases into one trial that explicitly drew upon what the judge would refer to as "traditional" and "cultural" law. It was an effort to try the practice of Great Lakes Indian Fish and Wildlife Commission (GLIFWC) wardens setting up full-scale models of deer, off the reservation, in places visible from the road, with the goal of enticing "tribal hunters" to shoot either from their vehicles or from within fifty feet of the centerline of the road, violating tribal code.[29] During this trial, issues of social class, differential access to policy-making bodies, and the nature of the usufructuary rights as property were addressed. The six defendants, most of whom were marginalized, underemployed, working-class men (there was also one woman), included a college-educated and increasingly bilingual spiritual leader. The defendants retained the services of a lay advocate with a lengthy history of political activity on this reservation.

Repeatedly using forms of the word *conceal* and the phrase *your place of concealment* in cross-examination of the tribe's witness (a fellow tribal member and warden), defense sought dismissal for reason of entrapment but failed, time after time, to get evidence admitted. The prosecutor had convinced the court that it was foundationless. The defense then put his expert witness on the stand: a widely respected, fully bilingual, local elder who was involved in the revitalization of the Ojibwe language on the reservation. This elder did most of the invocations at public events, lending them valuable legitimacy.

Counsel first asked him to describe the type of training he received "in the use of weapons in hunting" (quotations are from tape recording of court sessions), eliciting a discourse on traditional hunting education and technique. After testimony about the traditionality of hunting from an automobile, the defense counsel asked his witness to give an opinion, "as an elder and as a spiritual leader," of "putting a decoy deer or a make-believe deer out in the woods." The elder answered:

> Well, I'm going to give you my own opinion, my honest opinion, the way I feel. I think that's wrong. Because I was taught to respect the animal itself, that deer. When we killed a deer, we put tobacco down and made sure that the entrails were covered up and everything else. We didn't, I just can't see where a means of—I, I, I couldn't understand that part, because if you have to force somebody to commit a crime—and that would be a crime, I think, if you shot at a deer that was a stuffed deer. In the first place, we were taught to respect an animal and anything that you did contrary to that, like putting a stuffed deer out, that when I was trained, that would be what the Indian people would call Ishaa-bap-nadoah-nahwah-wehsee, which would mean that you're, in our way of thinking, that you're poking fun at that deer. That you're, and that isn't the way we did things. The fact that when we, when we, when we killed a deer, even when my grandfather was alive, when my grandfather killed a deer, he did things in the traditional way. He put tobacco out. And every portion of that deer was used. The

hooves, the hide, the neck, the everything, the legs, the shanks, heart, liver. Everything was used. And when I heard about that—I'll give you my opinion—I think that is wrong in the sense that I don't know what it's for, to teach safety or whatever it's for. I think that's wrong because I think that if you have to resort to something to that extent, to make somebody commit a crime, so that you, then I think maybe somewhere along the line its wrong and it's right that we have to create a crime or something that'll make a person commit a crime.

There is so many things I have heard about hunting seasons where people cut the hindquarters off the deer, take the hindquarters, or take the rest of the body. Rib cage, they leave it out in the woods. Or I heard of people killing illegal deer, dragging them under the trees to hide them to a later date. Those are the kinds of things that I think that should be enforced.

Now that's my opinion. And some of the things that we held sacred, we held sacred, an animal is sacred to us. And we didn't, to me, that having a stuffed deer is, I don't know, just against everything I have ever been raised with or taught.

Hunting animals with spirits rather like one's own is the condition of the possibility of human life for Ojibwe people. The relationship between hunter and prey is one of reciprocal obligation, entailing honor and respect for the animal's spirit, whose corporeal body sustains human beings.[30] It is very serious business. The emphatic incredulity with which the witness uttered the word *fun* makes the point forcefully in his testimony. To simulate the spiritual encounter that successful hunting represents, for the sake of the tribe's political and educational purposes, is disrespectful and spiritually dangerous.

Asked whether he had ever expressed his views on the use of decoy deer to the Voigt Task Force, the committee that develops policy for the GLIFWC, the witness said that he had never had the occasion ("I was never involved with it"), implicitly impugning the commission's thoroughness and the domains of local knowledge it had been able and inclined to access. This is a comment about division and diversity within communities. The representatives to the task force are typically appointed by the tribal council and are drawn from their own ranks or from others nearby in the tribal bureaucracy, not from the class of subsistence hunters.

The best-educated and most articulate defendant then took the stand. He was deeply committed to the maintenance of the local language and the defendants' traditional values. He elaborated themes introduced in the expert testimony of the elder, his teacher. He did not contest the fact that he had shot from his vehicle but testified that he thought he was shooting at a deer he had wounded earlier in the day as a member of "an organized hunting party that had been making drives." Thus, he implicitly ranked the orders of law that shape practice in this community. "I also seen an opportunity to take down a wounded animal.... My parents and others who were instrumental in my upbringing used automobiles and trucks for harvesting deer for purposes of feeding us, their children." He was rehearsing an account of customary practice:

> LAY ADVOCATE DEFENSE COUNSEL: I'm going to ask you one other question regarding, ah, you heard the testimony of Mr. Chosa, did you not, in regards to the hunting rights that Mr. Hoyt asked? Okay, what's your feeling about are they tribal rights or are they individual rights?
>
> DEFENDANT: In parallel with what I just commented on, when I leave, when I leave to harvest, I'm aware of rights that this tribe has negotiated with the state. And my feeling is that when those agreements were made, that this tribe lost great, a great amount of its privileges. I also feel that these rights are, are, are individual rights. I have the right to utilize the resources that the Great Spirit on the earth, not DNR or GLIFWC, that the resources were put here by the Great Spirit. We were told how to use the Great Spirit's gifts. I go out and hunt deer. I don't have to ask GLIFWC or the tribe or the DNR. I ask the Great Spirit. I use tobacco, and the deer comes to me. That's what happens. The spirit puts the deer in front of me. I then, I use a firearm to harvest the deer, and I try to use, as Joe had said, I also try to use all the parts of the deer. I tan hides. I use the buckskin. I use the hair off the deer. I used the insides of the deer. I use the brains in the deer. Try to use it all in a good way.
>
> LAY ADVOCATE DEFENSE COUNSEL: Do you then feel it's more of an individual right or a tribal right, or vice versa, or?
>
> DEFENDANT: I believe it is an individual right.

First, note the use of the word *feeling* by the defense counsel, who, at that time, was in his fifties (the defendant, a generation younger), asking whether the defendant meant "opinion" by that. Recall that the elder used the word *feeling* to preface his critique of the use of deer decoys. I suggest that the older man was using the closest English term to a local conception that is rooted in traditional epistemology. Briefly stated, authoritative knowledge is the outcome of disciplined, spiritual, personal experience. *To feel* communicates a certainty that *to know* does not.

As to the substance of his answers, the first not only is consistent with a common morality espoused by the likes of Thomas Aquinas, who assented to a man's stealing food if he is hungry, but also instantiates a deep, Algonquian legal disposition. Julian Lips reports that among the related Naskapi, a nonresident traveling Indian in need of food has the right to hunt "to provide for immediate needs...clean out a beaver house which has been marked by its owner" and take half the provisions of a food depot owned by another.[31]

The defendant's second answer reveals far more. Having to negotiate with the state, in itself, represents a loss for the Ojibwe communities, and this is an appraisal widely shared among members of the community who are not employed by the tribe. Suspicion of written documents and writing as certification process is part of this general concern. The statement "I use tobacco and the deer comes to me.... The spirit puts the deer in front of me" condenses an orientation toward the generalized reciprocity that organizes not only relations among close kin but also relations between humans and the nonhumans on whom they depend. The testimony bears witness to the presence of a small segment of this community that actually attempts to fulfill these metaphysical commitments. Also, it criticizes the assumptions and institutions that have effectively betrayed this insight—an insight that forms the very basis of those institutions.

The judge read his written decision aloud. He reviewed the course of the trial and explicitly repeated the Ojibwemowin term used by the elder. In doing so, he signaled his own commitment to tradition and capacity to evaluate orders of law. He then made a clear choice and recited the recent date and tribal council resolution authorizing the use of decoys. Finally, he rendered a judgment of guilty for all the defendants. Characteristically, he softened the blow by suspending $100 of their $150 fines.

Conclusions

"Public court sessions," writes Susan Philips, "are points of articulation between the state and civil society."[32] In local terms, the court is where the tribe meets the community. In two antagonistic ways of imagining the reservation, the tribe is an increasingly powerful bureaucracy, and the community, "a family of families," in the provocative words of one tribal member, recognizing the multiplexity and the inequalities inherent in that metaphor. The tribal court is the tribe's instrumentality that is most actively and thoroughly constituting the tribal state by "endowing" all the tribal departments with power and legitimacy, for each has the option of assuming plaintiff status in court.[33]

The tribal court seeks to socialize these "subsistence hunters," formerly called "violators," into the new regime. At the same time, the court encourages them to continue using the land in what is repeatedly represented as the traditional Indian way, because of the continual necessity to produce cultural distinctiveness, the ultimate condition of the tribe's separate legal status. These hunters and fishermen are the ones who supply the traditional foods required for the naming ceremonies, marriages, and ghosts feasts that reproduce the traditional order.

Like proceedings in Roma *kris*, conciliation is highly valued because both Ojibwes and gypsies see themselves as "surrounded by a foreign and essentially hostile environment and dependent upon mutual assistance and good fellowship."[34] Therefore, the court is lenient, with fines "kept low," in one judge's words. In the judgment of a warden, this is reportedly regarded as "the price of doing business," even as it generates convictions for display to external agencies interested in the accountability of tribal court.[35] In the process, the court gives a hearing to testimony that draws upon putative traditional values and dispositions, directly and indirectly indexing a widely shared understanding of the community as a distinct and egalitarian indigenous enclave, even though the tribe as state is dominated by a coalition of families whose interests are served by the reproduction of this image of the community.

Until the Voigt decision in 1983 and the institution of the tribal court, the government of the tribes took little interest in their members' hunting and fishing off the reservation, this being a matter of state jurisdiction, so the locus of opposition between the state and the civil society was forty miles from the reservation. In fact, early in the new regime, the tribal prosecutor's office, shared by a husband-and-wife team, was subject to an ethics inquiry initiated by a local district attorney. The couple was prosecuting tribal members in tribal court and also defending them in state court, simultaneously allying with and opposing arresting wardens. The tribe chose to find other prosecutors rather than abandon its members to the state courts. Now the state and civil societies meet within the borders of the reservation, a qualitatively different sociopolitical condition—the tribe no longer just gives, but also takes.

Before Voigt, regardless of the state's season, tribal members had harvested thousands of fish and hundreds of deer off the reservation, an activity referred to by Indians and non-Indians as "violating," but nonetheless a conscious exercise of stipulated rights under the provisions of the treaties of 1837 and 1842.[36] These typically nocturnal practices were elemental in the constitution of local Lac du Flambeau Ojibwe identity, in all their oppositional value, and were regulated by the customs that had evolved in the community over more than a century. As such, they were entirely separate from tribal government.

With Voigt, the animals that community members hunted became tribal property because the tribe asserted legal title "to the custody and protection of all wild plants and wild animals with the ceded territory...for purposes of regulating members' use, disposition and conservation thereof."[37] As tribal code was consolidated and natural-resource trial proceedings grew more routine, customary historical practices continued, abstractly referred to (in the context of this regulation) as "traditional" or "customary" law by defendants, defense lay advocates, the judge, and even the prosecutor from time to time. This process of redefinition was somewhat democratic, but it was also contested, revealing and consolidating differences in political power among the families in the community.

Though some important elements of the original commons have been reestablished in the Voigt process, there is also risk in transplanting any legal system. It has been argued that American Indians can participate in the American political economy as Natives and thereby be recognized as such in law, to the extent to which they are perceived to be culturally distinct. The external and internal pressure to maintain and display cultural difference is therefore ongoing.[38] Importing such a potentially volatile set of institutions as constitutional government—and now a court to endow those institutions with power and legitimacy—risks social changes that implicate the capacity and even interest in generating that cultural distinctiveness that is the dominant society's condition of the tribe's separate legal status.

This is why, for example, Ojibwe express such anxiety about losing their language on this reservation, even though only a few people in their eighties can converse in Ojibwe. This is also why the very few in their forties who have learned it as a second language enjoy such high status.[39] This is why symbolic and rhetorical cultural domains have proliferated. This is also why "traditional law," or "customary law," in the context of trials, wherein the facts are only perfunctorily tried, did not begin to emerge until the 1990s, several years after the importation of administrative law to regulate the off-reservation usufruct and eventually other relations within the community.

Marc Galanter points out that "the relation of official law and indigenous law is variable and problematic."[40] At Lac du Flambeau, indigenous (or "traditional") law is acknowledged and is being reproduced. It stands in an antagonistic relationship, however, to official tribal law because of the nature and structure of the relationship between the dominant society and the tribes and because of the diversity within the tribes. Similarly, in Clifford Geertz's analysis of the complexities of legal pluralism in Indonesia during the revolution in the mid-1960s, he concludes that the legal debates over issues like inheritance, interest, and marriage are particular instances of a singular issue: what sort of society will ex–East Indians be?[41] Much the same can be said of what is taking place in American Indian tribal courts today as sites of struggle over their ambivalence about the political and social changes that self-determination entails.

Acknowledgments

Research for this chapter was supported by a New Faculty Internal Grant at Ball State University, the Graduate School at the University of Wisconsin–Madison, and the American Council on Learned Societies/Mellon Junior Faculty Research Fellowship. I am grateful to Lawrence Rosen, Phyllis Morrow, Tom Biolsi, Neil Whitehead, Herb Lewis, Marc Gelernter, and Paul Nadasdy for comments and suggestions on its various incarnations. I would also like to thank especially Jane Beeler, Clerk of Courts at Lac du Flambeau, former tribal judges Tom Maulson and Ernie St. Germaine, and prosecutor Terry Hoyt for many hours of conversation about their court.

Notes

1. Frank Pommersheim, *Braid of Feathers: American Indian Law and Contemporary Tribal Life* (Berkeley: University of California Press, 1995); Robert Yazzie and James Zion, "'Slay the Monsters': Peacemaker Court and Violence Control Plans for the Navajo Nation," in *Popular Justice and Community Regeneration: Pathways of Indigenous Reform*, ed. Kayleen Hazelhurst (Westport, CT: Praeger, 1995), 57–88; Robert Yazzie and James Zion, "Navajo Restorative Justice: The Law of Equality and Justice," in *Restorative Justice: International Perspectives*, ed. Burt Galaway and Joe Hudson (Monsey, NY: Criminal Justice Press, 1996), 157–174; Thomas Biolsi, *"Deadliest Enemies": Law and the Making of Race Relations on and off Rosebud Reservation* (Berkeley: University of California Press, 2001); and Bruce Miller, *The Problem of Justice: Tradition and Law in the Coast Salish World* (Lincoln: University of Nebraska Press, 2001).

2. Bruce Miller, *The Problem of Justice*.

3. Tribal and state judges in Wisconsin were meeting, convened by then chief justice Heffernan as early as the mid-1980s, in response to a sudden increase in jurisdictional disputes between states and tribes nationwide at that time.

4. *Oliphant v. Suquamish Tribe*, 435 US 191.

5. R. Brian Ferguson and Neil Whitehead, *War in the Tribal Zone: Expanding States and Indigenous Warfare* (Santa Fe, NM: School of American Research, SAR Press, 1992), 6.

6. Ronald Cohen and Elman Service, eds., *Origins of the State: The Anthropology of Political Evolution* (Philadelphia: Institute for the Study of Human Issues, 1978). Also see Ronald Niezen, *The Origins of Indigenism: Human Rights and the Politics of Identity* (Berkeley: University of California Press, 2003).

7. See Charles Wilkinson, *American Indians, Time, and the Law: Native Societies in a Modern Constitutional Democracy* (New Haven, CT: Yale University Press, 1987); and David Wilkins and K. Tsianina Lomawaima, *Uneven Ground: American Indian Sovereignty and Federal Law* (Norman: University of Oklahoma Press, 2001).

8. See *Treaty with the Delawares*, 1778, 7 US Stat., 13.

9. For quote, see Thomas Blom Hansen and Finn Stepputat, *States of Imagination: Ethnographic Explorations of the Postcolonial State* (Durham, NC: Duke University Press, 2001), 14.

10. See Larry Nesper, *The Walleye War: The Struggle for Ojibwe Spearfishing and Treaty Rights* (Lincoln and London: University of Nebraska Press, 2002).

11. *Treaty with the Chippewa*, 7 Stat., 536.

12. See Marc Galanter, "Justice in Many Rooms: Courts, Private Ordering, and Indigenous Law," *Journal of Legal Pluralism* 19 (1981): 1–47, and "The Radiating Effects of Courts," in *Empirical Theories about Courts*, ed. Keith Boyum and Lynn Mather (New York and London: Longman, 1983), 117–142.

13. Elizabeth Joh, "Custom, Tribal Court Practice, and Popular Justice," *American Indian Law Review* 25, no. 1 (2000): 117–132. Tribes being "domestic dependent nations," the extent of tribal governmental powers has been curtailed but also intensely debated in Congress, the courts, and the executive and remains unsettled. Getches, Wilkinson, and Williams's *Cases and Materials on Federal Indian Law* (St. Paul, MN: West Publishing Co., 2005) is an excellent introduction.

14. See Milner Ball, "The Play's the Thing: An Unscientific Reflection on Courts under the Rubric of Theater," *Stanford Law Review* 28, no. 1 (1975): 81–115; Sally Merry, "Courts as Performances: Domestic Violence Hearings in a Hawai'i Family Court," in *Contested States: Law, Hegemony and Resistance*, ed. Mindie Lazarus-Black and Susan Hirsch (New York: Routledge, 1994), 35–58; and Susan Philips, "Local Legal Hegemony in the Tongan Magistrate's Court: How Sisters Fare Better Than Wives," in *Contested States* (see preceding citation), 59–88.

15. Sally Merry, "Legal Pluralism," *Law and Society Review* 22, no. 5 (1988): 888–889.

16. Victor Barnouw, *Acculturation and Personality among the Wisconsin Chippewa*, American Anthropological Association Memoir no. 72 (1950), 268; Arlie Schorger, "The White-Tailed Deer in Early Wisconsin," *Transactions of the Wisconsin Academy of Sciences, Arts and Letters* 42 (1953): 197–247; and Patricia Shifferd "A Study in Economic Change: The Chippewa of Northern Wisconsin: 1854–1900," *The Western Canadian Journal of Anthropology* 6, no. 4 (1976): 16–41.

17. One hundred years earlier, the secretary of the interior established courts on many Indian reservations to address the kinds of behavior the Indian Office found "antithetical to their assimilation and citizenship" (Troutman, chapter 5, this volume).

18. Morton Fried, *The Evolution of Political Society: An Essay in Political Anthropology* (New York: Random House, 1967); Stanley Diamond, *In Search of the Primitive: A Critique of Civilization* (New Brunswick, NJ: Transaction Books, 1974), 265; and Henry Sumner Maine, *Ancient Law* (New Brunswick, NJ: Transaction Publishers, 2002).

19. Sally Merry, *Colonizing Hawai'i: The Cultural Power of Law* (Princeton, NJ: Princeton University Press, 2000), 205–206. Helen Tanner's (chapter 10, this volume) pessimism about law generally concords with this insight.

20. Vine Deloria Jr. and Clifford Lytle, *American Indians, American Justice* (Austin: University of Texas Press, 1983), 120.

21. Russell Lawrence Barsh, "Putting the Tribe in Tribal Courts: Possible? Desirable?" *Kansas Journal of Law and Public Policy* 8, no. 2 (1999): 74–96. On this point, also see Pommersheim, *Braid of Feathers*, 66–75; and Miller, *The Problem of Justice*.

22. Wisconsin Statutes 806.245, Indian tribal documents: full faith and credit.

23. The tribes unilaterally credentialized Wisconsin's Department of Natural Resources wardens to enforce tribal law, because the ceded territories upon which the Lake Superior bands of Chippewa Indians have usufruct rights cover approximately one-third of the state, far too vast an area for the tribes' own conservation law enforcement capacity.

24. Between 1983 and 1992, when the court tabulated such data, the mean fine rose from $25 to $55; nearly every year, there were a few fines of more than $100 for second and third offenses. By 1992, after the first gaming compact was signed, creating more jobs in the community, the mean fine rose to $150. By 1991, however, the chief judge had begun to suspend at least one-third of the fine, pending no further citations for natural resource violations for the rest of the year. He continued the practice through the 1990s, so the mean fine by 1998 was $90, with seven fines of more than $200. Less than one-third had some portion suspended.

25. Susan Philips, "Evidentiary Standards for American Trials: Just the Facts," in *Responsibility and Evidence in Oral Discourse*, ed. Jane Hill and Judith Irvine (Cambridge: Cambridge University Press, 1993), 256.

26. Brian Tamanaha, *Understanding Law in Micronesia: An Interpretive Approach to Transplanted Law* (Leiden and New York: E. J. Brill, 1993), 128.

27. See William Leap, *American Indian English* (Salt Lake City: University of Utah Press, 1993), 85–86; and Roger Wilson Spielmann, *"You're So Fat": Exploring Ojibwe Discourse* (Toronto: University of Toronto, 1998), 76, 79.

28. J. Maxwell Atkinson and Paul Drew, *Order in Court: The Organization of Verbal Interaction in Judicial Settings* (Atlantic Highlands, NJ: Humanities Press, 1979), 36–81.

29. The commission is the agency created by the signatory tribes under inherent governmental powers recognized by the Indian Self-Determination and Education Assistance Act to assist in managing off-reservation harvests.

30. For an elaboration on this idea based on the Cree, see Robert Brightman, *Grateful Prey: Rock Cree Human–Animal Relationships* (Berkeley: University of California Press, 1993).

31. Julian Lips, "Naskapi Law: Law and Order in a Hunting Society," *Transactions of the American Philosophical Society* 37, no. 4 (1947): 379–442.

32. Susan Philips, "Local Legal Hegemony," in *Contested States*, 65.

33. This would minimally include GLIFWC and DNR wardens, of course, as well as the tribal police force, Enrollment Department, Child Welfare Office, Child Support Agency, Health Center, Conservation Law Department, Natural Resources Department, Forestry Program, Land Management Program, Historic Preservation Office, Housing Authority, and Water and Sewer Authority. With code for small claims and probate, the power accrues to the tribe as a guarantor of contracts.

34. When speaking of such matters, Indian residents of the reservation contrast "here" with either "the surrounding community" or "the dominant society." The quote is from Walter Weyrauch, *Gypsy Law: Romani Legal Traditions and Culture* (Berkeley: University of California Press, 2001), 80.

35. Duane Harpster, audiotaped interview by author, Boulder Junction, WI, February 23, 2005; Honorable Fred Ackley, audiotaped interview by author, Mole Lake, WI, March 14, 2005.

36. See Larry Nesper, "Ironies of Articulating Continuity at Lac du Flambeau," in *New Perspectives on Native North America: Cultures, Histories, and Representations*, ed. Sergei Kan and Pauline Turner Strong (Nebraska and London: University of Nebraska Press, 2006), 98–121.

37. So begins chapter III, section 26.301, "Title to Wild Animals and Wild Plants," of Lac du Flambeau's off-reservation conservation code.

38. Gerald Sider, *Lumbee Indian Histories: Race, Ethnicity and Indian Identity in the Southern United States* (New York: Cambridge University Press, 1993), 279–287; and Kirk Dombrowski, *Against Culture: Development, Politics, and Religion in Indian Alaska* (Lincoln: University of Nebraska Press, 2001), 11–12.

39. Contesting the cultural integrity and authenticity of indigenous communities in the United States has become virtually a cottage industry with the rise in value of federally recognized status in light of the Indian Gaming Regulatory Act. Jeff Benedict's *Without Reservation: The Making of America's Most Powerful Indian Tribe and Foxwoods, the World's Largest Casino* (New York: HarperCollins, 2000) is only the most recent and dramatic production in this genre.

40. Marc Galanter, "Justice in Many Rooms," 25.

41. Clifford Geertz, *Local Knowledge: Further Essays in Interpretive Anthropology* (New York: Basic Books, 1983), 230.

14 Florida Seminole Gaming and Local Sovereign Interdependency

Jessica Cattelino

The Seminole Tribe opened high-stakes bingo in 1979. Most tribes that have gaming operations make minimal profits, in contrast to the Seminoles. In fact, one study found that thirty-one facilities out of about two hundred account for 62 percent of the total Indian gaming revenue.[1] In 1988 Congress passed legislation to define and regulate several classes of gaming (see table 6). Since that time, scholarship has generally focused on the interactions between tribes and states from the standpoint of state opposition to or non-Indian attitudes toward gaming. Recent attention has also turned to the relationships between casinos and federal acknowledgment.[2] Jessica Cattelino's chapter focuses on the local context to examine the interface between the exercise of Seminole sovereignty and the sizable income from Class II gaming. She explores how Seminole charitable donations have given expression to indigenous identity concepts and altered power relationships with non-Indians.

The explosive growth of tribally operated, high-stakes gaming across Native North America has called new public and scholarly attention to the legal foundations of tribal sovereignty. Gaming also has brought into focus the importance of local and regional politics to American Indian political and economic action, because gaming reshapes political fields not only on Indian reservations but also between indigenous communities and their

262

non-Indian neighbors. For the Seminole Tribe of Florida, the American Indian tribe that first launched high-stakes gaming, casino success has brought more local scrutiny and journalistic attention, fostering local resentment of Seminoles' new economic and political power. At the same time, gaming has joined together Seminoles and non-indigenous Floridians in new political alliances, collaborative projects, and joint economic ventures. This chapter analyzes the intersection of locality and sovereignty in the context of Florida Seminole tribal gaming.

From newspaper headlines, it may seem that political controversies follow inevitably from tribal gaming. Many regions, most prominently, southern Connecticut, have endured gaming-related disputes over traffic congestion, tribal land purchases, crime, and federal recognition. In California and other states, hard-fought battles over ballot measures on Indian gaming fill the airwaves with increasingly sophisticated advertisements about "special rights," fairness, and, more recently, tribal sovereignty and self-reliance.[3] Yet gaming and sovereignty also come together in new relations of cooperation and interdependency between tribes and neighboring communities, from tribal philanthropy to intergovernmental cooperation, from local social-service delivery to job creation. Understanding the local dimensions of tribal sovereignty in the gaming context demands scholarly attention to the everyday politics of indigeneity and the ways that gaming has become a key point of engagement between Indian and non-Indian communities.

In legal and political analyses of tribal sovereignty, there is a pervasive emphasis on the tribal–federal relationship. The federal focus is based on the important principle that American Indian tribes have a nation-to-nation relationship with the United States, grounded in precolonial national orders, treaties and other forms of state recognition, and a long line of judicial rulings.[4] The scholarly emphasis on the formal legal dimensions of sovereignty has reinforced this federal focus and scale; studies of "federal Indian law" sideline or take as a "problem" the local as a site of legal action and entanglement.[5] Only recently has more attention been devoted to tribal–state relations as sites of sovereignty and to the internal tribal politics that shape sovereignty movements.[6] Still, the local and regional remain underanalyzed. Indeed, as Karen Blu wrote in 1980, and which still holds for the present, "the regional factor in Indian studies has been largely ignored or glossed over, as has the amount of influence Indians have on their localities."[7] Some important work has been done, such as Blu's work on Lumbee identity in North Carolina and Paula Wagoner's ethnography of regional identity in Bennett County, South Dakota.[8] Neither author takes sovereignty as a focus, but the methods and questions of each author suggest that further analysis of regional politics could refine our theories of sovereignty. This would show not only the ways that sovereignty escapes the "federal Indian law" framework and produces and challenges regional politics, but also how indigenous sovereignty is forged and maintained less through formal legal processes than by everyday relationships within and across communities, families, and generations.[9]

If the national remains the frame for most scholarship on tribal sovereignty, locality has emerged as an important analytic for thinking about indigeneity. The very category of indigeneity posits a spatial (and temporal) relation to colonialism. Also, anthropologists and others seek to understand the ways that people construct, are shaped by, and enact place.[10] In South Florida—where the Everglades dominate the Seminole Big Cypress Reservation, the cowboy culture of the central peninsula pervades the Brighton Reservation, Latin American migrant workers share history and space with the Immokalee Reservation, and the Hollywood Reservation has been surrounded by suburban development—local politics are unavoidable and not simply matters of clearly defined Indian and non-Indian interactions. Indigenous identity and political vision are produced partly (though by no means only) at a regional level, in interaction with others. That is, locality and indigeneity are related because the concept of indigeneity links people to place and because the local is a social field in which indigeneity is constituted, often challenged, and reproduced.

In the United States, localism has been recognized as a privileged site for identity and politics at least since Tocqueville and remains a vital force despite the twentieth-century expansion of the central government. Indeed, federalism renders the local constitutive of the nation-state. Therefore, it is especially important to consider the locality of tribal sovereignty.[11] This chapter offers an ethnographic argument for the importance of local politics to the ongoing practices, limits, and possibility of tribal sovereignty. I analyze two aspects of gaming in South Florida: the creation and continuing popularity of the Seminole Coconut Creek casino and the growth of gaming-based charitable giving by the Seminole tribal government.

From Bingo to Hard Rock,

with a View from Coconut Creek

In 1979 the Seminole Tribe of Florida opened Hollywood Bingo, a modest operation on a busy intersection of suburban Hollywood, a city situated along Interstate 95 between Fort Lauderdale and Miami. Hollywood Bingo was the first high-stakes gaming operation operated by an American Indian tribe, but within a decade tribal gaming would become an economic engine and political hot potato in many regions. Hollywood Bingo initially met with some local resistance, led by Broward County sheriff (and subsequent Florida attorney general) Bob Butterworth. But Seminoles successfully defended their sovereignty-based gaming rights in the path-breaking case *Seminole Tribe v. Butterworth*, which established the legal framework for tribal gaming and launched a casino revolution that soon spread across much (but not all) of Indian Country.[12]

By 2007 the Seminole Tribe was operating seven gaming facilities across its six urban, suburban, and rural reservations (figure 10). Some operations, such as the Brighton casino, are modest and cater to a local clientele. By contrast, new and massive Hard Rock casino-resorts on the Tampa and Hollywood reservations draw huge crowds to their gaming floors, convention centers, entertainment venues, shopping plazas, and restaurants. On an August 2004 Saturday night, it took me twenty minutes to drive less than a mile from the tribal headquarters in Hollywood to the casino, with casino-bound traffic backed up and the Seminole Police Department directing vehicles to overflow parking lots. Whereas the annual tribal budget had been less than $2 million in 1979, by 2000 it reached $300 million, almost entirely funded by gaming proceeds. By 2006, annual net revenues from Seminole gaming approached $600 million.[13] The elected tribal government allocates gaming funds to an array of social services (health care, education, elder services, crime prevention), administrative operations (the tribal bureaucracy, land management), cultural programs (a museum; language instruction in Miccosukee and Creek/Muskogee, the two Seminole languages; tribal and outreach cultural education programs), and economic development initiatives (agriculture, retail businesses and venture capital, tourism), as well as to each of the approximately three thousand tribal citizens in the form of monthly per capita dividends. After struggling for decades against endemic poverty, Seminoles moved into a period of economic security during the late twentieth century.

As never before, gaming compelled Seminoles and local communities to work together in sometimes tense, and often unequal, political and economic partnerships. Of course, Seminoles long had interacted with local non-Indians, for example in early-twentieth-century commercial activities such as tourism, hunting, and fishing; indeed, those relations shaped Seminoles' political and economic vision.[14] But with gaming, Seminoles increasingly relied on a non-Seminole consumer base for tribal income, and they courted public opinion during high-stakes political and legal battles over gaming rights.

Seminoles now sit on local tourism boards, administer educational programs in local high schools, travel abroad with economic development

Seminole Tribe of Florida
Reservations & Gaming Facilities

N

TAMPA

FORT PIERCE

BRIGHTON
Lake
Okeechobee

BIG CYPRESS
Coconut Creek (trust land)

IMMOKALEE

HOLLYWOOD

RESERVATIONS
Seminole Hard Rock Hotel & Casino
Seminole Bingo Casino
Seminole Casino - Immokalee
Big Cypress Casino
Hollywood Seminole Gaming
Seminole Hard Rock Hotel & Casino
Coconut Creek Casino

Created by: Joshua Sutterfield, 2007

Figure 10. This map locates the seven casinos operated on land owned by the Seminole Tribe of Florida as of 2007. Six of them are situated inside reservation boundaries. The Coconut Creek casino was established on land brought into trust by the tribe in Coconut Creek, Florida. Map courtesy of Joshua Sutterfield.

groups promoting South Florida, and run advertising campaigns listing their gaming-based contributions to the local economy in jobs, increased tourism, and payment for goods and services. Seminole Gaming holds well-attended job fairs and employs thousands of Floridians, mostly non-Seminole and of diverse races and neighborhoods. Seminoles are often represented in local, multicultural education programs and festivals—alongside whites and African Americans, Cubans and other Caribbean immigrants. As late as 2000, however, a respected local journalist wrote an oral history–based book titled *Race and Change in Hollywood, Florida* without including a single Seminole oral history and with only a few passing references to Indians.[15] The ritual enactment of Seminoles' local belonging has extended to displays of civic leadership and corporate citizenship, for example in the occasional and quite remarkable appearance of tribal leaders as parade marshals in reservation border towns. In 2001 Max Osceola (Panther), tribal council representative from Hollywood, was commodore of the high-profile Fort Lauderdale Winterfest Boat Parade, and in 2004 the Seminole Hard Rock took over the event's corporate sponsorship.[16] Such localizing relations can limit sovereignty by heightening local perceptions that tribes are private political and economic interest groups, not governments. These also threaten tribal sovereignty by putting tribes on a plane of equivalence with local governments, not national ones. This is risky business. Yet local gaming-based relations typically have reinforced sovereignty: through these relations, Seminoles have asserted their governmental status and achieved new regional power.

One example of local animosity over gaming that turned into a mutually beneficial relationship of sovereign interdependency was the development of the Coconut Creek casino (figure 11). In late 1999 the tribe prepared to open a modest casino on approximately five acres of trust land in the north Fort Lauderdale suburb of Coconut Creek. The land, which was located in an industrial and agricultural zone that soon became surrounded by suburban development, had been obtained in 1982 and placed in trust in 1985 as compensation for the eminent domain taking of Hollywood Reservation land for the Florida Turnpike. Turnpike construction had disrupted reservation sociality and space by bisecting tribal housing developments, reducing sightlines and mobility across reservation space, and increasing noise. Yet unintended consequences offered new opportunities. Most directly, tribal leaders in the 1990s correctly predicted that a casino at Coconut Creek would do brisk local business without reducing the Hollywood gaming market, located approximately fifteen miles to the south. Additionally, the turnpike may prove a boon to Hollywood Hard Rock casino business if the tribe successfully completes ongoing negotiations with the state to build a tribally funded exit ramp adjacent to the casino.

When news of the proposed Coconut Creek casino hit the press in the late 1990s, the local establishment in this retiree-filled suburb protested on the grounds that the casino would introduce crime, create traffic snarls, and reduce property values. Newspapers cited the tribe's nontaxable status and its sovereign immunity as dangers to the local economy and to unsuspecting casino patrons. They noted that tribal sovereignty generally prevents adjacent communities from regulating land use and business practices on Indian reservations and that tribal governments enjoy sovereign immunity, unless waived, for purposes of contract and liability. The Coconut Creek city manager termed the casino "a significant detriment to our community."[17] After initially failing to meet with city officials, tribal leaders

Figure 11. The history of the Coconut Creek casino in South Florida has revealed the potential for both conflict and cooperation between gaming tribes and local and state authorities. Photo courtesy of Jessica Cattelino.

began to promote their sovereignty through negotiation, reciprocity, and relations of interdependence. With this strategy, the tribe eventually won over Coconut Creek officials and secured tribal gaming rights. The city even bestowed upon the casino a plaque that read "esteemed corporate citizen"; the same city manager now lauded the casino's success. Also, the tribe managed to educate the local public about tribal sovereignty: in 2001 a local newspaper characterized tribal and city officials as being "as close as a flush hand to a riverboat gambler's vest."[18] Seminoles accomplished this financial and political success, in large part, by promising the city a $1 million annual voluntary contribution (later increased to $1.5 million). This "Municipal Service Provider Agreement" characterized the contribution as assisting the city of Coconut Creek in defraying the casino's municipal impacts on water, police and fire, garbage removal, and additional services. Importantly, tribal officers repeatedly asserted that this contribution was not a tax, emphasizing their sovereign, non-taxable status. The tribe also donated to a city park and to a local organization for abused children.

Under many circumstances, casino revenue sharing threatens to undermine tribal sovereignty because American Indian tribes feel compelled to negotiate with state and local, not federal, governments. This is particularly true when, under the 1988 Indian Gaming Regulatory Act, tribes must negotiate with states in order to operate the most lucrative class (Class III) of casino games. Taking advantage of Florida's persistent refusal to negotiate a compact, Seminoles have built a gaming empire based on Class II games, which the state cannot regulate. As a result, the tribe's revenue sharing with local governments is truly voluntary and thus is more powerful as a negotiating chip. In the Coconut Creek case, the tribe came to the table with sufficient power to negotiate favorable terms and emerged with substantial profits and regional goodwill. Such instances remind us that powerful sovereigns often negotiate with a range of actors, public and private. For example, the fact that foreign nation-states negotiate trade agreements with American mayors does not compromise state sovereignty, even as states enter into agreements with "lesser" governments. Tribal sovereignty is not necessarily threatened by tribes' participation in local politics or by negotiations with municipal governments. Instead, the political, symbolic, and ethnographic significance of these actions depends on the power relations that guide them.

The Coconut Creek casino opened in February 2000, fully under tribal management and with a Seminole manager, Jo-Lin Osceola (no clan known). Osceola had spent the preceding two years in leadership training at the Hollywood casino, working in every casino job on a rotating basis in order to learn the ins and outs of the business. She was twenty-nine years old at the time, the youngest manager and the only female manager of a tribal casino. Osceola emphasized that having a Seminole as the casino executive meant "being able to control the decisions" within the tribe.[19] The casino was earning about $60 million a year by 2003, had created 275 jobs by late 2000, and had sparked economic growth among local vendors.

The initial casino controversy died down quickly in Coconut Creek, and both the tribal and municipal governments touted the casino's benefits. A lawsuit settled in 2004 resolved a dispute between the tribe and its casino developer partner, making the tribe the sole owner and operator of the casino. Casino events, such as a December 2000 "Biker Bash," drew Seminole and non-Seminole participants (in this case, motorcyclists on the eve of a charity ride) and the casino instantly became a focal point for local senior-citizen socializing. As a sign of diplomatic respect, the mayor of Coconut Creek, Marilyn Gerber, was asked to serve as a "celebrity" judge for the 2000 Miss Seminole pageant. This pageant, like Seminole patchwork clothing contests and other judging events, traditionally has non-Seminole judges, often local non-Indian leaders or Indian leaders from across the continent. (According to several Seminoles, this externalizing practice avoids the inevitable—and moral—privileging of family members that would occur with Seminole judges.) The mayor's introduction by tribal chairman James

Billie (Bird) drew a loud round of applause from tribal citizens. Still, new tensions arose in 2006, when the Seminole Tribe submitted an Application for Trust Status to the US Department of the Interior. The application requested that approximately forty-four adjacent acres that the tribe and its subsidiaries had purchased and held in fee simple be placed into trust. Conversion to trust status would expand the tribe's local control and power while removing the land from property tax rolls. At the same time, the proposed expansion to create a destination resort with a larger casino, restaurants and retail, and 1,500 hotel rooms would anchor a new Coconut Creek economic development project, bringing tribal and city fortunes ever closer.

Beyond Coconut Creek, gaming wealth has enabled Seminoles to create new jobs and businesses, raising the tribe's standing and rendering local communities increasingly reliant upon it for economic growth. According to a June 1999 tribal report, the Seminole Tribe purchased more than $24 million in goods and services from more than 850 Florida vendors annually. It paid approximately $3.5 million in federal payroll taxes.[20] This gaming-based economic power has landed tribal officials a seat at the table when local governments discuss regional economic development and policy, for example, in negotiations over the massive Everglades restoration initiative. Beginning with the Hard Rock project, the tribal government issued municipal bonds to fund economic development, underlining the fact that tribal economic activity is driven by sovereign governmental action, not private entrepreneurship. The tribe's growing Seminole Police Department (SPD), which is funded with gaming proceeds, has entered into jurisdictional agreements with local law enforcement agencies, and the new rural emergency health services collaborate with regional hospitals.

Not surprisingly, gaming has not eliminated long-standing tensions between Seminoles and neighboring municipalities and individuals. At an interpersonal level, Seminoles complain that non-Indians falsely assume that they are rich. Moses Jumper Jr. (Snake) worried, "[Gaming] stereotyped us tremendously, not only among the locals here in the area." He told of tribal members who could not get favorable loan terms from local automobile dealerships because salespeople claimed to know how rich Seminoles were.[21] Tensions also characterize some intergovernmental relations. In fact, Jim Shore (Bird), the tribe's general counsel and the first Seminole to become a lawyer, viewed non-Indian local governments as the "biggest challenge" to Seminole self-determination, citing strained relations with municipalities and ongoing legal and political challenges to Seminole economic development projects. Still, he pointed out, "We're not going anywhere," so those governments must learn to coexist.[22] With gaming, the tribal government faces new pressures from local and state governments to finance road improvements and other public projects that are adjacent to reservations. The tribe is constantly fighting political and legal battles over local jurisdiction and sovereign immunity from suit. In such a climate, tribal leaders and constituents must determine whether and how strongly to push sovereignty claims. At issue is not whether gaming has "caused" strained intercommunity relations, but rather the significance of gaming as the key symbol and focal point of Seminoles' place in the social, political, and economic landscapes of South Florida.

From Receiver to Giver

Social scientists and policy makers are understandably eager to analyze the "economic impact" of tribal gaming, and several studies are currently under way. Although valuable, "economic impact" analyses often overlook the social and political dimensions of economy. The political significance of Seminole gaming cannot be grasped without taking into account the changes in *relative* economic power at a regional scale. Gaming-based tribal philanthropy is one example of how gaming has realigned local relations of dependency and sovereignty. Charitable giving illustrates ways that patterned transfers of material goods mediate power and sociality. Gaming-based indigenous philanthropy has the potential to reorganize the symbols and directionality of local economic relationships between American Indians and others.

At least since the early twentieth century, Seminoles had been recipients of charitable giving from local philanthropic groups, especially women's groups. Philanthropy often was coupled with political advocacy. The Friends of Seminoles, long led by the early settler and trader's wife Ivy Stranahan, collected clothing and other goods for Seminole children while advocating for Indian education and benefits (albeit with an assimilative agenda). Broward County community organizations raised money for Seminole housing during the mid-century, and women's groups donated household goods as prizes for Seminole homemaking contests.[23] Religious and secular groups donated clothing, toys, and other goods each year at Christmas. Middle-aged and elderly Seminoles frequently recalled individual donors with gratitude. This was in marked contrast to their accounts of government benefit programs, which most perceived to be inadequate compensation for the great losses of land and life endured by Indians at the hands of the US government.

In interviews and everyday conversation, Seminoles recounted many fond memories of local ranchers, religious leaders, and other private donors, even as they also told of the shame of wearing hand-me-down clothing to school. At one Big Cypress barbeque, tribal members lined up to greet an elderly white neighbor from a prominent ranching family who had donated to Seminole families. At a centennial celebration of the Stranahan House trading post, Seminoles spoke eloquently in public speeches and private conversation about Mrs. Stranahan's generous spirit and good heart. Charles Hiers (Bird) told me about the generosity of "pioneer" and trading families in southwest Florida and of the joint "cracker"–Seminole opposition to federal "meddling" in their shared way of life through restrictions on hunting and fishing in Everglades National Park.[24] Memories of philanthropy can blend seamlessly into trade and exchange, and it cannot be a coincidence that many leading philanthropists were also associated with trading posts, tourist enterprises, hunting and fishing operations, and other businesses.

Seminole gaming has altered the South Florida philanthropic landscape in at least two ways that implicate sovereignty. First, it has called attention to redrawn regional power relations as Seminoles assert political power in conjunction with their newfound economic status. This dimension of charity also reflects Seminoles' need to assert that they are not *simply* economic actors. In a neocolonial logic by which wealth undermines indigeneity, Seminoles' generosity operates both as a defense of gaming wealth and as an implicit, comparative critique of non-Indians' failures to share their wealth (this might be seen as a resignification of the racist phrase "Indian giving").[25] By donating to social and cultural causes, Seminoles also call attention to their own cultural distinctiveness and tribal governance, especially when they contribute to historic preservation, cultural programs, and social services.

Second, philanthropy reinforces sovereignty because it takes place at the level of the tribal government, not individual Seminoles. Individuals and families help one another within the tribe, within religious communities, and probably in other arenas, but it is rare to hear tribal citizens discuss individualized giving to non-Seminoles or to see Seminoles listed as donors to local organizations. By contrast, the tribal government frequently appears in local newspapers, the tribe's newspaper (the *Seminole Tribune*), and other publications as a donor to charitable causes, with pictures of tribal officials (always dressed in distinctive Seminole patchwork clothing) presenting physically enlarged checks, shaking hands, cutting ribbons, receiving plaques, and otherwise acting as generous donors and civic leaders.

Since the mid-1990s, when tribal revenue began to increase dramatically as a result of gaming success, tribal government charitable giving has grown. For example, in 2001 the tribe pledged $3 million toward the creation of a historical park adjacent to the former Stranahan House trading post (now a modest museum) in Fort Lauderdale. The tribal council also sponsored Smallwood Days, an annual public festival at a historic Gulf

Coast trading post, and the tribe underwrote a small permanent exhibit at the Smallwood Store. The tribe contributes to local schools, athletic teams, Indian River Community College, and health organizations; in 2006 Hollywood tribal council representative Max Osceola Jr. (Panther) was named to the Broward County Red Cross board of directors. The tribal council also sponsors civic events for the public, such as July Fourth fireworks displays and Veterans Day celebrations. In the poor farming town of Immokalee, home of many migrant farmworkers and a small Seminole reservation on the site of a former Indian farmworker camp, the tribe has contributed to programs for health care and education and to the Little League. Former tribal council liaison Elaine Aguilar (Otter) credited these tribal efforts with improving Immokalee's overall reputation and quality of life.[26] As former Hollywood casino manager Larry Frank (Otter) put it, "We have extended our hand to the community."[27] Seminoles also contribute to other American Indian tribes, sending hurricane-relief emergency crews— with a fire truck, an ambulance rescue unit, and four planeloads of food and supplies—to Gulf Coast tribes in the immediate aftermath of Hurricane Katrina, for example.[28] The tribe also donated large sums to South Florida hurricane relief efforts in the wake of Katrina and Wilma. At the same time, hurricanes revealed tensions over giving. Some Seminoles complained to me that non-Seminole neighbors improperly sought and received tribal emergency water distributions. The collective governmental character of rapidly growing, tribal charitable giving has encouraged local community members to conceive of the tribe *as* a tribe, and in this manner, it has buttressed tribal sovereignty.

As anthropologists repeatedly have demonstrated, gift giving often is a privileged mode through which power relations are articulated, established, or challenged.[29] Gifts are not simply economic transactions or expressions of selfless generosity but instead can be understood as constituting sociality, as creating relationships of obligation, care, power, and politics. This is not to say that charity is simply cynical, a mere ploy for recognition or a mode of coercive control over dependents. That Seminoles maintain close friendships and political alliances with past donors illustrates that charitable giving can move beyond relations of patronage to meaningful intercultural exchange. Nevertheless, the transition from Seminole charitable receiving to giving vividly illustrates shifting power relations in South Florida.

Some Seminoles understand charity to be a mechanism for responding to gaming critics and maintaining positive relations with local communities. James Billie (Bird), then tribal chairman, proposed that charity and generosity could help secure the goodwill of non-Seminoles, and he considered the tribal government to be responsible for creating such relationships.

Sympathy for Seminoles, he said, had deteriorated since gaming: before gaming, "a sympathetic atmosphere still existed. Today, no. Once the Indian got on his feet, made more money than most of the general public, that sympathetic feeling is gone." In a common refrain, Billie commented bitterly that local non-Indians never bothered Seminoles as long as they remained poor, but gaming wealth sparked scrutiny and jealousy. Billie viewed Seminole charity as one way to counter a newly hostile environment and to move beyond relations of sympathy to create reciprocity:

> So now comes the time to reverse the [former] sympathetic feeling to something good. When they're [non-Seminoles] trying to cut your throat, the Indian now needs to take that weird situation to his advantage and pay back and help the others around him. Sponsorships, scholarships, something little—just a mere thank you, hello. Go to their churches and help them or whatever. Just do something.[30]

For Billie, charity completes circuits of reciprocity with previously generous non-Seminoles, and in this sense, it returns obligation and speaks to history. At the same time, charity is a strategy for long-term tribal political and economic survival in the context of new Seminole wealth and shifting interracial tensions. Charity toward outsiders, for some Seminoles, is a mode of political protection in hostile times and a means for social reproduction both within the tribe and at a regional level.

Simmering beneath the surface of Seminole discourses and practices of charitable giving is the question of political power and authority. Seminoles are in a position to give charity after a long twentieth century in which charitable giving to Seminoles was among the more salient forms of interaction between tribal members and non-Seminoles; dependency characterized civic relations between the tribal government and local and state governments. In today's reorganized field of power, economy, and exchange, Seminole charity is a return or extension of past charity received, but the social meanings of philanthropy extend beyond an ongoing exchange relationship or the demonstration of goodwill. For Seminoles, charity takes on a special significance against the historical backdrop of centuries of economic destitution, dispossession, missionization, and failed economic development. At long last, they can give, not only receive, and with giving come respect and power. Seminole charitable giving also reflects the cosmic obligations and power that some Seminoles feel toward maintaining the whole world, not only their own families and communities.

Even as tribal citizens expressed irritation at local non-Seminole *expectations* that they should donate gaming proceeds to worthy causes—many noted bitterly that their own struggles often had been overlooked by others, and tribal citizens shared exasperated looks during tribal council meetings when guests appealed for money—they simultaneously leveraged this expectation toward political recognition. That is, Seminoles have effectively used their donor status to demand recognition and politicoeconomic consultation from municipal governments, civic organizations, and educational institutions. Seminole voluntary contributions to the Everglades restoration initiative have guaranteed them a place at the negotiating table on an issue that affects Seminole livelihoods (especially for cattle ranchers) and everyday lives on the Big Cypress and Brighton reservations. The Everglades contributions also have given Seminoles a forum for reminding South Floridians that Indians were the victims of natural resource mismanagement but, nonetheless, have been generous donors toward righting historic wrongs. Sometimes relations of giving and recognition are not grounded in monetary transfers but express reciprocal exchange structured by new power relations. For example, when the Seminole tribal council offered a 2005 resolution in support of Florida State University's use of the Seminole mascot, at a moment when FSU faced pressure from an NCAA investigation into Indian mascots, it also secured scholarships to FSU for Seminole students and ensured tribal input into the university's use of the Seminole name and image.

Other American Indian tribes also have become generous donors to local, national, and intertribal causes. For example, the San Manuel Band of Mission Indians donated to victims of a wildfire that ravaged an Apache reservation in Arizona and to survivors of the September 11, 2001, terrorist attacks. Mashantucket Pequots and Mohegans donated large sums to the Smithsonian National Museum of the American Indian, local historical preservation efforts, and other causes. By 2003 the Shakopee Mdewakanton Sioux Tribe had become one of Minnesota's top-twenty foundation and corporate grant makers (donating more than $7 million annually); the tribe's chairman called the giving "a cultural tradition."[31] Katherine Spilde, in a discussion of the relationship between gaming and American Indian activism, considers increased tribal giving at a local level to be "a model for philanthropy as a conduit to political power."[32] She demonstrates some ways that charitable giving has afforded tribes new access to political power and goodwill. As she notes, however, American Indian charitable giving is not always interpreted generously by local residents. Eve Darian-Smith reports that the Chumash Band of Mission Indians donates more than $1 million annually to a range of public organizations near Santa Barbara, California, but that such generosity is often overlooked by local residents, "or else they interpret the voluntary giving of money to nonprofit organizations as a purely political gesture made with insincere or manipulative intent."[33] Charitable giving signals a reinscription and reversal of dependency relations, which realigns power in ways that both threaten and reinforce indigenous sovereignty at a local level.

As a mode of engagement and a practice of exchange, charity represents Seminole generosity, strategic necessity, and, importantly, new political and economic power. Seminoles have mobilized this as governmental power, reversing ways that charity operated as a colonial technique during the twentieth century. Whether undertaking charity as a defense of the morality of gaming, a sovereign stance, a demonstration of economic power, a political strategy, a return for past generosity, an expression of neighborliness, or a form of participation in a regional community, Seminoles have enacted and localized sovereignty through philanthropy.

Conclusion

Focusing on the local dimensions of sovereignty does not undermine the nation-to-nation relationship between American Indian tribes and the United States. Quite the opposite: it points to the ways that national identities and polities everywhere are constituted in everyday, localized relations, not only for Indian tribes but also for other nations. By exploring gaming as a locus of political action, this chapter also calls attention to the material dimensions of sovereignty, or the ways that economic power, reciprocity, and exchange shape and are produced by sovereignty.

The Coconut Creek casino and charitable giving are only two examples of the many ways that gaming has shifted the economic and political landscape of South Florida, for Seminoles and for many other governments, individuals, and communities in the region. With Seminoles now serving on chambers of commerce, as honored guests at community events, and as players in regional economic development initiatives, new entanglements have tied the tribe and its members more closely to their non-Indian neighbors and simultaneously have provided the means by which Seminoles can assert tribal political status and authority. Of course, Seminoles' new gaming-based visibility also exposes them to criticism, threatening to undermine their political support and standing. To view these entanglements and interdependencies as merely undermining or, conversely, as only advancing tribal sovereignty would overlook the complex texture and particular histories of regional politicolegal relationships, simplifying the multiple meanings of Seminoles' overlapping citizenship and sovereignty. Like other events in South Florida, from the Elián González affair to the 2000 presidential election irregularities, Seminole gaming is a profoundly local story and also a window into larger political processes, in this case suggesting new ways of thinking about the localized and material dimensions of sovereignty.

Acknowledgments

Research for this chapter was part of a larger ethnographic and archival study of Florida Seminole economy and sovereignty, conducted in 2000–2001 (and on subsequent shorter visits) with tribal permission. The project was generously funded by a National Science Foundation Graduate Research Fellowship, an American Association of University Women American Dissertation Fellowship, a Woodrow Wilson Dissertation Grant in Women's Studies, a Smithsonian Institution Predoctoral Fellowship, an American Philosophical Society Phillips Fund Grant for Native American Research, a New York University Kriser Fellowship in Urban Anthropology, the Annette B. Weiner Graduate Fellowship in Cultural Anthropology, and a New York University Alumnae Club Scholarship.

Notes

1. Katherine Spilde, "Creating a Political Space for American Indian Economic Development: Indian Gaming and American Indian Activism," in *Local Actions: Cultural Activism, Power, and Public Life in America*, ed. Melissa Checker and Maggie Fishman (New York: Columbia University Press, 2004), 72, 79.

2. W. Dale Mason, *Indian Gaming: Tribal Sovereignty and American Politics* (Norman: University of Oklahoma Press, 2000); Eve Darian-Smith, *New Capitalists: Law, Politics, and Identity Surrounding Casino Gaming on Native American Land* (Belmont, CA: Thomson/Wadsworth, 2003); Renée Ann Cramer, *Cash, Color, and Colonialism: The Politics of Tribal Acknowledgment* (Norman: University of Oklahoma Press, 2005); and Stephen Light and Kathryn Rand, *Indian Gaming and Tribal Sovereignty: The Casino Compromise* (Lawrence: University Press of Kansas, 2005).

3. Paul Pasquaretta, *Gambling and Survival in Native North America* (Tucson: University of Arizona Press, 2003); Darian-Smith, *New Capitalists*; and Cramer, *Cash, Color, and Colonialism*.

4. Vine Deloria Jr. and Clifford Lytle, *The Nations Within: The Past and Future of American Indian Sovereignty* (New York: Pantheon, 1984); and David Wilkins and K. Tsianina Lomawaima, *Uneven Ground: American Indian Sovereignty and Federal Law* (Norman: University of Oklahoma Press, 2001).

5. One exception to this federal focus is Thomas Biolsi's *"Deadliest Enemies": Law and the Making of Race Relations on and off Rosebud Reservation* (Berkeley: University of California Press, 2001), though his is more a study of race and Indian–white relations than of the local dimensions of sovereignty.

6. Brad Bays and Erin Hogan Fouberg, eds., *The Tribes and the States: Geographies of Intergovernmental Interaction* (Lanham, MD: Rowman and Littlefield Publishers, 2002); and Loretta Fowler, *Tribal Sovereignty and the Historical Imagination: Cheyenne-Arapaho Politics* (Lincoln: University of Nebraska Press, 2002).

7. Karen Blu, *The Lumbee Problem: The Making of an American Indian People*, with a new preface by the author (1980; Lincoln: University of Nebraska Press, 2001), xii.

8. Paula Wagoner, *"They Treated Us Just like Indians": The Worlds of Bennett County, South Dakota* (Lincoln: University of Nebraska Press, 2002). Another foundational text is Niels Winthur Braroe's *Indian and White: Self-Image and Interaction in a Canadian Plains Community* (Stanford, CA: Stanford University Press, 1975).

9. For attention to the impact of state and regional processes, see Circe Sturm's chapter 12 and Larry Nesper's chapter 13 in this volume.

10. Keith Basso, *Wisdom Sits in Places: Landscape and Language among the Western Apache* (Albuquerque: University of New Mexico Press, 1996).

11. Alexis de Tocqueville, *Democracy in America*, edited and with an introduction by Harvey Mansfield and Delba Winthrop, transl. Harvey Mansfield and Delba Winthrop (Chicago: University of Chicago Press, 1994); and Thomas Sugrue, "All Politics Is Local: The Persistence of Localism in Twentieth-Century America," in *The Democratic Experiment: New Directions in American Political History*, ed. Meg Jacobs, William Novak, and Julian Zelizer (Princeton, NJ: Princeton University Press, 2003), 301–326.

12. 658 F.2d 310 (5th Cir. 1981).

13. Figures courtesy of the Seminole Tribe of Florida, Legal Department.

14. Harry Kersey Jr., *Pelts, Plumes, and Hides: White Traders among the Seminole Indians, 1870–1930* (Gainesville: University Presses of Florida, 1975); and Patsy West, *The Enduring Seminoles: From Alligator Wrestling to Ecotourism* (Gainesville: University Press of Florida, 1998).

15. Kitty Oliver, *Race and Change in Hollywood, Florida* (Charleston, SC: Arcadia Publishing, 2000). This is all the more remarkable because one of the author's community meetings, which I attended, was hosted by the Seminole Tribe at the Hollywood Reservation library. Worse, the organizers' attempt to generate immigrant, black, and white interracial solidarity turned to outright disregard for indigeneity in the event's title: "We're All from Somewhere Else."

16. Seminoles' matrilineal clan affiliations are indicated after their names.

17. Paul Brinkley-Rogers, "Coconut Creek Fighting Full-Scale Indian Casino," *Miami Herald*, April 25, 1999, 1A, 13A.

18. Robert Nolin, "Casino, Creek Come Up Winners," *South Florida Sun-Sentinel*, February 5, 2001, 1A, 12A.

19. Jo-Lin Osceola, interview with author, November 29, 2000.

20. Seminole Tribe of Florida, Briefing on Secretarial Procedures for Class III Gaming (n.p.: 1999).

21. Moses Jumper Jr. (Snake), interview with author, January 16, 2001.

22. Jim Shore (Bird), interview with author, August 10, 2001.

23. Rex Quinn Papers, University of Florida Archives, unaccessioned, Gainesville.

24. Charles Hiers (Bird), interview with author, March 31, 2001.

25. I thank Tony Clark for urging me to incorporate "Indian giving" into this chapter.

26. Elaine Aguilar (Otter), interview with author, January 8, 2001.

27. Larry Frank (Otter), interview with author, October 11, 2000.

28. Nery Mejicano, "Seminole Tribe Sends Help to Band of Choctaw Indians," *The Seminole Tribune* 26, no. 13 (September 23, 2005): 1, 25.

29. For example, see Franz Boas, "The Potlatch," in *Indians of the North Pacific Coast*, ed. Tom McFeat (1895; Seattle: University of Washington Press, 1967), 72–80; Marcel Mauss, *The Gift: The Form and Reason for Exchange in Archaic Societies* (1950; New York and London: Norton, 1990); and Maurice Godelier, *The Enigma of the Gift* (Chicago: University of Chicago Press, 1999).

30. James Billie (Bird), interview with author, April 13, 2001.

31. Robert Franklin, "Shakopee Tribe among Minnesota's Largest Sources of Charitable Dollars," *The Star Tribune* (Minneapolis), December 29, 2003, www.startribune.com (accessed

December 29, 2003).

32. Spilde, "Creating a Political Space," 72.

33. Darian-Smith, *New Capitalists*, 86.

15 Miami Indian Language and Cultural Research at Miami University

Daryl Baldwin and Julie Olds

Language loss is one of the most pressing concerns among indigenous peoples today. An estimated 89 percent of the languages spoken in North America at the time of contact with Europeans are now "dormant" or "sleeping."[1] Revitalization efforts, sparked by a combination of Native activism and legislative support from the federal government, ultimately speak to larger issues concerning the rights of indigenous peoples (see table 4, 1968, and table 6, 1990).[2] Recent scholarship addresses tensions surrounding language revitalization and, in particular, tensions that reflect intratribal divisions and conflicts resulting from the legacies of colonialism.[3] These studies focus on communities with a population that includes native speakers, often from several generations. Baldwin and Olds write about the Miami community, one with a "sleeping" language. They describe the Myaamia Project, a cooperative research initiative between the Miami Tribe of Oklahoma and Miami University in Oxford, Ohio, to support the tribe's language and cultural revitalization goals. All the research is tribally directed. It asks questions and addresses issues that Miami people consider most important and strives to apply the results in practical, community-relevant ways. The partnership between the Miami Tribe and Miami University

is an example of Indian activism in an institutional arena outside the governmental sphere.

The Miami Tribe of Oklahoma has been engaged in language and culture revitalization since the mid-1990s. In July 2001 the tribe and Miami University agreed to develop a research initiative, the Myaamia Project. Its mission is the advancement of the language and cultural research needs of the Miami Tribe of Oklahoma. How a project of this nature came to be, and to what extent it truly serves the needs of the Miami people, is what we cover briefly. We would like to note that our experiences directing tribal scholarship through the Myaamia Project are new, so we are learning a great deal as it evolves. With that said, we will present the fundamental building blocks that make this project unique and successful as a tribal effort in an academic setting and will describe how this experience is impacting the tribal community.

The Miami people, or as we say in our language, Myaamiaki, were historically located throughout the southern Great Lakes region. The northern portion of the Wabash River in north-central Indiana geographically defines the heart of our ancestral homeland. After years of treaties, the Miami lost their rights to occupy these historic lands and finally, in 1846, were forcibly removed to an unwanted reservation in the Kansas Territory. The Miami's time in the Kansas Territory was brief; white settlement forced a second removal to Indian Territory (Oklahoma) by the late 1870s. The next several years would bring about further hardships, including the allotment of tribal lands, boarding schools, and continued social and governmental pressures to suppress all aspects of being Miami. By the 1960s the Miami were landless, and the last of the native speakers of their language had passed on.

This history is important because everything we do today as a nation, including our language and cultural efforts, is in direct response to this oppressive history. It became clear by the 1980s that we were losing an entire generation of elders who grew up among those who spoke the language, harvested traditional plants, and still maintained a worldview that was uniquely Miami. If we were going to learn from our elders, we had to move quickly because their time with us was limited. Additionally, we also understood that we needed to begin making use of the vast historical record. Today our language and cultural efforts incorporate both living and written knowledge.

In 1996 the Miami Tribe of Oklahoma began to pursue language and culture reclamation. The desire to reclaim traditional language and culture was motivated by several factors: the Native American Languages Act of 1990, which was the initial source of funding for the Miami Language

Teacher Training Program; the authors' completion of a dissertation at the University of California at Berkeley, which outlined the morphology and phonology of the Miami language; and a growing desire among tribal members to learn something of their heritage language and culture.[4] What we did not know at the time was the amount of work that lay ahead of us. But one thing was certain. Whatever shape our effort took, it had to be community driven and in direct support of community desires and needs.

Some of our initial efforts have included organizing language camps, developing basic lessons, and identifying families who are willing to create a home environment conducive to Miami language and culture. It also became very clear that a tremendous amount of research, training, and material development would be needed over time in order to reverse language loss. The Miami Tribe is small, only 3,250 citizens. Populations are scattered across the country, with concentrations living in Oklahoma, Kansas, and Indiana, reflecting the removal route. Like many other Great Lakes tribes that suffered removal, the Miami Tribe has historically had very limited monetary resources. This status changed with the long-awaited arrival of economic development in the late 1990s, which has become more important as the effort grows. Although monetary support was given to the reclamation effort in the beginning, community cultural leaders determined early on that available tribal resources needed for conducting research and developing educational materials were minimal, for the tribe had no educational infrastructure.

After much discussion and debate among community leaders, a decision was made to turn to our friends at Miami University for help. This seemed the most appropriate avenue to pursue because the tribe and the university have had a long-standing relationship dating back to the 1970s. This has slowly grown over the years into a strong, mutually beneficial relationship. Tribal officials regularly visit campus, and the university has been involved in a number of service learning projects designed to benefit the tribe in Oklahoma. In other words, a level of trust was already well established, which was essential in creating a climate that would enable tribal officials and cultural leaders to feel comfortable bringing something as important as our traditional language and culture into an academic setting, far from the tribe.

Finally, after a few months of negotiations between university and tribal representatives, the Myaamia Project for language and cultural revitalization became a reality at Miami University in the summer of 2001. Tribal representatives had only two requirements for the operation of the Myaamia Project. The first was that research projects be initiated and directed through the tribe's cultural preservation office. This would ensure that our research was of direct interest and benefit to the tribe. It would also ensure that academic interests would never take priority over community interests and needs. The second requirement was that the Miami Tribe of Oklahoma hold the copyright to all printed and published materials produced through the project. We felt that our ancestors' intellectual knowledge should not be the property of Miami University. All these stipulations were verbally agreed upon and continue to be honored by both parties today.

In exchange for these stipulations, we were asked to share our research and knowledge in the classroom, and we are happy to do so. We also encourage university students to participate in research projects conducted through the Myaamia Project. Through these, students are exposed to the tribal community, including its government, traditional language and culture, and our esteemed elders and leaders. Over the years, we have witnessed benefits to students who become involved in projects directly affecting our community. Their experiences through the Myaamia Project are real and tangible, often leading to a deeper understanding of how community-driven research can positively contribute to the welfare of the entire community.

It did not take long for a wide range of projects to be initiated. One example is the extensive ethnobotany project undertaken by a very talented graduate student in botany at Miami University. One aspect of his graduate project was to create an ethnobotany database to catalog and store all the references we had collected from the vast historical and linguistic records. When we spoke with our elders about this work, they began to recall plants they had harvested in their youth. Suddenly, we realized that there was still a good deal of living botanical knowledge of which we were unaware. This living knowledge enabled us to take our research one step further, and we began looking at traditional harvesting practices. We also began preparing and cooking several of these native plants under the direction of community elders, and out of this activity arose information about seasonal diets. Typically, these projects would start out with a simple goal in mind and then blossom into much bigger and potentially more meaningful projects.

For example, during a recent planned gathering, we prepared and cooked a variety of corn soups and hominy dishes among a group of tribal members. During this gathering, we learned that two of the elders could not agree on whether heat was used during the lye process in preparation of hominy. We tried both methods of preparation, with and without heated lye, and there seemed to be no difference in the effect on the hominy. A few days later, we turned to the language record and found that, in fact, there was specific language for preparing hominy with heated lye, *peelaki-inkweesaakani*, and hominy where no heat is used in the lye process, *peelaki-inkwaakani*. We arrived at the conclusion that both elders were correct and probably had different personal recollections of the process. This is an excellent example of how living knowledge and the historical language record can combine to help us better understand traditional practices.

The success of the ethnobotany project goes beyond good documentation. Crucial parts of the success were the researcher's personality, research objectives, and ability to build and maintain relationships of trust within the community. We were fortunate to find an individual, although not a Miami Indian, who maintained a high degree of respect for our intellectual knowledge and the elders who possess that knowledge. His personal skills and respectful behavior deepened and extended his research beyond what most can accomplish. In addition, his own innocence in regard to our traditional culture caused him to ask questions many of us would not have thought of asking. Our collective desire to fulfill the mission of the tribe's language and cultural needs allows for the participation of non-Native scholars. But that participation must be rooted in appropriate research objectives and healthy relationships. Both elements are essential for success. Our notion of success is based on what is good for the people, not necessarily what is good for academia or the researcher.

In 2004 we launched an in-depth geography project that will result in a number of information layers created through geographic information systems (GIS) technology. These layers will include a reconstruction of the historic vegetation of the historic homeland region, a place name layer of all the traditional names for rivers, lakes, streams and other significant places, and a layer showing permanent and temporary village locations over time. This will directly benefit our understanding of the past and also help us satisfy current needs related to the National Historical Preservation Act and the Native American Graves Protection and Repatriation Act (see table 6). This project is still very much in its infancy, and we welcome the challenges of using GIS technology to represent a historical, cultural, and ancestral landscape.

Another project is a compilation of more than fifteen years of language research into a dictionary of the Miami language, which became our first major publication, in 2005.[5] We are also on schedule to complete a publication of nearly thirty traditional narratives in a bilingual format. These examples represent only a sampling of the projects and research efforts currently under way, all of which were born from the needs identified by community leaders and through the Miami Tribe's Office of Cultural Preservation.

One exciting and unanticipated outcome of our work involves our own tribal students on campus. The university offers a Miami Indian heritage award for tribal members who choose to attend Miami, and in the 2006–2007 academic year, we had fifteen tribal students on campus. Three graduated in May 2007 and we anticipate another six entering the university during the fall 2007 semester. Many of these students did not grow up near Miami lands in Oklahoma, so they have been unable to participate in tribal functions. We felt that it would be a shame if these young adults came to Miami University, got their degrees, and moved on without ever having the opportunity to learn from the work being done through the Myaamia Project.

In response to this need, we created a series of one-credit independent study opportunities for our tribal students, beginning during the 2003–2004 school year. This includes two semesters of history and ecological perspectives, two semesters of language and culture, two semesters of tribal economic development, government, and sovereignty, and, in their fourth year, a topic of their choice. We have had incredible success with our tribal students and have been able to work with them on a more personal level in the areas of language, culture, and history.

We are proud to say that we have thus far had two graduate students at Miami University who are tribal members and have been supported and encouraged to direct their research for tribal benefit. One is set to complete a degree in geography in 2007. His work explores the use of technology for cultural resource management. The other, a history major, completed a master's thesis in 2006, using his knowledge of our traditional language to interpret our tribal history. He then chose to continue his work at one of the nation's leading history doctoral programs. It is important for us that our young adults feel intellectually challenged and connected to their community. We want them to know that the Miami Tribe community is also a place to grow and learn in many ways, and we hope that one day they can serve their nation as we rebuild. Our needs are great; as with any nation, we need all forms of talent and knowledge.

The Myaamia Project has created an atmosphere of learning and sharing among those of us who have a vested interest in the continuation and survival of our community's traditional language and culture. As we have already pointed out, one does not have to be Miami to have that vested interest and to work within that circle of commitment. In the spring of 2006, we held our second biannual conference on Miami Tribe Scholarship at Miami University and had presenters from across the country and local presenters who then became connected in some way with the Myaamia Project and the Miami Tribe. Several of the presenters were tribe members, and many were not, but all presented their work to both tribal and university community members.

Admittedly, when the Myaamia Project was created, we did not know what it would look like or the effect it would have on both the tribal and academic communities. The creation of the Myaamia Project has profoundly affected our tribal community at large. Before its conception, there were few, if any, tribal members specializing in fields related to language and culture. Because of exposure to the Myaamia Project, we now have several tribal members specializing in a multitude of fields relating to our culture, language, and history.

On a more personal note, we would like to make some observations regarding our experience directing a Native-driven research project in an academic setting, including some of the tangible outcomes of this kind of work for the community. The success of this project really does depend on the ability of both parties to maintain a degree of mutual respect for and understanding of each other. We as Myaamiaki (Miami People) are challenged to understand the needs and purpose of a socially and economically driven academic institution, and, likewise, university faculty who become involved with the tribe must understand our community needs and motivations, which can be very different.

We also find that our research objectives can differ from a typical academic focus, which is often on broad topics of research on indigenous communities. What we mean by this is that almost all our research has direct application to the community. For example, researching the origins of the Miami people or whether we have biological connections to the prehistoric mound builders of Ohio is, in our view, nonessential research. It may have academic or historic value to some, but it has little or no community value to us at this time. Reconstructing our traditional lunar calendar, however, as a means of strengthening our relationship with the landscape by preserving traditional ecological knowledge is very useful and has direct application for Miami people on Miami lands today.

It is the applied aspect of our work that forces our research to be interdisciplinary. The Myaamia Project does not have a strictly linguistic, anthropological, or historical research focus but instead crosses many disciplines. A people's worldview does not function as a set of defined, analytically segmented pieces but instead is an interaction between a people and their physical world, their empirical knowledge of that physical world, and the interpretation of their unique experience. Learning about the "interconnectedness" of a people's world cannot be accomplished through any single academic discipline. The research used to understand a Miami worldview requires an understanding of all facets of the human experience in a given place. Understanding this concept is important to understanding why it would be inappropriate to place the Myaamia Project within the philosophical constraints of any single academic discipline.

Perpetuating and strengthening Miami identity through adult and youth education is the ultimate goal of the language and cultural reclamation effort. As researchers, we are challenged not only to understand the intricacies of our traditional ways of knowing but also to develop ways of teaching traditional concepts to the community at large. We often find ourselves creating educational models as a means of teaching concepts such as time, space, relationship, leadership, and ecological perspectives. Through our independent study programs for tribal students on Miami University's campus and with our programs in Oklahoma, we have the opportunity to test these cultural models and observe how our people respond to and internalize traditional concepts. This experience ultimately allows us to be more effective when we share this kind of cultural information in the classrooms at Miami University. The power and energy generated when our community becomes involved and informed are what drive and motivate the Myaamia Project and its many research initiatives.

Our traditional language must always serve as the lens through which we develop our understanding of traditional concepts. In other words, we are not just teaching language, but also a worldview that is based on the language. We find that when students are learning these unique concepts through the language, the language becomes the primary means for understanding traditional knowledge. We want students to value the *ideas*, which are best expressed through the language. Thought and knowledge are essential to cultural learning, and if done well, our traditional language will do for our traditional culture something English has not evolved to do. Being Miami is about many things, but when cultural knowledge is presented to youth in appropriate ways, a new worldview is opened and diversity is truly experienced. We have seen how this enlightening experience can inspire a tribal member to learn his native language. At this point, it becomes something experienced and felt, not something one does solely for posterity or to honor one's ancestors.

In the summer of 2006, we had the opportunity to introduce a cultural landscape model through the tribe's Eewansaapita Summer Education Program. The program is a weeklong summer educational opportunity for tribal youth ages ten through sixteen. Students live together for a week in a small community setting on the tribe's cultural grounds, located within the tribal jurisdiction area in northeast Oklahoma. The cultural grounds consist of a wide range of habitats, including native tall-grass prairie, woodlands, creeks, wetlands, and riparian areas. Our objective is to see whether we can help the students experience this unique landscape in a Miami way, which means to know and see the land as a place where our traditional culture is practiced and maintained. We want them to begin developing the ability to interact with our lands through a Miami cultural lens. Through this activity, we seek to replace the objectified, quantified, and linear Western view of land with a Miami view of land, which is based on sustainable interdependence within a spatial orientation of culturally significant places. The outcome of this experience is a student-generated map of the site that reflects their interactions, created with group consensus. The only stipulations we impose are that the map not show trails (forcing spatial site orientation) and that place names be in the Miami language (based on the location of an activity or a geographical feature).

A complete description of this exercise, in and of itself, would require a paper, but generally speaking, the exercise involves observation, awareness, traditional use of the land, understanding the interactions that take place on the landscape, and the use of sight, sound, and smell—all taught within a cultural context. At first, it is difficult for students to break free from thinking about the land from an overhead "satellite" perspective, which consists of absolute borders, "perfect" representation of trails, and a general focus on representing all the "things" in the landscape. In the first summer program, it took most of the week before they were able to break from these linear and objectified notions and start talking about their personal interactions with the landscape. This educational process encouraged them to start thinking of the land as a place where they interact through cultural activities (figure 12).

Throughout the week, the students harvested plants from the land, established culturally significant places, and observed other natural interactions that took place. By the end of the week, as the map began to emerge, places were identified by such labels as "the place where we harvested *wiinhsihsiaki* [onions]" or "harvested *mihtekwaapiminiiki* [mulberries]." Students also learned the importance of other beings' interactions within the landscape, in their recognition of the *alenaswa waali* (buffalo wallow) and the *mahkoteewi* (tall-grass prairie). Uniquely, Miami landmarks were also emphasized as students marked the place of the *mihšiinkweemiši* (Burr Oak), a tree of historical and cultural importance, as a place of significance to them.

Our hope is that through continued and expanded programs, students will develop a deeper sense for a cultural place and that one day this will form the basis for how we, as a community, interact with our lands. As staff and teachers, we found the experience very rewarding. We were able to witness cultural learning taking place, by watching our youth experience a landscape, guided by a culture model developed from our research initiatives through the Myaamia Project. As educators, the experience reinforced the importance of maintaining a cultural landscape for community use and education. On a gloomier note, it sharpened our perception of what forced removal did to our ancestors, who were so intimately tied to their historic homelands in the lower Great Lakes. It became clearer, as we observed the students throughout the week, that this forced removal from an ancestral and cultural landscape was a

Figure 12. During the Miami Tribe's Eewansaapita Summer Education Program in 2006, students generated this map, which reflects tribal ways of conceptualizing space and relating to the land. Photo by Karen Baldwin. Courtesy of Miami Nation Archives.

form of cultural genocide and one of the most important historical events leading to the decline of Miami language and culture.

We realize that our work in language and culture revitalization goes beyond the restoration of a worldview. It includes the cultural restoration of a landscape. For us, a Miami form of ecological restoration embraces the recovery of culturally significant flora and fauna, as well as the revitalization of the interactions between these beings and the land. Only when these inhabitants are present and the interactions are restored to a natural stability will our physical environment be intact enough for the continuation and growth of our way of life. Our research and educational programs serve to rebuild these elements in a way that recognizes and continues to add to ancestral knowledge. Many of us believe that ancestral knowledge is not just "knowledge of the past" but instead a "way to be" that takes us well into the future, sustaining our place and us.

Fundamental to our culture is the concept of relationship. The concept of relationship is expressed in our language in ways not solely defined by genetics. It is more about interaction and how we treat one another. Our very future and survival as a people depend on our ability to relate well to others, including the land. The success of the Myaamia Project also depends on the ability to maintain respectful relationships. As the Myaamia Project grows and expands in scope and depth, we will no doubt be challenged to deepen and strengthen our relationship with Miami University and the researchers with whom we work.

The future of the Miami, and therefore our survival, as a nation is dependent on our success in cultural preservation work. We must continue to find ways to reach out to a scattered community and help them learn how to connect to one another. Many of our youth are raised far from the nation's home in Oklahoma. It is from our Oklahoma home that all cultural education materials are distributed, and currently, tribal members must come to Oklahoma to participate in tribal community events such as language programs, reunions, political meetings, and seasonal gatherings. These gatherings are important if tribal members want to come into contact with elders and experience their oral traditions before they leave us.

The Myaamia Project is a tool of immeasurable value to the Miami Nation. Born of a respectful relationship between a sovereign nation and an educational institution located on the lands of our ancestors, the Myaamia Project is acknowledged by our people as the cornerstone to our ultimate success in reclaiming our language and restoring our traditional worldview, which will ensure the perpetuation of our great Miami Nation.

Notes

1. James Crawford, "Endangered Native American Languages: What Is to Be Done, and Why?" in *Language and Politics in the United States and Canada: Myths and Realities*, ed. Thomas Ricento and Barbara Burnaby (Mahwah, NJ: Lawrence Erlbaum Associates, 1998), 151–170.

2. See Leanne Hinton and Ken Hale, eds., *The Green Book of Language Revitalization in Practice* (San Diego: Academic Press, 2001). For an eloquent statement that situates language in the context of global indigenous rights, see Article 14 of the United Nations Declaration on the Rights of Indigenous Peoples, http://www.ohchr.org/english/issues/indigenous/docs/declaration.doc (accessed August 21, 2006).

3. James Collins, "Language," in *A Companion to the Anthropology of American Indians*, ed. Thomas Biolsi, Blackwell Companions to Anthropology (Malden, MA: Blackwell Publishing, 2004), 490–525.

4. In response to a community survey taken in 1998, it was determined that the most important thing to the community was language and cultural development.

5. Daryl Baldwin and David Costa, *myaamia neehi peewaalia kaloosioni mahsinaakani: A Miami-Peoria Dictionary* (Oxford, OH: Myaamia Project at Miami University, 2005). Copyright Miami Tribe of Oklahoma.

16 Conclusion
Education, Art, and Activism
Della C. Warrior

Della Warrior has been engaged in issues revolving around Indian education since the 1960s. The first woman elected as chairperson and as chief executive officer of the Otoe-Missouria Tribe, she has been director of Indian Education for the Albuquerque Public Schools, a board member of the National Museum of the American Indian, the Smithsonian Institution, and the American Indian Higher Education Consortium, an appointee to President George W. Bush's Board of Advisors on Tribal Colleges and Universities, and a chartering member of the World Indigenous Nations Higher Education Consortium. In this chapter, Warrior reflects on how her experiences as a youth shaped her professional career and particularly her tenure as president of the Institute of American Indian Arts (IAIA) in Santa Fe, New Mexico, a position she held from 1993 to 2006. Warrior's conclusion brings the volume full circle by emphasizing the importance of leadership and the production of knowledge discussed in Don Fixico and Fred Hoxie's opening chapters (1 and 2, respectively). Here we gain an inside perspective on the personal dimension of being an advocate for change, the ways in which art and education can be seen as forms of activism, and the role women have played in the politics of community survival.

Ha! Hintado. That is "Hello, my friends" in Otoe-Missouria language. My Otoe-Missouria name is Wa^unPiMi, which is from the Beaver Clan. Its generic meaning is "somebody that is busy always doing something, always got something going." Through my later years, I realized that I was appropriately named. My grandparents saw to it that I had a good Indian name.[1]

In this conclusion, I want to address what I see as the relationship of art, education, and community persistence in Indian Country. When Dan Cobb initially invited me to give a talk on this topic at Miami University, he asked me to draw upon my four decades of involvement in this area (figure 13).[2] For some reason, this made me stop and think. I remember saying to myself, "Four decades. That is forty years." I still find it difficult to imagine that I have been doing this for forty years. It reminded me of home, how when I go home to Oklahoma, they call on me to pray. You never get called on unless you are considered an elder, so I am coming to grips now with being a Native elder woman. It is an adjustment because I do not see myself at that point of having that stature. And from another perspective, a traditional perspective, in my community and culture, a woman's role is not to get up and speak before the public. If you have something to say or you want to get a message across, it is tradition to get a male elder of your clan or your family to "voice for you." So that is something that I constantly have to overcome, to step out of that role, in order to be a leader.

Within the past forty years, I have seen the passage of legislation that has greatly affected American Indian people, such as the Indian Education Act, the Indian Self-Determination and Education Assistance Act, and the Tribally Controlled Community Colleges Act, as well as laws dealing with resource development, religious freedom, legal jurisdiction, taxation, repatriation, and gaming (see table 5, 1975 and 1978, and table 6, 1988 and 1990; Helton and Robertson, chapter 3, this volume). In each of these cases, grassroots people—people from local communities—served as the catalysts for change. Through their efforts came requirements for parental involvement in school systems, tribal control over programs that used to be operated by the Bureau of Indian Affairs (BIA), power over decisions regarding the use of tribal resources, and the chartering of some thirty-five tribally controlled colleges and universities. All of these have led to the revitalization of tribal communities.

Today if you go to visit a tribal headquarters, you will see Indian people running their own governments and in control of nearly all the services these provide. But it was not always that way. The young people who are coming up today take it for granted. They think that it has always been that way, but that is not the case. Take my tribe, the Otoe-Missouria, for example.[3] Forty years ago, the only business that my little tribal council had to do was to consider who was going to get the leases—to whom the tribal government would award leases to farm and plant crops. That was essentially all the business our tribal government could conduct back then.

Figure 13. Della Warrior (Otoe-Missouria) speaks on the intersection of art, education, and activism at Miami University in Oxford, Ohio, April 2006. Photo courtesy of Hugh Morgan.

Programs and services for the tribe were completely under the control of the Bureau of Indian Affairs and later the Indian Health Service (IHS), when health programs moved out of the BIA over to Public Health Services.

In order for you to understand, I would like you to imagine yourself traveling back in time. It is the mid-1950s, and you are about twelve years old.[4] You are going to go down to the Pawnee Indian Agency with your aunt, about forty miles from your home in Red Rock, Oklahoma. Red Rock is not really even a town but more like a village. Your aunt is going down to the Indian agency to ask the BIA superintendent whether she can have some of her money because she needs to buy some groceries. You are a "ward" of the federal government. They act as though you are a child, as though you are not competent to handle your own affairs. So you go with your aunt to the superintendent's office, and she explains why she needs the funds. It is your money, but he has to approve letting you draw down on it. After talking with your aunt, he decides that she really does need the money, and he orders a check cut.

You are twelve, and you walk down the hallway of the Pawnee Indian Agency office and look around. You see that the only Indians working there are a couple secretaries and the janitor. Then you go with your aunt over to the Indian hospital because you need to get some immunizations and she needs some meds. Again, you notice that the only Indians working there are in menial positions. When you get back to Red Rock, you begin looking around at the little businesses there—the grocery store, three small cafés, a couple service stations, a hardware store, a post office, and then the co-op where the farmers bring their wheat crops. And you notice that there are no Indians running any of these businesses, even though the town is predominantly Indian, because that was how it was started. It was originally set up as a reservation.

So you begin to wonder about this. Why is this? Why, in a community that is predominantly Native, don't we have any doctors or nurses or teachers or principals? Why aren't we running the café? Why don't some of us own the grocery store? You begin thinking about this, so you ask your mother, "Why is this? Why don't we have jobs?" Your mother basically tells you and your aunt, "Well, that's just the way it is now. That is why you need to go to school, and maybe you can do something to help your people—go to school and come back here and help in some way." You make up your mind that you are going to get an education and go to college. You work hard. You earn good grades in high school and get on the pre-college track. You take all the required courses. In about the eleventh grade, the school counselor calls you to her office to review your scores on the achievement tests. She says to you, "I know you are planning to go to college, but based on these test scores, I think it is highly unlikely that you can be successful in college." She tells you to consider going to a technical school to become something like an X-ray technician.

As you may have guessed, I have been describing what it was like for me growing up in Kansas and Oklahoma. Those were the words my school counselor said to me. That is what she advised me to aspire to—or what she told me not to aspire to. Here I had been making something like a 3.8 grade point average in high school. I had begun planning to be a medical doctor, and she tells me that I am not college material, based on these test scores (this was long before the whole cultural bias issue involving standardized testing came up). I remember talking to my mother about this. I asked her, "What am I going to do? I don't want to be an X-ray technician. I want to go to college." My mother said, "Don't listen to her. Don't listen to her. Maybe she doesn't want you to go to college." "I think that if you work really hard, you can probably do it," she told me. "Those tests don't tell everything."

I decided that I was not going to listen to my school counselor. This was in Wichita, Kansas. We used to move around quite a bit. My folks would go out and look for jobs, and then my mother would get lonesome for home, so we would move back to Red Rock. I went to six different high schools, and sometimes I wonder how I ever managed to graduate. But I did. I was the first person in my extended family to get a high school education. Out of all my aunts and uncles' children, my mother's generation, I was the first one to graduate from high school and then go to college.

Another experience that made an impression on me was a trip I took to Ponca City, about sixteen miles north of Red Rock, to apply for a job. I went into the employment office and filled out an application. After my interview, I watched as the job counselor wrote on a piece of paper "neat, clean, pretty." And then he said, "You are not from around here, are you." In that part of Oklahoma, we have five tribes, the Otoe-Missouria, Pawnee, Tonkawa, Kaw, and Ponca. I said, "Yes, I'm just from Red Rock. I'm just from south of here." He shook his head. What it communicated to me at that age—I think that I was seventeen—was "You're not like the rest of these Indians," meaning that there was something wrong with Indians. I was one of them, so there must be something wrong with me—that was what I went away with. And, by the way, it didn't help me get the job.

The point is that one's community helps shape your definition of yourself, and it helps shape your future. Because I had strong family and communal support, I made it through high school. That was remarkable. The majority of Indian people do not graduate. Percentages vary from state to state, but even today Indian young people continue to have high dropout rates. When I attended college in the early 1960s, there were probably fewer than a thousand Indian students enrolled across the entire United States (today only 17 percent of American Indian students who graduate from high school go on to college). There were twelve of us in my high school graduating class. Eight of us were American Indians, and of that eight, two went on to earn college degrees.

In 1961 I went to Cameron College in southwestern Oklahoma. All the Indian students boarded at the Ft. Sill Indian School and took the bus to campus. By my sophomore year, I had some really good friends, Native people like Clyde Warrior (Ponca), Katherine Red Corn (Osage), Gloria Keliaa (Washo-Shoshone), and Jereldine Cross (Caddo), who is a potter now. I remember them talking about this program called the Workshop on American Indian Affairs. They kept telling me that I needed to go because I would meet all these other Indian college students from all over the United States and that it was something I had to do, I must do. They finally convinced me that if I did not go, I would be missing out on something that was really important. I applied and was selected. Despite my mother's strong objections, I went to the University of Colorado in Boulder in June 1963. It was quite a change from Red Rock, Oklahoma, and I have to tell you that it was a life-changing experience for me (Cobb, chapter 9, this volume).

I mentioned earlier that I had been planning to go to medical school. At Cameron, I was on a pre-med track. But after the workshop, I had a burning desire to make a better world for Indian people. That summer, I met thirty-five other Indian college students for the first time, and for the first time I became proud of who I am as an Indian person. It was an amazing thing just to see and learn from these Indian students from Alaska, Washington, North Dakota, South Dakota, and Montana. And here I was thinking that there were "just us" in Oklahoma. So I learned a lot from the students, as well as from the workshop's formal curriculum. I learned about the numerous federal Indian policies that were designed to fix the so-called Indian problem. I came to understand the detrimental impact of policies, from allotment to termination, that were designed to "fix" the Indian problem by taking away our land and resources (see tables 1 and 3; Troutman, chapter 5, and Kidwell, chapter 7, this volume).

During this workshop, we also learned to analyze Native communities, based on anthropologist Robert Redfield's folk-urban continuum and other social scientific theories. Bob Thomas and the other instructors would ask us to analyze our community, and we wrote papers on what we wanted our communities to look like in ten years. We all did that. We began to analyze what policies like allotment and termination had done to our people. And we got mad. We got very angry because we understood that we were not the people to blame. It was not our problem, and we were not at fault for high dropout rates, poverty, or any of the other negative statistics. We came to understand that these were the results of policies that had been forced on us. So we became excited about education and what we could do to help our people.

The workshops went on about eight years, and many of the individuals who attended went on to make remarkable contributions to their communities. If you look out over that eight-year period, you have approximately three hundred students from one hundred tribes. Many of them went into leadership positions, and they have contributed to many changes. They have not only been instrumental to the passage of the positive legislation I mentioned in my introduction, but have also done constructive work within Native communities. At the workshop, we became passionate about helping to change our communities and to improve the standard of living of our people. We also came to understand that it could be done only by changing policies, changing systems, and changing institutions.

In 1964, one year after I attended the workshop, I married Clyde Warrior and became involved in the National Indian Youth Council (NIYC). Clyde and eleven of his counterparts formed the NIYC in the summer of 1961, shortly after the American Indian Chicago Conference. Clyde at the time was visiting college campuses and talking to students. He was stirring up things, to put it mildly. He was saying such purportedly outrageous things (these are not his words but just taken from what I remember): "Let us make our own mistakes. We couldn't possibly do any worse than the federal government." "We have the right to make our own choices and decisions. We don't need the Bureau of Indian Affairs doing this for us." "We could be 'educated' and not lose our Indianness." "Our heritage and culture are important. They need to be incorporated into the school curriculum." "Indians need to be able to determine their own destiny. They need to run their own educational systems. They need to take charge of their future."

Today Clyde's statements sound very logical; they make total sense. But at the time, they were considered radical. Remember, this was just a decade after the termination policy—that policy that basically said, "Okay, we are terminating the treaties we made with you. We are cutting off all our obligations to you tribes." They were intent on assimilating Indians into the mainstream as quickly as possible because they really believed that you have all these other peoples coming from all over Europe and coming to this country and they were making it, so why can't Indians make it? Why can't they live the American dream? Today we know that the melting pot theory did not work. You still have distinct societies within the general society. But during the 1960s we were still fighting this fight. And we were determined to fight for the right to be Indian however we wanted. All Clyde ever wanted —this man whom so many people called a radical and found so threatening—was to ensure that Indians could improve their standard of living without having to abandon their Indianness.

Clyde passed away in the summer of 1968. I lost my husband, and the Indian youth movement lost its leader. I remember friends calling and asking me, "What are we going to do now?" My work has always operated from the premise Clyde articulated time and again—that we have value as a people and that our history, language, and culture are critical to our survival and to our prosperity. We have seen that the attempt to take it away from us was destructive, because we did not want to give that up. We just pulled back and did not want to take part in becoming "educated" as white people understood it.

During my tenure as president of the Institute of American Indian Arts (see table 4, 1962), we operated on the assumption that our students must come to grips with their own identities as Native people and that they must be able to function effectively in any cultural context. Indian role models are and always have been essential to making this happen. As a tribal leader, a college president, and a member of national educational advisory committees, I have stressed the importance of having Native teachers and administrators. It is imperative that Indian students know the history of Native people, that they know and understand their own culture. They must know where they came from and who they are before they can determine where they are going. No matter their grade level, students need to feel that their histories, languages, and cultures are important.

I sometimes wonder what my life would have been like had I not gone to the workshop, if I had not learned to value who I was as a Native person. I probably would have graduated from college and then assimilated into the general society. And I probably would not be doing what I have been doing for the past forty years. I would imagine that I would be unsure of who I am. I would still be trying to fit in without recognizing and valuing my own Indianness. Most certainly, I would have continued wondering, "What is wrong with Indian people? Why couldn't we conform? Why were we the people whom they had negative things to say about?" Everyone has seen it on television, all the stereotypes of war-whooping, backward Indians. It is so detrimental to the way Indian children perceive themselves, because they come to realize that the general society still sees them as savages. Yet we are living here today. We did not die, despite all the wars waged to kill us. We are still here.

I began working at the Institute of American Indian Arts in Santa Fe, New Mexico, in late 1993. I was hired as the tribal liaison in the development office because I had just left the position of chairperson of the Otoe-Missouria. The IAIA felt that it needed someone to strengthen relationships with the tribes. I was in that position for three or four months, then became the director. During that time, I interviewed about fifty of our most successful alumni. The institute was in dire straits and about to go over the cliff. We were losing our funding, and I had to be able to convince Congress and the public what was important about this school, why it was worth saving. In order to do that, I had to go talk to the alumni and hear about their experiences, what they were doing. I worked with Tim Giago, the editor of *Indian Country Today*, in order to print an alumni profile every week. In almost every instance, the people we interviewed said that the institute was a life-changing force. Here was an institutional space for them to come to and learn about being Indian, to be proud of who they are. And once they were proud of who they were, they could do anything. Their art just flourished.

The Institute of American Indian Arts is devoted to cultivating contemporary Indian arts. Our museum, in the heart of Santa Fe, features the work of IAIA students, alumni, and others. It is interesting. Many people come to the museum with all these preconceived notions about what "real" Indian art is. And then they see our exhibitions. When they discover that these are not works created during the eighteenth or nineteenth centuries, they immediately say, "This isn't Indian art." But it *is* Indian art. It is by Indians and tells about who we are today. The stories alumni told for *Indian Country Today* made a huge difference. We conveyed the message that the institute was critically important, not only to Indian people but also to all people, because this is the art of the first peoples of this country.

I find myself comparing the experience of students at the institute with my own at the Workshop on American Indian Affairs during the 1960s. Even though their connection to Indianness is primarily through art, I see a strong correlation. We have all come to realize that the strength of our culture contributed to our survival as Native people. The institute has revolutionized American Indian education by creating a curriculum that emphasizes students' pride in their heritage—I like to think of it as a kind of "boot camp" for Indianness. Students are encouraged to create art that communicates profound ideas on a global scale. The visionary leader during the institute's early years was the late Lloyd Kiva New, a Cherokee man who was a guiding force that led to IAIA's being recognized as a flagship for creative expression.

The institute has produced nationally recognized artists who have contributed greatly to the national art scene by enriching Indian and mainstream cultures. It has created a living legacy of artistic expression built on traditional cultures, while reflecting contemporary life. Lloyd Kiva New once wrote that IAIA's real legacy, expressed by many of its graduates, lies in the sense of personal strength students have found through the arts and the reinforcement of pride and their identities as people. This is why I loved working at the institute. It reflected what I had been working on all my life, my life's work. I had spent my life fighting to have Indian teachers in the classroom and arguing why a Native-centered curriculum is important. At IAIA, these ideas were already the premises underlying the school's philosophy.

My beliefs were similar to those of Lloyd Kiva New. I am so honored that I had the pleasure of working with him, because he was very inspirational. He was a remarkable man, much like my late husband, Clyde Warrior, was remarkable. It would have been wonderful had they been able to work together. We have seen the empowerment that has come about by merging education with arts and culture. I think that it would have happened sooner if they could have collaborated at an earlier point in time. There is no doubt that Clyde was a leading force in initiating a cultural revolution that reopened deep feelings of pride in the distinctiveness of being Indian. The

Institute of American Indian Arts led the renaissance of American Indian art. It has maintained the philosophy that culture is inseparable from human expression, that art is inseparable from culture. Therefore, the arts are integral expressions of living Native American cultures. The arts have enabled Native cultures to survive the onslaught that sought to destroy them. Without the music, the stories, the dances, the beauty expressed in the material culture, the culture of Native people would have been destroyed. So it is the arts that carried forth the culture. Without that, our spirits would not have had the nourishment they needed in order to continue. I believe that our people would have given up and become assimilated.

In reflecting on my life's work, I would like to think that I have made some contributions, that I have solved more problems than I made. I get highs from my students' growth and their success, and I always feel that I am a small part in their success. I feel blessed when they thank me for my role in their education. My life's work—because what I have been doing is life's work—has been exciting, engaging, and rewarding. I have had many challenges, but I have been committed to my goal of helping to make a better life for Native people. There is no telling what I would have done had I not gone to the workshop back in the 1960s. I might have been more "successful" or at least had more money in the bank. But I may not have loved my life's work. So that is what I ask young people to think about: "What are you doing now? What are you learning in high school and college? At the end of your life's work, you need to look back and ask, what did I contribute? what did I do to help others?" To me, education is not merely a way to get a job. For me, going to school and earning a degree was also a way for me to give back to my people.

Because our old ways are continually threatened, we depend heavily on an upcoming generation of rising visionary artists, authors, and poets to help remind us of both the tragedies and glories of the past, as well as to help us maintain perspectives and the human spirit for negotiating the road ahead. Without the arts, there would be little evidence of our past, and our present and future would be very bleak indeed. The arts not only reflect the state of any culture but also define the very challenging realities of the present and future. The strength of Native cultures is directly tied in to how well the arts describe Native peoples. As our languages continue to fall dormant and young people are not geared to the values and traditions of Native people, the culture will continue to diminish, and along with that will go the arts. You cannot have the beautiful art without strong cultures and proud people.

This is exactly why the institute was founded during the 1960s and why it exists today. It provides an institutional space for Native creativity to continue. It provides support for youths as they struggle to define an identity of their own. Taking pride in Indianness is as important now as it was when I was young. They need to grapple with fundamental questions about who they are, where they come from, and where they want to go. They must come to terms with these questions in a nurturing learning environment, embraced by traditions of community and values of respect, responsibility, relevance, and reciprocity.

For our communities to survive, we must strive to build a sense of self-esteem in our youths. We must think about our tradition of education, what guided us in the past to produce people on whom we could rely. Beginning in the late nineteenth century, the federal government's boarding schools took that responsibility away from Indian families, away from parents and grandparents and the kinship networks. More recently, relocation did the same by breaking families apart and moving them into cities. People like my grandparents did not see themselves as educators, but they were, because they taught their children and their grandchildren how to live. We are still struggling with that in many of our communities. We need to look at the past in order to produce people of today whom we can rely on—people who will complete high school and earn college degrees.

We need to create environments that constantly teach young people their traditions, their histories, and their values. And youths must seek out their elders and listen to their stories about life. The arts, the cultures, and the languages are what have enabled tribal people to survive and to retain their beliefs and ways of life. The wisdom and strength of our ancestors and elders of today are profound. They have been overlooked. Some scholars are beginning to recognize that Indians have always had knowledge, they have always known about the earth, about medicines, about stars, about the environment. But the profound wisdom that Indians have always had speaks to the value we have placed on knowledge, the way we value teaching respect, sharing, reciprocity, community responsibility, spirituality, humility, and appreciation. G. K. Chesterton, an English man of letters, once wrote, "Education is simply the soul of a society as it passes from one generation to another."[5] This is precisely why we must be in control of the education of our young people. The survival of our communities and of our respective cultures depends upon it.[6]

Notes

1. The editors would like to thank linguist Jimm GoodTracks (Ioway/Otoe) for his help in ensuring the appropriate spelling of the Otoe-Missouria words.

2. Editors' Note: This chapter originated in a lecture Della Warrior delivered at Miami University in Oxford, Ohio, during the spring of 2006.

3. Editors' Note: The original Otoe and Missouria homelands encompassed present-day Nebraska. After signing several treaties to protect a portion of their aboriginal lands, they yielded to pressures by the US federal government to accept removal. In 1881 the Otoe and Missourias agreed to a new reservation in the Indian Territory and since that time have reestablished a homeland in present-day north-central Oklahoma. Today they refer to themselves as the Otoe-Missouria Tribe of Oklahoma (http://www.omtribe.org/history.htm, accessed November 16, 2006).

4. Editors' Note: During the 1950s the federal government put tremendous pressure on Indian people to assimilate (Helton and Robertson, chapter 3, this volume; table 3).

5. G. K. Chesterton wrote a column for the *Illustrated London News* between 1905 and 1935. For this quotation, see his column in the *Illustrated London News*, July 5, 1924.

6. Editors' Note: On how the retention of cultural knowledge intersects with the goal of decolonization and realizing sovereignty, see Waziyatawin Angela Wilson, *Remember This! Dakota Decolonization and the Eli Taylor Narratives*, with translations from the Dakota text by Wahpetunwin Carolynn Schommer (Lincoln: University of Nebraska Press, 2005), 1–22, 236–241; and Taiaiake Alfred, *Peace, Power, Righteousness: An Indigenous Manifesto* (New York: Oxford University Press, 1999). For a critical view, see Vine Deloria Jr., "Intellectual Self-Determination and Sovereignty: Looking at the Windmills in Our Minds," *Wicazo Sa Review* 13, no. 1 (1998): 25–31.

About the Contributors

Daryl Baldwin (Miami Tribe of Oklahoma) is director of the Myaamia Project at Miami University in Oxford, Ohio. He has worked with Miami people for more than ten years, developing language- and culture-based educational materials, including *myaamia neehi peewaalia kaloosioni mahsinaakani: A Miami-Peoria Dictionary* (with David Costa).

Jessica Cattelino is an assistant professor in the Department of Anthropology at the University of Chicago. Her book, forthcoming from Duke University Press, is *High Stakes: Seminole Tribal Gaming, Sovereignty, and the Social Meanings of Casino Money*.

D. Anthony Tyeeme Clark (Sac and Fox Tribe of the Mississippi in Iowa) is a veteran of the US Marine Corps and an assistant professor of American Indian Studies at the University of Illinois, Urbana-Champaign. His current book project is titled *Roots of Red Power: American Indian Protest and Resistance, From Wounded Knee to Chicago*.

Daniel M. Cobb is an assistant professor in the Department of History at Miami University and former assistant director of the D'Arcy McNickle Center for American Indian History in Chicago. His book, forthcoming from the University Press of Kansas, explores the politics of tribal self-determination during the 1960s.

Donald L. Fixico (Shawnee, Sac and Fox, Muscogee Creek, and Seminole) is Distinguished Foundation Professor of History at Arizona State University, Tempe. He is the author of numerous articles and several books, including most recently *The American Indian Mind in a Linear World: American Indian Studies and Traditional Knowledge* and *Daily Life of Native Americans in the Twentieth Century*.

Loretta Fowler is currently an ethnohistorical consultant at the D'Arcy McNickle Center for American Indian History and Professor Emerita at the University of Oklahoma, Norman. Her books include *Arapahoe Politics: Symbols of Crisis and Authority, 1851–1978*, *Shared Symbols, Contested Meanings: Gros Ventre Culture and History, 1778–1984*, *Tribal Sovereignty and the Historical Imagination: Cheyenne-Arapaho Politics*, and *The Columbia Guide to American Indians of the Great Plains*.

Taiawagi Helton (Cherokee) is an associate professor of law and an adjunct associate professor of Native American Studies at the University of Oklahoma. His scholarship focuses on nation-building in Indian Country.

Frederick E. Hoxie is Swanlund Professor of History at the University of Illinois, Urbana-Champaign, and former director of the Newberry Library's D'Arcy McNickle Center for American Indian History. He is the author of *A Final Promise: The Campaign to Assimilate the Indians, 1880–1920*, *Parading through History: The Making of the Crow Nation in America, 1805–1935*, and *The People: A History of Native America* (with Neal Salisbury and R. David Edmunds).

Clara Sue Kidwell (Choctaw) is currently director of the Native American Studies program at the University of Oklahoma. From 1993 to 1995 she was assistant director of cultural resources at the National Museum of the American Indian. She is the author of *Choctaws and Missionaries in Mississippi, 1818–1918* and co-author (with Alan Velie) of *Native American Studies*.

Larry Nesper is an assistant professor of anthropology and American Indian Studies at the University of Wisconsin, Madison. He is the author of *The Walleye War: The Struggle over Spearfishing and Treaty Rights* and is currently doing research on the emergence and significance of the tribal court system in Wisconsin among the Ojibwe bands.

Julie Olds (Miami Tribe of Oklahoma) is the cultural preservation officer and former secretary-treasurer of the Miami Tribe of Oklahoma. An accomplished artist, she produces works using oil, acrylic, gouache, watercolor, egg tempera, ink, pastel, and graphite from her "*alamooni* Studio" in Miami, Oklahoma. Her subject matter is inspired by her Miami heritage and cultural knowledge.

Katherine M. B. Osburn is a professor of history at Tennessee Technological University, Cookeville. She is the author of *Southern Ute Women: Autonomy and Assimilation on the Reservation, 1885–1934* and is currently working on a project that analyzes the emergence of the Mississippi Choctaw as a viable Indian nation in the biracial south.

Lindsay G. Robertson is the Orpha and Maurice Merrill Professor of Law and faculty director of the Center for the Study of American Indian Law at the University of Oklahoma. He is the author of *Conquest by Law: How the Discovery of America Dispossessed Indigenous Peoples of Their Lands*.

Sherry L. Smith is a professor of history and an associate director of the Clements Center for Southwest History at Southern Methodist University, Dallas, Texas. She is the author of *Reimagining Indians: Native Americans through Anglo Eyes, 1880–1940*. Her current book project is titled *Discovering the Nations Within: Indians, the Counterculture, and Progressive Reformers, 1960–1975*.

Circe Sturm is an associate professor of anthropology and Native American Studies at the University of Oklahoma and the author of *Blood Politics: Race, Culture, and Identity in the Cherokee Nation of Oklahoma*. Her work examines the complex histories and understandings of race, culture, blood, and indigeneity at work in Native North America.

Helen Hornbeck Tanner is a senior research fellow at the Newberry Library, Chicago. Along with part-time teaching, she began research for federal Indian Claims Commission litigation in 1962, becoming probably the first professional historian to join anthropologists in presenting evidence in these cases. She has been associated with the Newberry Library since 1976 and is the author of *The Atlas of Great Lakes Indian History*.

John Troutman is currently an assistant professor of history at the University of Louisiana, Lafayette. He was assistant director of the D'Arcy McNickle Center for American Indian History in Chicago and a Mellon postdoctoral fellow at Wesleyan University, Middletown, Connecticut. His current book project is tentatively titled *"Indian Blues": American Indians and the Politics of Music, 1890–1935*.

Della C. Warrior (Otoe-Missouria) brought more than thirty years of professional experience in administration and development to her role of president of the Institute of American Indian Arts (IAIA) in Santa Fe, New Mexico, a position from which she retired effective January 2006. The first and only woman elected as chairperson and to serve as chief executive officer of the Otoe-Missouria Tribe, she has extensive experience in education within Native American communities. In 2007 she was inducted into the Oklahoma Women's Hall of Fame.

References

Adams, David Wallace
1995   Education for Extinction: American Indians and the Boarding School
        Experience, 1875–1928. Lawrence: University Press of Kansas.
2001   More Than a Game: The Carlisle Indians Take to the Gridiron. Western
        Historical Quarterly 32(1):25–53.

Alfred, Taiaiake
1999   Peace, Power, Righteousness: An Indigenous Manifesto. New York: Oxford
        University Press.

Ambler, Marjane
1990   Breaking the Iron Bonds: Indian Control of Energy Development. Lawrence:
        University Press of Kansas.

American Friends Service Committee
1970   Uncommon Controversy: Fishing Rights of the Muckleshoot, Puyallup, and
        Nisqually Indians. Seattle: University of Washington Press.

American Indian Chicago Conference
1961   Declaration of Indian Purpose: The Voice of the American Indian. Chicago:
        University of Chicago Press.

Andrews, Thomas G.
2002   Turning the Tables on Assimilation: Oglala Lakotas and the Pine Ridge Day
        Schools, 1889–1920s. Western Historical Quarterly 33(4):407–430.

Atkinson, J. Maxwell, and Paul Drew
1979   Order in Court: The Organization of Verbal Interaction in Judicial Settings.
        Atlantic Highlands, NJ: Humanities Press.

Axtell, James
1992   Colonial Encounters: Beyond 1992. William and Mary Quarterly, 3rd series,
        49(2):335–360.

Bad Heart Bull, Amos
1967   A Pictographic History of the Oglala Sioux. Text by Helen H. Blish. Lincoln:
        University of Nebraska Press.

Baldwin, Daryl, and David Costa
2005 *myaamia neehi peewaalia kaloosioni mahsinaakani:* A Miami-Peoria Dictionary. Oxford, OH: Myaamia Project at Miami University.

Ball, Milner S.
1975 The Play's the Thing: An Unscientific Reflection on Courts under the Rubric of Theater. Stanford Law Review 28(1):81–115.
1987 Constitution, Court, Indian Tribes. American Bar Foundation Research Journal 135(1):1–140.

Banks, Dennis, with Richard Erdoes
2004 Ojibwe Warrior: Dennis Banks and the Rise of the American Indian Movement. Norman: University of Oklahoma Press.

Baringer, Sandra K.
1997 Indian Activism and the American Indian Movement: A Bibliographical Essay. American Indian Culture and Research Journal 21(4):217–250.

Barnouw, Victor
1950 Acculturation and Personality among the Wisconsin Chippewa. American Anthropological Association Memoir no. 72. Menasha, WI: American Anthropological Association.

Barsh, Russell Lawrence
1999 Putting the Tribe in Tribal Courts: Possible? Desirable? Kansas Journal of Law and Public Policy 8(2):74–96.

Barsh, Russell Lawrence, and James Youngblood Henderson
1979 The Betrayal: *Oliphant v. Suquamish Indian Tribe* and the Hunting of the Snark. Minnesota Law Review 63(4):609–640.
1980 The Road: Indian Tribes and Political Liberty. Berkeley: University of California.

Barthes, Roland
1972 Mythologies. New York: Noonday Press.

Basso, Keith H.
1996 Wisdom Sits in Places: Landscape and Language among the Western Apache. Albuquerque: University of New Mexico Press.

Bauman, Robert Alan
1998 Race, Class, and Political Power: The Implementation of the War on Poverty in Los Angeles. Ph.D. dissertation, University of California, Santa Barbara.

Bays, Brad A.
2002 Tribal-State Tobacco Compacts and Motor Fuel Contracts in Oklahoma. *In* The Tribes and the States: Geographies of Intergovernmental Interaction. Brad A. Bays and Erin Hogan Fouberg, eds. Pp. 181–209. Lanham, MD: Rowman and Littlefield.

Bays, Brad A., and Erin Hogan Fouberg, eds.
2002 The Tribes and the States: Geographies of Intergovernmental Interaction. Lanham, MD: Rowman and Littlefield.

Beck, David
2002   Developing a Voice: The Evolution of Self-Determination in an Urban Indian Community. Wicazo Sa Review 17(2):117–141.

Beck, Susan Abrams
1987   The Limits of Presidential Activism: Lyndon Johnson and the Implementation of the Community Action Program. Presidential Studies Quarterly 27(3):541–557.

Bee, Robert L.
1969   Tribal Leadership in the War on Poverty: A Case Study. Social Science Quarterly 50(3):676–686.

Belvin, Harry J. W.
N.d.   Choctaw Tribal Structure and Achievement, August 18, 1948, to August 25, 1975. Durant: Choctaw Bilingual Education Program, Southeastern Oklahoma State University.

Benedict, Jeff
2000   Without Reservation: The Making of America's Most Powerful Indian Tribe and Foxwoods, the World's Largest Casino. New York: Harper Collins.

Berkhofer, Robert F.
1971   The Political Context of a New Indian History. Pacific Historical Review 40(3):357–382.

Bernstein, Alison
1991   American Indians and World War II: Toward a New Era in Indian Affairs. Norman: University of Oklahoma Press.

Biolsi, Thomas
1992   Organizing the Lakota: The Political Economy of the New Deal on the Pine Ridge and Rosebud Reservations. Tucson: University of Arizona Press.
2001   "Deadliest Enemies": Law and the Making of Race Relations on and off Rosebud Reservation. Berkeley: University of California Press.
2004   Political and Legal Status ("Lower 48" States). In A Companion to the Anthropology of American Indians. Thomas Biolsi, ed. Pp. 231–247. Blackwell Companions to Anthropology. Malden, MA: Blackwell Publishing.
2005   Imagined Geographies: Sovereignty, Indigenous Space, and American Indian Struggle. American Ethnologist 32(2):239–259.

Biolsi, Thomas, ed.
2004   A Companion to the Anthropology of American Indians. Blackwell Companions to Anthropology. Malden, MA: Blackwell Publishing.

Blu, Karen I.
2001   The Lumbee Problem: The Making of an American Indian People. With a
[1980]   new preface by the author. Lincoln: University of Nebraska Press.

Boas, Franz
1967   "The Potlatch." In Indians of the North Pacific Coast. Tom McFeat, ed. Pp.
[1895]   72–80. Seattle: University of Washington Press.

Bodinger de Uriarte, John J.
2003   Imaging the Nation with House Odds: Representing American Indian Identity at Mashantuckett. Ethnohistory 50(3):549–565.

Boxberger, Daniel L.
2000   To Fish in Common: The Ethnohistory of Lummi Indian Salmon Fishing. With a new afterword by the author. Seattle: University of Washington Press. First published 1989 by University of Nebraska Press.

Bradford, William
2004   "Another Such Victory and We Are Undone": A Call to an American Indian Declaration of Independence. Tulsa Law Review 40(1):71–136.

Brand, Stewart
1988   Indians and the Counterculture, 1960s–1970s. In The Handbook of North American Indians, vol. 4: History of Indian–White Relations. Wilcomb E. Washburn, ed. Pp. 570–572. Washington DC: Smithsonian Institution Press.

Brando, Marlon, with Robert Lindsey
1994   Brando: Songs My Mother Taught Me. New York: Random House.

Braroe, Niels Winther
1975   Indian and White: Self-Image and Interaction in a Canadian Plains Community. Stanford, CA: Stanford University Press.

Braunstein, Peter, and Michael William Doyle, eds.
2002   Imagine Nation: The American Counterculture of the 1960s and 70s. New York and London: Routledge.

Brewton, Barry
1963   Almost White: A Study of Certain Racial Hybrids in the Eastern United States. New York: Macmillan.

Brightman, Robert Alain
1993   Grateful Prey: Rock Cree Human–Animal Relationships. Berkeley: University of California Press.

Britten, Thomas A.
1997   American Indians in World War I: At Home and at War. Albuquerque: University of New Mexico Press.

Brooks, Elbridge S.
1887   The Story of the American Indian: His Origin, Development, Decline and Destiny. Boston: Lothrop.

Brown, Dee
1970–   Bury My Heart at Wounded Knee: An Indian History of the American West.
1971   New York: Holt, Rinehart, and Winston.

Browner, Tara
2002   Heartbeat of the People: Music and Dance of the Northern Pow-wow. Urbana: University of Illinois Press.

Burt, Larry
1982   Tribalism in Crisis: Federal Indian Policy, 1953–1961. Albuquerque: University of New Mexico Press.

Cahn, Edgar, ed.
1969   Our Brother's Keeper: The Indian in White America. New York: A New Community Press Book.

Campisi, Jack
1991   The Mashpee Indians: Tribe on Trial. Syracuse, NY: Syracuse University Press.

Castile, George Pierre
1998   To Show Heart: Native American Self-Determination and Federal Indian Policy, 1960–1975. Tucson: University of Arizona Press.

Cattelino, Jessica
2006   Florida Seminole Housing and the Social Meanings of Sovereignty. Comparative Studies in Society and History 48(3):699–726.

Chase, Hiram
1897   O Mu Hu W B GRa Za: The Chase System of Reading and Recording the Omaha and Other Indian Languages. Pender, NE: Republic Press.

Chase, Robert T.
1998   Class Resurrection: The Poor People's Campaign of 1968 and Resurrection City. Essays in History 40. Electronic document, http://etext.lib.virginia.edu/journals/EH/EH40/chase40html, accessed February 11, 2003.

Claiborne, Colonel John F. H.
1964   Mississippi as a Province, Territory, and State, vol. 1. Pp. 512–513. Baton Rouge: Louisiana State University Press. First published 1880 by Power and Barksdale, Publishers and Printers.

Clark, C. Blue
1994   Lone Wolf v. Hitchcock: Treaty Rights and Indian Law at the End of the Nineteenth Century. Lincoln: University of Nebraska Press.

Clark, D. Anthony Tyeeme
2004   Representing Indians: Indigenous Fugitives and the Society of American Indians in the Making of Common Culture. Ph.D. dissertation, University of Kansas.

Clarkin, Thomas
2000   Federal Indian Policy in the Kennedy and Johnson Administrations, 1961–1969. Albuquerque: University of New Mexico Press.

Clemmer, Richard O.
1995   Roads in the Sky: The Hopi Indians in a Century of Change. Boulder, CO: Westview.

Clifford, James
1996 Routes: Travel and Translation in the Late Twentieth Century. Cambridge, MA: Harvard University Press.

Clinton, Robert N.
2002 There Is No Federal Supremacy Clause for Indian Tribes. Arizona State Law Journal 34 (Spring):113–260.

Cobb, Daniel M.
1998 Philosophy of an Indian War: Indian Community Action in the Johnson Administration's War on Indian Poverty, 1964–1968. American Indian Culture and Research Journal 22(2):71–103.
2002 "Us Indians understand the basics": Oklahoma Indians and the Politics of Community Action, 1964–1970. Western Historical Quarterly XXXIII(1):41–66.
2006 Indian Politics in Cold War America: Parallel and Contradiction. Princeton University Library Chronicle LXVII(2):392–419.
2007 Devils in Disguise: The Carnegie Project, the Cherokee Nation, & the 1960s. American Indian Quarterly 31(3): 201-237.

Cobb, James C., and Michael Namorato, eds.
1984 The New Deal and the South. Jackson: University Press of Mississippi.

Cohen, Fay G.
1986 Treaties on Trial: The Continuing Controversy over Northwest Indian Fishing Rights. Seattle: University of Washington Press.

Cohen, Ronald, and Elman Service, eds.
1978 Origins of the State: The Anthropology of Political Evolution. Philadelphia: Institute for the Study of Human Issues.

Coker, William Sidney
1965 Pat Harrison's Efforts to Reopen the Choctaw Citizenship Rolls. Southern Quarterly 3 (October):36–61.

Cole, Terrence
1992 Jim Crow in Alaska: The Passage of the Alaska Equal Rights Act of 1945. Western Historical Quarterly 23(4):429–449.

Collins, James
2004 Language. In A Companion to the Anthropology of American Indians. Thomas Biolsi, ed. Pp. 490–525. Blackwell Companions to Anthropology. Malden, MA: Blackwell Publishing.

Cornell, Stephen
1988 The Return of the Native: American Indian Political Resurgence. New York: Oxford University Press.

Cowger, Thomas W.
1999 The National Congress of American Indians: The Founding Years. Lincoln: University of Nebraska Press.

Cramer, Renée Ann

2005   Cash, Color, and Colonialism: The Politics of Tribal Acknowledgment. Norman: University of Oklahoma Press.

Crawford, James

1998   Endangered Native American Languages: What Is to Be Done, and Why? *In* Language and Politics in the United States and Canada: Myths and Realities. Thomas K. Ricento and Barbara Burnaby, eds. Pp. 151–170. Mahwah, NJ: Lawrence Erlbaum Associates.

Crum, Steven

2006   Almost Invisible: The Brotherhood of North American Indians (1911) and the League of North American Indians (1935). Wicazo Sa Review 21 (Spring):43–59.

Daniel, Pete

1990   Federal Farm Policy and the End of an Agrarian Way of Life. *In* Major Problems in the History of the American South, vol. 2: The New South. Paul D. Escott and David R. Goldfield, eds. Pp. 397–406. Lexington, MA: D. C. Heath and Company.

D'Arcy McNickle Center for the History of the American Indian

1989   The Struggle for Political Autonomy: Papers and Comments from the Second Newberry Library Conference on Themes in American Indian History. Occasional Papers in Curriculum, 11. Chicago: The Newberry Library.

Darian-Smith, Eve

2003   New Capitalists: Law, Politics, and Identity Surrounding Casino Gaming on Native American Land. Belmont, CA: Thomson/Wadsworth Learning.

Debo, Angie

1951   The Five Civilized Tribes of Oklahoma: Report on Social and Economic Conditions. Philadelphia: Indian Rights Association.

1961   The Rise and Fall of the Choctaw Republic. 2nd edition. Norman: University of Oklahoma Press.

1968   And Still the Waters Run: The Betrayal of the Five Civilized Tribes. Princeton,
[1940]   NJ: Princeton University Press.

1970   A History of the Indians of the United States. Norman: University of Oklahoma Press.

Deloria, Philip J.

1998   Playing Indian. New Haven, CT: Yale University Press.

2004   Indians in Unexpected Places. Lawrence: University Press of Kansas.

Deloria, Philip J., and Neal Salisbury, eds.

2002   A Companion to American Indian History. Blackwell Companions to American History. Malden, MA: Blackwell Publishing.

Deloria, Vine, Jr.

1988   Custer Died for Your Sins: An Indian Manifesto. New York:
[1970,   Macmillan; reprs., New York: Avon Books; Norman: University of Oklahoma
1969]   Press.

1998   Intellectual Self-Determination and Sovereignty: Looking at the Windmills in Our Minds. Wicazo Sa Review 13(1):25–31.

2000   Singing for a Spirit: A Portrait of the Dakota Sioux. Santa Fe, NM: Clear Light Publishers.

Deloria, Vine, Jr., ed.

2002   The Indian Reorganization Act: Congresses and Bills. Norman: University of Oklahoma Press.

Deloria, Vine, Jr., and Clifford M. Lytle

1983   American Indians, American Justice. Austin: University of Texas Press.

1984   The Nations Within: The Past and Future of American Indian Sovereignty. New York: Pantheon Books.

Deloria, Vine, Sr.

1987   The Establishment of Christianity among the Sioux. In Sioux Indian Religion: Tradition and Innovation. Raymond J. DeMallie and Douglas R. Parks, eds. Pp. 91–111. Norman: University of Oklahoma Press.

Denson, Andrew

2004   Demanding the Cherokee State: Indian Autonomy and American Culture, 1830–1900. Lincoln: University of Nebraska Press.

Diamond, Stanley

1974   In Search of the Primitive: A Critique of Civilization. New Brunswick, NJ: Transaction Books.

Dombrowski, Kirk

2001   Against Culture: Development, Politics, and Religion in Indian Alaska. Lincoln: University of Nebraska Press.

Drinnon, Richard

1987   Keeper of Concentration Camps: Dillon S. Myer and American Racism. Berkeley: University of California Press.

Driving Hawk Sneve, Virginia

1977   That They May Have Life: The Episcopal Church in South Dakota, 1859–1976. New York: Seabury Press.

Du Bois, William E. B.

1903   The Talented Tenth. In The Negro Problem: A Series of Articles by Representative Negroes of Today. Pp. 33–75. New York: James Pott and Company.

1948   The Talented Tenth Memorial Address. Boulé Journal 15 (October):3–13.

Duthu, N. Bruce

1994   Implicit Divestiture of Tribal Powers: Locating Legitimate Sources of Authority on Indian Country. American Indian Law Review 19(2):353–402.

Eastman, Charles A.

1915   The Indian To-Day: The Past and Future of the First American. Garden City, NY: Doubleday, Page and Company.

Ellis, Clyde
1999   "We Don't Want Your Rations, We Want This Dance": The Changing Use of Song and Dance on the Southern Plains. Western Historical Quarterly 30(2):133–154.

Ellis, Clyde, Luke Lassiter, and Gary Dunham, eds.
2002   Powwow: Native American Performance, Identity, and Meaning. Lincoln: University of Nebraska Press.

Ellis, George E.
1882   The Red Man and the White Man in North America, from Its Discovery to the Present. Boston: Little Brown.

Erikson, Patricia Pierce, with Helma Ward and Kirk Wachendorf
2002   Voices of a Thousand People: The Makah Cultural and Research Center. Lincoln: University of Nebraska Press.

Ferguson, R. Brian, and Neil L. Whitehead
1992   War in the Tribal Zone: Expanding States and Indigenous Warfare. Santa Fe, NM: School of American Research, SAR Press.

Fey, Harold E., and D'Arcy McNickle
1959   Indians and Other Americans: Two Ways of Life Meet. New York: Harper and Brothers.

Fixico, Donald L.
1986   Termination and Relocation: Federal Indian Policy, 1945–1960. Albuquerque: University of New Mexico Press.
1998   The Invasion of Indian Country in the Twentieth Century: American Capitalism and Tribal Natural Resources. Niwot: University Press of Colorado.
2000   The Urban Indian Experience in America. Albuquerque: University of New Mexico Press.
2003   The American Indian Mind in a Linear World: American Indian Studies and Traditional Knowledge. New York: Routledge.
2004   Federal and State Policies and American Indians. In A Companion to American Indian History. Blackwell Companions to American History. Philip J. Deloria and Neal Salisbury, eds. Pp. 379–396. Malden, MA: Blackwell Publishing.

Fixico, Donald L., ed.
1997   Rethinking American Indian History. Albuquerque: University of New Mexico Press.

Fortunate Eagle, Adam
2002   Heart of the Rock: The Indian Invasion of Alcatraz. Norman: University of Oklahoma Press.

Fowler, Loretta
1982   Arapahoe Politics: Symbols of Crisis and Authority, 1851–1978. Lincoln: University of Nebraska Press.

1987   Shared Symbols, Contested Meanings: Gros Ventre Culture and History, 1778–1984. New York: Cornell University Press.
2002   Tribal Sovereignty and the Historical Imagination: Cheyenne-Arapaho Politics. Lincoln and London: University of Nebraska Press.
2004   Politics. In A Companion to the Anthropology of American Indians. Thomas Biolsi, ed. Pp. 69–94. Blackwell Companions to Anthropology. Malden, MA: Blackwell Publishing.

Frickey, Philip P.
1990   Congressional Intent, Practical Reasoning, and the Dynamic Nature of Federal Indian Law. California Law Review 78(5):1137–1242.
1997   Adjudication and Its Discontents: Coherence and Conciliation in Federal Indian Law. Harvard Law Review 110(8):1754–1784.

Fried, Morton H.
1967   The Evolution of Political Society: An Essay in Political Anthropology. New York: Random House.

Friedman, Moses
1910   Indians Who Have "Made Good": Charles E. Dagenett, National Supervisor of Indian Employment. Red Man 2(8):39–45.

Gaddis, John Lewis
1997   We Now Know: Rethinking Cold War History. New York: Oxford University Press.

Galanter, Marc
1981   Justice in Many Rooms: Courts, Private Ordering, and Indigenous Law. Journal of Legal Pluralism 19:1–47.
1983   The Radiating Effects of Courts. In Empirical Theories about Courts. Keith O. Boyum and Lynn Mather, eds. Pp. 117–142. New York and London: Longman.

Garroutte, Eva Marie
2003   Real Indians: Identity and the Survival of Native America. Berkeley: University of California Press.

Geertz, Clifford
1983   Local Knowledge: Further Essays in Interpretive Anthropology. New York: Basic Books.

Getches, David H.
1996   Conquering the Cultural Frontier: The New Subjectivism of the Supreme Court in Indian Law. California Law Review 84(6):1573–1656.
2001   Beyond Indian Law: The Rehnquist Court's Pursuit of States' Rights, Color-Blind Justice and Mainstream Values. Minnesota Law Review 86(2):267–362.

Getches, David H., Charles F. Wilkinson, and Robert A. Williams, eds.
2005   Cases and Materials on Federal Indian Law. 5th edition. St. Paul, MN: West Publishing Co.

Gibbon, Guy
2003   The Sioux: The Dakota and Lakota Nations. Malden, MA: Blackwell Publishing.

Gillette, Michael L., ed.
1996   Launching the War on Poverty: An Oral History. New York: Twayne Publishers.

Godelier, Maurice
1999   The Enigma of the Gift. Chicago: University of Chicago Press.

Goldberg, Carole E.
1975   Public Law 280: The Limits of State Jurisdiction over Reservation Indians. UCLA Law Review 22(3):535–594.

Gonzales, Angela
1998   The (Re)articulation of American Indian Identity: Maintaining Boundaries and Regulating Access to Ethnically Tied Resources. American Indian Culture and Research Journal 22(4):199–225.

Green, Adriana Greci
2001   Performances and Celebrations: Displaying Lakota Identity, 1880–1915. Ph.D. dissertation, The State University of New Jersey.

Green, Elna, ed.
2003   The New Deal and Beyond: Social Welfare in the South since 1930. Athens: University of Georgia Press.

Greenbaum, Susan
1991   What Is a Label? Identity Problems of Southern Indian Tribes. Journal of Ethnic Studies 19 (Summer):107–126.

Greenwald, Emily
2002   Reconfiguring the Reservation: The Nez Perces, Jicarilla Apaches, and the Dawes Act. Albuquerque: University of New Mexico Press.

Gregory, Dick
1976   Up from Nigger. New York: Stein and Day.

Grobel, Lawrence
1991   Conversations with Brando. New York: Hyperion.

Hafen, P. Jane
2001   Gertrude Simmons Bonnin: For the Indian Cause. In Sifters: Native American Women's Lives. Theda Perdue, ed. Pp. 127–140. New York: Oxford University Press.

Hagan, William T.
1993   Quanah Parker, Comanche Chief. Norman: University of Oklahoma Press.

Hansen, Thomas Blom, and Finn Stepputat
2001   States of Imagination: Ethnographic Explorations of the Postcolonial State. Durham, NC: Duke University Press.

Hanson, Randel D.

2004   Contemporary Globalization and Tribal Sovereignty. *In* A Companion to the Anthropology of American Indians. Thomas Biolsi, ed. Pp. 284–303. Blackwell Companions to Anthropology. Malden, MA: Blackwell Publishing.

Harmon, Alexandra

1998   Indians in the Making: Ethnic Relations and Indian Identities around Puget Sound. Berkeley: University of California Press.

2003   American Indians and Land Monopolies in the Gilded Age. Journal of American History 90(1):106–133.

Hastain, E.

1908   Index to Choctaw-Chickasaw Deeds and Allottments. Muskogee, OK:
–1910   E. Hastain.

Hauptman, Lawrence

1981   The Iroquois and the New Deal. Syracuse, NY: Syracuse University Press.

1986   The Iroquois Struggle for Survival: World War II to Red Power. Syracuse, NY: Syracuse University Press.

Haynes, Joshua S.

2001   Power of the Blood: Identity Construction and the Cherokee Tribe of Eastern North Carolina. Master's thesis, University of Mississippi.

Herring, Helen Baldwin

1943   History of Lincoln County. Master's thesis, University of Oklahoma.

Hertzberg, Hazel

1971   The Search for an American Indian Identity: Modern Pan-Indian Movements. Syracuse, NY: Syracuse University Press.

Heth, Charlotte, ed.

1992   Native American Dance: Ceremonies and Social Traditions. Washington DC: National Museum of the American Indian, Smithsonian Institution, with Starwood Publishing, Inc.

Hightower-Langston, Donna

2003   American Indian Women's Activism in the 1960s and 1970s. Hypatia 18(2):114–132.

Hinton, Leanne, and Ken Hale, eds.

2001   The Green Book of Language Revitalization in Practice. San Diego: Academic Press.

Hoikkala, Päivi

1995   Mothers and Community Builders: Salt River Pima and Maricopa Women in Community Action. *In* Negotiators of Change: Historical Perspectives on Native American Women. Nancy Shoemaker, ed. Pp. 213–234. New York: Routledge.

Holler, Clyde
1995   Black Elk's Religion: The Sun Dance and Lakota Catholicism. Syracuse, NY: Syracuse University Press.

Holm, Tom
1996   Strong Hearts, Wounded Souls: Native American Veterans of the Vietnam War. Austin: University of Texas Press.
2005   The Great Confusion in Indian Affairs: Native Americans and Whites in the Progressive Era. Austin: University of Texas Press.

Holm, Tom, Diane Pearson, and Ben Chavez
2003   Peoplehood: A Model for the Extension of Sovereignty in American Indian Studies. Wicazo Sa Review 18(1):7–24.

Hoover, Herbert T., and Carol Goss Hoover
2000   Sioux Country: A History of Indian–White Relations. Sioux Falls, SD: Center for Western Studies, Augustana College.

Hosmer, Brian C.
1999   American Indians in the Marketplace: Persistence and Innovation among the Menominees and Metlakatlans, 1870–1920. Lawrence: University Press of Kansas.
2004   "Dollar a Day and Glad to Have It": Work Relief on the Wind River Reservation as Memory. *In* Native Pathways: American Indian Culture and Economic Development in the Twentieth Century. Brian A. Hosmer and Colleen O'Neill, eds. Pp. 283–307. Boulder: University of Colorado Press.

Houghton, Louise Seymour
1918   Our Debt to the Red Man: The French-Indians in the Development of the United States. Boston: Stratford Company.

Hoxie, Frederick E.
1992   Exploring a Cultural Borderland: Native American Journeys of Discovery in the Early Twentieth Century. Journal of American History 79(3):969–995.
1995   Parading through History: The Making of the Crow Nation in America, 1805–1935. New York: Cambridge University Press.
2001   A Final Promise: The Campaign to Assimilate the Indians, 1880–1920.
[1984] Cambridge: Cambridge University Press; Lincoln: University of Nebraska Press.
2001   "Thinking like an Indian": Exploring American Indian Views of American History. Reviews in American History 29(1):1–14.

Hoxie, Frederick E., ed.
2001   Talking Back to Civilization: Indian Voices from the Progressive Era. Boston: Bedford/St. Martin's.

Iverson, Peter
1983   The Navajo Nation. Albuquerque: University of New Mexico Press.
1985   Building toward Self-Determination: Plains and Southwestern Indians in the 1940s and 1950s. Western Historical Quarterly 16(2):163–173.

1994   When Indians Became Cowboys: Native Peoples and Cattle Ranching in the American West. Norman: University of Oklahoma Press.
2001   Carlos Montezuma and the Changing World of American Indians.
[1982] Albuquerque: University of New Mexico Press.
2002   "For Our Navajo People": Diné Letters, Speeches and Petitions, 1900–1960. Albuquerque: University of New Mexico Press.
2002   Diné: A History of the Navajos. Albuquerque: University of New Mexico Press.

James, Harry C.
1974   Pages from Hopi History. Tucson: University of Arizona Press.

Janda, Sarah Eppler
2007   Beloved Women: The Political Lives of LaDonna Harris and Wilma Mankiller. DeKalb: Northern Illinois University Press.

Joh, Elizabeth
2000   Custom, Tribal Court Practice, and Popular Justice. American Indian Law Review 25(1):117–132.

Johnson, Lyndon B.
1970   The Public Papers of the Presidents of the United States: Lyndon B. Johnson, Containing the Public Messages, Speeches, and Statements of the President, 1968-1969, book 1. Washington DC: GPO.

Johnson, Troy
1997   The Occupation of Alcatraz Island: Indian Self-Determination and the Rise of Indian Activism. Urbana: University of Illinois Press.

Johnson, Troy, ed.
1999   Contemporary Native American Political Issues. Walnut Creek, CA: Alta Mira.

Johnson, Troy, Joane Nagel, and Duane Champagne, eds.
1997   American Indian Activism: Alcatraz to the Longest Walk. Urbana: University of Illinois Press.

Jorgensen, Joseph G.
1990   Oil Age Eskimos. Berkeley: University of California Press.

Josephy, Alvin, Jr.
1961   The Patriot Chiefs: A Chronicle of American Indian Leadership. New York: Viking.

Josephy, Alvin, Jr., ed.
1971   Red Power: The American Indians' Fight for Freedom. New York: American Heritage Press.

Kappler, Charles J., ed.
1904   Indian Affairs: Laws and Treaties. Washington DC: Government Printing
[1892] Office (GPO).

Kauffman, L. Jeanne
2001   State Recognition of American Indian Tribes. Denver: National Conference of State Legislatures.

Kavanagh, Thomas W.
1992   Southern Plains Dance: Tradition and Dynamism. *In* Native American Dance: Ceremonies and Social Traditions. Charlotte Heth, ed. Pp. 105–123. Washington DC: National Museum of the American Indian, Smithsonian Institution, with Starwood Publishing, Inc.

Kelly, Lawrence C.
1968   The Navajo Indians and Federal Indian Policy, 1900–1935. Tucson: University of Arizona Press.

Kersey, Harry A., Jr.
1975   Pelts, Plumes, and Hides: White Traders among the Seminole Indians, 1870–1930. Gainesville: University Presses of Florida.
2001   The Havana Connection: Buffalo Tiger, Fidel Castro, and the Origin of Miccosukee Tribal Sovereignty, 1959–1962. American Indian Quarterly 25(4):491–507.

Kesey, Ken
1995   One Flew over the Cuckoo's Nest. New York: Signet.
[1962]

Kesey's Garage Sale
1973   Introduction by Arthur Miller. New York: Viking Press and Intrepid Trips.

Kickingbird, Kirke, and Karen Ducheneaux
1973   One Hundred Million Acres. New York: Macmillan Books.

Kidwell, Clara Sue
1995   Choctaws and Missionaries in Mississippi, 1818–1918. Norman: University of Oklahoma Press.
1995   Choctaw Women and Cultural Persistence in Mississippi. *In* Negotiators of Change: Historical Perspectives on Native American Women. Nancy Shoemaker, ed. Pp. 115–134. New York: Routledge, Inc.

Kidwell, Clara Sue, and Alan Velie
2005   Native American Studies. Lincoln: University of Nebraska Press.

Kotlowski, Dean J.
2003   Alcatraz, Wounded Knee, and Beyond: The Nixon and Ford Administrations Respond to Native American Protest. Pacific Historical Review 72(2):201–227.

LaGrand, James
2002   Indian Metropolis: Native Americans in Chicago. Urbana: University of Illinois Press.

Lassiter, Luke, Clyde Ellis, and Ralph Kotay
2002   The Jesus Road: Kiowas, Christianity, and Indian Hymns. Lincoln: University of Nebraska Press.

Latham, Michael
2000   Modernization as Ideology: American Social Science and "Nation Building" in the Kennedy Era. Chapel Hill: University of North Carolina Press.

Lawson, Michael
1982   Dammed Indians: The Pick-Sloan Plan and the Missouri River Sioux, 1944–1980. Norman: University of Oklahoma Press.

Lazarus, Edward
1991   Black Hills/White Justice: The Sioux Nation versus the United States, 1775 to the Present. New York: Harper Collins.

Leap, William
1993   American Indian English. Salt Lake City: University of Utah Press.

Legters, Lyman H., and Fremont J. Lyden, eds.
1994   American Indian Policy: Self-Governance and Economic Development. Westport, CT: Greenwood.

Lewis, David Rich
1991   Reservation Leadership and the Progressive–Traditional Dichotomy: William Wash and the Northern Utes. Ethnohistory 38(2):124–148.

Liberty, Margot, ed.
1978   American Indian Intellectuals of the Nineteenth and Early Twentieth Centuries. Norman: University of Oklahoma Press.

Lieder, Michael, and Jake Page
1999   Wild Justice: The People of Geronimo v. The United States. Norman: University of Oklahoma Press.

Light, Stephen, and Kathryn Rand
2005   Indian Gaming and Tribal Sovereignty: The Casino Compromise. Lawrence: University Press of Kansas.

Lippard, Lucy
2003   Esthetic Sovereignty, or, Going Places with Cultural Baggage. In Path Breakers: The Eiteljorg Fellowship for Native American Fine Art. Pp. 1–10. Seattle: University of Washington Press.

Lips, Julian
1947   Naskapi Law: Law and Order in a Hunting Society. Transactions of the American Philosophical Society 37(4):379–442.

Lomawaima, K. Tsianina
1994   They Called It Prairie Light: The Story of the Chilocco Indian School. Lincoln: University of Nebraska Press.

Lopach, James J., Margery Hunter Brown, and Richmond L. Clow
1998   Tribal Government Today: Politics in Montana. Boulder: University Press of Colorado.

Lurie, Nancy Oestreich
1961   The Voice of the American Indian: Report on the American Indian Chicago Conference. Current Anthropology 2(5):478–500.
1978   The Indian Claims Commission. Annals of the American Academy of Political and Social Science 436 (March):97–110.
1999   Sol Tax and Tribal Sovereignty. Human Organization 58(1):108–117.

Macleod, William Christie
1928   The American Indian Frontier. London: Kagan Paul, Trench, Tribner and Co.

Maddox, Lucy
2005   Citizen Indians: Native American Intellectuals, Race, and Reform. Ithaca, NY: Cornell University Press.

Magliocca, Gerard N.
2003   The Cherokee Removal and the Fourteenth Amendment. Duke Law Journal 53(3):875–966.

Maine, Henry Sumner
2002   Ancient Law. New Brunswick, NJ: Transaction Publishers.

Martin, Calvin, ed.
1987   The American Indian and the Problem of History. Oxford: Oxford University Press.

Mason, W. Dale
2000   Indian Gaming: Tribal Sovereignty and American Politics. Norman: University of Oklahoma Press.

Mauss, Marcel
1990   The Gift: The Form and Reason for Exchange in Archaic Societies. New York
[1950] and London: Norton.

Maxfield, Peter C.
1993   *Oliphant v. Suquamish*: The Whole Is Greater Than the Sum of Its Parts. Journal of Contemporary Law 19(2):391–441.

McDonnell, Janet
1991   The Dispossession of the American Indian, 1887–1934. Bloomington: University of Indiana Press.

McLaughlin, Daniel
1992   When Literacy Empowers: Navajo Language in Print. Albuquerque: University of New Mexico Press.

McNickle, D'Arcy
1975   They Came Here First: The Epic of the American Indian. Philadelphia:
[1949] J. P. Lippincott; repr., New York: Harper and Row.

1993   Native American Tribalism: Indian Survivals and Renewals. New York: Oxford
[1973] University Press.

McSloy, Steven Paul
1994   Revisiting the "Courts of the Conqueror": American Indian Claims against the
        United States. American University Law Review 44(2):537–644.

Meadows, William C.
1999   Kiowa, Comanche, and Apache Military Societies: Enduring Veterans, 1800 to
        the Present. Austin: University of Texas Press.

Means, Russell
1995   Where White Men Fear to Tread: The Autobiography of Russell Means. New
        York: St. Martin's.

Meisner, Kevin
1992   Comment: Modern Problems of Criminal Jurisdiction in Indian Country.
        American Indian Law Review 17(1):175–208.

Mellis, Allison Fuss
2003   Riding Buffaloes and Broncos: Rodeos and Native Traditions in the Northern
        Great Plains. Norman: University of Oklahoma Press.

Meriam, Lewis, ed.
1928   Institute for Government Research Studies in Administration: The Problem of
        Indian Administration. Baltimore, MD: Johns Hopkins University Press.

Merrell, James H.
1989   Some Thoughts on Colonial Historians and American Indians. William and
        Mary Quarterly, 3rd series, 46(1):94–119.

Merrill, Pierce Kelton
1940   The Social and Economic Status of the Choctaw Nation. Ph.D. dissertation,
        University of Oklahoma.

Merry, Sally Engle
1988   Legal Pluralism. Law and Society Review 22(5):869–901.
1990   Getting Justice and Getting Even: Legal Consciousness among Working-Class
        Americans. Chicago: University of Chicago Press.
1994   Courts as Performances: Domestic Violence Hearings in a Hawai'i Family
        Court. In Contested States: Law, Hegemony and Resistance. Mindie Lazarus-
        Black and Susan Hirsch, eds. Pp. 35–58. New York: Routledge.
2000   Colonizing Hawai'i: The Cultural Power of Law. Princeton, NJ: Princeton
        University Press.

Metcalf, R. Warren
1996   Lambs of Sacrifice: Termination, the Mixed-Blood Utes, and the Problem of
        Indian Identity. Utah Historical Quarterly 64(4):322–343.
2002   Termination's Legacy: The Discarded Indians of Utah. Lincoln: University of
        Nebraska Press.

Meyer, Melissa L.
1994 The White Earth Tragedy: Ethnicity and Dispossession at a Minnesota Anishinaabe Reservation, 1889–1920. Lincoln: University of Nebraska Press.

Mihesuah, Devon A., ed.
1998 Natives and Academics: Researching and Writing about American Indians. Lincoln: University of Nebraska Press.

Miller, Bruce G.
1992 Women and Politics: Comparative Evidence from the Northwest Coast. Ethnology 31(4):367–383.
1994 Contemporary Tribal Codes and Gender Issues. American Indian Culture and Research Journal 18(2):43–74.
2001 The Problem of Justice: Tradition and Law in the Coast Salish World. Lincoln: University of Nebraska Press.
2003 Invisible Indigenes: The Politics of Nonrecognition. Lincoln: University of Nebraska Press.

Miller, Mark Edwin
2004 Forgotten Tribes: Unrecognized Indians and the Federal Acknowledgment Process. Lincoln: University of Nebraska Press.

Momaday, N. Scott
1968 House Made of Dawn. New York: Harper and Row.

Mooney, James
1896 The Ghost Dance and the Sioux Outbreak of 1890, part 2. 14th Annual Report of the Bureau of Ethnology, 1892–1893. Washington DC: GPO.
1996 The Ghost Dance. Repr., North Dighton, MA: JG Press.
[1896]

Moorehead, Warren K.
1914 The American Indians in the United States, Period 1850–1914. Andover, MA: The Andover Press.

Nagel, Joanne
1996 American Indian Ethnic Renewal: Red Power and the Resurgence of Identity and Culture. New York: Oxford University Press.

Native American Development Corporation (NADC)
2004 Tribal Economic Contributions to Montana. N.p.

Nesper, Larry
2002 The Walleye War: The Struggle for Ojibwe Spearfishing and Treaty Rights. Lincoln and London: University of Nebraska Press.
2006 Ironies of Articulating Continuity in Difference among the Anishinabeg at Lac du Flambeau. In New Perspectives on Native North America: Cultures, Histories, and Representations. Sergei Kan and Pauline Turner Strong, eds. Pp. 98–121. Lincoln and London: University of Nebraska Press.

Newton, Nell Jessup
1992   Indian Claims in the Courts of the Conqueror. American University Law
        Review 41(3):753–854.

Nichols, Deborah
1997   Richard C. Adams: "Representing the Delaware Indians." *In* Legends of the
        Delaware Indians and Picture Writing. Deborah Nichols, ed. Pp. xv–xlv.
        Syracuse, NY: Syracuse University Press.

Niezen, Ronald
2003   The Origins of Indigenism: Human Rights and the Politics of Identity.
        Berkeley: University of California Press.

O'Brien, Greg
2002   Choctaws in a Revolutionary Age, 1750–1830. Lincoln: University of
        Nebraska Press.

O'Gara, Geoffrey
2002   What You See in Clear Water: Indians, Whites, and a Battle over Water in the
[2000] American West. 2nd edition. New York: Vintage.

Oliver, Kitty
2000   Race and Change in Hollywood, Florida. Charleston, SC: Arcadia Publishing.

O'Neill, Colleen
2005   Working the Navajo Way: Labor and Culture in the Twentieth Century.
        Lawrence: University Press of Kansas.

Parker, Dorothy R.
1992   Singing an Indian Song: A Biography of D'Arcy McNickle. Lincoln: University
        of Nebraska Press.

Parman, Donald
1976   The Navajos and the New Deal. New Haven, CT: Yale University Press.

Pasquaretta, Paul
2003   Gambling and Survival in Native North America. Tucson: University of
        Arizona Press.

Passel, Jeffrey S.
1997   The Growing American Indian Population, 1960–1990: Beyond Demography.
        Population Research and Policy Review 16(1/2):11–31.

Pavlik, Steve, ed.
1998   A Good Cherokee, A Good Anthropologist: Papers in Honor of Robert K.
        Thomas. Contemporary American Indian Issues, 8. Los Angeles: UCLA
        American Indian Studies Center.

Peroff, Nicholas
1982   Menominee DRUMS: Tribal Termination and Restoration, 1954–1974.
        Norman: University of Oklahoma Press.

Peterson, John H., Jr.
1970   The Mississippi Band of Choctaw Indians: Their Recent History and Current Relations. Ph.D. dissertation, University of Georgia.

Philips, Susan U.
1993   Evidentiary Standards for American Trials: Just the Facts. *In* Responsibility and Evidence in Oral Discourse. Jane Hill and Judith Irvine, eds. Pp. 248–259. Cambridge: Cambridge University Press.
1994   Local Legal Hegemony in the Tongan Magistrate's Court: How Sisters Fare Better Than Wives. *In* Contested States: Law, Hegemony and Resistance. Mindie Lazarus-Black and Susan Hirsch, eds. Pp. 59–88. New York: Routledge.

Philp, Kenneth R.
1977   John Collier's Crusade for Indian Reform, 1920–1954. Tucson: University of Arizona Press.
1999   Termination Revisited: American Indians on the Trail of Self-Determination, 1933–1953. Lincoln: University of Nebraska Press.

Philp, Kenneth R., ed.
1995   Indian Self-Rule: First-Hand Accounts of Indian–White Relations from Roosevelt to Reagan. Salt Lake City, UT: Howe Brothers, 1988; repr., Logan: Utah State University.

Pickering, Kathleen Ann
2000   Lakota Culture, World Economy. Lincoln: University of Nebraska Press.

Pipestem, F. Browning, and G. William Rice
1978   The Mythology of the Oklahoma Indians: A Survey of the Legal Status of Indian Tribes in Oklahoma. American Indian Law Review 6(2):259–328.

Pommersheim, Frank
1995   Braid of Feathers: American Indian Law and Contemporary Tribal Life. Berkeley: University of California Press.

Porter, Joy
2001   To Be an Indian: The Life of Iroquois-Seneca Arthur Caswell Parker. Norman: University of Oklahoma Press.

Price, A. Grenfell
1950   White Settlers and Native Peoples. Melbourne: Cambridge University Press.

Prucha, Francis Paul
1973   Americanizing the American Indians: Writings by the "Friends of the Indian." Cambridge, MA: Harvard University Press.
1984   The Great Father: The United States Government and the American Indian. 2 vols. Lincoln: University of Nebraska Press.

Quinn, William W.
1990   The Southeast Syndrome: Notes on Indian Descent Recruitment

Organizations and Their Perceptions of Native American Culture. American Indian Quarterly 14(2):147–154.

Reinhart, Christopher
2002   Effect of State Recognition on an Indian Tribe. Office of Legislative Research Report, no. 2002-R-0118, Connecticut General Assembly.

Resnick, Judith
1995   Multiple Sovereignties: Indian Tribes, States, and the Federal Government. Judicature 79(3):118–125.

Richardson, James D., ed.
1917   A Compilation of the Messages and Papers of the Presidents. 20 vols. Washington DC: Bureau of National Literature and Art.

Rogel, Amy Lyn
1990   "Mastering the Secret of White Man's Power": Indian Students at Beloit College, 1871 to 1884. Beloit, WI: Beloit College, Archives Publication Number One.

Rosenthal, Harvey
1976   Their Day in Court: A History of the Indian Claims Commission. Ph.D. dissertation, Kent State University.
1985   Indian Claims and the American Conscience: A Brief History of the Indian Claims Commission. In Irredeemable America: The Indians' Estate and Land Claims. Imre Sutton, ed. Pp. 35–86. Albuquerque: University of New Mexico.
1990   Their Day in Court: A History of the Indian Claims Commission. New York: Garland.

Rosier, Paul C.
2001   The Rebirth of the Blackfeet Nation, 1912–1954. Lincoln: University of Nebraska Press.
2006   "They Are Ancestral Homelands": Race, Place, and Politics in Cold War Native America. Journal of American History 92(4):1300–1326.

Roszak, Theodore
1995   The Making of a Counterculture. Berkeley: University of California Press.
[1969]

Royster, Judith V.
1994   Mineral Development in Indian Country: The Evolution of Tribal Control over Mineral Resources. Tulsa Law Journal 29(3–4):541–638.
1995   The Legacy of Allotment. Arizona State Law Journal 27(1):1–78.

Saito, Natsu Taylor
2002   The Plenary Power Doctrine: Subverting Human Rights in the Name of Sovereignty. Catholic University Law Review 51(4):1115–1176.

Satz, Ronald N.
1986   From the Removal Treaty Onward. In After Removal: The Choctaw in Mississippi. Samuel J. Wells and Roseanna Tubby, eds. P. 3. Jackson: University of Mississippi Press.

Savagian, John C.
1993 The Tribal Reorganization of the Stockbridge-Munsee: Essential Conditions in the Re-creation of a Native American Community, 1930–1942. Wisconsin Magazine of History 77(1):39–62.

Schorger, Arlie W.
1953 The White-Tailed Deer in Early Wisconsin. Transactions of the Wisconsin Academy of Sciences, Arts and Letters 42:197–247.

Scott, James C.
1990 Domination and the Arts of Resistance: Hidden Transcripts. New Haven, CT: Yale University Press.

Seminole Tribe of Florida
1999 Briefing on Secretarial Procedures for Class III Gaming.

Sheffield, Gail K.
1997 The Arbitrary Indian: The Indian Arts and Crafts Act of 1990. Norman: University of Oklahoma Press.

Shifferd, Patricia
1976 A Study in Economic Change: The Chippewa of Northern Wisconsin: 1854–1900. The Western Canadian Journal of Anthropology 6(4):16–41.

Shoemaker, Nancy, ed.
2002 Clearing a Path: Theorizing the Past in Native American Studies. New York: Routledge.

Shriver, Sargent
1966 Tribal Choice in War on Poverty: Rubber Stamp or Communal Decision? Journal of American Indian Education 5(2):8–13.

Sider, Gerald M.
1993 Lumbee Indian Histories: Race, Ethnicity and Indian Identity in the Southern United States. New York: Cambridge University Press.

Smith, Dean Howard
2000 Modern Tribal Development: Paths to Self-Sufficiency and Cultural Integrity in Indian Country. Walnut Creek, CA: Alta Mira.

Smith, Linda Tuhiwai
1999 Decolonizing Methodologies: Research and Indigenous Peoples. New York: Zed Books.

Smith, Paul Chaat, and Robert Allen Warrior
1996 Like a Hurricane: The Indian Movement from Alcatraz to Wounded Knee. New York: The New Press.

Smith, Sherry L.
2000 Reimagining Indians: Native Americans through Anglo Eyes, 1880–1940. New York: Oxford University Press.

Smithsonian Institution, Bureau of American Ethnology
1907   Handbook of American Indians North of Mexico. Vol. 1. Bulletin 30.

Snipp, C. Matthew
1989   American Indians: First of This Land. New York: Russell Sage Foundation.

Speroff, Leon
2003   Carlos Montezuma, MD: A Yavapai American Hero. Portland, OR: Arnica
        Publishing, Inc.

Spielmann, Roger Willson
1998   "You're So Fat": Exploring Ojibwe Discourse. Toronto: University of Toronto
        Press.

Spilde, Katherine A.
2004   Creating a Political Space for American Indian Economic Development:
        Indian Gaming and American Indian Activism. *In* Local Actions: Cultural
        Activism, Power, and Public Life in America. Melissa Checker and Maggie
        Fishman, eds. Pp. 71–81. New York: Columbia University Press.

Standing Bear, Luther
1975   My People the Sioux. E. A. Brininstool, ed. Lincoln: University of Nebraska
[1928] Press.

Steiner, Stan
1968   The New Indians. New York: Dell Publishing; New York, Evanston, IL, and
        London: Harper and Row Publishers.

Stetson, Catherine B.
1981   Decriminalizing Tribal Codes: A Response to *Oliphant*. American Indian Law
        Review 9(1):51–82.

Stewart, Omer
1987   Peyote Religion: A History. Norman: University of Oklahoma Press.

Straus, Terry, ed.
2002   Native Chicago. 2nd edition. Chicago: McNaughton and Gunn, Inc.

Strickland, Rennard, editor-in-chief
1982   Felix S. Cohen's Handbook of Federal Indian Law. Charlottesville, VA: Michie
        Bobbs-Merrill.

Sturm, Circe
2002   Blood Politics: Race, Culture, and Identity in the Cherokee Nation of
        Oklahoma. Berkeley: University of California Press.

Sturtevant, William, ed.
1988   Handbook of North American Indians, vol. 4: Indian–White Relations.
        Washington DC: GPO.

Sugrue, Thomas J.
2003   All Politics Is Local: The Persistence of Localism in Twentieth-Century America. *In* The Democratic Experiment: New Directions in American Political History. Meg Jacobs, William J. Novak, and Julian E. Zelizer, eds. Pp. 301–326. Princeton, NJ: Princeton University Press.

Sutton, Imre, ed.
1985   Irredeemable America: The Indians' Estate and Land Claims. Albuquerque: University of New Mexico Press.

Swanton, John
1931   Source Material for the Social and Ceremonial Life of the Choctaw Indians. Bureau of American Ethnology, Bulletin 103. Washington DC: GPO.

Taliman, Valerie
2006   UN Human Rights Council Adopts Declaration on Indigenous Rights. Indian Country Today, July 10.

Tamanaha, Brian Z.
1993   Understanding Law in Micronesia: An Interpretive Approach to Transplanted Law. Leiden and New York: E. J. Brill.

Tanner, Helen Hornbeck
1999   History v. The Law: Processing Indians in the American Legal System. University of Detroit Mercy Law Review 76(3):693–708.

Taylor, Alan
2006   The Divided Ground: Indians, Settlers, and the Northern Borderland of the American Revolution. New York: Knopf.

Taylor, Graham D.
1980   The New Deal and American Indian Tribalism: The Administration of the Indian Reorganization Act, 1934–1945. Lincoln: University of Nebraska Press.

Thomas, Cyrus
1903   The History of North America, vol. 2: The Indians of North America in Historic Times. Philadelphia: George Barrie and Sons.

Thomas, Robert K.
1966/   Colonialism: Classic and Internal. New University Thought 4(4):37–44.
1967
1966/   Powerless Politics. New University Thought 4(4):45–53.
1967

Thornton, Russell
1990   The Cherokees: A Population History. Lincoln: University of Nebraska Press.

Thornton, Russell, ed.
1998   Studying Native America: Problems and Prospects. Madison: University of Wisconsin Press.

Tocqueville, Alexis de
1994   Democracy in America. With an introduction by Harvey C. Mansfield and Delba Winthrop. Harvey C. Mansfield and Delba Winthrop, eds. and transls. Chicago: University of Chicago Press.

Tollefson, Kenneth D.
1992   The Political Survival of Landless Puget Sound Indians. American Indian Quarterly 16(2):213–235.

Trafzer, Clifford, Jean A. Keller, and Lorene Sisquoc, eds.
2006   Boarding School Blues: Revisiting American Indian Educational Experiences. Lincoln: University of Nebraska Press.

Ulrich, Roberta
1999   Empty Nets: Indians, Dams, and the Columbia River. Corvallis: Oregon State University Press.

Vizenor, Gerald
1984   The People Named the Chippewa: Narrative Histories. Minneapolis: University of Minnesota Press.

Wade, John Williams
1904   The Removal of the Mississippi Choctaws. Publications of the Mississippi Historical Society 8:397–426.

Wagoner, Paula L.
2002   They Treated Us Just like Indians: The Worlds of Bennett County, South Dakota. Lincoln: University of Nebraska Press.

Washburn, Wilcomb
1971   Red Man's Land/White Man's Law: A Study of the Past and Present Status of the American Indian. New York: Scribner.

Washburn, Wilcomb, ed.
1973   The American Indian and the United States: A Documentary History. New York: Random House.

Weibel-Orlando, Joan
1999   Indian Country, LA: Maintaining Ethnic Community in Complex Society. Urbana: University of Illinois Press.

Wells, Samuel J., and Roseanna Tubby, eds.
1986   After Removal: The Choctaw in Mississippi. Jackson: University of Mississippi Press.

West, Patsy
1998   The Enduring Seminoles: From Alligator Wrestling to Ecotourism. Gainesville: University Press of Florida.

Weyrauch, Walter O.
2001   Gypsy Law: Romani Legal Traditions and Culture. Berkeley: University of California Press.

White, Richard
1991   It's Your Misfortune and None of My Own: A New History of the American West. Norman: University of Oklahoma Press.

White Face, Charmaine
2006   Indigenous Peoples Still Lack Human Rights. Indian Country Today, July 21.

Wilkins, David E.
1997   American Indian Sovereignty and the United States Supreme Court: The Masking of Justice. Austin: University of Texas Press.
2002   American Indian Politics and the American Political System. Lanham, MD: Rowman and Littlefield.

Wilkins, David E., and K. Tsianina Lomawaima
2001   Uneven Ground: American Indian Sovereignty and Federal Law. Norman: University of Oklahoma Press.

Wilkinson, Charles F.
1987   American Indians, Time, and the Law: Native Societies in a Modern Constitutional Democracy. New Haven, CT: Yale University Press.
2000   Messages from Frank's Landing: A Story of Salmon, Treaties and the Indian Way. Seattle: University of Washington Press.
2005   Blood Struggle: The Rise of Modern Indian Nations. New York and London: W. W. Norton and Co.

Wilkinson, Charles F., and Eric R. Biggs
1977   The Evolution of the Termination Policy. American Indian Law Review 5(1):139–184.

Wilkinson, Glen A.
1966   Indian Tribal Claims before the Court of Claims. Georgetown Law Journal 55(3):511–528.

Williams, Robert A., Jr.
1986   The Algebra of Federal Indian Law: The Hard Trail of Decolonizing and Americanizing the White Man's Indian Jurisprudence. Wisconsin Law Review 1986(2):219–299.
1999   Linking Arms Together: American Indian Treaty Visions of Law and Peace, 1600–1800. New York and London: Routledge.

Wilmouth, Stanley Clay
1987   The Development of Blackfeet Politics and Multiethnic Categories. Ph.D. dissertation, University of California, Riverside.

Wilson, Raymond
1983   Ohiyesa: Charles Eastman, Santee Sioux. Urbana: University of Illinois Press.

Wilson, Waziyatawin Angela
2005   Remember This! Dakota Decolonization and the Eli Taylor Narratives. With translations from the Dakota text by Wahpetunwin Carolynn Schommer. Lincoln: University of Nebraska Press.

Wilson, Waziyatawin Angela, and Michael Yellow Bird, eds.
2005   For Indigenous Eyes Only: A Decolonization Handbook. Santa Fe, NM: School of American Research, SAR Press.

Wise, Jennings C.
1931   The Red Man in the New World Drama: A Politico-Legal Study with a Pageantry of American Indian History. Washington DC: W. F. Roberts.

Wolfe, Tom
1969   The Electric Kool-Aid Acid Test. New York: Bantam Books.

Wright, Rolland Harry
1972   The American Indian College Student: A Study in Marginality. Ph D. dissertation, Brandeis University.

Yazzie, Robert, and James W. Zion
1995   "Slay the Monsters": Peacemaker Court and Violence Control Plans for Navajo Nation. In Popular Justice and Community Regeneration: Pathways of Indigenous Reform. Kayleen M. Hazelhurst, ed. Pp. 57–88. Westport, CT: Praeger.
1996   Navajo Restorative Justice: The Law of Equality and Justice. In Restorative Justice: International Perspectives. Burt Galaway and Joe Hudson, eds. Pp. 157–174. Monsey, NY: Criminal Justice Press.

Young Bear, Severt, and R. D. Theisz
1994   Standing in the Light: A Lakota Way of Seeing. Lincoln: University of Nebraska Press.

Zanjani, Sally
2001   Sarah Winnemucca. Lincoln: University of Nebraska Press.

Index

Page numbers in *italics* refer to tables.

Archaeological Resources Protection Act, 46
Arkansas, and recognition of tribes, 231, 234
Army Corps of Engineers, xv, 63, 195
art, as form of political activism, 291–301
Ashley, Dean, 99
assimilation and allotment era, of federal policy (1871–1934), xiii, 36–38, 58–60, 91–104
Assiniboine Tribe, 205–206, 217–18, 219–20
Association on American Indian Affairs, 64
Atoka agreement (1897, 1902), 129, 131
Axtell, James, 57, 58

Baldwin, Daryl, 203
Ball, Milner, 50n19
Banks, Dennis, 5
Barsh, Russell Lawrence, 31n2, 249
Barthes, Roland, 89n54
Battice, Walter, 77, 78, 79, 88n37
Beaulieu, Gustave H., 81, 82–83
Belindo, John, 171–72
Bellmon, Henry, 135
Belvin, Harry J. W., 126, 127, 130–32, 133, 134–35, 136, 137
Benedict, Jeff, 261n39
Bennett, Ramona, 155
Berkhofer, Robert F., 69n25
Bellecourt, Clyde, 5
Big Cypress Reservation (Florida), 272, 275
Bilingual Education Act (1968), xvi
Billie, James, 269–70, 273–74
Biolsi, Thomas, 201, 277n5
Blackfeet Tribe, 206, 214–15, 226n10
Black Hills lands claim case, xiii, 193, 196, 204, 212, 213, 218, 224
Black Hills Treaty Council, 58
Black Panthers, 152, 155
Blu, Karen, 263
boarding schools, and federal policy of assimilation, 92, 95, 96, 97, 104, 301. See also Carlisle Indian Industrial School; education
Boldt, George, 156
Bonnichsen decision (2002), xix
Bordeaux, Earl, 211
Bradford, William, 50n19
Branch of Acknowledgment and Research (BAR), xvii, 228, 240n9
Brand, Stewart, 157n2, 158n10

Brando, Marlon, 145, 148–49
Braroe, Niels Winthur, 277n8
Braunstein, Peter, 158n5
Breuninger, August, 82
Bridges, Al, 152, 153
Bridges, Alison, 153
Bridges, Maiselle, 153
Bridges, Suzette, 153, 154
Bridges, Valerie, 153
Brightman, Robert, 260n30
Brighton casino (Florida), 265
Brighton Reservation (Florida), 275
Brooks, Elbridge S., 23
Brosius, Samuel, 81
Brotherhood of Christian Unity, 75
Brotherhood of North American Indians, 71, 80–84, 88n45
Brown, Charles, 135, 136–37
Brown, Dee, 6–7, 19
Brown, H. Rap, 150
Brown, John, 101, 102
Bureau of Indian Affairs (BIA): assimilation policy and Indian culture, 59; and Branch of Acknowledgment Research, xvii; control of Indians' lives in first half of twentieth century, 8; and Indian Adoption Project, xv; and Institute of American Indian Arts, xvi; march on Washington in 1972 and takeover of offices, x; and Mississippi Choctaw Indian Federation, 109–21; and recognition of tribes, 229; and tribes in eastern Oklahoma during termination era, 127–28, 130, 131, 132, 137; trust management suit against (1994), xix, 46; and Voluntary Relocation Program, xv
Burke, Charles H., 101, 103, 105n11
Burke Act (1906), xiii
Burleson, Bishop, 96
Bury My Heart at Wounded Knee (Brown 1970), 6–7, 19
Butler, Hugh, 4
Butterworth, Bob, 265

Cabazon Band of Mission Indians, xviii, 45
Cahn, Edgar, 7
California: and Cherokee entities, 232; and disputes over tribal gaming, xviii, 45, 263

California v. Cabazon Band of Mission Indians (1987), xviii, 45
Cameron College (Oklahoma), 295
Campbell, Ben Nighthorse, 12
Canada: Indian Claims Commission and Potawatomi descendants living in, 196–99; and protests against Indian policies, 64; treaties and lawsuits of aboriginal peoples in, 199
Carl, John, 82
Carlisle Indian Industrial School, xiii, 50n22. See also boarding schools
Carmichael, Stokely, 150
Carpenter, Louis Joseph, 82
Carpenter v. Shaw (1930), 49n6
Carter, Charles David, 83
Cattelino, Jessica, 202, 203, 230
Charleston, Mike, 137–38
Chase, Hiram, 77
Cherokee Nation, 22, 28, 40, 49n6, 83, 228–39, 240n8–9, 245
Cherokee Nation v. Georgia (1831), 40, 49n6, 245
Chesterton, G. K., 301, 302n5
Cheyenne-Arapaho Tribes v. United States (1975), 54n90
Cheyenne Nation, 54n90, 202, 214, 218–19, 221, 222, 227n19
Cheyenne River Reservation (South Dakota), 99, 195, 211, 213
child custody, and tribal sovereignty movements, 211. See also Indian Child Welfare Act
Childers, Ernest, 3
Chippewa Tribe, 260n23. See also Saginaw Chippewa
Chitto, Joe, 110, 113–14, 115–16, 118, 120
Choctaw Tribe, 28, 63, 109–21, 126–38, 139n14
Choteau, Luzena, 74
Chumash Band of Mission Indians, 275
citizenship: and history of Indian political activism, 28, 91–92, 97; and membership criteria for tribes, 205–206; and military service, 105n5; and resistance to assimilation, 103, 104. See also American Indian Citizenship Act (1924)
Civilian Conservation Corps, 60–61

civil rights movements, and Indian political activism, 35–36, 49n9, 132, 144–45. See also Indian Civil Rights Act of 1968
Clean Air and Clean Water Acts, 45
Clifford, James, 29
Clinton, Robert, 50n19
Cobb, Daniel, 64, 175n19, 292
Cobb, Samuel, 115
Coconut Creek casino (Florida), 264–71, 276
Cohen, Felix, xiv
Cohen, Ronald, 245
Cold War: and political activism in Native America, 161–73; and public schools in 1950s, 4; tribal nationalism and language of, 63
Collier, John, 18, 38, 60, 110, 113, 163
Colmer, Bill, 119
colonialism: and concept of indigeneity in context of Florida, 264; and debates over tribal recognition and sovereignty, 230, 241n14; and views of Indian history, 65; and Workshop on American Indian Affairs, 164–65, 172–73. See also decolonization
Comanche Nation, 60, 205, 221, 223
community: and art education, 291–301; and legal definitions of "Indianness," 229
Community Action Programs (CAP), 64, 132, 168–69
Connecticut: and tribal gaming, 263; and tribal recognition, 235, 236, 242n24
constitutions: adoption of by tribes, 60–61, 215, 216, 217, 218, 219–20, 223, 224, 247; US and Indian policy, 33–34, 42, 44, 79
contracting, and federal policy, 201–202
Coolidge, Rev. Sherman, 73
Cotton Petroleum v. New Mexico (1989), xviii
Council of Energy Resources Tribes (CERT), xvii, 8, 204
counterculture: definition of, 158n5; and fish-in movement in Pacific Northwest, 142–57
Court of Indian Claims, 40, 128, 129, 139n14
Courts of Indian Offenses, xiii
Craig, Joseph, 82
Creek Tribe, 241n19

legal history: and denial of rights of Indians to testify in court, 51n34; and expert witness view of Indian Claims Commission, 178–99; and federal policy in history of US-Indian relations, 33–48. *See also* criminal justice; tribal courts

Leupp, Francis Ellington, 77

Lips, Julian, 255

Little Big Horn Battlefield National Monument, 204

Little Big Horn College, 216

localism, and tribal sovereignty, 264

Locke, Victor, 129–30

Lone Wolf, Delos, 59

Lone Wolf v. Hitchcock (1903), *xiii*, 37, 53n73, 59

Longest Walk (1978), x, *xvii*

Louisiana, and tribal recognition, 233

Lumbee Tribe, 63, 239n5

Lummi Tribe, 145

lunar calendar, and Miami culture, 286

Lurie, Nancy O., 167, 179, 182

Lyng v. Northwest Indian Cemetery Association (1988), *xviii*, 43

Lytle, Clifford, 248–49

Macleod, William Christie, 25

Maine, Henry, 248

Major Crimes Act (1885), *xiii*, 36

Makah Tribe, 145, 202

Mankiller, Wilma, 234–5, 237

Maori (New Zealand), 199

Mardock, Robert William, 19, 21–22

Margold, Nathan, *xiv*

Marshall, John, 34, 35, 48

mascots, Indians as, 275

Mashantucket Pequots, *xviii*, *xix*, 275. *See also* Pequot Tribe

Mashpee Wampanaog Tribe, 241n19

Mattaponi Tribe, 239n5

McCarren, Patrick, 4

McCloud, Janet, 150, 151, 155

McCormack, Mary, 12

McDonald, James, 28

McKenzie, Fayette Avery, 78–79

McLaughlin, Daniel, 202

McLaughlin, James, 96

McNickle, D'Arcy, 7, 10, 17, 19, 28, 31n11,

163, 165, 166, 167, 173

McWhorter, Lucullus V., 81

Means, Russell, 5

Medicine, Bea, 10

Medicine Lodge, Treaty of (1867), 37

membership criteria, for tribes, 205–206, 223

Menominee Restoration Act (1973), *xvi*, 43

Menominee Tribe, *xvi*, 41, 53n73, 62

Meriam Report (1928), 38, 180

Merrell, James, 57, 65

Merrion v. Jicarilla (1982), *xvii*

Merry, Sally, 247, 248

Meskuotis, George, 154

Meyer, Melissa L., 82

Miami Language Teacher Training Program, 281–82

Miami Tribe, 182–83, 188, 280–90

Miami University, 203, 280–90

Michigan, and historical research by expert witness for Indian Claims Commission, 179–91

Miller, Bruce, 201, 207, 226n7

Miller, Esther, 81

Miller, Mark, 228

mineral resources: and Choctaw Nation during termination era, 129–30, 131, 135; and tribal sovereignty movements, 214, 215, 217, 218, 219, 220, 222, 223

Mississippi Choctaw Indian Federation (MCIF), 109–21

Mississippi Choctaw Welfare Association (MCWA), 110

Missouri, and recognition of tribes, 234

Missouria Tribe. *See* Otoe-Missouria

Missouri River: and Army Corps of Engineers, *xv*, 63; Sioux reservations on and Indian Claims Commission, 191–96

Mitchell, George, 5

Mitchell I (1980) and *Mitchell II* (1983), 46, 54n90

Mohegan Tribe, 275

Mohr, James, 244

Momaday, N. Scott, 6, 10, 19

Monroney, Mike, 136

Montana: and comparison of tribal sovereignty movements, 210, 214–20; and conflicts between Indian nations, 204; and limits on tribal civil jurisdiction, *xvii*,

47; and taxation of tribal mineral leases, *xviii*

Montana v. Blackfeet (1985), *xviii*

Montana v. United States (1981), *xvii*, 47

Montezuma, Carlos, 22, 63–64, 71, 72–76, 84, 88n30, 105n6

Montgomery, Jack, 3

Moorehead, Warren K., 24

Morton v. Mancari (1974), *xvii*, 44

Muckleshoot Tribe, 149, 155

Murphy, Charles, 213

Myaamia Project, 280–90

Myer, Dillon S., 40, 52n41

Naskapi Tribe, 255

Natalish, Vincent, 74

National Collegiate Athletic Association, *xix*

National Congress of American Indians (NCAI), *xiv*, *xv*, 8, 61, 65, 155, 166, 168–73

National Council of American Indians, 76

National Endowment for the Humanities, 192–93

National Historical Preservation Act, 284

National Indian Forest Management Act of 1990, 45

National Indian Gaming Commission, 46

National Indian Gaming Regulatory Act (1988), *xviii*

National Indian Republican Association, 74

National Indian Youth Council (NIYC), *xvi*, 8, 18, 64, 65, 148, 297

nationalism, and concepts of sovereignty, 230

National Museum of the American Indian, *xix*

Native American Church, *xiii*, 59, 144

Native American Free Exercise of Religion Act (1993), 241n19

Native American Graves Protection and Repatriation Act (1990), *xviii*, 46, 284

Native American Language Act (1990), *xviii*, 281

Native American Rights Fund, *xvi*, *xviii*, *xix*, 64, 156, 197, 203, 228

Native American Tribalism: Indian Survivals and Renewals (McNickle 1993), 7

Navajo Community College, *xvi*, 9, 64

Navajo Nation, 22, 202, 203, 204, 206, 240n8

Nesper, Larry, 203

Neuberger, Richard, 4

New, Lloyd Kiva, 299

New Deal, 38, 109, 117, 163

New Indians, The (Steiner 1968), 7

New Left, and fishing rights movement in Pacific Northwest, 142–57

New Mexico, and right of Indians to vote in state elections, 63

New Republic (periodical), 81

New York, and tribal recognition, 232, 239n5

New York Times (newspaper), 171

New Zealand, and Maori, 199

Nichols, Roland, 76

Nisqually Tribe, 145, 150, 152, 153, 159n24

Nixon, Richard, *xvi*, 42

North Carolina, and Cherokee groups, 237, 239n5

North Carolina Commission on Indian Affairs, 233

Northern Arapaho, 220–1

Northern Cheyenne, 214, 218–19

Northwest Federation of American Indians, 58

Nuyen, France, 151, 159n23

Oahe Dam (South Dakota), 213

Occam, Samson, 22

Office of Economic Opportunity (OEO), 132, 133, 134, 169–70, 171

Office of Indian Affairs (OIA), 92, 93–95, 96, 97, 99, 110, 111, 118, 120

Oglala Lakota College, 213

Oglala Sioux, 75, 211–13

Ohio: and Cherokee entities, 232; and historical research by expert witness for Indian Claims Commission, 179–91

Ojibwe Tribe, *xvii*, *xviii*, 10–11, 197, 203, 243–58

Oklahoma: and Choctaw Nation, 116, 126–38; and comparison of tribal sovereignty movements, 210, 221–3, 225; and conflicts among tribal nations, 204; and Miami summer education program, 287–88, 290; sovereignty and recognition of tribes in, 228–39

Oklahoma City Council of Choctaws, 135, 136–37

Oklahoma Indian Welfare Act, 132, 222, 223
Oklahomans for Indian Opportunity (OIO), 132, 133, 134–35
Olds, Julie, 203
Oliphant v. Suquamis Indian Tribe (1978), xvii, 47, 245
Omaha Tribe, 77, 106n16
O'Neal, Minnie, 78
One Flew over the Cuckoo's Nest (Kesey 1962), 145–47
Oneida Indian Nation, 44
O'Neil, Floyd, /
O'Neill, Colleen, 206
oral tradition, and hearings of Indian Claims Commission, 187–88
Oregon, and fish-in movement, 148–57
Oregon v. Smith (1990), xviii
Ortiz, Alfonso, 10
Osage Tribe, 106n16
Osceola, Jo-Lin, 269
Osceola, Max, 267
Osceola, Max, Jr., 273
Otoe-Missouria Tribe, 291, 292–93, 302n3
Ottawa Tribe, 182, 185
Our Brother's Keeper: The Indian in White America (Cahn 1969), 7

Pacific Northwest, and fish-in movement, xvi, 63, 142–57
Pamunkey Tribe, 234, 239n5
Paris, Treaty of (1783), 181
Parker, Arthur, 22, 81, 88n38, 88n41
Parker, Quanah, 59
Parkman, Francis, 184
PARR (Protect Americans' Rights and Responsibilities), 11
Passamaquoddy Tribe, 241n19
Patriot Chiefs, The (Josephy 1961), 18
Paucatuck Eastern Pequot, 235, 242n24
Pawnee Tribe, 106n16
Peace and Freedom Party, 152, 153
Peckham, Howard H., 184
Penobscot Nation, 241n19
Pequot Tribe, 205, 235, 242n24. *See also* Mashantucket Pequots
philanthropy, and Seminole gaming industry, 271–76
Philips, Susan, 255

Pickering, Kathleen, 203
Pick-Sloan Plan (Missouri River), xv
Pierce, Earl Boyd, 166, 167
Pine Ridge Reservation (South Dakota), x, 100, 194, 211–13
Pipestem, Browning, 165
Plains tribes, and comparison of sovereignty movements, 209–25
plenary power doctrine, 37, 49–50n19
Poarch Band of Creek Indians, 241n19
politics and political activism: academic experts and misunderstanding of, 16–30; art and education as forms of, 291–301; and assimilation and allotment era of federal policy (1871–1934), xiii; and civil rights movements, 35–36; and Cold War, 161–73; dance and music as resistance among Lakota, 91–104; multidisciplinary history of, xi–xii; and non-Native participation in Indian reform movement, 142–57; personal reflection on past fifty years of, 2–14; and recent studies on sovereignty, 201–207; and reorganization era of federal policy (1934–1946), xiv; and resistance to termination of Choctaw Nation of Oklahoma, 126–38; and self-determination era of federal policy (1961–2006), xvi, xvii, xviii, xix; self-determination as focus of, 35; and Society of American Indians, 71–85; and termination and relocation era of federal policy (1946–1961), xv, 42
Ponca Tribe, 106n16
Poor People's Campaign, xvi, 172
Porter, Joy, 32n25
Potawatomi Tribe, 182, 196–99
Poteete, Troy Wayne, 231
poverty, and Choctaw in Oklahoma, 128
power: and charitable giving by Seminoles, 273, 274–76; and debates over tribal recognition and sovereignty, 230; Seminole gaming and relative economic, 271, 273; tribal nations and differentials of, 206
Powers of Indian Tribes opinion (1934), xiv
Pratt, Richard Henry, 74
Price, A. Grenfell, 25
Progress, The (newspaper), 82–83

property law, concepts of English, 184–85
Prucha, Francis Paul, 7, 19, 22, 41
Public Law 280 (1953), *xv*, 41, 242n23
Pueblo Nation, 59
Puyallup Tribe, 145, 152, 153, 155

Quakers (Society of Friends), 150, 152, 155–56, 157. *See also* American Friends Service Committee
Quinones, Joseph, 151–52, 154

race: and status of Choctaws in South, 111; and visibility of Seminoles in South Florida, 266
Race and Change in Hollywood, Florida (2000), 266
Rebirth of the Blackfeet Nation, 1912–1954, The (Rosier 2001), 32n25
Redfield, Robert, 163, 296
Red Man's Land/White Man's Law: A Study of the Past and Present Status of the American Indian (Washburn 1971), 7
Red Man and the White Man in North America, from its Discovery to the Present, The (Ellis 1882), 23
Red Power: The American Indians' Fight for Freedom (Josephy 1971), 7
Red Power era, *x. See also* Alcatraz Island; American Indian Movement; politics and political activism; sovereignty; Wounded Knee
Reed College, 152
Reinhart, Christopher, 242n24
Rehnquist, William H., 47
Religious Freedom Restoration Act (1993), *xviii*, 47
removal: and Cherokee history, 231, 236–37; and Choctaw Nation, 126–27; and Indian political history in nineteenth century, 27; and Miami Tribe, 281; and Otoe-Missouria Tribe, 302n3; and relocation during termination era of federal policy, 62
reorganization era, of federal policy (1934–1946), *xiv*, 38–39, 60–61
resistance: to assimilation and allotment policies, 59–60; and politics of dance and music among Lakota, 91–104

revitalization movements, during assimilation and allotment era, xiii
Richardson, Earl, 110, 114
Road: Indian Tribes and Political Liberty, The (Barsh & Henderson 1980), 31n2
Robertson, Lindsay, xi, 63, 203
Rolling Thunder (Cherokee), 151
Roosevelt, Theodore, 37
Rosebud Reservation (South Dakota), 97, 211, 213
Rosenthal, Harvey, 51n33
Rosier, Paul, 32n25
Ross, John, 22
Roszak, Theodore, 158n5
Rough Rock Demonstration School, 64
Rural Poverty Demonstration project, 134
Russell, Bertrand, 150

Saginaw Chippewa, 182, 187–88. *See also* Chippewa Tribe
St. Germaine, Ernest, 244
Saito, Natsu Taylor, 50n19
Salway, Harold, 212
Sand Creek Massacre (Colorado 1864), 219
San Manuel Band of Mission Indians, 275
Santa Clara Pueblo v. Martinez (1978), *xvii*, 44
Satiacum, Bob, 148, 149, 155
Saul, Thomas, 77–78, 87n28
Scholder, Fritz, 64
Scott, James C., 92, 105n7
Search for an American Indian Identity: Modern Pan-Indian Movements, The (Hertzberg), 7
Seattle Legal Services, 156
Seattle Liberation Front, 155
Seattle Post-Intelligencer (newspaper), 154–55
self-determination era, of federal policy (1961–2006), *xvi, xvii, xviii, xix*, 35, 42–48, 63–65, 161–73, 243–58
Sells, Cato, 99–100, 101
Seminole Tribe, *xix*, 2, 4, 8–9, 202, 203, 262–76
Seminole Tribe v. Butterworth (1979), 265
Seminole Tribe v. Florida (1996), *xix*, 46
Seminole Tribune (newspaper), 272
Seneca Tribe, 182
Shakopee Mdewakanton Sioux Tribe, 275
Shaw, Dallas, 96–97
Shawnee Tribe, 182

They Came Here First (McNickles 1949), 17–18, 28

Thom, Mel, 165, 172–73

Thomas, Cyrus, 24, 32n19

Thomas, Elmer, 129

Thomas, Robert K., 132, 134, 163–65, 173, 296

Three Stars, Clarence, 75, 86n13, 87n16

Tlingit Tribe, 207

To Be an Indian: The Life of Iroquois-Seneca Arthur Caswell Parker (Porter 2001), 32n25

Tomahawk, The (newspaper), 81

tourism, and Indian imagery in Oklahoma, 221

traditionalism, and tribal sovereignty movements, 219

Trail of Broken Treaties (1972), x, *xvi*

Trail of Tears, 231, 236–7. *See also* removal

Treated as a state (TAS) status, 45

treaty rights, and controversies over fishing and hunting, 148–57

Tribal College Journal, 10

tribal courts, and conflicts in Ojibwe communities of Wisconsin, 243–58, 260n24. *See also* criminal justice; legal history

tribal government: and Choctaw Nation in Oklahoma during termination era, 130, 137–38; and comparison of sovereignty movements in Plains region, 209–25; and Mississippi Choctaw under Indian Reorganization Act, 110–21; Oklahoma statehood and dissolution of, 127. *See also* constitutions

Tribally Controlled Community College Act (1978), xvii, 43, 45, 292

tribal museums, 202

Tribal Self-Governance Act of 1994, 45

tribal politics, as distinct from Indian politics, 5. *See also* politics and political activism

tribes: location of communities discussed, *xi*; and membership criteria, 205–206; recognition of by states, *xx*, 228–39, 241n13–15; and value of internal tribal histories, 13. *See also* tribal courts; tribal government; tribal museums; tribal politics; *specific tribes*

Truman, Harry S., 39, 162

Tucker Act (1887), 51n33

Udall, Stewart, 170

United Keetoowah Band of Cherokee Indians, 238

United Nations. *See* Declaration of the Rights of Indigenous Peoples

United States v. Kagama (1886), *xiii*, 36–37

United States v. Lara (2004), *xix*, 47

United States v. Navajo Nation (2003), 54n90

United States v. Nice (1916), *xiii*, 38

United States ex rel. Hualapai Indians v. Santa Fe Pacific Railroad Co. (1941), 41

United States v. Washington (1974), *xvii*, 44, 156

University of Colorado, 296

University of Oklahoma, 133

University of South Dakota, 64

University of Washington, 149, 152

University of Wisconsin–Milwaukee, 10–11

Upper Skagit Tribe, 205

urban centers, in Oklahoma, 221

Urban Indian Experience in America, The (Fixico 2000), 7

Ute Tribe, 62

Utley, Robert, 19

Vietnam War, 143, 144–45, 153, 159n30

Virginia, and tribal recognition, 232, 234, 239n5

Vizenor, Gerald, 82

Voight decision (1983), *xviii*, 243, 246, 256, 257

Voluntary Relocation Program, *xv*

Wade, Delos, 135

Wagoner, Paula, 263

"Walking on Common Ground: Pathways to Equal Justice" conference (2005), 244

War on Poverty (1960s), *xvi*, 64, 132, 168–69

Warrior, Clyde, 148, 165, 297, 299

Warrior, Della, 64, 165, *293*

Washburn, Wilcomb, 7, 17

Washington, and fish-in movement, 148–57

water rights, 50n21, 220–1

Watkins, Arthur V., 4, 189–90

Wax, Murray, 170

webs of relationships, and Society of American Indians, 72–76, 84–85